MW00763425

Future Concepts of Library and Information Services

Changes, Challenges and Role of Library Professionals

Future Concepts of Library & Information Services
Changes, Challenges and Role of Library Professionals

J. Danrita

V. P. Ramesh Babu

T. Marichamy

Ess Ess Publications

4837/24, Ansari Road, Darya Ganj,
New Delhi-110002
Tel. : 23260807, 41563444
Fax : 011-41563334
E-mail: info@essessreference.com
www.essessreference.com

Ess Ess Publications
4837/24, Ansari Road,
Darya Ganj,
New Delhi-110 002.

Tel.: 23260807, 41563444
Fax: 41563334
E-mail: info@essessreference.com
www.essessreference.com

© **Editor/s**

Rs.1475/-

First Published - 2009

ISBN: 978-81-7000-558-2

Published By Ess Ess Publications and printed at Salasar Imaging Systems

Cover Design by Patch Creative Unit

PRINTED IN INDIA

Contents

TECHNICAL SESSION – III
Applications of ICT in LIS

TECHNICAL SESSION – IV

**Globalization, Knowledge Industry and
Management and Other Related Topics in LIS**

TECHNICAL SESSION – V

**Collection Development Management in
Electronic Environment**

Contents   13

Preface

The book "Future concept of Library and Information Services : Changes, Challenges and Role of Library Professionals" is a compilation of papers presented at the National Conference by library professionals from universities and colleges. The papers cover vital issues, problems and challenges and are presented under five subtitles. They are

1. Public, Academic, Special Libraries and Information Centers
2. Self development of Librarians and Library Professionals and Human Resource Development
3. Application of Information Communication Technologies (ICT) in Library and Information Services
4. Globalization, Knowledge industry and Management
5. Collection development management in electronic environment

Hosting the National Conference was a rich experience for Rev. Jacob Memorial Christian College, located in a rural area called Ambilikkai in Dindigul District, Tamil Nadu. The careful documentation and meticulous follow up by the College librarian Mr. V. P. Ramesh Babu and Economic lecturer Mr. T. Marichamy has culminated in the publication of the book. I feel hounoured and privileged to be part of this venture and wish to record my appreciation for the colossal contribution by my colleagues to the enrichment and growth of library professionals.

Prof. J. Danrita
Principal
Rev. Jacob Memorial Christian College

Acknowledgements

The librarians are the backbone for the country's educational development. For the updation and enhancement of knowledge, the librarian plays a vital role. Any societal or institutional development can be assessed only with the help of the readers' status. Enrichment of the readers' status is possible only through the accomplishments of the librarians. The two day national conference proved to be a successful venture due to the support given by the management and cooperation of faculty friends and student volunteers.

In this juncture we are very much thankful to the members of the organizing and national advisory committee for their encouragement and moral support.

We express our heartfelt thanks to Dr. S. Srinivasa Ragavan, University Librarian and Head in charge, Department of Library and Information Science, Bharathidasan University, Trichy, Dr. A.Ganesan, Librarian and Head, PG Department of Library and Information Science, A.V.V. M Sri Pushpam College, Poondi and Dr. S. Ally Sornam, Head, Department of Library and Information Science, Bishop Heber College, Trichy for their constant support and suggestions for conducting the conference.

Our thanks are also due to all the participants who have presented the papers and all the sponsors for extending their supporting hands for the conference.

Finally our sincere thanks goes to Ess Ess Publications, New Delhi who agreed to publish this volume in a book format for the benefit of the readers.

Prof. J. Danrita
Mr. V.P. Ramesh Babu
Mr. T. Marichamy

List of Contributors

Dr. J. Abraham
Deputy Librarian , Gandhigram Rural University
Gandhigram – 624 302, Dindigul Dist

Dr. S. Ally Sornam
Head, Department of Library and Information Science
Bishop Heber College, Trichy

Mr. M.S. Amanulla
Librarian, The New College (EVE)
Chennai.14

Ms. G. Amudha
Librarian, V.H.N.S.N.College
Virudhunagar

Mr. L. Arun Kumar
II M.L.I.Sc Student
Department of Library and Information Science
A.V.V.M Sri Pushpam College (Autonomous)
Poondi, Thanjavur Dt

Ms. Babita Garg
Librarian, PT.BD. Sharma PGIMS
Rotak 124 001, Hariyana

Mr. P.S. Baghath Singh
Advocate (Madurai High Court)
No.56, G.N. Mansion
K. Pudur, Alagar Kovil Road , Madurai-7

Mr. C.P.S. Balamurugan
Librarian, Kendira Vidhyalaya
CECRI Campus, Karaikudi

Mr. N. Baskaran
Librarian, Kamaraj College of Engineering and Technology
Virudhunagar.

Mr. S.Chinnaiyan
Librarian, Vikram College of Engineering
Sreenivasan Nagar, Madurai

Mrs. P. Clara Jeyaseeli
Librarian (SS), V.V. Vanniaperumal College for Women
Virudunagar – 626 001

Mr. R. Daniel Prince
Assistant Librarian, Institute of Ophthalmology
Joseph Eye Hospital, Trichy

Ms. T. R. Deivanai
Lecturer, Department of Library and Information Science
A.V.V.M Sri Pushpam College (Autonomous)
Poondi, Thanjavur Dt

Mr. M. Dorairajan
Librarian, St. Joseph's College
Autonomous, Trichy-2

Mrs. P. Eps
Librarian, All India Radio, Tirunelveli

Mr. J. Franklin
Librarian, Evening Session
Bishop Heber College, Trichy

Dr. A. Ganesan
Head and Librarian
Department of Library and Information Science
AVVM Sri Pushpam College (Autonomous), Poondi,
Thanjavur Dt.

Mr. A.G. Ganesan
Librarian, KLN College of Information Technology
Pottapalayam -630 611
Madurai Dt

Mr. P. Ganesan
Assistant Librarian, Central Library
Alagappa University, Karaikudi-3

Mr. M. Gangatharan
Librarian, Sardar Vallabhbhai Patel Institute of Textile
Management, Peelamedu, Coimbatore

Ms. E.Gajalakshmi
II M.L.I.Sc, Department of Library and Information Science
A.V.V.M Sri Pushpam College (Autonomous)
Poondi, Thanjavur Dt

Mr. A. Gopinath
M. Phil Research Scholar
Bishop Heber College, Trichy

Ms. M. Gowri
I M.L.I.Sc Student,
Department of Library and Information Science
A.V.V.M Sri Pushpam College (Autonomous)
Poondi, Thanjavur Dt

Mr. P. Ilangumaran
Librarian, Erode Sengunthar Engineering College
Thuduppathi – 638 057, Erode Dt

Mrs. P. Indirani
Librarian, Arulmigu Palaniandavar Arts College for Women
C.K.Puthur, Palani – 624 615

Mr. R. Jayabal
Librarian, Sri Ramakrishna Mission Vidhyalaya College of
Arts and Science, Coimbatore

Mr. R. Jayaraman
Assistant Librarian (S.G)
Agricultural College and Research Institute (TNAU)
Madurai - 625 104.

Mr. R. Jeysankar
Lecturer, Department of Library and Information Science
Alagappa University, Karaikudi -630 003

Ms. B. Jyothi
Manager, Library and Information Services
Tata Consultancy Services Ltd., Velacherry, Chennai

Mr. S. Kallimuthu Kumaran
M.L.I.Sc Student
Department of Library and Information Science
AVVM Sri Pushpam College, Autonomous
Poondi, Thanjavur Dt

Mr. K. Kamalanathan
National Engineering College, Kovilpatty
Tuticorin Dt

Dr. M. Kanakaraj
Librarian & Head, PSG College of Technology
Coimbatore

Mr. M. Kannan
Plot No.28, Door No.3, I Cross Street
Vanamamali Nagar, By-Pass Road, Madurai-625 016.

Dr. S. Kanthimathi
SG Librarian & Research Guide
Rani Anna Government College for Women
Tirunelveli-627 008

Mr. P. Karuppusamy
Assistant Librarian, The Standard Fireworks Raharatnam
College for Women, Sivakasi- 626 123

Ms. M. Kodeeswari
Libarian, Swamy Dayananda College of Arts and Science
Thiruvarur

Mr. E. Krishnamoorthy
Librarian, District Central Library, Trichy.20

Ms. M. Kurunji
II M.L.I.Sc Student
Department of Library and Information Science
AVVM Sri Pushpam College (Autonomous), Poondi
Thanjavur Dt

Dr. A. Lawrence Mary
Research Guide & Librarian(SGL), TDMNS College
Kallikulam, Valliyoor, Tirunelveli District

Mrs. R. Maheswari
Plot No.4, 2/166A 5th North Street, Viraiya Koil Street,
Rajakambadi, Palkalai Nagar , Maduai-21

Mr. V.T. Mani
Library, Tamil Nadu Agricultural University
AC & RI, Madurai -625 104

Ms. S.Mathurajothi
Assistant Librarian(Sl.Gr), Dr. Ramachandra Library
Ganhigram Rural University, Gandhigram- 624 302
Dindigul Dt.

Mr. M.Mariraj
Assistant Technical Officer, School of Management
Bharathiar University, Coimbatore-46

Dr. S. Mohammed Esmail
Reader, Department of Library and Information Science
Annamalai University, Annamalainagar, Chidhambaram

Dr. N. Murugesa Pandian
Librarian, Ganesar Senthamil Kalloori,
Melaisivapuri - 622 403,
Pudukkottai District.

Mr. P. Muthu Mari
Librarian, G.S.A. College, Rajagambeeram
Manamaduari – 630 606

Mr. R.Muthukrishnan
Librarian (SG), Sivanthi Aditanar College
Virapandian Patnam, Tiruchendur – 628 216.

Mr. R. Muthuraj
National Engineering College, Kovilpatty, Tuticorin Dt

Mr. P. Nagamani,
Assitant Librarian, Adhiyamaan College of Education
Dr. M.G.R. Nagar, AERI Campus, Hosur-635 109

Ms. R. Nagarathinam
Assistant Librarian, Cherraan's Institute of Health Sciences
Telugupalayam Pirivu, Coimbatore

Mr. M. Palaniappan
Library Assistant, Central Library
Alagappa University, Karaikudi

Ms. G. Pandi Selvi
Librarian, ICFAI National College, Madurai

Mr. S. Paramasivam
Librarian, GGR College of Engineering,
Pillaiyarkulam, Vellore.9

Ms. S. Praba Devi
II M.L.I.Sc Student
Department of Library and Information Science
AVVM Sri Pushpam College (Autonomous)
Poondi, Thanjavur Dt

Mr. R. Prabu
M. Phil Student, Bishop Heber College, Trichy

Mr. K. Paulraj
Research Scholar, (P.M.T.College Melaneelithanallur-627953), Manonmaniam Sundaranar University
Tirunelveli-627 012

Mr. P. Pounraj
Librarian, Victory Teacher Training Institute and College
of Education, Kambiliyampatty (PO), Dindigul Dt – 624
306

Mr. M.Prabhakaran
Librarian, Vivekananda College (Autonomous)
Tiruvedagam West, Madurai Dt

Ms. R. Radha
Librarian, Tamil Nadu College of Engineering, Coimbator

Mr. P. Raghavan
Librarian, National College, Trichy

Mr. B.Rajaseelan
M.L.I.Sc Student
Department of Library and Information Science
AVVM Sri Pushpam College, Autonomous, Poondi
Thanjavur Dt

Mr. V. Rajavel
Student, Department of Library and Information Science
AVVM Sri Pushpam College (Autonomous), Poondi
Thanjavur Dt.
Email: chinthapriyan@yahoo.co.in

Mr. M. Rajeevgandhi
I M.L.I.Sc Student
Department of Library and Information Science
A.V.V.M Sri Pushpam College, (Autonomous)
Poondi, Thanjavur Dt

Mr. A. Rajinikanth
Library Assitant, PSNA College of Engineering and
Technology, Muthanampatty
Dindigul – 624 622

Mr. B. E. Rajkumar
Librarian, Institute of Ophthalmology
Joseph Eye Hospital, Trichy

Mr. G. Ramadas
Librarian, Noorul Islam College of Arts and Science
Kumaracoil, - 629 180

Mr. N. Ramasabareeswari
Assistant Libarian, Kongunadu Arts and Science College
(Autonomous), Coimbatore-29

Mr. R.U. Ramasamy
Librarian, SACS M.A.V.M.M. Engg. College
Kidaripatty (PO), Madurai – 625 301

Mr. R. Ramesh
Assistant Tehcnical Officer, University Library
Bharathiar University, Coimbatore

Mr. J. Ramesh
Librarian, Park's College, Chinnakkarai
Tirupur – 641 605

Dr. B. Ramesh Babu
Professor, Department of Information Science
University of Madras, Chennai – 600 005

Mr. V.P. Ramesh Babu
Librarian, Rev. Jacob Memorial Christian College
Ambilikkai – 624 612, Dindigul Dt

Mr. S. Ramkumar
Assistant Tehcnical Officer, University Library
Bharathiar University, Coimbatore

Ms. S. Rani
Library Assistant,
Agricultural College and Research Institute, Melur road
Madurai -625 104

Mr. M.Ravichandran
Librarian, Mohamed Sathak Engineering College
Kilakarai – 623 806, Ramnad Dt

Ms. A. Rekha
II M.L.I.Sc. Students,
Department of Library and Information Science
AVVM Sri Pushpam College
Poondi, Thanjavur Dt

Ms. D. Revathi Selvi
Librarian, S.T.E.T. Women's College
Sundarakkotai, Mannargudi – 614 061
Thanjavur Dt

Mr. A. Robert William
Assistant, Bharathiar University, Coimbatore-46

Mrs. J. Rosalind
Librarian (S.G), JKK Nataraja College of Arts and Science
Komarapalayam, Namakkal Dt

Mr. M. Sankar
Assistant Librarian
Tamil Nadu Agricultural University AC & RI
Madurai-625 104

Ms. M. Sangeetha
I M.L.I.Sc Student
Department of Library and Information Science
A.V.V.M Sri Pushpam College, (Autonomous)
Poondi, Thanjavur Dt

Ms. J. Santhi
Librarian, Cherraan's Institute of Health Sciences
Teluguppalayam Pirivu, Coimbatore

Ms. N. Santhi
Librarian, N.S. College of Arts and Science
P.B. No.55, Vadapupatti – 625 531, Theni.

Ms. M. Santhi
Librarian, Erode Sengunthar Engineering College
Thuduppathi – 638 057, Erode Dt

Mr. R.R.Saravanakumar
5/1546, Subathra Street, Sadhasiva Nagar
Maduri-625 020

Mr. K. Sekar
Librarian, Tamil Nadu College of Engineering
Karumathampatty, Coimbatore – 641 659

Mr. K. Sekar
Librarian, Christian College of Engineering
Oddanchatram- 624 619, Dindigul Dt

Mr. J. Selvam
Lecturer, Department of Library and Information Science
AVVM Sri Pushpam College (Autonomous)
Poondi, Thanjavur Dt.

Mr. R. Senthil Kumar
Librarian (SS), Kongunadu Arts and Science College
(Autonomous), Coimbatore-29

Dr. T.Selvanayaki
S.G.Lecturer in History
Arulmigu Palaniandavar Arts College for Women, Palani

Ms. M. Sharmila
Library Trainee, University Library
Mother Teresa University, Kodaikanal
Dindigul Dt

Ms. N. Shyamala
Librarian, Nadar Saraswathi College of Education
Vadapuduppatti – 625 531, Theni

Mr. S. Sivaraj
Head, Learning Resource Centre
Bannari Amman Institute of Technology
Sathyamangalam, Tamil Nadu

Ms. Sreelatha Purushothaman
Asst.Librarian
Sri Krishna College of Engineering and Technology
Coimbatore- 641 008

Dr. S. Srinivasa Raghavan
Librarian, Bharathidhasan University, Trichy

Mr. T. Stephen
Librarian, Malankara Catholic College, Mariagiri
Kanniyakumari Dt. 629 153

Mr. M. Subramaniyan
II M.L.I.Sc Students, Department of Library and
Information Science , A.V.V.M Sri Pushpam College
(Autonomous)
Poondi, Thanjavur Dt

Mrs. G. Sudha
No.789, 5th North Street, Thiagaraja Nagar
Tirunelveli

Ms. S. Suguna
II M.L.I.Sc Student
Department of Library and Information Science
A.V.V.M Sri Pushpam College (Autonomous)
Poondi , Thanjavur Dt

Ms. Sumukki Padmanabhan
Librarian, Chevalier T Thomas Elizabeth College for Women
Perambur, Chennai

Mr. S.K. Sundar
Executive, Library and Information Services
Tata Consultancy Services Ltd
Velacherry-Taramani Road
100 Feet Road, Velacherry, Chennai- 600 042

Dr. M. Tamizhchelvan
Librarian, Sri Krishna College of Engineering and Technology
Coimbatore- 641008.

Ms. K. Thilahavathi
II M.L.I.Sc. Student
Department of Library and Information Science
AVVM Sri Pushpam College, Poondi
Thanjavur Dt

Ms. T.Thilagavathi
Assistant Librarian, Faculty of Education
Avinashilingam University for Women
Varappalayam, Thadagam (PO), Coimbatore, 641 108

Mr. Thirunavukkarasu
Assistant Librarian, Bharathiar University
Coimbatore – 641 046

Mr. R.Thiruppathi
Librarian, SRM College of Arts and Science
Kattankulathur, Kanchipuram Dt

Ms. L. Uma
Assistant University Librarian
Anna University, MIT Campus, Chennai

Mrs. D. Umamaheswari
Librarian, Christian College of Nursing , Ambilikkai- 624 612
Dindigul Dt.

Ms. P. Umarani
Faculty ICFAI National College, Madurai

Ms. K. Vanitha
I M.L.I.Sc Student
Department of Library and Information Science
A.V.V.M Sri Pushpam College (Autonomous), Poondi
Thanjavur Dt

Mr. N. Vasantha Kumar
Assistant Librarian
Thiagarajar School of Management (TSM)
Centre for Higher Learning, Thirupparankundram
Madurai – 625 005

Mr. S. Venkatesh
Assistant Librarian, PSG College of Technology
Coimbatore

Mr. A. Victor
Lecturer, Department of Library and Information Science
Bishop Heber College, Trichy

Ms. R.T. Vijaya
Librarian (SG), Pope John Paul II College of Education
Reddiarpalayam, Pondicherry – 605 010

Ms. V. Vijayalakshmi
I M.L.I.Sc Student
Department of Library and Information Science
A.V.V.M Sri Pushpam College, (Autonomous)
Poondi, Thanjavur Dt

OTHER PARTICIPANTS

Mr. C.S. Vijayakumar
Librarian, Sourashtra College
Villachery Main Road, Pasumalai Post
Madurai – 625 004

Mr. S. Suburamani
Library Assistant, PSNA College of Engineering and
Technology, Kothandaraman Nagar, Muthanampatty
Dindigul Dt – 624 622

Mrs. P. Padma
Library Assistant, Dr. T.P.M. Library
Madurai Kamaraj University, Palkalai Nagar
Madurai – 625 012

Ms V. Sasikala
Guest Lecturer, Dept. of Library and Information Science
Madurai Kamaraj University, Palkalai Nagar
Madurai – 625 012

Ms M. Kavitha
Guest Lecturer, Dept. of Library and Information Science
Madurai Kamaraj University, Palkalai Nagar
Madurai – 625 012

Mr. Selvakumar
Librarian, Matha Memorial Education Trust
Vannpuram, Manamadurai, Sivagangai Dt.

Dr. A. Sokkalingam
Librarian, Ramkrishna Mission Vidyalaya Polytechnic
College, P.N. Palayam, Coimbatore- 641 020

Herald BrowineThomas
#M-118, Phase-2, Muthampalayam H.U., Kasipalayam
Erode – 638 009

Ms. M. Gayathri
Librarian, PEACE College of Education
Opp. Every Ready Mill, Vittalnaickenpatty
Sukkampatty (PO), Vedasandur Road, Dindigul Dt

Ms. S. Pauline Upahara Rani
Library Assistant
PSNA College of Engineering And Technology
Kothandaraman Nagar, Muthanampatty

Mrs. T. Narmadha
Librarian, Periyar Maniammai University
Periyar Nagar, Vallam
Tanjavur – 619 403

Technical Session – I
Public, Academic, Special Library and Information Centers

A-01
Role of Public Libraries in the Modern Society

E. Krishnamoorthy
Librarian, District Central Library, Trichy.20
R. Senthil Kumar
*Librarian, Kongunadu Arts and Science
College (Autonomous), Coimbatore-29.*

ABSTRACT

Public libraries are institutions that support democracy and development in the society by offering free access to information. This paper discusses the purposes, features, initiatives, services and different roles of public libraries in the modern era in accordance with UNESCO manifesto and model library act of Dr. S.R. Ranganathan. This paper also highlights highbrid library concept and new public library concept with naming synonyms of public libraries in the knowledge era. It highlights the present situation encouraged in the public library system at state and national level with more emphasis on District Central Library, Trichy with its collections, services and user expectations.

INTRODUCTION

Public libraries are institutions that support democracy and development in the society by offering free access to information. The public library the local gateway to knowledge, provides basic conditions for life-long learning, independent decision – making and cultural development of the individual and social groups. In this paper, meaning, purpose, function, types, systems and services of public libraries are discussed. Expectations of readers covering the knowledge era are presented.

MEANING

As per the "Model Public Libraries Act" of Renganathan Public Library means

- State Service library
- Any library established by a Local library authority and service stations.
- Any library opening to the public free of charge.
- An aided library receiving grant-in-aid from the Government.
- Any other library notified by the government as a public library.

PURPOSES OF THE PUBLIC LIBRARY

- Serve as a centre of culture and information in the community.
- Provide service for all sections of the community.
- Encourage and promote books or information.
- Facilitate continuing education and life long learning.
- Cater to the information needs of the general public or lay person.

FUNCTIONS OF PUBLIC LIBRARY

- To ensure nation wide coordination and cooperation.

- To promote a national library network based on agreed standards and services.
- Public library network must be designed in relation to National, Regional and Special, Schools, Colleges in University Library Etc.
- Organize and promote library and users as a whole society
- Promoting education, disseminating information and providing recreation.

NEW PUBLIC LIBRARY CONCEPT

In recent times, general development has taken place in the area of Information and Communication Technologies (ICT).

- Fulfill the traditional role of the public library
- Apply ICT to its functions / activities so as to facilitate access to general information to its user in the most cost effective manner possible.
- Assure new roles so as to help the general public / lay persons.

HYBRID LIBRRY CONCEPT

Hybrid library contains a practical blend of traditional and electronic documents/materials and provides document – oriented and electronic – based services to its users.

DIFFERENT NAMES OF PUBLIC LIBRARY

- Learning centers
- Information centers
- Resource centers
- Knowledge centers
- Access Centers
- Knowledge Cleaning centre

- Information society
- Service organization etc.,

TYPES OF PUBLIC LIBRARIES IN TAMIL NADU

- State Central Library
- District Central Library
- Mobile Libraries
- Branch Libraries
- Village Libraries
- Part-time Libraries

PUBLIC LIBRARY SERVICES

- Issue of documents
- Inter library loan
- Provisions of General and Specific information
- Reference service
- Referral service
- Compilation of bibliography
- Extension services
- Publicity
- Information Display
- Mobile library
- Children's Library
- User assistance in the use of library resources
- News paper clipping services
- Photocopying services
- Computer assisted services such as
  - On – line books renewal
  - OPAC
  - Internet – browsing service.
  - Books, CD reference service etc.,

ROLE OF PUBLIC LIBRARIES IN MODERN SOCIETY FORMAL EDUCATION

- Must be an institution
- Provides books for recreational reading
- Library can be approached for service reading, for educational purposes.
- Library must encourage the teachers and students of educational institutions by acquiring books.

LIFE LONG SELF EDUCATION

- Everybody has to keep himself/herself abreast of the continuous development in their respective fields.
- Education is described as a life long process.
- It is possible only if they have access to public libraries in the branches of knowledge.

EDUCATION OF WORKING GROUPS

- Should stock books relevant to the needs of people engaged in different vocations.
- They will become better informed and educated in their areas of work
- It will increase their work efficiency.
- This will lead to greater productivity

DISTANCE EDUCATION

- It basically involves self study for which library support is absolutely essential
- A Well- stocked public library.
- Diversified knowledge provided by public library.

ADULT EDUCATION

- To provide literacy by all means with a view to improve the economic conditions of the masses

- Eradication of illiteracy is necessary
- It must be associated with literacy campaign both with the adult and neo - literates.
- To produce wall pictures and charts representing the news and the latest facts and ideas.
- To use T.V, Radio, and motion pictures which are useful in adult education programmes.

CULTURAL ROLE

- It plays a vital role in collecting and preserving the cultural heritage of the locality.
- The public library must be readily available to the people of the locality to enrich its cultural awareness.

RECREATION ROLE

- To offer certain recreational facilities so that they can spend their leisure time with profit.
- It helps people get rid of the stress and strain of modern complex life.
- The public library is required to organize various social functions to entertain people and attract them toward the use of libraries.

CIVIC ROLE

- Role to play as informed and intelligent citizens.
- Helps them to know, define, and enjoy their rights and realize and discharge their duties in a free society.
- The people must have civic education to participate intelligently in activities like municipalities, panchayats etc.,
- Knowledge of political, social, economic and technological affairs.

SOCIAL ROLE

- Role to play in social education to prepare people for social adjustment
- Offers materials and services to the public to understand social phenomena.
- Live a successful social life and to avoid social evils.
- Provides opportunities to the people to understand social diseases and how to control them.

INFLUENCE OF INFORMATION TECHNOLOGY ON PUBLIC LIBRARIES

- Computer Literacy
- Multimedia access
- Network technology
- WEB technology
- Bar code technology
- Digital library access

USERS EXPECTATIONS FROM PUBLIC LIBRARIES IN MODERN SOCIETY

Types of Users

- General public
- Teachers and Students
- Research scholars
- Children
- Layman to Scientist

Users Expectations

Community information : Local charts, activities, education, opportunities, employment visits, civil rights etc.,

Consumer information : Consumer associations, government bodies, financial advice, tours, law, holidays, buying and selling etc.,

Government information : Governor, chief minister, MPs, MLAs, government orders, public utility forms, tender notices, information rights, state government department's welfare schemes etc.,

Health information : For women, children, health institutions, diseases, reference to some specialist etc.,

Education & Training :

- Travel information
- Business & finance information
- Local history information
- Weather information
- Tsunami and earthquake information as a whole

RRRLF FOUNDATION

Raja Ram Mohan Roy Library foundation is located in the National library at Kolkata. This foundation has provided lot of services to the public libraries throughout the country. Mainly it develops the public libraries and also gives financial assistance.

Main Assistance of RRRLF

- Book assistance
- Accommodation
- Aid to acquire T.V cum VCR sets for educational purpose.
- As voluntary organization
- Assistance to children's libraries and sections.
- Assistance toward organization for seminar/ conference
- RRRLF award
- Computerization

HIGHLIGHTS OF DISTRICT CENTRAL LIBRARY (TRICHY)

- Established : 1952.
- Locality : City Corporation
- Total Population (2001 Senses) : 7,460,62
- Literacy : 6,16,798
- Staff : 14
- Books : 1,52,725
- Members : 24,950
- Average visitors - 450
- Average books issue - 250
- Average books reference - 125

DIFFERENT SECTIONS

- Reading
- Lending
- Reference
- Civil service
- Visitor
- Children's section
- Binding
- Computer

SERVICES

- Books lending by computer
- Reference books
- Civil service books
- News paper Reading
- Children's book service
- OPAC search
- On-line book renewal

- Internet – Browsing
- TNPSC bulletin, Gazette service
- Xerox service
- Telephone

CONCLUSION

In view of the above the people in the modern society have been benefited to a large extent from public libraries. More over the Government should take steps for making available the advanced information by providing the facilities like computerization of library, bar coding, internet etc., to get up-to-date information and save the time.

REFERENCES

* **Sri Devi and Shalini Vyas** Library and Society. New Delhi : Shree Publications, 2005

* **Shayamala Balakrishnan and P.K. Paliwal (Eds)**. Public library system in India . New Delhi : Anmol, 2001.

* National Seminar in new public library in the information age.

* Indian journal of library studies by RRRLF.

A-02

Open Access System in College Libraries: An Overview

R.Senthilkumar
Librarian (SS), Kongunadu Arts and Science College (Autonomous), Coimbatore -29

E.Krishnamoorthy
Librarian, District Central Library, Trichy – 20.

ABSTRACT

In the modern days, the concept of library is changed in to Knowledge Resource Centers. The meaning of the library i.e. the store house of books is changed to the store house of knowledge. So the services of the library must be improved to fulfill the user's requirement. One of the best practices of the library and information center is to implement OPEN ACCESS SYSTEM in all types of libraries, especially in the college and university libraries. This will enable the users to use the library without any hesitation and with full liberty. The under utilization of the available resources in the library and information center is also to be eliminated.

INTRODUCTION

Open access system is an useful concept for all type of

libraries .Especially in the academic libraries, it is very much useful for the users to use the library without any hesitation. But many libraries in India are not ready to introduce open access system due to many reasons like manpower shortage, safety angle, decision taken by the management etc. In this paper we will discuss all the pros and cons of open access system.

OPEN ACCESS SYSTEM

Once upon a time the libraries had only printed books. Now the modern libraries have all type of study materials and services like periodicals, CDs DVDs, cassettes, online journals, e-books, internet, cable TV, Mini theatre etc. By introducing the open access system in the college libraries all the users can come and use the services available in the library without the assistance of library staff and feel free to use the resources available in the libraries. They can use all type of services like OPAC,INTERNET,CD,DVD Access, online journal access, e books access etc., without seeking the help from the library staff.

NEED FOR THE IMPLEMENTATION OF OPEN ACCESS SYSTEM

Management Support

The management of the college must whole heartedly welcome the open access system, then only the library staff can actively introduce the same and attract the students to make use of all the available facilities with full interest and freedom.

Modernisation Like Computerization and Barcoding etc

The modernization of the college libraries is very much important these days. Because many modern concepts in all the fields of higher education are being introduced, the library also must adopt the modern concepts to cope with. The OPAC facility is the base for open access by using the OPAC, the students themselves can know the availability of the materials, location, circulation status etc., through the computers. So, computerization is essential for implementing the open access system in the college libraries.

Adequate Manpower

Sufficient manpower is essential to implement the open access system. Because, the book used by the users must be replaced in the same location by the library staff only. Also the supervision activity must be strengthened by using adequate number of staff.

Well Structured Library Building

The library building should be well planned. This must include all the sections like circulation counter, reference section, book storage ie stock section, internet section, back volumes section, periodicals section, audio-visual section etc.,

Also by introducing the safety concepts like dividers in between the sections, all the windows having sliding glass doors with mesh etc., to protect the books and other materials from being misused. All the safety concepts must be introduced and then the users can be allowed to the library with open access to use the materials.

Library Staff Support

Supporting library staff with sincerity and hard work is essential to implement the open access system. Because, effective supervision and control only leads to success for open access system,

Adequate Training to the Users

Through the proper user education programmes like library orientation programme, the students are educated about the available facilities, services and how to use the same. This type of user education helps the users to use the library open access system in a positive way.

The open access system is very useful to the users to use the available resources in a library with full freedom. This system has the following merits and demerits.

MERITS

User Satisfaction

The library users especially the college library users can use the material any time without delay because they can take the materials by themselves. They can take more than one title for the same purpose and enjoy reading them. Other services like OPAC, internet browsing, periodical reference etc., can be used by themselves without seeking any help from the library staff. So, the users are highly satisfied and are ready to visit the library frequently.

Effective Utility of the Available Resources

Open access system gives full freedom to the users for using all the available facilities in the library by themselves. This freedom results in more effective utilization of the available resources.

Good Image About the Library Services

The open access system creates a good image among the users about the library and its activities.

Motivation to the Users

This open access system motivates the users to visit the library frequently.

Discipline

Allowing the users to make use of the facilities without any restriction makes the user understand the faith, the department has in him. This develops discipline among the users while using the library.

DEMERITS

Lack In The Safety Angle

The open access system is a very sensitive concept. Different types of users visit the library daily. So effective monitoring system must be introduced.

Tough Maintenance

This system is a challenging one. Many library staff must be involved to maintain the library materials like books, periodicals etc. and to replace the materials after usage by the users.

More Expense For Manpower

The open access system requires more number of staff for maintenance, monitoring activity etc. so more number of staff must be appointed which is an additional burden to the management.

CONCLUSION

Every good concept has its own merits and demerits. So, by considering the merits and finding out the solution to overcome the demerits one can implement the good concept like the open access system in the college libraries. In these modern days, without the open access system, the library services will not get any recognition from the users.

REFERENCES

* **Ranganathan, SR.** *Reference service.*Ed.2.Bangalore:Sarada Ranganathan Endowment for library science,1999

* **Ranganathan, SR.** *Elements of library classificaton.* Bangalore: Sarada Ranganathan Endowment for library science,1998

* **Ranganathan, SR.** *Library book selection.* Bangalore:Sarada Ranganathan Endowment for library science,1998

* **Ranganathan, SR.** *Library administration.* Bangalore:Sarada Ranganathan Endowment for library science,1998.

A-03
A Study of Sources and Services of College of Education Library: Future Concept

P. Nagamani
Assitant Librarian, Adhiyamaan College of Education,
Hosur-635 109.

P.S. Baghath Singh
Advocate (Madurai High Court), No.56,
G.N. Mansion, K. Pudur, Alagar Kovil Road, Madurai-7.

ABSTRACT

In ancient days, libraries are considered as store houses and librarians are considered as custodians. After the invention of printing technology information reached each and every place in the world. Slowly library has developed. Collection of documents will not satisfy the user needs. A library should be well versed in its services. According to the fourth law of library science saving of time satisfies the users in searching and getting their information. Collection, processing and retrieval plays a key role. So this paper deals with the sources and services of Adhiyamaan College of Education, Hosur.

INTRODUCTION

The Education Library of Adhiyaman Colege of Education is located in the AERI Campus at Hosur. Its services and collection of books are very good. From the starting of the college library in 2004, till now, the library has vastly developed.

OBJECTIVES

- To develop the collection of books
- To develop the internet facilities
- To develop the automation of library
- To provide the reprography services
- To provide web services

SOURCES / BOOK COLLECTION

Total number of volumes of books	-	15,000
Total number of Titles	-	4,000
Dictionaries	-	1,500
Total number of Reference Books	-	3,000
Total number of Encyclopedia	-	50 sets
Total number of year Books	-	20

PERIODICALS

The library has good collection of periodicals. They consist of

National Journals	-	38
International Journals	-	13
Subject Magazines	-	17
General Magazines	-	15

NON-BOOK – MATERIALS

1. CD's   -   65
2. Cassettes   -   20

3. Floppy   -   05
4. Diskettes   -   19

LIBRARY SERVICES

The library is equipped with a number of services such as:

- Issue and Return services
- Reference services
- Reprography services
- Technical service
- Abstracting service
- Indexing service

FUTURE CONCEPT

In the future the college plans to provide other facilities or services. They are as follows.

- Internet facilities
- Adding number of volumes / Books.
- Automation
- Reprography services
- Link with society at primary level and higher secondary levels.

CONCLUSION

I would like to conclude that in the near future, we plan to develop our college Library with enormous facilities.

REFERENCES

* **Sharma, JB.** *Organisation and development of libraries.* New Delhi : Vedam Books Publications, 1995

* **Dhiman, Anil K and Sinha, Suresh C.** *Academic Libraries.* New Delhi : Ess Ess Publications, 2002

A-04
Sources and Services of District Central Library : An Over View

K. Sekar
Librarian, Christian College of Engineering,
Oddanchatram- 624 619

D. Umamaheswari
Librarian, Christian College of Nursing,
Ambilikkai- 624 612

ABSTRACT

Library is a center of learning which gives enormous information to the users. Users may be looking for the information in various aspects. So, the libraries should contain variety of information and it has to be analysed in a perfect manner to satisfy the user's needs. A proper service alone satisfies user's expectations. Therefore, collection, processing and retrieval are playing a vital role in giving the right information to a right user at the right time. Users in general are entirely different from the potential and academic users. They may give irrelevant keywords to the library professionals in searching their needs. To satisfy this kind of users needs, the library professionals should be well equipped in searching and finding information. According to the fourth law of Library science, only reduction in the time consumed for retrieval may fully satisfy the users. This study deals with identifying the sources and services of Dindigul District Central Library and gives suggestions to improve the same.

INTRODUCTION

Retrieval is like a transaction of money in a bank. A good deposit of money will lead good withdrawal in time. It is a good concept, the same concept may be used in Library or in a Information Centre and Documentation Centre. The sources of all information or organization of information, may be categorized as mentioned below.

- Text Book,
- Reference Book,
- Document
- Old document like
    - Manuscript of Palm Leaves
    - Stone Scripts
    - Clay Tablets
- Periodicals
    - Journals and Magazines
    - Bulletin
    - News Letters
    - Patents and Copy rights

All these sources should be stored or arranged or preserved systematically in these centers and can be retrieved effectively for the purpose of good reference to help betterment of human activities.

Here the authors try to connect the link between organizing the information and importance of library.

DETAILS OF THE STUDY SOURCES AND SERVICE OF DINDIGUL DISTRICT LIBRARY

Public Libraries gives reading materials to the people without any creed or caste or religion status of education and economical background. So it is called people University. Library is the center of learning which gives various information to the users. User may be looking for information in various interested aspects. So the libraries should add variety of information like text of subjects and reference materials. It should be arranged in a perfect manner to satisfy user needs.

Dindigul central library was **opened on 10th of April 1954**.It has a total number of **11, 97,798 (Eleven Lakhs Ninety Seven Thousand Seven Hundred and Ninety Eight Volumes)** volumes and these volumes are distributed in 50 branches, all over the District. The central library has 96,004 volumes located at West Govindapuram Dindigul City,

THE DETAILS OF LIBRARIES IN THE DISTRICT

Central library	-	1
Branch libraries	-	50
Village libraries	-	72
Part-time libraries	-	18
Total	-	141

Among the libraries all the taluk head quarter libraries are computerized and controlled by central library.

USERS OF THE DINDIGUL LIBRARIES

Dindigul Public Library System has its members from various places of Dindigul District as mentioned below.

- Members(Users) - 12,720

- Total no. of readers - 1,66,744 (As per the report of October 2007)

INFORMATION SOURCES

1. Books

Containing novels, short stories and text books of Arts and Science in both English and Tamil Languages written by various authors.

2. Reference Books

- *Encyclopedia*

This Library is having a good number of Encyclopedias for various subjects.

- *Dictionaries*

Also the Library is having a good collection of Dictionaries.

3. Periodicals

- This Library is having number of periodicals for the users under the section "Reference and Recreation". The following periodicals are displayed for the purpose of the same.
  - Kumutham
  - Kalaimagal
  - Health
  - Anandha Vigadan
  - Tamil Computers
  - Mangaiyar Malar
  - Aval Vigadan
  - Reader's Digest
  - India Today
  - Valar Kalvi

— Valar Thozhil
— Velan Vingnanam
— Employment News
— Daily Magazines of
  * Dina Malar
  *Dina Karan
  *Dina Thanthi
  *Dina Mani
  *Malai Malar
  *Malai Murasu
  *Indian Express
  *The Hindu
  *Cinema Express, etc.,

INFORMATION SERVICES

The district center library has provided the **indexing services** of its collection and users **current awareness services** in the field of employment opportunities and guide to the student communities and youth. **Reprographic service** is also provided to the users on their request.

SUGGESTION OR RECOMMENDATION

In general the public libraries have insufficient furniture for the users. And it is found that the latest facility of internet system is provided only to the urban users. It should be extended to rural areas also.

REFERENCES

* **Anil Redd, DC.** *Organisation and management of public libraries.* New Delhi : Vedam Books Publications, 1998
* **Shayamala Balakrishnan and P.K. Paliwal (Eds).** *Public library system in India.* New Delhi : Anmol, 2001.

A-05

Niscair-an Information Centre : A Case Study

E. Gajalakshmi

II M.L.I.Sc, Department of Library and Information Science,
A.V.V.M Sri Pushpam College, (Autonomous),
Poondi, Thanjavur Dt.

T.R. Deivanai

Lecturer, Department of Library and Information Science,
A.V.V.M Sri Pushpam College, (Autonomous),
Poondi, Thanjavur Dt.

ABSTRACT

Nowadays we are in information era. So we are aware of all fields. As a Library Professional we have a responsibility to know about all types of information. Many Information centres can provide information about various fields. In this article, we discuss about NISCAIR an Information centre. They provide various services like CAPS, Document Copy Supply Service, Readers Service, Copying Service, Inter-Library Loan Service & E-Journals Access service. They have finished various projects related to the field of Science & Technology (TKDL), E-Journals Consortia, Directory of S&T awards in India and Database of R&D Projects. Not only Library Professionals but also all persons in the field can become aware of the functions of Information Centre.

INTRODUCTION

Information is nothing but the task of handling information for all disciplines. The major objective is, in libraries, archives and in information centers they provide storage and retrieval services to the user. Any institution that can handle information for storage and retrieval activities, is termed as information centre.

DEFINITION

According to Cohan & Crowen, Information centre has been defined as, "the demand of laboratory and administrative personnel for expanded, more efficient and better integrated information services. As a result effort has been made to unify Libraries, Patent, Report Writing, Archival, Abstracting, Literature Search, Editorial, Communication & Publication activities with in a single facility. The centralization of all the above leads to the formation of Information centre".

HISTORICAL CONCEPT OF NISCAIR

- In older days, NISCAIR was known as INSDOC.
- NISCAIR came into existence on 30th September 2002 with the merger of NISCOM & INSDOC.
- It was initiated in 1952 and was engaged in providing S&T information and Documentation Services.
- Through myriad activities such as Abstracting & Indexing, Design & Development of Databases, Translation, Library Automation, Providing access to International information sources, Human source development, Consultancy Services, Setting up modern Library-cum-Information centres.
- INSDOC was also host to the National Science Library and the SAARC Documentation Centre.
- NISCOM & INSDOC the two premier institutes of the

Council of Scientific & Industrial Research (CSIR) were devoted to dissemination and documentation of S&T information.

- NISCOM had been in existence for the last six decades. In 1996 it was termed as NISCOM.

- It diversified the activities through a host of its information products, comprising research & popular science journals, encyclopedic publications, monographs, books and information services.

- It had been reaching out to researchers, students, entrepreneurs, industrialists, agriculturists, policy planners and also common man.

FUNCTIONS OF NISCAIR

Following are the functions and activities of NISCAIR.

- To provide formal linkages of communication among the scientific community in the form of research journals in different areas of S&T.

- To disseminate S&T information to general public, particularly school students and to inculcate the spirit of science among them.

- To develop human resources in the field of Science Communication, Library & Information Science, Documentation and S&T information management systems and services.

- To harness information technology applications in information management with particular reference to science communication and modernizing.

- To act as a facilitator in furthering the Economic, Social, Industrial, Scientific and Commercial development by providing timely access to relevant and accurate information.

- To collaborate with International institutions &

agencies having objectives and goals similar to those of NISCAIR.

VARIOUS SERVICES PROVIDED BY NISCAIR

NISCAIR can give various services related to the field of S&T. Following are the services,

ELECTRONIC PUBLISHING

- Using newer tools for producing many products on CD-ROM including Wealth of India, ISA, NUSSSI.
- In future, other NISCAIR Journals, popular science books and monographs will also be published in CD-ROM format.
- Back issues of the journals will also be made available on CD-ROM format.

EDITING

- They provide editorial services for conference proceedings, scholarly books etc for other organizations on man hour basis.
- The charges for editing services are decided on case to case basis.
- This editing job covers content editing as well as copying editing and stylization.

PRINT & PRODUCTION

- It takes up editing, composing, designing and printing jobs from its clients preferably in digitized form.
- Its clientele include INSA, DRDO, DNES, DST, DSIR,DBT, DOD, NBOGR, ICAR, IAMR, COSTED, NAMS & T, IIT DELHI,RANBAXY LABORATORIES, CAG, INDIA METEROLOGICAL DEPT etc besides various CSIR labs.

CONTENT, ABSTRACT, PHOTOCOPY SERVICES (CAPS)

- It is an innovative personalized information services provided by NISCAIR.
- In this centre,7000 journals from various disciplines are identified.
- Select the journal from the list of your choice.
- You will receive at your doorstep every month the table of contents of your chosen journals.

DOCUMENT COPY SUPPLY SERVICE

- In this service, they one obtains the abstract or full text of desired articles through NISCAIR's Document copy supply service.
- It provides yoeman services to Indian Scientific Community by supplying copies of articles from Indian & Foreign journals at nominal charges.
- NISCAIR can obtain copies of Indian & Foreign patents and Standards.

LITERATURE SEARCH SERVICE

- It offers its service in compiling bibliographies on demand from indigenous as well as from international databases in the areas of S&T, Engineering, Industry etc.
- It charges some nominal amount based upon the cases.

TRANSLATION SERVICES

- It provides translation of S&T documents from 20 Foreign languages into English Language.
- It provides services of reverse translation i.e. English to Foreign languages.
- It also undertakes interpretation and consultancy assignments in Japanese language.

- It charges some nominal fees for translation services and for interpretation.

BIBLIOMETRIC SERVICES

- It carries out studying of growth, development and spread of any area of research.
- It also identifies centres of excellence, influential authors etc.
- These services are useful for Heads of Depts / Institutions, Research Planners, Policy makers and Individual scientist.

CONSULTANCY SERVICES

- This service is provided in the area of automation, modernization and re-organizations of libraries and Information centres.
- The design and development of specialized databases for organizations on turnkey basis.
- Areas of editing, designing, production and printing.

These are the services given by NISCAIR for various scholars of different fields.

VARIOUS PROJECTS OF NISCAIR

In NISCAIR they do several projects and also they arrange various programmes in all emerging fields.

TKDL:(Traditional Knowledge Digital Library)

- The main aim for doing this project was to safeguard ancient inventions of Ayurveda.
- To address this problem of grave national concern NISCAIR and the Dept of Indian Systems of Medicine & Homeopathy are collaborating.
- A Separate agency is constituted for this project.
- The responsibilities include providing user-friendly

software, setting up TKDL hardware & Software
Platform for data entry.

- Digitizing images of slokas, making a directory on
  TKRC and hosting the database in web/portal.
- It will be available in English, German, French, Spanish
  and Japanese Languages.
- It would encompass in addition to ayurveda, siddha,
  unani, yoga, naturopathy and folklore medicine.

E-JOURNALS CONSORTIA

- NISCAIR is the nodal organization for developing a
  "consortium for CSIR laboratories for accessing e-
  journals"
- The journal resources will play a vital role and
  strengthen research and development in CSIR
  laboratories.
- The objectives are to strengthen the pooling, sharing
  & electronically accessing the CSIR library resources.
- To provide access to world S&T literature to CSIR.
- To nucleate the culture of electronic access resulting
  into evolution of digital libraries.

NISCAIR has started this project with an agreement
from the following publishers. They are listed below

S. No	PUBLISHER	No. of sub. labs	No. of labs for e-access	Number of journals for access	Number of subscribed journals
1.	Elsevier	38	ALL	1500	399
2.	Springer	32	ALL	800	120
3.	American Institute of Physics	8	8	16	17
4.	Black Well	23	23	355	55
5.	American civil Engg	8	8	30	20
6.	American Chemical Society	24	ALL	41	31

7.	John Wiley	28	ALL	374	84
8.	Cambridge University Press	11	11	74	18
9.	Oxford Univr Sity Press	15	ALL	69	28
10.	American Society of Mechanical Engg	6	6	20	19
	Total: 10			3316	813

DIRECTORY OF S&T AWARDS IN INDIA

- The Directory of S&T awards in India (DSTAI) is being updated by NISCAIR under the sponsorship of National Science & Technology Management Information System (NSTMIS), Dept. of S&T, Govt. of India.

- The Directory will fulfill a long standing demand of S&T workers in the country.

- It is a good tool to provide necessary information about S&T awards available to R&D workers of India.

- The major objectives of DSTAI are to update the database and keep it current and to widen up the coverage of the database.

DATABASE OF R&D PROJECTS

- This project was developed by NISCAIR under the sponsorship of (NST MIS) Department of Science and Technology & Government of India.

- The databases are available on CD-ROM

- It provides information nearly 8000 R&D projects in S&T institutions and other disciplines from pure science to applied science.

- The updated database will be extremely useful to organizations and individuals for identifying areas of research and subject specialists and will help in optimal utilization of Government funds.

- The data about ongoing research projects is being collected through questionnaires which can be downloaded and filled in questionnaires can be sent through E-mail.

These are the projects run by NISCAIR in the field of Science & Technology.

CURRENT EVENTS &PROGRAMMES OF NISCAIR

- CSIR- WIPRO Workshop on Negotiating Technology Licensing agreement.
- CSIR Programmes on Youth for Leadership in Science.
- Digital database on genetic resources of India.
- Visit of five high level South African member delegation to NISCAIR.
- NISCAIR participates in most of the Book Fairs organized in the country at State National and International level.
- It also has an exhibition-cum-sale through a van for display-cum-sale of NISCAIR publication.
- It is done on regular basis in schools, colleges, IIT, Delhi University and CSIR labs
- They give special discount at the buyer's doorstep of 10% too.

VARIOUS PRODUCTS GIVEN BY NISCAIR

- PROCEEDINGS OF FIRST INDO-US WORKSHOP ON GREEN CHEMISTRY
- WEALTH OF INDIA
- NUCSSI ON CD-ROM
- INDIAN PATENTS ON CD-ROM
- ISA ON CD-ROM
- THE TREATISE ON INDIAN MEDICINAL PLANTS
- COMPENDIUM OF INDIAN MEDICINAL PLANTS

- THE USEFUL PLANTS OF INDIA
- STATUS REPORT ON CULTIVATION OF MEDICINAL PLANTS IN NAM COUNTRIES
- PLANTS FOR RECLAMATION OF WASTE LANDS
- MISCELLANEOUS PUBLICATIONS

VARIOUS WEBSITES PROVIDED BY NISCAIR

- *www.aicte.ernet.in*
  (All India Council for Technical Education)
- *www.aiuweb.org*
  (Association of Indian Universities)
- *www.csir.res.in*
  (Council of Scientific & Industrial Research)
- *www.mit.gov.in*
  (Department of Information Technology)
- *www.dst.gov.in*
  (Department of Science & Technology)
- *www.dsir.nic.in*
  (Department of Science & Industrial Research)
- *www.iisc.ernet.in*
  (Indian Institute of Science, Bangalore)
- *www.iitb.ac.in*
  (Indian Institute of Technology, Bombay)
- *www.iitd.ernet.in*
  (Indian Institute of Technology, Delhi)
- *www.iitk.ac.in*
  (Indian Institute of Technology, Kanpur)
- *www.iitkgp.ernet.in*
  (Indian Institute of Technology, Kharagpur)
- *www.iitm.ac.in*
  (Indian Institute of Technology, Madras)

- *www.ignou.ac.in*
  (Indira Gandhi National Open University IGNOU)
- *www.mst.nic.in*
  (Ministry of Science and Technology)
- *www.nic.in*
  (National Informatics Centre)
- *www.unesco.org*
  (United Nations Educational Scientific and Cultural Organization UNESCO)
- *www.ugc.ac.in*
  (University Grants Commission)

FINDINGS

- Now a days we are in Information Era
- We must be aware of all Information related to our emerging fields.
- Library is otherwise known as Information Centre
- NISCAIR can give brief information about the field of Science & Technology
- They assist all scholars from various disciplines to be aware of current events in the related fields
- Lot of programs, exhibitions and projects are done by NISCAIR
- They publish various products related to the field of S & T
- It is highly useful to the Research Scholars and Scientists to know the current information and update information related to one's field

CONCLUSION

The purpose of this study is stress that all scholars from different disciplines must be aware of Information Centre.

Information Centre can give updated and current events of information related to one's field. In this article, we discuss about NISCAIR which gives various services like conducting programs, projects and exhibitions. They also give various products related to the field of S&T. They provide various website addresses of different disciplines. Through these activities the user can easily attain the current information related to one's field.

REFERENCES

* http://www.niscair.ac.in
* http://www.google.com
* http://www.yahoo.com
* http://www.infolibrarian.com

A-06
Information Services in Information Centres with Special Reference io INCOIS – A Case Study

M. Subramaniyan
L. Arun Kumar
S. Suguna
II M.L.I.Sc Students, Department of Library and Information Science,
A.V.V.M Sri Pushpam College, (Autonomous), Poondi, Thanjavur Dt.

ABSTRACT

This paper discusses the need and importance of information services in the information age and also analyzes Indian National Centre for Ocean Information Services (INCOIS) in India and its various models like organization, advisory services, information bank, ocean observation and ocean sciences. It also describes various components of information bank in INCOIS like In-situ data, satellite data, ARMEX-1 COMAPS, Model outputs, Historical data sets, maps, metadata.

INFORMATION SERVICES

It is advantageous to discuss information services on the basis of information units. Here the traditional units of libraries are excluded. However it is to be noted that these units do provide information services depending upon the nature of users and nature of the parent unit.

The main purposes served by these units are:

- To identify as accurately as possible all information of potential interest to users.
- To ensure that users receive the information.
- To help them find the primary documents
- To answer their queries.

INFORMATION CENTRE

The task of handling information for storage and retrieval have been the major objectives of libraries, archieves and information centres. "If any institution handles information for storage and retrieval activities, it is termed as information centre". Information centre is classified in the following way

- Data centre
- Retrieval Centre
- Clearing house
- Information analysis centre
- Translation centre
- Reprographic centre

OBJECTIVES OF THE STUDY

- To study about information services
- To study and evaluate

INCOIS

Indian National Centre for Ocean Information Services.

It is an autonomous body under the Ministry of Earth Sciences, Govt. of India.

MISSION OF INCOIS

To provide ocean information and advisory services to the society, industry, government and scientific community through sustained ocean observations and constant improvements through systematic and focused research.

ACTIVITIES OF INCOIS

i. INCOIS is providing information services to the following

- Potential Fishing Zone (Mission – mode)
- Experimental Ocean State Forecast (Mission – mode)
- Marine Meteorogical Advisory Services
- Web-based Ocean Information Services
- Value added services and Decision Support Systems

ii. Contribute to

- Storm surge prediction and Disaster Management
- Climate / Monsoon / Weather Forecast
- Monitoring of Pollution / Oil Spill
- Global Ocean Observing System

iii. Establish

- Infrastructure for ocean information, Modeling
- Regional Argo Data Centre
- National Agro Data Centre
- Ocean Portal

INFORMATION BANK

INCOIS has a separate bank for information. INCOIS, being the central repository for marine data in the country, receives voluminous oceanographic data in real time from a variety of in-situ and remote sensing observing systems. The ocean information bank provides information on physical, chemical, biological and geological parameters of ocean and coasts on spatial and temporal domains that is vital for both research and operational oceanography. The ocean information bank is supported by the data received from ocean observing systems in the Indian Ocean (both the in-silu platforms and satellites) as well as by a chain of Marine Data Centres.

Further, INCOIS has been designated as the National Oceanographic Data Centre by the International Oceanographic Data Exchange Programme (IODE) of International Oceanographic Commission (IOC), Also INCOIS serves as the National Argo Data Centre, the regional data centre and clearing house for the Indian Ocean region for the IOGOOS programme.

INCOIS Ocean information Bank has the following data sets

- In-situ data
- Satellite Data
- ARMEX-1
- COMAPS
- Model Outputs
- Historical Data Sets
- Maps
- Meta Data

STAFFING

INCOIS has a separate leader (Head) for providing Information Services in Ocean and also it has executive members and support services staff groups.

FINDINGS

- INCOIS has a separate information bank
- INCOIS is providing very effective and fruitful services to its members
- INCOIS is providing web based information services.
- It has a global organization for oceanography.

SUGGESTIONS

All librarians take necessary steps for providing information services.

CONCLUSION

The effectiveness and efficiency of information centre is largely dependent upon the competence of staff and facilities and environment provided for their work and development.

REFERENCES

* **Venkataraman, P.** *Information technology application in libraries.* New Delhi : Ess Ess Publications, 2004

* **Murthy and Sonal Singh.** *Information services, Library education and research in India.* Jaipur : RBSA Publications, 2003

A-07
Dr. S. R. Ranganathan's Five Laws of Library Science: Applicability in the College Libraries

R. Senthilkumar
*Librarian (SS), Kongunadu Arts and
Science College (Autonomous), Coimbatore – 641 029*

N. Ramasabareswari
*Asst. Librarian, Kongunadu Arts and
Science College(Autonomous), Coimbatore – 641 029*

ABSTRACT

Dr. S.R. Ranganathan derived FIVE LAWS OF LIBRARY SCIENCE and through this, he enabled the librarians to serve in a better way to the user community. By implementing the concept of each and every law in today's academic libraries, one can get the best results and also establish all the BEST PRACTICES in the library field. These laws are more applicable to the modernized services in the library and information centers and also to meet tomorrow's expectations. In this paper, we have discussed more

*on this aspect. This paper discusses the applications
of the facets of five laws in contemporary library
environment.*

INTRODUCTION

Dr.S.R.Ranganathan devised five Laws of Library
Science. These five laws are useful for today's modernized
library. Each and every law is useful for the day to day
operation of the library and development of library activities.
All the best practices being introduced in today's libraries
are originating from these laws only. Each and every law is a
useful tool to build any modern library. In this paper, we
discuss the five laws and their applicability in today's library.

BOOKS ARE FOR USE

This first law clearly stresses the importance of open
access system and modernization. The open access itself is
to facilitate the **utilisation of all the books & other
materials** available in the library. By using the open access
facility the users can make use of all the materials and
facilities available in the library without any hurdle and
hesitation.

The modernization, like computerization, bar-coding,
RFID technology implementation etc., in the college libraries,
facilitates the users to know the materials available
immediately. So, today's technology and yesterdays concepts
like classification, open access system etc., are very much
useful to the college libraries.

EVERY READER HIS BOOK

In these days, all the libraries are ready to procure
various types of materials & update the services like providing
different subject books, e-books, internet, online journals,
back volumes of journals, periodicals etc. It will really attract
the users, because users' needs are fulfilled. Dr.S.R.
Ranganathan through his second law i.e. every reader his

book, points out the satisfaction of users by building the collection of materials based on the users requirements. Today's concept of various types of collection services is really based on the second law of library science only.

EVERY BOOK ITS READER

Through this third law, Dr.S.R.Ranganathan points out the utility of the available materials and the materials collection updating is based on the users needs only.

Dr. S. R.Ranganathan through his third law, has said that each and every material and service available in the library should be useful to the user. No materials and services must be underutilized. Through the modernization like providing Online Public Access Cataloguing facility, by conducting Library orientation programme, User Awareness Test, Library Resource Awareness Quiz etc., all the materials and services available can be advertised (or) promoted among the users. These are all motivational activities to make use of the available materials and services. Not only these, but also the procurement of collection must be based on the users' requirements only.

Dr.S.R.Ranganathan's third law supports today's library services promotional activities like OPAC, Library orientation programme, Library resource awareness Test, Library user awareness Quiz etc., in the college libraries.

SAVE THE TIME OF THE READER

Dr. S. R. Ranganathan through his fourth law, tells the importance of Quick service to the users. Todays modern concept is also useful to establish this law in the college libraries.

Today's modern concept of OPAC, Barcoded user entry, Barcoded circulation system, scrolling facility of important news through computers, proper classification system & maintenance of the books etc., are based on this fourth law only. Quick service only attracts the users and motivates them to visit the library again and again, in all type of libraries, especially in the academic libraries.

LIBRARY IS A GROWING ORGANISM :

Every care must be taken to develop the library is the message from this law. Today's concept of "Library is a nerve centre of any institution" is based on this law only. Proper care to procure the collection, proper care to implement different services and maintenance, no limit to provide the facilities and collection development etc., are all stressed through this law. Mainly **"Updation is very important"** is the message through this law. So, today's concept of "Vast development" is really based on this law only. The expansion activity to face the future collection development and facilities updation is to be planned well in advance is the main theme of this law for all kinds of libraries.

CONCLUSION

Dr.S.R.Ranganathan devised the Five Laws of Library Science by predicting the need of future libraries needs and wants. These five laws are really useful for all types of libraries and by following these laws, any library can be elevated to the best level, because today's developments are really based on these five laws only. These five laws match all the best practices being implemented in today's library development.

REFERENCES

* **Ranganathan, SR.** *Reference service*. Ed. 2. Bangalore:Sarada Ranganathan Endowment for library science,1999

* **Ranganathan, SR.** *Elements of library classificaton*. Bangalore:Sarada Ranganathan Endowment for library science,1998

* **Ranganathan, SR.** *Library book selection*. Bangalore:Sarada Ranganathan Endowment for library science,1998

* **Ranganathan, SR.** *Library administration*. Bangalore:Sarada Ranganathan Endowment for library science,1998

A-08
Academic Librray and Information Centers in The Digital Era

K. Paulraj
Research Scholar, (P.M.T.College, Melaneelithanallur-627953)
Manonmaniam Sundaranar University, Tirunelveli-627 012,

Dr. S. Kanthimathi
SG Librarian & Research Guide,
Rani Anna Government College for Women, Tirunelveli-627 008

ABSTRACT

Dr. Johnson says "Knowledge is of two kinds: We know a subject ourselves, or We know where we can find information upon it". The amount of information generated today is astronomical and the problems relating to its storage, dissemination and analysis are beyond human ingenuity. The current knowledge proliferation rightly called 'the era of Knowledge explosion', is expanding at a tremendous speed and it is not humanly possible to keep the whole upsurge of knowledge at one's fingertips. It is in this context that the "Intellectual Workshops" or Libraries play an important role.

Information Communication Technologies through satellites, e-mail, computer and other multimedia technologies have made libraries more dynamic. The next logical step is the application of computers to library operations. The information super highways have made 'Virtual office' and 'virtual classroom' possible. Thus the end-user or the actual user can sit at the terminal and search or retrieve bibliographic records without the help of an intermediary like the library professional. The databases are so designed that they can serve the end-user though he is not a computer expert. These User-friendly databases save time not only for the library professional but also for the user who can also obtain a hard copy of the document needed. This paper discusses the uses of digital technologies for the provision of library and information services.

INTRODUCTION

Dr. Johnson says, "Knowledge is of two kinds: We know a subject ourselves, or We know where we can find information upon it". The amount of information generated today is astronomical and the problems relating to its storage, dissemination and analysis are beyond human ingenuity. The current knowledge proliferation rightly called 'the era of Knowledge explosion', is expanding at a tremendous speed and it is not humanly possible to keep the whole upsurge of knowledge at one's fingertips. It is in this context that the "Intellectual Workshops" or Libraries play an important role.

For centuries libraries remained passive storehouse of books accessible only to the elite. Public libraries after the first world war were dynamic institutions open to all free of charge and maintained out of public funds by the local governments. After the Second World War extension programmes were introduced to reach out to the potential users through branches and bookmobiles. Resource sharing became a common practice through inter-library loan. The real breakthrough came with the invention of the microcomputers, optical discs and other mass storage media worldwide computer and library networks. Information

Communication technologies through satellites, e-mail, computer graphics and other multimedia technologies have made libraries more dynamic information providers. The next logical step was the application of computers to library operation. The information super highway made 'virtual office' and a 'virtual classroom' possible. Thus the end-user or the actual user who sits at the terminal can search or retrieve bibliographic records without the help of an intermediary like the library professional. The databases are so designed that they can serve the end-user though he is not a computer expert. These User-friendly data bases save time not only of the library professional but also of the user who can also obtain a paper copy of the document needed.

The invention of CD-ROM has enabled a thousand page book or document to be recorded on it which are machine readable (read through a computer) and print out taken instantly at a nominal cost. Now the electronic media or the "Expert System" comprising Knowledge base, User Interface', Inference Engine, Explanation Facility, Knowledge Acquisition and External Interface, does provide circulation of books and journals, Reference Service, Selective Dissemination of Information (SDI), Current Awareness Services (CAS), Indexing and abstracting services.

Hence the work of information professional becomes convenient, systematic and easy. It helps in saving the time of the users.

USER EDUCATION

In this technological scenario, libraries are renamed as "Intellectual Workshops". They are no longer "shrines of worship" as Socrates would have us believe. Paul Buck, an eminent Harward University Librarian remarked, "a good collection of books attracts a good faculty, a good faculty in turn attracts good students". An ordinary teacher tells, a good teacher explains but an excellent teacher inspires. So also a good book raises your spirit and inspires you to inculcate noble and intellectual thoughts. Evidently if the breakthrough in information technology is to be fully taken advantage of, then, changes need to be brought about in our policies regarding teaching, research and educational administration. A corollary is that there had to be a revamping of the infrastructure and appropriate changes in procedure and methodologies. The reputation of an academic institution depends on the status of its library. Hence the need of the hour for libraries is to function as 'Intellectual workshops' rather than a museum of books.

Knowledge has become a critical resource. The radical structural transformation currently reshaping our society had necessitated changes in the types of work we are all engaged in, increasingly demanding knowledge intensive skills. A higher degree of information literacy is required. People need to be able to seek out, retrieve, reorganize, assimilate, interpret and utilize data information and knowledge. However they often lack both the time and the inclination to pursue these activities. The librarians as providers of information and as premier information experts have to act as strategic intermediaries.

COMPONENTS / CONSTITUENTS OF USER EDUCATION

The librarian of the future is quite often a practicing librarian of today, grappling with the issues that are reshaping the profession. In this context the American Library Association (ALA) in 'ALA Goal 2000' (1994) insists that the librarians must "transform themselves into a force capable of engaging (society) in the age of information". Library Information Professional, apart from being a gatherer and provider of information from materials both in the print and electronic form, has to act as an interpreter to those who are users of information. As librarianship is reinvented, the term 'librarian' continues to be a useful employment title in the Indian scene, describing the role of the information professional. Many alternative titles as Knowledge Counselor, Chief Information Officer, Information Broker, Information Navigator, Information Manager and Information Designer are in use.

The librarian can discharge his/her obligation only by shaping the library users into self-directed learners thereby transforming the library into an intellectual workshop. To do this he/she has to introduce the learner to the world of exploration. He/she has to initiate the process of such exploration both personal and participative. He/she has also to inspire him to undertake arduous tasks for the purpose. Above all he/she should help him to chart the course of action and make the needed breakthrough on his way. In this journey of the student for KNOWLEDGE the-library, its resources, its personnel, its modalities of work; 'its climate and culture' and its various services have to provide him support which will prove critically vital in sustaining his morale, his patience, his commitment and his will to learn on his own. Such tactical support will reinforce his faith in himself and in his ability to pursue his goals of learning. The aim of libraries should be not to have up-to-date information but up-to-minute information. The growing role of the Intellectual Workshop lies in information counseling, individual training, advising the users on services and products appropriate to their needs and how best to use them. Any Intellectual Workshop should play a vibrant role giving room for cross-fertilization of ideas and for serving as a centre for perpetuating and extending the horizons of knowledge.

DAMOCLE'S SWORD – A PARADIGM SHIFT

As the metamorphical change is from collection management to knowledge management the need of the hour of the Librarians or Knowledge Managers is to compete with the threatening situation due to the surfacing of Information Technology in libraries. The "internet" is the Damocles' sword for the knowledge navigators.

WHAT IS KNOWLEDGE MANAGEMENT

Knowledge "creation" is providing productive new knowledge through innovative thinking experimenting and researching. Technology plays a vital role in analyzing and translating results into products and services.

Knowledge "capturing" is a very important activity in Knowledge management. This enables the Knowledge managers to identify the sources as to the know-hows, the competitor's intelligence, marketing and customer information etc.

Knowledge "sharing" or transfer is very effective due to the advancement of Information Technology. Internet plays a prominent role here E-mail, video-conferencing, on-line discussion, forums etc. enable the users' participation in decision making.

Knowledge "retention" is a very important activity, which again involves technology such as designing of Data base, management, Information systems and Expert systems.

"Leveraging" of knowledge depends on the ability to shape and organize the captured and stored information and in utilizing the knowledge to its fullest.

KNOWLEDGE MANAGEMENT CAPABILITIES

The Internet is an abundant source of information and the biggest depository of knowledge and is an ideal platform for communication and collaboration. As creating knowledge portals have become an inevitable task of Knowledge Managers they should develop skills to sustain in this competitive world. Organizations no longer depend on printed books for enhancing their capabilities but believe in resource sharing.

Another very important function of information personnel is to provide the users with what is known as Repackaging of Information, catering to the varied demands and needs of the users on inter-disciplinary basis. The librarians should be effective Information Managers. The key factor that permits librarians to metamorphose into information manager is their ability to organize conceptually, to evaluate, to select and to channelise information to the point where it is needed. Thus "the information professionals do more than just providing information and information services, they help people do what they do, better".

Dilemma of change in library management has to be recognized. The librarian as Thought Navigator is faced with accelerating change in both the external environment supra-system and internal organizational subsystems, which a effect the managerial process. These lead to increasing complexity involving the manager more vigorously in maintaining equilibrium between the need for organizational stability and continuity and the need for adaptation and innovation. He/she needs to be a benevolent leader to facilitate an easy organizational and environmental change.

TOTAL QUALITY MANAGEMENT

Enhancing library services through an evaluating technique is a must. As responsive service to users is identified as the primary goal of professional libraries it is important to incorporate TQM mechanism to evaluate the achievement of this goal. Total Quality Management is a systematic process, which focuses on understanding customer's needs and improving customer service and satisfaction. In addition, the emphasis of TQM is a continuous improvement rather than meeting specific standards. Given a library's commitment to customer satisfaction, TQM could serve as a practical and useful strategy for the ongoing evaluation and improvement of library services.

CONCLUSION

Information Designer should be characterized by visibility and vitality. The new role of librarian will be that of a provider of "expertise in the relevance, veracity and meaning of resources". These Information Brokers should be valued as essential to the teaching, learning and research activities. The Thought Navigators should be seen as part of the solution – contributing to quality education. There should be visionaries in conceiving the present and imaging the future and they should be willing to take the risks inherent in translating their vision to action. Nothing is permanent in this world except "CHANGE". People may come and go into the portals of any institution but the institution remains for posterity.

REFERENCES

* **Newton, Robert & Dicon and David** (1999). "New Roles of Information Professional User Education as a core professional competency within the new information Environment". *Journal of Education for Library & Information Science,* 1999.pp.157-160..

* **M. Kramer (Series Ed) & D.W Former & T.F. Mech. (Vol. Eds)** New dimension for Higher Education, No.78 Information Literacy, developing students as independent learners, San Fransisco Jossey – Ban.

* **SALIS 2006** – *National Conference on Initiatives in Libraries and Information* Centers in the Digital Era.

A-9
Library on the Wheels; Best Practice of A College Library

R. Jayabal
*Librarian, Sri Ramakrishna Mission Vidhyalaya
College of Arts and Science, Coimbatore.*

M. Prabhakaran
*Librarian, Vivekananda College, Autonomous,
Tiruvedagam, Madurai Dt*

S. Chinnaiyan
Librarian, Vikram College of Engineering, Madurai

ABSTRACT

*Reassessing the professional practices followed by the academic libraries and in particular in college libraries is the main thirst to compete with the academic institutions and also to serve the nation better. One among the best practices of the Vivekananda College Library is Mobile Library System. **Vivekananda College,** Thiruvedagam, the only registered Gurukula institute of Life training in modern India has launched an extension service **"Library on Wheels"** in July 2006 for the benefit of the rural students and the public.*

INTRODUCTION

"The development and implementation of outreach services and reading-enhancement services (such as adult literacy and children's programs)", is one of the long-term issues indicated by Wikipeida, the free encyclopedia. The Academic libraries in the country are on the threshold of facing big challenges as a result of globalization and liberalization trends in higher and professional education. The higher and professional education is moving more and more towards privatization. Educational institutions no longer wish to make their budget requirements a liability on their national exchequer, but on the contrary are trying to mobilize their own resources to provide better services by following best practices. The libraries in this regard have become part of this strategy and the parent organisations are investing sizable sum on the development of libraries to improve the services with better infrastructure, yet they are also conscious of their Return on Investment (ROI). This calls for the standardisation of services offered by libraries. This calls for reassessing the professional practices followed by the academic libraries and particular college libraries. One among the best practices of the Vivekananda College Library is Mobile Library System. **Vivekananda College**, Thiruvedagam, the only registered Gurukula institute of Life training in modern India has launched an extension service *"Library on Wheels"* in July 2006 for the benefit of the rural students and the public with the following objectives,

- To improve the reading habits
- To remove ignorance
- To provide awareness about the environment and nation
- To improve the educational and social status
- To provide library services on demand

    To this noble cause, the SBI has donated a Van worth

of Rs.5.00 Lakhs. With the contributions from the Old Students Association, and the College Management additional books were procured. The beneficieries are 8-10 standard students of Government Higher Secondary School, Sholavandan, Vivekanda Matriculation Higher Secondary School, Sholavandan, and Seva Bharathi - Self Help Groups (SHG) located both in Thiruvedagam, and Madurai. The beneficiaries either do not have library facilities at all or the existing facility is not adequate enough to supplement their information needs. Total number of beneficieries includes 350 students, and 330 public in all. The beneficieries utilize the services through 'in-charges'; the class teachers in the case of schools, and the team leaders in SHGs.

At specific intervals, this Library on Wheels goes to the service locations, meets the respective in-charges, and the circulation of books is carried out till the appointed hours. For any type of specific requirement (beyond the collection on the wheels) the said requirements are noted down and the circulation of such materials are made available subsequently. Using regular interactions with the users and the in-charges, necessary changes are incorporated as and when necessary. In the case of *Library on the Wheels*, the Library professional has to cope with the specific group that he serves. One should be willing to work beyond his regular timings. This requires commitment and social responsibility on the part of the professional. The cross section of the rural users may be heterogeneous and more complex that warrant a good understanding of the environment that one has to deal with. The following are the specific skills needed for school and SHG environment.

SKILLS FOR SERVING SCHOOL STUDENTS

In the college environment, the library provides textbooks and reference books for the curriculum needs. Also it supplements extra reading for knowledge and recreation.

But in the school environment students may not need books for their curriculum. The students normally own copies for their curriculum needs. The role of the library is restricted to materials for extra reading, for knowledge and recreation. It is the duty of the library professional to assess the user needs and to provide reading materials, and also, make them habitual readers. It requires adequate motivation, communication, and interpersonal relationship (soft skills).

SKILLS FOR SERVING SHGS

Team Building, Interpersonal relationship, Communication and Motivation (soft skills), are the foundations on which SHGs are built. If the library professional is equipped with these soft skills, he/she can play an important role in the knowledge transfer process. In the SHG environment growth and prosperity could be improved by adequate input of knowledge. The library professional if he/she is skillful enough in analyzing the user needs and their behavior, the individual user needs could be satisfied. Thus the entire group gets required inputs which can result in further growth of the group as a whole. Presently this service deals with books only. In the long run the service may have to include other type of materials also. i.e. non-book materials. Such a situation will warrant more familiarity in the other areas such as Technology skills, Processing Skills, Financial Management skills and Marketing skills.

CONCLUSION

Serving the rural people through education is not only for present but also for future generation. The best practice followed in the library of Vivekananda Collge, Thiruvedagam is the one among the outreach programs. "Library of Wheels" or mobile library makes the rural students move towards the goal of 'education to all' by the Government.

REFERENCES

* **Dawra, Manisha.** *Libraries in India.* New Delhi : Rajat, 2004
* **Mohanraj, V.** *Library services for children.* New Delhi : Ess Ess Publications, 2004

A-10
Special Library –
Saraswathi Mahal

V. Vijayalakshmi
M. Sangeetha

*I M.L.I.Sc Students, Department of Library and Information Science,
A.V.V.M Sri Pushpam College, (Autonomous), Poondi, Thanjavur Dt.*

ABSTRACT

Saraswathi Mahal, the granary of Tamilnadu is famous for its multi faceted activities in Literature, Fine arts, Native Medicine, Dance and numerous other fields. Special Library is devoted to special subject and offers specialized service to the specialized clientele. This paper discussed about the history of the Saraswathi Mahal and also deals with the administration, services, manuscripts, Dhanvantari Mahal, Modi Documents, conservation, museum and other activities.

LIBRARY

The literary treasures of ancient India in Sanskrit and other Indian languages were written by hand on various materials such as palm-leaves, paper etc., They were preserved in the houses of Pandits and other Scholars, in private possession and also in public institutions like Mutts, temples and last but not least, in the Palaces of Kings who were patrons of arts and letters. Without exception, all kings had their manuscript collections in their Library called Sarasvati Bhandara, which varied from one another only in respect of size.

SPECIAL LIBRARY

The most accepted definition of the Special Library "is devoted to special subject and offers specialized service to the specialized clientele". This paper discussed about special services of Saravathi Mahal, Tanjavur.

SARASVATHI MAHAL LIBRARY

Introduction

The Tanjore Maharaja Serfoji's Sarasvati Mahal Library is one among the few medieval libraries in the world. It was started as a Royal Palace Library during the Nayak Kingdom over Thanjavur and was developed by Maratha kings of Tanjore. It is a repository of culture and unexhaustive treasure house of knowledge. The Library houses rich, rare and valuable collections of manuscripts on all aspects of art, culture and literature. In 1918, this library was made as Public Library.

History

During the reign of Nayaks of Thanjavur (1535-1675 A.D.), "Sarasvati Bhandar"(Collection place of Manuscripts) was formed and developed. The Maratha rulers who captured Thanjavur in 1675 A.D. patronised the culture of Thanjavur and developed the Royal Palace Library till 1855 A.D. Among the Maratha Kings, King Serfoji II (1798-1832), was an eminent scholar in many branches of learning. In his early age, he studied under the influence of Rev. Schwartz and learned English, French, Italy, Latin etc., and also was interested in Arts, Science and Literature. With great enthusiasm he took special steps for the enrichment of the Library. During his pilgrimage to Banares, he employed many

Pandits to collect, buy and copy a vast number of works from all renowned Centres of Sanskrit learning in the North and other far-flung areas. It is a fitting tribute to the great collector Serfoji that the Library is named after him. After last Maratha Queen, the Royal Family members voluntarily came to dedicated this Library to the public with one lakh rupees for its maintenance and upkeep. Accordingly, the Government of Madras in their G.O. Ms. No.1306 Home (Education) dated 5th October 1918, took possession of the Library under the Charitable Endowment Act and has framed a scheme for the management of the Library. A five member committee under the ex-officio Chairmanship of the District Collector was appointed to maintain the Library. The name of the Library was changed to "The Thanjavur Maharaja Serfoji's Sarasvati Mahal Library".

Administration

The Society was constituted and got registered on 9-7-1986 under the Registered Societies Act of 1975. The Society consists of ex-officio members of both Central and State Governments, nominated scholars, members from the Royal family and the Director of the Library. The Hon'ble Education Minister of the Government of Tamilnadu is the Chairman and the Director is the Secretary of the Society. There are 48 staff members working in this Library. They are classified under three divisions namely. Administration, Technical and Academic. Director is the Head of the Library.

Fund

The Library receives fund from the Government of Tamilnadu for the maintenance and from Government of India for its developmental activities.

Functions

- To preserve our traditional cultures hidden in the books and non book materials

- To promote the research activities for the users of society
- To publish books from manuscripts available in different languages
- To preserve all the manuscripts in microfilm
- To conserve all the books, manuscripts and other rare artificats
- To catalogue and classify books and assist the research scholars
- To sell the publications
- To conduct seminars and training course on manuscriptology, conservations etc.

MANUSCRIPTS

Collection

This Library has the richest collection of manuscripts in Sanskrit, Tamil, Marathi and Telugu that reflect the history and culture of South India. The manuscripts are available both in palm-leaf and paper, on different forms, on different subjects in Tamil, Telugu, Marathi and Sanskrit languages. The Major parts of the manuscripts are in Sanskrit language, which exceed 39,300 written in Grantha, Devanagari, Nandinagari, Telugu scripts etc. The total number of Tamil manuscripts is 3780 comprising titles of literature and medicine. In Marathi Manuscripts, 3076 Marathi manuscripts are of South Indian Maharastrian of the 17th, 18th, and 19th centuries. There are 846 Telugu manuscripts in this Library, which are mostly on palm leaves and a few in papers. Apart from these manuscripts there are 1342 bundles of Maratha Raj records available at the Library.

NATURE OF MANUSCRIPTS

Palm-leaf Manuscripts

Palm leaves were commonly used as writing material

in ancient India and were known as tada patra, tala patra or panna. The leaves of the palm tree, available all over India, were collected and dried and cut into the same convenient length. Two holes were made to pass a string, which tied the leaves together.

Paper Manuscripts

Paper was introduced quite late in India, but had appeared by the time Ekoji I took over Thanjavur. It was made by hand from cellulose vegetable material; masi or mela was the ink used for writing, available in red, black, gold and silver. The permanent black ink was prepared by mixing the lamp soot of sesame (Sesamum indicum) oil with the gum of acacia and rainwater. The pens were made of either wood, bamboo or goose quill. The papers were dipped in turmeric water for protection from insects.

Sanskrit Manuscripts

The Sanskrit Collection of the Sarasvati Mahal, which is the largest collection, contains not only the major works of Sanskrit literature beginning with the Vedas but it is also especially noteworthy for the history of later Sanskrit literature and copies of works which were produced directly under the patronage of the Telugu and Maratha Rajas of Thanjavur. The manuscripts are in palm leaves and paper form which are written in Devanagari, Nandinagari, Grantha and Telugu scripts.

Marathi Manuscripts

The Marathi Paper Manuscripts collected during the reign of Marathas of Thanjavur i.e., from 1676 to 1855 A.D. are preserved in this Library. The total number of 3076 Marathi Paper Manuscripts are compiled in 6 volumes of catalogues called "The Descriptive Catalogue of Marathi Manuscripts" and classified into many subjects like Philosophy, Literature, Drama, Music, Lexicon, Medicine, Science etc.

Tamil Manuscripts

The Tamil Manuscript Section comprises of 3780 manuscripts of which 2083 are Literary and the rest are Medical. All these are in palm leaves and are of the following categories: -

a. Rare Works like Kambaramayana, Kalingathu Bharani, Moovarula etc., are   available in palm leaf manuscripts

b. Unpublished portions of classics.

c. Saiva, Vaishnava and Jain works.

d. Later poetry of all descriptions.

DHANVANTARI MAHAL

Sage Dhanvantri was the Father of Indian medicine. To honour the memory of Dhanvantri Raja Serfoji ran a medical institution called "Dhanvantri Mahal". Besides research on many ailments, excellent work was done on diseases like cancer, polio, diabetes and tuberculosis by the Institution of Ayurvedic and Siddha medicines. Raja devoted himself to the progress of research in Dhanvantri Mahal by bringing together Siddha, Ayurveda and Unani physicians of repute. As a result of physicians discussions, the best among tried and effective remedies are embodied in the series of works named Sarabhendra Vaidhya Muraigal. These works are composed in lucid Tamil verse form to facilitate easy memorisation. This Library has published many of them. The Dhanvantri Mahal also had a wing of research for animal husbandry. Many prescriptions for the disease of domestic as well as wild animals and birds show the broad scope of interests supported by the Rajah and implemented by the Dhanvantri Mahal. The concept of research, especially of a clinical nature is comparatively modern. Some modern systems carry out research only on rabbits and other animals. But at a comparatively early period Rajah Serfoji's doctors were confident enough to use their drugs on human beings.

TELUGU MANUSCRIPTS

The Tanjore Telugu manuscripts collection is unique and it represented the home productions of royal patrons of art, their court pandits and other scholars domiciled in the Tanjore country. It may be said that the collection represents the southern school of Telugu literature.

MODI DOCUMENTS (MARATHI RAJ RECORDS)

Modi is a type of script used for writing the Marathi court language during the Maratha rulers of Maharashtra as well as Thanjavur. The court records are called Modi documents and they are all paper manuscripts. Letter correspondences, Orders, Daily accounts, Diaries, Petitions etc., were written only in Modi script.

OTHER MANUSCRIPTS

Along with the manuscripts in Sanskrit, Tamil, Telugu and Marathi languages, manuscripts written in various scripts like Grantha, Devanagari, Nandinagari, Tamil, Telugu, Malayalam, Oriya, Bengali, Burmese are also available. This Library also has few manuscripts in Persian, Urdu and Hindi languages.

RAJAH'S COLLECTION OF BOOKS

The old books in European languages in this Library are mostly collected by Maharaja Serfoji. Maharaja was a scholar and patronised many scholars. He was taught by Danish Missionary Father C.F. Schwartz. He learnt English and many other languages. In his collection there are more than 4500 books in English, French, Italy and Danish languages. These books deal with many subjects including Musical Notations.

GENERAL COLLECTION

The general collection of this Library has been started

from 1918. This general collection comprises rare books in six major languages Sanskrit, Tamil, Telugu, Marathi, Hindi and English. The earliest printed books, mostly the first editions are available in this collection. Books are added to this Library by the following ways

    a. Purchase of Reference Books from the Government of India's grant.

    b. Donation of old books by Private Institutions, Mutts and Individuals.

    c. Books received as complimentary from the Department of Culture, Government of India.

    d. Books purchased by the library from the publishers.

Now the reference section has 54,009 books in various languages. Card catalogues are prepared according to Title, Author and Subject for each language books. Books are issued only for reference under closed access system.

Sanskrit	-	154
Marathi	-	43
Telugu	-	22
Tamil	-	205
English	-	8
Total	-	**432**

Generally10 percent to 30 percent discount is allowed for the sale of books. 50 percent discounts on sale of their publications are allowed during every September 24th - the birthday of Raja Serfoji II. This Department has three units namely, Printing, Binding and Marketing Units. In 1998, DTP equipment and electronic copy printer have been purchased to expedite the publication work.

VARIOUS SECTIONS

Conservation Section

Conservation Section of this Library has been

functioning since August 1980. The main functions of this
section are :

    a. To keep the Manuscripts, Books, Cupboards, Show
        cases etc., clean.

    b. To restore damaged books and manuscripts.

    c. To preserve the manuscripts from deterioration.

Cleaning

The Manuscript cupboards are cleaned twice a year and
therein kept insect repellents and indigenously prepared
insect repellent mixture i.e., Sweet flag, Pepper, Black cumin,
Bark of Cinnamon, Cloves with Camphor are kept. Dried
neem leaves are also used as Insect repellent.

Guarding

Teak wood reapers are fixed on both sides of the palm
leaf manuscripts to safe guard them from damages. Similarly,
paper manuscripts are protected with acid free hand made
board after getting them repaired and fumigating them.

Rebinding

Rare books are repaired and rebound according to the
condition of the books. Paintings, drawings and maps are
also dust cleaned, repaired and strengthened for
preservation.

Reprography Section

The Microfilming unit was installed in the year 1980
with one DK5 Microfilm camera, Developing machine,
Photocopier, Film copier and one Reader. In the first phase
5000 rare manuscripts of Sanskrit, Tamil, Telugu and
Marathi were selected and microfilmed for preservation.

Museum

A Museum is located in the Library building to reveal
the importance of the Library to the Public. This Museum

has seven sections such as ancient manuscripts, Illustrated Manuscripts, Old books, Printed copies of the Original Drawings, Atlases, Thanjavur style of Paper Paintings, Canvass Paintings, Wooden Paintings, Glass paintings, Portraits of the Thanjavur Maratha kings, Daniel Paintings, Fraser prints of Indian Scenarios, Punishments of China depicted in picture, Physiognomy charts of Charles Le-Brun, Bathing ghats of Banaras and other Antiquities. These materials will give an idea about the total and variegated collections of the Library to the public.

Interesting Manuscripts

This Library has more than 46,000 manuscripts both in palm leaf and paper form. In palm leaf manuscripts there are the following manuscripts are available:

- Phalavathi
- Thiruvaimozhi Vachakamalai
- Valmiki Ramayanam
- Kamba Ramayanam
- Panchpakshi sastram
  In Paper Manuscripts,
- Bhamati
- Bhagavat Gita
- Tattuva chintamani
- Amber Hussaini
- Rigveda manuscripts with illustrated title sheet
- Shivaji & Ramadoss
- Dasbodam
- Siva para pancharatna slokas

MAPS AND ATLASES

The Library not only has books and manuscripts but also rare maps, atlases and historically important documents.

The atlases and maps preserved in this Library are more important. Most of them were collected and purchased by Raja Serfoji. They were compiled with survey materials in land and sea. These materials dealt with ancient historical, geographical details, sea routes, political divisions, ancient names and their boundaries etc. The oldest printed book available in this Library is an atlas dated back to 1692, 1693 and 1696.

PICTURES AND DRAWINGS

Along with paintings and illustrated manuscripts this Library is also having drawings and lithographic pictures and most of them were collected by Raja Serfoji .

- Daniel Prints
- Charles Le Brun's Human Physiognomy charts
- Chinese punishment
- Ophthalmic case sheets
- Botanical Album
- The 64 Bathing Ghats on the Gates at Banaras

CONCLUSION

A library working for a special purpose is called special library. The researches and students are coming here to consult the primary sources, college students for their dissertations and research scholars for preparing critical editions.

Steps are being taken to extend the computerization of the library. The books and non-books materials available in this library are our national wealth. It becomes the duty of one and all to preserve it property for the use of future generations.

REFERENCES

*   http://www.sarasvatimahallibrary.tn.nic.in

A-11
Public Library

K. Vanitha
M. Gowri
M. Rajeevgandhi

*I M.L.I.Sc Students, Department of Library and Information Science,
A.V.V.M Sri Pushpam College, (Athonomous), Poondi, Thanjavur Dt.*

ABSTRACT

Library is storage of knowledge. We have a universal belief that education is for one and all and that it is essential for social change. Thus we make effort to promote education to get rid of the evils of illiteracy. This paper discusses about the Public Library definition, objectives, collection, functions, services etc.

INTRODUCTION

Public Library is considered as an essential part of modern society and plays a very important role in the community. It is basically a service library. It provides free service or charge a nominal fee for its service

DEFINITION

"The public library is a product of modern democracy and by its nature and scope it is a library for every citizen". It is freely open to every person irrespective of class, creed or age or sex.

CHARACTERISTICS OF MODERN PUBLIC LIBRARY

The collection of a Public Library is built on the basis of the educational level, occupation, interest and needs of the mass population. It serves to the individual or groups.

OBJECTIVES

- To offer free access to services
- To meet the potential needs of its community
- To provide facilities and materials for free research
- To aid formal education
- To develop adult and self education
- To promote reading habits

FUNCTIONS

- Acting as an agency of adult education
- Acting as an agency of perpetual self education
- Functioning as a community centre
- Meeting place to commemorate public events
- Display books or lists
- Defining as a centre for developing reading habit
- Promote popular enlightment of all the people

USER'S NEEDS

- Homogeneous and heterogeneous people need general and special information
- Public Library users need inter library loan
- Public Library is a Public University
- A Public Library user needs books and novels for recreational reading.
- Users needs up to date information on various branches of knowledge

- Organizing reading clubs (books will be read out to them), holding exhibitions, educating through films, radio, television etc. to educate people

ROLE

- A Public Library can play an important role in helping different sectors of the community
- It can help farmers to improve production by providing simple and useful information on agricultural techniques and product in local languages
- A Public Library can create in children a love for reading which can lead to formation of reading habits at an early age
- It can enable a businessman to improve business prospects
- It can help student of all ages. It can provide career information helping people looking for better prospects or those who are unemployed
- Public Library is the only institution accessible for self learning

DOCUMENTS

A Public Library has to cater to a vide variety of users and perform challenging functions. The expectation is that a user of every age and educational attainment should be able to find documents of his interest. The total collections should include documents on all subjects. A public library acquires a large variety of documents such as books, pamphlets, periodical publications, visual materials, audio visual materials, audio and video cassettes, films and slides for educational purpose. New forms of documents are becoming increasingly important part of a public library's collections.

PRODUCTS

The public library may bring out the following products:

- Brochure / hand books about the library
- Products of current awareness service for retrospective searching
- Bibliographic Surveys
- Accession Lists
- Bare documentation List
- Literature Survey
- Duplicate contents of periodicals
- Library catalogue and union catalogues
- Newspaper Clippings
- Data Books
- Translations

AUTHORITY

The following types of authorities are possible

- State and Union Government
- Local Government
- Representative body
- Private Body

ACTIVITIES

- Issue of Documents
- Inter Library Loan
- Provision of general and specific information
- Assistance in searching
- Readers advisory service
- Compilation of Bibliographies
- Referral Orientation and Bibliographic instruction

- Extension service

ORGANISATION

A Public Library System should have a central Library. It should have branches. In addition mobile libraries should serve rural and sub urban areas. In urban areas where library buildings do not exist mobile libraries can be used. Mobile libraries are extremely useful for rural areas having dispersed population. Mostly mobile libraries are used to provide only lending facilities.

Usually a Public Library is organized into lending, reference, periodicals, acquisition, technical and maintenance sections. In large Public Libraries, the libraries may be organized on the basis of subject departmentation. In addition, there would be a children section.

CONCLUSION

The Library is a living Organism humming with activity. The Public Library is a product of modern democracy. The Public Libraries' out reach services dealing with illiterates, disadvantaged, aged and handicapped and deprived are to be organized and designed to suit the specific user group and closely allied to the main purpose of Libraries as provider of knowledge.

REFERENCES

* **Kumar, PSG.** *A Student Manual of Library and Information Science.* New Delhi : B.R. Publications, 2002

A-12
The Concept and Construct of Resource Division in Special Libraries

Mrs. J. Rosalind

Librarian (S.G), JKK Nataraja College of Arts and Science.
Komarapalayam, Namakkal Dt.

ABSTRACT

In this I.T. era of specialization and super specialization, in the development of any research field, science and technology or social science specialization plays a major role. Education and research activities make an individual worthy in recognizing right and wrong. Thus it makes an individual capable of progressing in life. The main object of the special library is to disseminate special information to specialists as per their demands and needs. In recent times it has been well realized that to accelerate the speed of socio economic development, it is not only necessary to promote scientific and technological research but to disseminate information at a competing pace to achieve the targets of the utilization.

Hence the resource division is the most important to

share the resources through inter library-loan. It is not a new one, earlier it was called library cooperation or inter library loan or library resource sharing concept. It is very true that no special libraries can be perfect in its stock collection. It has to get help from other special libraries in the same field. All the special libraries should come forward to co-operate and share the available resources and services of the effective and instant services to meet the increasing demands. Such an integrated service will surely help to bring a new revolution in the field of information.

This paper attempts to analyse inter dependence and inter relatedness in the filed of knowledge sharing.

INTRODUCTION

Generally special libraries are part of research institutions of various fields of sciences and technology. Their objectives, collections and even clients differ from one type of special libraries to other types of special libraries depending upon various fields, type of special libraries and their clients.

According to Thomas Laudu "Special library is a service unit devoted to the important requirement both present and future. A special librarian is one who has administrative as well as technical and professional duties".

Earlier the request has been made through postal system which was time consuming. With the progress of communication media services like Fax, E-mail and now internets connected through satellites and on-line services are available which has made the entire world quite closer. But these services are only available when all these special libraries are interconnected through computer networking using LAN, WAN and satellite connections. All these special libraries holdings must be on computer disks through library automation.

MEANING OF RESOURCE DIVISION

With the realization of importance of information in R and D organizations, there is a need of the information consciousness amongst the scientists. No special library, how so ever, well- stocked, can never declare itself self sufficient in its library holding and therefore it has to stake claim from other existing libraries in the locality, regional and other cities, states and even abroad.

For this division, it is a must that the library must have a knowledge of stocks of other special libraries. Some times back BARC, INSDOC, DESIDOC complied the union catalogues of different regional libraries and finally National Unions Catalogue of periodicals was complied, which is to be kept updated periodically.

For the Resource Division, it is essential that it must have the information of other special library's collections. Earlier INSDOC, DELHI complied a National Union Catalogue of Serials in the year 1968, first in the form of Regional Union Catalogues of Special Libraries where the participants gave details of their Serial and Periodicals holdings and to get this information a detailed questionnaire was prepared to collect information.

This division should have the facilities of transfer of communication through Fax, E-mail, internet communication service and on-line services to make full use of various special libraries holdings connected with these facilities. Of course, the research fields of these libraries should be the same or inter related to each other, within the country or abroad.

AIMS, OBJECTS AND PURPOSE OF RESOURCE DIVISION

In order to establish a Resource Division, its aims, objectives and the purpose are detailed out as under:

1. In this the needs and requirements of the readers are taken into account and their objectives are collectively achieved by providing various library services on cooperative basis. These needs are carefully studied and analysed by which the information required should be met keeping in view in which library that information is available. To obtain this information, all electronic equipments which are available in the parent organisation may be used inorder to fulfill the aims and objectives of parent research organisation to which these special libraries are attached.

2. By providing effective library services to its clientele: Maximum needs of these clientele should be met to provide these services to other special libraries as well like CAS (Current Awareness Services), SDI (Selective Dissemination Information), reprographic services so that clientele of other special libraries might make use of these services to get required information.

3. To fulfill the required information need immediately without wasting time.

4. Keeping in view of rising cost of books and subscriptions of current foreign periodicals, the information contained in these must be provided at a reasonable cost without wasting time.

5. To achieve special information from the subject specialist of research organisation through their special libraries' channels.

SCOPE OF RESOURCE DIVISION

The library cooperation is not only achieved for exchange of information for readers/ client ales. Further to achieve these goals of parent organizations of its users, cooperation of various special libraries is must, through their services. These concepts are developed to increase the efficiency and utility of these special libraries collections on cooperative basis. Therefore, these resources divisions are activated to achieve these objectives.

   a. Cooperative acquisition

   b. Issue and return of information and reading material

   c. Cooperative reference and documentation service

   d. Through inter-library loan service

   e. Use of specific tools and tables.

   f. To obtain cooperative reference services

   g. Establishment of cooperative network amongst various special libraries in the technical work.

   h. To establish resource division in special libraries

   i. Cooperation in meeting the immediate information needs.

   j. Cooperative binding of reading material.

   k. Cooperative professional training for library personnel.

   l. Cooperative financing

COOPERATIVE PROVISION READING MATERIAL AMONGST PARTICIPATING SPECIAL LIBRARIES

In the modern era prices of books and periodicals are touching the sky and also the price of electronic equipments used. No special library how so ever large it may be, cannot claim that it is self sufficient in their holdings. This has led to the concept of Resource Divisions. In the Special Libraries, Mr. Framington suggested a plan under which different libraries have special stock holding viz. Books, Current periodicals, back bound volumes, and these special libraries function on cooperative basis.

EXCHANGE OF READING MATERIAL

Under the Framington plan, there is a provision of exchange of reading material amongst the participating special libraries. Whenever the reading material is required by a library, these are exchanged as per rules and regulations of these libraries. If some of the reference books are not allowed to be sent out of the library, the photocopies of the required information is sent on exchange free of cost within reason able limits.

REFERENCE AND DOCUMENTATION SERVICES

Some special libraries bring out, documentation list after scanning the articles in the current periodicals subscribed in the libraries and these articles will be related to the projects which the research organisations are pursuing. The main objective of bringing these documentation lists is to bring to the notice of the scientists the latest information on the project. Similarly these special libraries also receive more information published in the form of articles in the current periodical which are not being, subscribed in their libraries. These documentation lists are only meant for the internal circulation of these libraries. Some these special libraries also provide the facilities of SDI Services, CAS Services. By bringing these services, lot of duplication, time and money can be saved. In this way the different types of information services can be better utilized by the Scientists.

INTER –LIBRARY –LOAN/CREDIT SERVICES

This concept is very commonly prevalent for a long time. To make this concept active, cooperation amongst various special libraries is a must. Under this reading material can easily be achieved on short loans for the scientists whenever such demands by them are received by the libraries. This service is not only available on local level but can be extended to regional level, national level and even at international level. Knowledge of the stock of these libraries are available through their union catalogue of serials and periodicals.

CONGENIAL ENVIRONMENT TO ESTABLISH RESOURCE DIVISIONS AMONGEST SPECIAL LIBRARIES

In order to establish the resource division the co-operation of various libraries are sought. Acceptable library rules should be framed according to the convenience of participating libraries which are willing to send their material on inter library loans.

USE OF SPECIAL EQUIPMENT AND OTHER DEVICES

In most of these special libraries some specialized equipment are not available. Therefore under this plan, scientists are allowed to use their facilities in order to carry out their experiments and specialists can train these scientists to better utilize equipment in an effective way to achieve the best results.

CO-OPERATIVE IN REFERENCE SERVICES

There are some information which are available only in a particular library in the form of reference tools which can be received on telephone calls on demand by scientists through resources division of these libraries.

SOLUTION OF IMMEDIATE PROBLEMS

This is possible if a resource division is established with a well equipped latest tools in their respective fields of specialization of their organisation.

CREATION OF CO-OPERATION NET WORK

Present era is said to be an era of computer and these are being utilized to handle the information explosion effectively, available in the form of research articles. It is only feasible by making these libraries stock holdings available in computers under the library automation programme, because this is the first step towards the creation of net working among the participating special libraries to utilize their data. By creating computer net work among these libraries the exchange of data will be possible at a greater speed effectively. This net working can be created at local level, national level and at the inter-national through on line services. The arrangements of exchange of data can be arrived at by mutual co-operation among these libraries.

CO-OPERATION IN THE AREA OF TECHNICAL PROCESSING

In order to technically process the reading material of the cooperating libraries by the participating libraries viz, in the areas of classification, cataloguing, accessioning and abstracting of reading material which requires intelligent handling by the experts working in the libraries which can be achieved by mutual co-operation.

CO –OPERATION IN BINDING OF READING MATERIAL

Money spent on binding the reading material of these libraries can be saved and the duplication of the stock is avoided and the binding can be done at on a cooperative basis and thereby lot of money can be saved on binding.

TRAINING PROGRAMME FOR LIBRARY ACTIVITIES IN PARTICIPATING SPECIAL LIBRARIES

All the special library staff members have the same type of professional programme to run their respective libraries. It is found that these library professional members posses different I.Q in their professional achievements for serving their users. Due to scarcity of funds these professional don't receive the appropriate professional training or don't get chance to attend refresher courses to make their knowledge upto date. It is proposed that if the participating libraries can pool some portion of their budget to train their staff, the special library association can come forward to arrange short term courses or alternatively some library departments can be contacted to train these professional staff members at a reasonable cost by offering short term courses according to their requirements.

BACKGROUND OF SUCCESS IN RUNNINGS RESOURCE DIVISION EFFECTIVELY

It is not very easy to implement the programme of library cooperation. The following points should be borne in mind.

1. It is essential to see that there is an agreement on all points of the rules they follow and must have common acceptance among the participating libraries.

2. It must have an effective communication and postal system to communicate the information on exchange requirement by the clients of participating libraries.

3. There should be an agreement on all common rules framed by the participating libraries.

4. Exact reading material should be sent by the participating libraries as per the requirements of all the clientele, no substitute material should be provided.

5. The required information must be passed by the participating libraries to the library from where the material is being asked, immediately without delay.

6. It is very essential for the participating libraries to have the Union Catalogue from which the information might be extracted.

7. There should be a common consensus on the common expenditure to be incurred and postal expenses which should be discussed, mutually.

8. Computer networking at the local level is a must to know the data base of participating libraries which

might be connected directly on computers to their readers, so that they themselves can find out their requirement. In this age of computerization such an arrangement on library co-operation is very easy. Lot of money spent on various libraries on getting such information from abroad can be saved but this expenditure can only be reduced by having an independent resource division with an effective library networking.

REFERENCES

* **Krishan Gopal.** *Library collections: Conundrums and contractions.* New Delhi : Authors Press, 2003

* **Suresh C Singha and Anil K Dhiman.** *Special libraries: Research & Technical* libraries. New Delhi : Ess Ess Publications, 2002.

A-13
Public, Academic Special Library and Information Centers

R. Muthuraj
National Engineering College, Kovilpatty.
K. Kamalanathan
National Engineering College, Kovilpatty.

ABSTRACT

This paper discuss about the Public libraries, Academic libraries and Special libraries service and facilities to various people like students, research scholars, laymen etc. And also it discusses the current facility of **IASLIC** *(INDIAN ACADEMIC SPECIAL LIBRARY INFORMATION CENTRE) - like professional development, education and training, bibliography and translation service etc.*

INTRODUCTION

The subjects of the Public Libraries are the users. Their diverse need for an undisputable social change, either wholly or partially is being fulfilled, solved or achieved by the interaction of the users with the books, documents, ideas, information of any type for the liquidation of illiteracy, advancement of education, cultivation of knowledge and for a perpetual self-education of the mass. Public libraries are the nerve centers of the society and their role in social transformation is undisputable and vital.

Prof. Kaula has said that "Library develops literacy, increases productivity and sustains democracy"

"Public Library must be readily accessible and its door open, for free and equal use by all members of the community regardless of race, colour, nationality, age, sex, religion, language, status and educational attainments"

"Public libraries should be maintained wholly out of public funds, so that they can render free service to one and all in the society".

MADRAS PUBLIC LIBRARIES ACT

In recognition of the importance of the library service the Government of Madras Passed the Madras Public Libraries Act as early as in 1948 for the establishment and organization of a comprehensive rural and urban library service. This is the first of its kind in India and was brought into force from the year 1950.

TYPES OF PUBLIC LIBRARIES

The present set up of public library service in Tamil Nadu as on 1991-92 are as follows.

(A) State Central Library (Connemara Public Library)

(B) District Central Libraries

(C) Branch libraries (including circle Libraries)

(D) Mobile Libraries

(E) Part – time libraries. There was no separate regional libraries in the state covering a few districts.

BOOK SELECTION COMMITTEE FOR PUBLIC LIBRARY

A recognized library may be paid additional grant at

the rate specified, provided the library purchased more books from the lists of books issued by the Director.

"The public library should spend 50% of the grant on books, provided not less than 25% should be spent on books from not less than two lists approved by the Director during the year"

ACADEMIC LIBRARIES

In most modern libraries however many of the library personnel are not known to the clientele. They are acquisition personnel, the catalogue classifiers, the binding men, the photographic assistants and certain members of the circulation staff.

It will be useful at the outset to define certain terms which are used in connection with the work as a library. The literature on Librarian ship contains reference to such words as work routine treatments, procedures, actions, activities, operations method, services, techniques and processes.

FAIRLEIGH DICKINSON UNIVERSITY

Function	1992 LIBRARY (Yesterday)	2007 LIBRARY (Today)
Integrated Library System	Provided MARC, patron, and circulation records	Web-based: metadata; resource links; cross data-base searching
Information available	The print collection; Inter-Library Loan : CD Abstracts & Indexes	Print collection plus online data- bases; Document Delivery; extensive E-resources
Access to information	Walk-in to OPAC, PC's, stacks	Remote, wireless
Study space	Quiet areas	Group study areas
Information Instruction	Bibliographic Instruction, by instructor request	Information Literacy; hands-on "learning"

Information printouts	Dot matrix printer	Laser printer
Organizational	Bureaucratic; functional; hierarchical	Services oriented; Teams
Orientation	Local	Regional, consortial
Computer access	OPAC; Online access to DBs	Information Commons
Financial	"Parent" dependent	Participates in fund raising
Consortia	Test and buy databases	Negotiate special DBs

THE LIBRARY OF 2012 (TOMORROW)

Integrated Library System

The system of 2012 will feature interfaces customized for the patron with visualized searching, multi-media resources and "on call" knowledge management tools. The system will recognize the patron and quickly adapt and respond to the patron's new questions and needs.

Information Available

Collections will undergo dramatic transformations. They will be largely patron-selected, featuring multi-media resources and databases, many provided collaboratively through extensive consortia arrangements with other libraries and information providers. Collection management tools will concentrate holdings where they are used, evolving with changes in curriculum and instructors. New "weed, harvest, and migrate" schemes will enable widespread title swapping to get unused titles off the shelf and into circulation elsewhere.

ACCESS TO INFORMATION

Print-on-demand schemes will be developed utilizing the dissertation production experience of UMI but providing mechanisms by which the reader can return the fresh, undamaged manuscript for credit, and for binding and future use if appropriate. Out-of-print collections will be created for similar utilization.

STUDY SPACE

Space for work and study will be adaptable, with easily reconfigured physical and virtual spaces. Multi-media "smart-boards" will facilitate "conferencing" with contemporary and global scholars, artists, and intellectuals as well as digitally created personas from history and fiction, including science fiction. Portable devices and media delivery systems will allow the library to reach out to classrooms and other locales.

INFORMATION INSTRUCTION

Training and learning support, delivered both in person and through appliance-delivered (desktop, hand-held, and small-group) videoconferencing, will characterize learning commons and learning incubators, facilitating information literacy, media competency and socio-technical fluency as the new core competencies. Personalized learning-support programs will utilize preferred modes of learning as time and the situation allow and "stretch" the learning competencies of the patron. Science-technology-art ateliers will offer sophisticated visualization tools, training, and collaboration support for cross-disciplinary research and projects.

INFORMATION PRINTOUTS

Patron-desired copies will be in color or, more frequently, in multi-media DVDs (or the technology that supercedes them). Articles, videos, audios, and on-demand printing of articles and books will be commonplace. Additionally, displays of new academic titles in various formats will be coordinated with publishers and booksellers to enhance information currency, to market small-run monographs and to generate revenues.

ORGANISATIONAL ASPECTS

The library staff will be engaged, networked, matrix-structured, and largely "transparent" unless the patron is standing inside the facility facing the individual. Research and Information Management Services (such as data mining) will displace "reference" as the front-line service for the patron.

ORIENTATION

The library's perspective will be global; ubiquitous automatic translators will facilitate truly global information-accessing programs.

COMPUTER ACCESS

Wireless and laser-enhanced access for collapsible laptops and personal appliances will be ubiquitous.

FINANCIAL

The viable library will have developed dependable revenue streams to facilitate ongoing innovation and advancement.

CONSORTIA

Library consortia will be deeply involved in collaborating to create and publish academic journals and resources, particularly e-journals, e-books, and collections of visual resources in various media. Niche Publishers of academic monographs and journals will be active partners in these endeavors.

Many of these projections will prove too cautious in their impact. Others will not materialize. But what can be stated with confidence is that the library of 2012 will be both very similar to, and yet very different from, the library of today.

INDIAN ASSOCIATION OF SPECIAL LIBRARIES AND INFORMATION CENTRES (ISALIC)

After independence there was a spurt in scientific research. Several scientific and industrial research centres were established all over India. As a result a large number of Special Libraries and Information Centres have cropped up. Research in the field of documentation was initiated by Dr. Ranganathan.

OBJECTIVE

IASLIC has the following major objectives:-

1. To encourage and promote the systematic acquisition, organization and dissemination of knowledge.

2. To improve quality of library and information services and dissemination work.

3. To coordinate the activities and foster mutual cooperation and assistance among special libraries, information centres etc.,

4. To serve as a field of active contact for librarians, information bureaus documentation centres etc.,

5. To improve technical efficiency of workers in special libraries, information centres, etc. and look after their professional welfare.

6. To act as a centre for research for special library and documentative techniques.

7. To act as a centre for information in scientific, technical and other fields.

8. To take such action as may be incidental and conducive to the attainment of the objective of the association.

PROFESSIONAL DEVELOPMENT

IASLIC has drafted the Inter-Library loan code for

facilitating mutual exchange of books between different institutions and organizations in the country that are entrusted with the responsibility of dissemination of information. In order to help foster better standards and quality service in the field of special librarians, it has evolved a code of conduct and ethics for special libranship in the country.

EDUCATION AND TRAINING

In the past IASLIC used to conduct regular training courses in foreign language and in library science, at post graduate level. Now it is engaged in continuing education programme only.

BIBLIOGRAPHY AND TRANSLATION SERVICES

IASLIC offers translation and bibliography compilation services to individuals and institutions in a non-profit basis. It maintains a library devoted to library and information science literature.

CONCLUSION

A part from finance, there are several problems which stand in the way of public library development in India of which the foremost are multiplicity of languages, low level of literacy and problems of books production. But when compared to the conditions that existed in 1947, the prevailing conditions have improved considerably. Now the level of literacy is more than 30% as against the 15% at the time of independence.

REFERENCES

* **Dillon, Dennis,** "Digital Books: Making Them Work for Publishers and Libraries", *College & Research Libraries News*, No.61 (May 2000),pp.391-393.

* **Dillon, Dennis,** "E-books: The UT-Austin Experience," *Texas*

LibraryJournal, No.76 (Fall 2000), pp. 112-115.

* **Ditlea, Steve,** "The Real E-Books", *Technology Review*, July/ August, 2000.Accessed on the web at *http:// www.technologyreview.com/magazine/juloo/ditlea.asp>*. Accessed August 25, 2000.

* **Gibbons, Susan,** "E-books: Some Concerns and Surprises," *portal: Libraries and the Academy*, 1 (2001), pp.71-75.

* **William R. Kennedy,** "Metaphor Factory." Available: *<http:// alpha.fdu.edu/~marcum/metaphorfactory.doc>*.

* **Thomas T. Surprenant and Claudia A. Perry,** "The Academic Cybrarian in 2012:A Futuristic Essay." Available: *<http:// alpha.fdu.edu/~marcum/supernant_perry.doc>*.

* **Harold Billings,** "The Wild Card Academic Library in 2013," College and Research Libraries 64:2 (March 2003), pp. 105-109.

* **Steven E. Gromatzky,** "Academic Librarians 2012: Researchers, Technologies and Proactive Partners." Available: *<http:// alpha.fdu.edu/~marcum/gromatzky.doc>*.

* **Shayamala Balakrishnan and P.K. Paliwal (Eds).** *Public library system in India* . New Delhi : Anmol, 2001.

* **Sreenidhi - Iyengar.***Academic Libraries And Budgetary Control.* New Delhi, 1996.

Technical Session – II

Self Development of Librarian,
Library Professionals and HRD

B-01
Library Professionals As A Knowledge Worker

Babita Garg

Librarian, PT. B. D. Sharma PGIMS, Rohtak 124 001, Hariyana

ABSTRACT

All human beings around the world have some knowledge and with the help of that knowledge, they survive, they provide help to others, they serve the nation and they also try to improve and update it through various sources available world wide. The Librarian, Information officer or Documentation officer working in any library plays different role under a single title such as Planner, Manager, Administrator, Coordinator, Director, Finance Officer, Knowledge Worker, etc. The library professionals identify, acquire, manage, and disseminate knowledge available globally to the needy community at the right time and at the right place. To develop the day-to-day knowledge, library professionals surf and filter world wide knowledge readily available in different formats. There is no doubt that the word knowledge worker can be used for an information professional. This paper describes the role of Library professionals as Knowledge

Workers. The guidelines, which would help the Librarian to become the knowledge worker are also explained.

INTRODUCTION

Information, knowledge, management and librarian are interrelated terms. Information is knowledge available in any managed way but unknown to its receiver. Receiver may be a librarian, information scientist or a user. To identify, verify, acquire, manage and disseminate the information or knowledge to its end users, are the main traditional services being provided by a librarian since the emergence of this discipline. Librarians have traditionally dealt only with explicit books and periodicals. When a librarian receives an item for cataloguing, that item is already in a final, and usually static, form, the book is already written, the audio track written in a tape or digital file and even multimedia web pages are in concrete and explicit state. Librarians again had to expand their area of expertise to include digital information, including areas of the World Wide Web. And they are being asked to redefine themselves again.

Librarians have the perfect background to appreciate the issues brought up by knowledge taxonomy design and development. Librarianship in its most basic form is about providing services- both through direct reference works, and by organizing their libraries in a way that makes sense for their users. Librarians are generally driven by the desire to provide access to information sources and match this desire with values that assume that information sharing is good. This is also the driving force behind Knowledge Management.

Librarians often have a background which covers the management of day to day activities in a library office or department, but this can be radically different from the business processes of a large scale company or organization. Most librarians today are comfortable with online search engines and library databases, but they should not be limited to one or two particular applications.

LIBRARY PROFESSIONALS

A library professional with managerial skills can easily grow. In the info-tech age the concept of library is totally changed. So all library professional are required to possess the following managerial skills to perform their duties in a better way:-

a) Communication Skills

Communication skills are most important and necessary at all levels of management. Communication is the way library leaders can bridge the gaps, stay in touch, build trust, monitor performance and attain the consolidated vision. Proper communication helps in controlling misunderstandings, conflicts and improving co-ordination among groups. Reading, writing, learning, speaking, listening, presenting are also the important forms of communication skills.

b) Technical Skills

It involves specialized knowledge and analytical ability with in the area of specialty and facility in the use of the tools and techniques of the specific discipline. Vocational and on the-job training programmes largely do a good job in developing the skills. These skills basically involve the use of knowledge, methods and techniques in performing a job efficiently and effectively. For example to become a librarian a person must have formal education in library and information science with some experience and technical degree.

c) Decision Making Skills

Decision making skills are very important to library professionals. No decision will be successful without the cooperation commitment and enthusiasm of other colleagues, team or users. Making a decision begins when we realize that something needs to be done. The decision should be firm to achieve the objectives in right direction.

d) Motivating Skills

Motivation starts when someone consciously or unconsciously recognizes an unsatisfied need. This need establishes a goal and action is taken accordingly to achieve that goal. Motivational skills are also important part of managerial skills. Motivation also improves the working capacity of an employee.

e) Leadership Skills

Leadership skill can be considered as the personal qualities, behaviours styles and decision making of the leader. The function of leadership is to produce more leaders not more followers. Leadership skills are very important for 21st century's library professionals.

f) Performance Skills

Performance management is a term being used increasingly to cover a number of personal techniques. Performance development provides a means of communication to what is happening with the organization and demonstrating its future direction in a way that has immediate meaning to the individual members or staff. Only that library professional who is performing well is called truly librarian.

g) Time Management Skills

According to S.R.Ranganathan's fourth law "save the time of the user", indicates importance of the time management for library professionals & users both. In this turbulent world we never seem to have enough time. Working long hours is not necessarily a sign that you are overloaded with work. It can mean that you need to develop your time management. So planning is a vital element of time management.

KNOWLEDGE WORKER

The concept of knowledge worker is explored not only as relating to key workers-typically well educated and highly skilled- but also as a more inclusive notion of any one employee working with 'knowledge'. A knowledge worker is anyone who works for a living at the task of developing or using knowledge. For example, a knowledge worker might be someone who works at any of the tasks of planning, acquiring, searching, analyzing, organizing, storing programming, distributing, marketing, or otherwise contributing to the transformation and commerce of information and those who work at using the knowledge so produced. A term first used by Peter Drucker in the book, published in year 1959, "Landmarks of tomorrow", the knowledge worker includes those in the information technology fields, such as programmers, system analysts, technical writers, academic professionals, researchers, and so forth. The term is also frequently used to include people outside of information technology, such as lawyers, teachers, scientists of all kinds and also students of all kinds

WHO CAN BE KNOWLEDGE WORKER?

1. A problem solver or a production worker.
2. A person who uses intellectual rather than manual skill to earn a lively hood.
3. An individual who requires a higher level of autonomy.
4. A manipulator of symbols: someone paid for quality of judgment rather than speed of work.
5. A worker who uses unique processes.
6. Someone who possesses un-codified knowledge, which is difficult to duplicate.

7. Someone who uses knowledge and information to have deeper knowledge and information.

TYPES OF KNOWLEDGE WORKERS

From a practical perspective, it can be useful to consider two distinct types of knowledge workers as mentioned below:-

1. Core knowledge workers are those in specific knowledge management roles Examples include Chief information/ knowledge officers, knowledge managers, librarians, content managers, information officers, knowledge analysts, etc

2. Everyone else constitutes all the other knowledge workers- doctors, nurses, dentists, pharmacists, managers, technicians, administrators etc.

Of course there is not always a clear dividing line between the two, but the distinction can be useful when starting out. It can be particularly useful in helping people to understand that everyone is a knowledge worker to some degree and knowledge work is everyone's responsibility, not just that of a few people with " information" or "knowledge " in their job title.

LIBRARY PROFESSIONAL VS KNOWLEDGE WORKERS

Knowledge managers or library professionals can work very closely with the expert team in any library, information center or documentation center for developing a knowledge management environment. Library professionals are the best personnel who can apply the principles of management to create various new knowledge management systems. Their knowledge in information techniques can be utilized by the professionals of an organization to create a knowledge management environment. Library professionals are the person who actually connect the information sources by their services with the experts in their organization. Librarians in the course of their work come to understand a great deal about various knowledge needs of their organization

Information professionals have to recast their roles as knowledge professional. In other words librarians need to work as knowledge workers. Knowledge work is characterized by variety and exception rather than routine and is performed by professional or technical workers with a high level of skill and expertise. So those who exercise their intellects in any of these types of activities are knowledge workers. If librarian's work can be or is totally routinized, then they are administrative workers (for example, gatekeeper), not a knowledge worker. That means that librarian" roles should not be limited to being the custodians or gatekeepers of information. Knowledge professional will have to move from the background to the center of the organizational stage, to jointly hold the reins of knowledge management with users and the technology experts, to help steer and shape knowledge policies, structures, processes and system that will nurture organizational learning. Knowledge professional should be able to extract, filter and disseminate vital external knowledge. They also will design and develop workgroup application suites that are effective platforms for knowledge management.

Peter Drucker, author of Managing for the Future and Post Capitalist Society, writes that "the future belongs to knowledge workers." Because new technologies bring information overload. "knowledge workers are the people who tell you what you ought to use, which requires trust," said White. Librarians must ask whether they deal with content, or containers. " We are perceived to be in the wine bottle business, " said White. " So, what business are we in, and how well do we operate in it? If it is making better buggy whips, there is no market for it, nor will there be a market for information containers," said White. Technology provides the ability to be an excellent library, " he continued. "There need no longer be such a thing as a bad library. But good libraries will require more people. Nothing can be done with nothing," said White.

White's final advice to federal librarians was to aim high and stop focusing on the bottom line. "Your job is not to run a cheap library but to run a good one!" he said. "If you stood in the shower shredding $20 bills all day long, you could not affect the Defense Departments budget. So run the best library you know how to run. In the absence of money, there is always money. If it is worth doing, someone will find money to do it," said White.

Tamsen Dalrymple, department manager of product planning and communications at OCLC, discussed the organizations history and products. OCLCs mission is to "create and enhance services that accommodate member libraries' needs just as they create and enhance services to accommodate users needs," said Dalrymple. Keys to implement a successful mission include listening, observing, and providing libraries with products and tools which allow patrons access.

"Do not just be a library home page manager, but get actively involved in making agency information available online," said David Brown, Director of Government Services for Knight-Ridder information.

Brown predicted that the information center of the future would include a 24-hour virtual library, just-in-time document delivery, and an internal/external home page. Librarians will provide information synthesis —managing external search services, performing data analysis, and creating research reports. They will serve as organization knowledge managers, developing a framework for leveraging employee knowledge, building internal knowledge management systems, and facilitating internal creation of knowledge.

The information professional who is working as the knowledge worker has the knowledge of emerging tools and techniques available world wide in the relevant area or make necessary efforts to get it as early as possible.

QUALITIES IN LIBRARY PROFESSIONAL TO BECOME A KNOWLEDGE WORKER

1. Information Identification and Gathering:- Knowing how to find information and identifying essential information selecting books and other materials with the members of library committee or selection committee. Acquire and manage materials in various formats to add to the library collection.

2. Information organization:- Finding ways to structure or classify multiple pieces of information. Organize collection of books, publication, documents, audiovisual aids, stored files/database in computer and other reference materials for convenient access in a systematic way.

3. Service Orientation:- Actively looking for ways to help people with smiling face. If the required information is not available, the best referral services can be provided.

4. Reading Comprehension:-Understanding written sentences and paragraphs in work related documents. Quarry or user profile should read or understand carefully and solved.

5. Category Flexibility:- The ability to produce many rules so that each rule tells how to group or combine a set of things in a different way.

6. Information Ordering:- The ability to correctly follow a given rule or set of rules in order to arrange things or actions in a certain order.

7. Instructing:- Proper guidelines and instructions related to retrieval techniques and best utilization of different types of available collection. Orientation programmes with theoretical and practical experience for users as well as for staff may also be conducted time to time.

8. Resource Sharing:- Sharing the information and understanding with other professional colleagues to meet their information needs.

9. Acquire and Update:-To acquire and keep update about the current advances at national and international level in information systems and technologies and their application in libraries.

10. Using Standards:- Building the indexes based on standards and using standard vocabulary for easy access of world wide information.

ULTIMATELY WE ARE ALL KNOWLEDGE WORKERS

Over the centuries, the librarian and teaching professionals have become elite groups that are currently losing their exclusive privileges in the access to knowledge. We see the emergence of figures that reinvent the old role of "guide to the sources" coming from the varied fields. Consider the human guide of "About.com" What are they? Reference librarians? Journalists? Teachers? Engineers? Psychologists?

Creating, acquiring and managing information have emerged as the central focus of the digital economy. Now we are all knowledge workers. We create and use information using web sites, e-mail, databases, forums etc. Creating and sharing information are the basis of social relationships within the specific virtual communities. This sets up an enormous long-term challenges for every library or information center as well as for every professional involved in information sector. We need a new mind-setup and we are all learning as we go 'Like cats moving through their fabled nine lives'. I think that teachers and learners should redefine their own roles beyond the confines of their respective traditions. In my opinion the most promising road today is that of helping people develop their own cognitive abilities, understand their own needs, and learn how to express them correctly

REFERENCES

* **Amanulla M.S & Palani S.** "Health Science Information & Knowledge Managers", *National Convention,* 9-11 December, 2004. pp474-475.

* **Anand Parkash Yadav.** "Knowledge Management in Libraries Emerging Perspective & Challenges", *51st All India Conferences*, ILA, December 16-18, 2005. pp.390.

* **Rajesh Kumar.** "Need of the Managerial Skills for Library Professional", *51st All India Conference*. ILA, December 16-18, 2005. pp314-315.

* Librarians & Knowledge Management. GLIS 692 Assignment1, Sep 25, 2003 http://www.Majnik .org

* **Valerie Florance and Nina W Matheson.** "Health Science Librarian as knowledge worker", *Library Trends*, Summer 1993.

* Western Management Consultants, Herding Knowledge workers? 2002, http://www.wmc.on.ca

* **Burnella Longo.** "How a Librarian can Live Nine Lives in a Knowledge Based Economy", *Human Factors in Computing System*, Massachusetts, USA, April 24-28, 1994

* "Interest area: Professional and Managerial", *California Occupational Guide*, Number 154, 2002.

B-02
Self Development of Librarian and Library Professionals:

N. Shamala
Librarian, Nadar Saraswathi College of Education, Theni.

ABSTRACT

Self development is the key concern of any professional to accomplish social recognition and carrier prospects. Libraries being a service industry, it is imperative the librarian should be a multifaceted personality. To attain this multifaceted skills, life long self learning and self development become significant. This paper discusses the needs and factors of self development and emphasizes the concept of independent learning. Further, the paper highlights on internal and external elements taking part in professional development in the field of library. The importance of HRD and role of information are also highlighted.

INTRODUCTION

Self development is a key area for any librarian or information manager. Library and information staff needs to be seen not merely as signposts to sources. The information department of a legal or accounting practice could easily be involved in a range of developments across the firm.

The library services which operate off site, takes information out to particular areas of the community. Librarians are being called upon to streamline procedures and become more cost effective, introducing more value-added services for which charges are increasingly likely to be made to the ultimate user of the information. All these activities require a variety of skills and knowledge over and above basic information on seeking and finding skills which are in themselves becoming more complex, yet at the same time more exciting, the range of sources and formats now available, including the ability to manipulate data as well as store it.

NEED OF DEVELOPMENT

All types of library and information service benefit from the encouragement and support of training, but in addition to skills and knowledge there is another vital objective. An information manager or a librarian with a variety of experience, knowledge, interests and skills brought into the organization, enhances both the service and job. However his involvement will not only benefit the individual and the organisation : the process of training and self-development will also be instrumental for

- Visionary potential
- Ability to enlist others
- Confidence and encouraging trust
- Risk taking potential
- Empowering skills

SELF DEVELOPMENT FACTORS

Self development program includes on the job training and attendance at meetings as well as visits to other library and information centers. There are number of useful training techniques and methods, ranging from the formal course involving lectures interspersed with group and individual activities, to task based training with constant feedback.

There are number of activities as listed below

- Lectures
- Demonstrations
- Participation, discussion in group activities
- Role playing
- Data tablet and computer graphics
- CDs
- Computer packages

INDEPENDENT LEARNING

An increasingly popular and flexible means of development opportunities is by the use of self study, often through computer based learning for specific areas or through distance learning packages. This form of self-driven learning requires considerable commitment and discipline. Self-study is an appropriate method for both the professionals and information managers to consolidate the process of continuing professional development.

COURSES

Internal Courses

Working on an internal course with people from various departments with whom there has been little previous contact, can add to each participant's knowledge and understanding of the organization. It is also likely to increase and improve communication across departments, increasing the assistance that each can provide to the other and enhancing work relationships.

External Courses

External courses provide networks of contacts for future reference. It is also useful to talk to those in other organizations who might have used the external courses. Their intention is to guide new entrants to the LIS profession through the basic skills required, to update the experience of LIS workers on various topics; to provide a means of refreshing those returning to work after a career break.

DEVELOPMENT IN PROFESSION

Libraries are using many kinds of groups in the workplace, both to improve personal satisfaction and to improve organizational problem solving. Technology equipments and software are helpful when they are needed to support or improve personal and professional effectiveness. Technology is a broader concept; it implies the conceptual framework in which technology exists, so the librarian should make intelligent decisions about when and how to employ it for the development of the profession.

ROLE OF INFORMATION CENTERS

Information is needed for a variety of purposes contributing to decision-making or problem solving. The distribution of information by providing telecommunication facilities and software and finally those who are able to repackage information economically and quickly in a form wanted by the user can expect increase in demand and growth in their activities,

- Creation of information and knowledge further subdivides in to information, transmission and communication with its different functions of storage, value adding, presentation (cataloguing, indexing etc) and dissemination of information.
- It consists of redistributors of information, companies that aggregate available information, which are

generated by the Government and public held companies.

- It includes companies that collect, analyze and distribute the information. It also includes critical support activities, such as company manufacturing, software development and telecommunications.

- It influences increasingly the environment i.e. user group environment, study environment and research environment which operates inside the community through projects and through regulations

- Creation of knowledge by itself has no immediate economic impact However it becomes a major component of economic progress, as soon as it is turned into a source for innovative process of decisions of whatever kind

- The Compact Disc Read Only Memory is another revolution in the field of information.

- A typical digital library is built on client server model, having linkage to various other sources of information in digital format, connectivity and computing services to multiple users.

- In modern days digitization technology for data capture or content creation, includes data storage and management, searching and accessing digital data, publishing, distributing contents over networks and rights management.

- Global organization creates the uniform strategic planning and quality control which allows anybody to post anything in the internet and thereby creates organized knowledge documents.

- Globalization of information has overcome the problem of physical limitations of library facility and the fragility of the materials of collections.

HUMAN RESOURCE DEVELOPMENT

The key human resource development issues will need to be addressed either through the creation of new programs or by making improvements to existing ones. Well conceived programs and upgrade organizational capacities and faculty skills as these changes occur. Through networking, electronic publication and distribution as it promises universal and unified access to information. It enables the editors to send the manuscripts of articles to reviewers and to receive responses more quickly. It also induces the communications to help in the technological development of various fields like education, science, political, social etc.

Resource sharing through internet, includes sharing documents, information, manpower and cost. If the libraries or information centers in India share their catalogue and bibliographies by an electronic device, it makes its users and it leads to information sharing. The information centers and the library have to be digitized their information for of resource sharing. The resource sharing concept is a revolution of the information centers. Every information centers has to be aware of resources sharing. All the information around the world coming under a single roof is possible only by the resource sharing. The communication between the information centers definitely leads to Human Resource Development.

CONCLUSION

Through the networking the librarian can be made skillful and talented to render service to the user group. The up to date knowledge about the information will increase the worth of the library. Developing library will attract its users and helps to develop the human resource.

REFERENCES

* **Christine, Gorman.** *Stock development in library.* New Delhi : Dominent Publishers, 2003

* **Patel, Santhosh**. *Library information reservation and access.* New Delhi : Authors Press, 2005

* **Janakavalli, C.** "Information dissimination", *EduTracts*, Vol.5. No.11 july, 2006

* **Rani Shamalamba**, "Academic library in higher education", *EduTracts*, Vol.5. No.12 August, 2006

B-03
Librarian is an Information Specialist: A View

S. Praba Devi
M. Kurunji
*II M.L.I.Sc Students, Department of Library
and Information Science, AVVM Sri Pushpam College,
Poondi, Thanjavur Dt.*

ABSTRACT

This paper discusses, how librarian can act as an Information Specialist?. Information specialist includes the amalgamation of information policy (IP), knowledge building (KB), information literacy (IL), and knowledge Management (KM). It also explains various skills, professional competencies, information resources and role of information specialists.

INTRODUCTION

According to Dr. S.R.Ranganathan "Librarian ship is a noble profession". Librarian as a teacher occupies an important place in the modern educational system, His aim is to educate by providing the proper information services through the reading material and the modern technologies available in the library. Librarian's important work is collecting, storing, organizing, processing, analyzing, presenting and disseminating information to his use.

INFORMATION

In simple terms, the processed data is information.

Data → Process → Information

Information consists of data that have been retrieved, processed or otherwise used for informative or inference purpose, argument or as a basis for forecasting or decision making. The way in which the data is processed, is crucial to their effect as information.

It may be a message, a signal, a stimulus, it assumes a response in the receiving organism and therefore, possess response potential.. its motivation is inherently utilitarian ..it is instrumental and usually is communicated in an organized or formalized pattern, mainly because such formalization increases potential utility.

COMPONENTS OF INFORMATION SPECIALIST

Information Specialist is an important concept in the information era.

Information specialist can be seen as the amalgam of : Information policy (IP), Knowledge Building (KB), Information literacy (IL), and knowledge Management (KM), as illustrated in the following figure.

IP + KB + IL + KM → Information Specialist

SKILLS

Librarian is otherwise known as information specialist. So he needs some skills then only he can lead his career in a successful way. Following are the skills related to Information specialist.

- To identify action opportunities

- To develop information projects, programmes, plans, and policies.
- To develop research projects.
- To be part of the strategic planning of the organization.
- To manage economic, human and physical resources.
- To select and evaluate information resources and services according to the needs of the information units.
- To capture information needs and petitions from users offering new services and / or products to satisfy them.
- To measure the user satisfaction level.
- To measure the information services and products impact on the decision of the organization.
- To identify, compile, evaluate, organize and diffuse the information.
- To create and to manage information nets and systems through new technologies and applications
- To contribute to the knowledge management in the organization.
- To know, to explain, to teach and to advise in all professional matters.

PROFESSIONAL COMPETENCIES

We may classify professional competencies in accordance with six categories as given below.

PROFESSIONAL AREA

Information Resources

- Expert knowledge of the content of information resources including evaluating and filtering.
- Subject knowledge of organization or client

INFORMATION MANAGEMENT

- Provide excellent instruction and support for library and information service users.
- Assess information needs, designs and markets, value added information services and products to meet identified needs.
- Use appropriate business and management approaches to communicate the importance of information services to senior management.
- Improve information services in response to changing needs.

INFORMATION ACCESS

- Develop and manage convenient accessible and cost effective information services that are aligned with the strategic directions of the organization.

INFORMATION SYSTEM AND TECHNOLOGY

- Use appropriate information technology to acquire, organize and disseminate information .

RESEARCH

- Evaluate the out comes of information, use and conduct research related to the solution of information management problems

INFORMATION POLICY

- Consultant to the organization on information issues.

INFORMATION RESOURCES

Information resources in the IT Environment are categorized in the following way,

- Aggregated full – text – e –journal data – bases.
- e- journals (direct from publishers)

- Bibliographic data bases.
- Company Industry databases (Corporate information services)
- Value added information services (portals etc)

ROLE OF INFORMATION SPECIALIST

- Librarians should organize and design an efficient teaching environment.
- Collaboration is essential as Information specialist works with teachers to plan, conduct and evaluate learning activities that incorporate Information literacy.
- They must be conversant with the curriculum , be able to connect learning objectives with information literacy and establish a good relationship with teachers.
- They provide leadership in changing from text book based learning to information based learning and act as a technologist, who can collaborate to design instructional experience that fully integrates technology.
- They present the information literacy standards to audiences like parents, teachers, and administrators. The two greatest areas of impact have been in teacher / SLMS (school library media specialist) collaboration and the awareness of the need for "hand and glove" teaching of information literacy skills and subject matter content.
- If we are to teach information literacy, we must teach students to sort, to discriminate, to select and to analyze the presented message.

CONCLUSION

Information comes out from data. Data comes out from wisdom, wisdom comes out from universe of knowledge so we are in the information era. As a librarian we need some skills to run the library, Library professional must be aware of current and updated information. Librarian is other wise known as information specialist.

REFERENCES

* **Awasthy, GC,** *Broad casting in India*, Bombay : Allied publishers Pvt. Ltd., 1965.
* http://www. yahoo.com
* http://www.goegle.com
* pk@yahoo.com
* http: //flitch librarian.

B-04
Self Development of Professionals in Modern Libraries

S. Paramasivam

Librarian, GGR College of Engineering, Pillaiyarkulam, Vellore.

A. Rajinikanth

Library Assitant, PSNA College of Engineering and Technology,K Muthanampatty, Dindigul

ABSTRACT

Modern Libraries are providing information function and services. Due to the development of communication technology, the society is moving towards knowledge based society for which information is considered as the primary source. Libraries began developing web pages to organize and publicize internal and external links to information. Web based information and CD-Rom databases are increasing and play a vital role in the libraries to satisfy the user's requirements as quickly as possible, effectively and efficiently. So the self development of professionals in modern libraries is an essential one and it includes various form of skills like administrative skills, communication skills, developing personal qualities, leadership, appropriate technical training, developing library websites, and non-web technologies including M-Office software, time management, evaluation skills and developing network between the libraries and information centers.

INTRODUCTION

Emergence of computers and communication technology have great impact in every facet of library activities and services. In this area new technologies are replacing the old method of collection, storage and retrieval. Developments in information technology have played a crucial role and will continue to a play a central role in restructuring of the libraries. Library is an extremely important entity in an ever changing society and it must be responsive to the needs of society. Due to the revolution of information communication technology library and information science professional must develop themselves in various categories and work effectively and efficiently.

COMPETENCIES FOR LIBRARIANS

Competencies have been defined as the interplay of knowledge, understanding, skills and attitudes on the part of so called information persons required to execute their job effectively from the viewpoint of both the performer and observer.

ADMINISTRATIVE SKILLS

Librarian must be able to analyze and solve problems, to demonstrate organizational ability, to demonstrate team building skills, manage fiscal resources/budgets.

COMMUNICATION SKILLS

Communication skill is an essential part of library and information centers. Without communication one can't solve the user's requirements. Librarian should be able to communicate effectively with staff/public (good interpersonal/people skills) through oral and written presentation skills.

CREATIVITY

Librarian should have creativity skills to fund new ways to solve the problems (web creation, web services)

KNOWLEDGE BASE

Knowledge managers or Information officers should have broad knowledge of issues (1) Scholarly communication (2) Financial management (3) Planning (4) Digital libraries (5) IT collection, management and development (6) Out come assessment (7) User expectations (8) Information needs (9)Intellectual Property Rights (10) Fund raising (11) Public relations (12) Service Quality measurement (13) Goal setting (14) Information Delivery system and publishing.

LEADERSHIP

Leadership is an integral part of management and plays a vital role in managerial operations.

MOTIVATING EMPLOYEES

Motivating is an important factor for achieving goal, to create an environment that fosters accountability, to generate various sources of funds (grants, gifts etc.)

PERSONAL QUALITIES

Librarian must develop the following personal qualities

(i)   To treat people with dignity and respect.

(ii)   To be diplomatic

(iii)   To be a good listener and good facilitator.

(iv)   To be an open minded person, work effectively in groups (appropriate timing)

(v)   To be persuasive and committed to a set of values

(vi)   To take initiative and self awareness of strength and weakness

(vii) Should have sense of proper perspective and commitment

IT SKILLS

Librarian should have the following skills. Creating library website skills. Skills in HTML, XML, SMIL, PERL, PHP, ASP, SQL, JSP, JAVASCRIPT, COLD FUSION, JAVA, DREAMWEAVER, FLASH AND VISUAL BASIC and Non-web technologies, including MSWORD, EXCEL, ACCESS, POWERPOINT.

PROFESSIONAL COMPENTENICES

1. Knowledge of content of information resources available both in print and non-print formats.

2. Systematic and scientific organization of different formats of collection.

3. Appropriate information technology for information management and retrieval capabilities.

4. Management techniques.

5. Conducting user studies and imparting user education.

RELATIONSHIP AND NETWORK BUILDING

Build relationship with customers, internal colleagues, external colleagues, vendors and others, to help us to do our work better, to assist other colleagues and for personal development.

EVALUATION

Evaluation shows the progress of institution and individual activity based on clear realistic objectives, shared sense of purpose and best use of resources

TIME MANAGEMENT

Time management is an essential part of library and information centers. It includes following points (1) Set goals (2) daily priority list (3) handle every piece of paper only once (4) Use prime time for doing top priorities (5) Should have protected time.

CONCLUSION

The professional librarian will have to ascertain the impact of information technology on the library and will have to monitor and acquire skills to cope intelligently and objectively for effectiveness and efficient function of a library. Librarians must prepare themselves to meet the changing scenario and update the latest skills. Library and information science people must be well equipped with up-do-date skills, knowledge on the basics of computer and networking with other libraries. Librarians should take positive approach to provide better services and continue to prove their usefulness before the non-professionals take over their roles.

REFERENCES

* **Peter Heron, Ronald R Powell and Arthur P Young**, *The Next Library Leadership*, London Libraries unlimited, 1995.

* **Karl Bridges**. *Expectations of libraries in the 21st century*. London: Greenwood press, 2001.

* **Kaul, HK and Baby,MD**. *Library and Information Networking NACLIN 2002*. NewDelhi: Delnet,2003.

* **Vijayraghavan,GK and Sivakumar, P.** *Principles of Management*, Chennai : Lakshmi Publications, 2005.

* **Raju, AAN, Ramaiah, Laxman Rao, and Prafullachaudra,TV.** *New vistas in Library and information science*. Ne Delhi:Vikas Publishing House Pvt ltd, 1995.

B-05
Role of Librarians in the Modern Electronic Era

S. Rani

Library Assistant, Agricultural College and Research Institute, Madurai -625 104.

A.G. Ganesan

Librarian, KLN College of Information Technology, Pottapalayam -630 611.

ABSTRACT

A librarian is a mediator or an ambassador who provides valuable and reliable information service at the right time to the right person. During this century there is an innumerable growth in recorded knowledge. In managing the increasing information flow, the modern electronic revolution is playing a vital role. Librarians act as a bridge linking the recorded knowledge and the knowledge seeker. Hence the library professionals are in need of developing their knowledge on new technologies. Use of computers, telecommunication and storage facilities such as CD-ROM, microfilm, micro card, microfiche etc. have improved the knowledge transfer. In the same way, dissemination of knowledge in machine readable forms such as online databases like OPACs, electronic journals, Usenet newsgroups and newsletters are also coming in use. A brief discussion on the role of library professionals in information service in the electronic environment is made in this paper.

INTRODUCTION

The explosion of information and the technology of information are increasing day by day, and so it is essential to develop the appropriate information infrastructure. Application of technologies to information handling for efficient and effective information management is termed as information technology. It encompasses the activities like generation, storage, processing, retrieval, dissemination etc. The merging and integration of modern information technologies of telephone, computer, facsimile, television, video-discs, and electronic mail service is leading to a vast re-organization in the modes of communication. The impact of new trends and techniques in informatics has elevated the modern day librarians to a top position. The advancement of computer technologies, microprocessors, electronic databases, software packages etc. have been developed to automate the library functions. The modern techniques in the storage systems like magnetic tapes, discs, microfilms, microfiche, optical and magnetic storage systems have impacted the library and information centers to face the need of the twenty-first century. Hence some of the storage systems and dissemination services through electronic medium are going to be discussed.

COMPUTER ERA

To-day, we are living in computer era evolving from the industrial/machine age to the age of electronics. Many of the routine activities in to-day's society have been performed by computers. Now-a-days we consider computer knowledge as second literacy even in the developing world.

The computer and telecommunication systems have rolled into the area of library and information activities in a big way. The irresistible invasion of this technology into the library scene has triggered a revolution in our traditional methods in the developing countries like India as well. Now, computer can successfully be put to use for providing library services efficiently and effectively.

Computers can be used for house-keeping operations of the library like acquisition, cataloguing, circulation, serial control, public access system, etc. sparing valuable time of the professionals for more productive functions.

STORAGE SYSTEMS IN ELECTRONIC MODE

The need for stack area to store a large number of books and journals have been very much compressed using the electronic storage media like magnetic taps, magnetic discs, CD –ROM discs, microfilms, microfiches etc.

NOVEL SYSTEM STORAGE

i.   A data storage unit made of Plexiglas exhibits a diameter of 30cm and can store 10, 000- fold more data than floppy or video discs.

ii. The super storage unit opens up immense possibilities for data processing. Theoretically, 100 billion bits per sq cm can be registered. This capacity surpasses that of the human mind.

iii. The storage medium for compressed video determines the degree of compression. A compact Read Only Memory offers a good tradeoff between performance and cost.

A CD-ROM stores nearly 650 megabytes and reads it out at the rate of 150 kilobytes per second which yields a playing time up to 72 minutes.

OPTICAL AND MAGNETIC STORAGE SYSTEMS

Optical discs offer a huge storage capacity and that too at a low cost. One disc can record as much digital data as 25 magnetic disks is error-free and has high density and capacity for recording, i.e., One Giga byte for a 20 cm disc is equal to 104 sheets of A4- paper.

ICI UK has developed an optical film which can store data up to one million bytes in a magnetic tape of 2400 feet.

KINDS OF OPTICAL DISCS

i   CD-ROM Read only memory

ii   Reading but which also offers the facility to record once called WORM Technology. (Write once and read many)

iii Permits rewriting, called the erasable disc.

OPTICAL DISC'S DATA STORAGE

SERODS *(Surface Enhanced Roman Optical Data Storage)* was developed in United States which could increase the average compact data disc's capacity by more then a 1000 fold, from about 600 megabytes to 1000 billion bytes. It provides extra data security because any drive to read a given disc or block will have to be tuned to read the specific frequency at which molecules vibrate. This technology is new and yet to be proto typed.

DISSEMINATION SERVICE THROUGH ELECTRONIC MODE

Computers and the telecommunication through satellites have introduced new trends and techniques and offered new means of information transfer such as e-mail, electronic journals, online scarch and networking systems. Libraries and information centres cannot dream of acquiring all the literature published worldwide individually. Hence libraries have to co-operate to share their resources of information.

Libraries and information centers and network communication are the newly improved techniques for the sharing of expensive resources to provide information at optimal cost.

ELECTRONIC PUBLISHING

The advent of e publishing has brought a revolution in journals, publication, subscription and access to scholarly literature and the age of library consortia is at the doorsteps to prove cooperation locally, regionally, nationally and internationally. Library consortium is one of the emerging toolkits for libraries to survive. FORSA is an Indian Astrophysics consortium called Forum for resource sharing in Astronomy. The council of Scientific and Industrial Research (CISR) in India has 40 scientific laboratories involved in basic and applied research in various disciplines. The CSIR consortium provides access to globally available electronic journals to the entire science and technology staff of CSIR.

INDEST CONSORTIUM

Electronic resources for 38 institutions including IISC, IITs, NITs, RECs, IIM s and few other centrally funded government institutions are sharing their resources through this Indian National Digital Library in Science and Technology (INDEST) Consortium.

UGC INFONET CONSORTIUM

INFLIBNET is an UGC Infonet consortium and is providing remarkable access in sharing of both print and electronic resources amongst university libraries

ONLINE RETRIEVAL

During this decade there has been a revolutionary change and development in information technology products and we must utilize them properly to provide an effective and efficient information retrieval service to the users.

The following are some of the software packages of library and information – technology products available in Indian market.

LIBMAN

LIBMAN was developed by M/s. Kasbah System, Chennai. It is a user friendly package designed for small and medium libraries. It is menu driven and is handling 60,000 books, periodicals, etc.

UNILIB

It was developed by Hindustan computers Limited, Bangalore for medium and big size libraries, under UNIX / XENIX environment. It is a menu driven and multi-user package.

CDS/ISIS

It is an information storage and retrieval package developed by UNESCO and distributed to the library and information centres free of cost. It runs on IBMDC/XT compatibles. It has been provided with a stock module to give the status of stocks at a given periodicity including the valuation of books.

ARCHIVES

It was developed by M/s. Minafax Electronics Systems, Mumbai. It can run in an IBM- PC /XT & AT in the MS DOS environment.

LIBRARIAN

It is library management software developed by M/s. Mundra Electronics, New Delhi. It can be operated in a LAN environment.

LYBSYS

It is available on a variety of platforms like UNIX, NOVELL LAN or in DOS. It has improved user interface and menu bars and more window facilities are available. It has an incredible OPAC.

CD –ROM DATABASES

DIALOG – ON DISC, PROQUEST, UMI, CAS, etc. have developed various databases like, Ei compedex Plug INSPEC, Abstracts, Indexes, Dissertations, etc on CD-ROM and they are available in the market.

SIGNIFICANT SERVICES OF LIBRARIANS THROUGH ELECTRONIC DEVICES

Significant services provided by the librarians in the electronic environment to the users of the library are as follows.

- Electronic journals
- Pre – prints
- Technical reports
- Numeric and graphical data
- Library catalogues
- Software
- Other Libraries
- Campus vide Information Systems (CWIS)
- Table of contents of journals
- Databases
- Institutions
- Electronic discussion forums (consortium)
- Electronic publishing
- Marketing and Publicity of products and services
- Online education

- Tools for integrating access to internal and external information
- Access to multimedia information

CONCLUSION

Technology can bring three important benefits. The first of these is an improvement of the efficiency of our service to library users. The second benefit is that we are able to use our limited resources more sensibly and the third benefits in the improvement of the nature of the work of those engaged in cataloguing and other technical services. Thus the technology developments are friendlier to the library professionals and the library users. Technologies are giving the growing information in a meaningful and manageable way. So, developing our knowledge in growing technologies has made easy our day to day activities at library.

REFERENCES

* **Kochar, RS.** *Library Science today.* New Delhi : Vedam Books, 1999

* **Thillainayagam, V.** *New Dimensions of Library Scenario in India.* New Delhi : Vedam books, 1994

* **Satyanarayana, B.** *Multimedia: its applications in library and Information Science.* New Delhi : Ess Ess Publications, 2002

B-06
Smile – Learning Techniques in Digital Age

P. Indirani

Librarian, Arulmigu Palaniandavar Arts College for Women, Palani

Dr. T. Selvanayaki

S.G.Lecturer in History, Arulmigu Palaniandavar Arts College for Women, Palani

ABSTRACT

In this modern era of knowledge explosion Information and Communication Technologies play a vital role in the dissemination of resources and sharing of information to the learners. SMILE refers to Simple, Motivating, Interactive and Learner Centre Environment. We need strategies to implement SMILE and it should help to shape the vision of learning for the future wherein the students enjoy learning with SMILE and get themselves free from mental stress caused by learning with out understanding. For this ICT centers have to create an environment which prepares the students for lifelong learning with curiosity, learn how to learn by learning to share and sharing to learn. The high quality e-learning resources provide consistent and enhanced learning environment for students and teachers. The schools and colleges are to be connected with the network and resource sharing facilities and is to be placed under the management of well qualified people. On-line systems now enable the user to establish communication link directly in a conversational mode with the help of a computer. Libraries will have to cope up with the current trends that are taking place at the global level and particularly Indian libraries are to be created in the changed ICT environment. Librarians can no longer afford to remain as an institutionalized passive spectator. All the activities will now have to be tailored to give long distance and often home delivered information through on-line services. In this article an attempt is made to promote and develop the learning techniques among various sections of people in the society.

INTRODUCTION

In this modern era of knowledge explosion, information and communication technologies play a vital role in the dissemination of resources and sharing of information to the learners. **Learning** is the acquisition and development of *memories* and *behaviors*, including *skills, knowledge, understanding, values,* and *wisdom*. It is the goal of *education*, and the product of *experience*. Digital technology makes informative content easier to find, to access, to manipulate and remix, and to disseminate. All of these steps are central to teaching, scholarship and study. Together, they constitute a dynamic process of "digital learning."

SHARING KNOWLEDGE IN THE DIGITAL AGE

Digital children do not learn in isolation. They might work alone, but they learn in groups (even if some of the group members live in other countries). For them, knowledge is like dropping a pebble in a pond. Waves of understanding wash over the digital classroom. The learning environment should help the people to share their knowledge and this type of sharing helps them not only enhances their knowledge but improve their reading habits. Now a days group discussions are made compulsory while selecting a person for a job. In this era of information science and knowledge explosion life long learning is essential. Here we have to remember the proverb, ' known is little and unknown is an ocean'. The children of this digital age need to update their knowledge and widen their mental horizon to remain relevant and productive in this new economy.

Learning strategy needs to be different in the digital age to leverage adavances in ICT for innovative learning solutions "learning to learn helps us to pursue life long learning and enjoy learning'. An old proverb says, "Fish can't see the water." Likewise, our digital child swims in an ocean of changing technologies. The ebb and flow of new gizmos and scientific discoveries are merely punctuated by occasional technological typhoons reminiscent of the Y2K storm.

The major focus of digital learning research is to extract information from data automatically, by computational and statistical methods. Digital children are more independent, more intellectually open, more tolerant, and more adventurous than most 20th-century children. They hold strong views and expect instant gratification. At the same time, they are at greater risk from AIDS, school shootings, terrorism, depression, and suicide than their 20th-century predecessors. And they represent a larger population segment than those analog "baby boomers" who dominated the 20th century. Their collective voices are heard above all others.

SMILE

SMILE refers to simple, motivating, interactive and learner centric environment. SMILE blends the best of both the worlds-classrooms learning and network enabled e-learning. Learning theories, models and the science of instruction are embedded in SMILE to create an environment that empowers learners and teachers.

SIMPLE

Learning with understading requires the teacher to present and explain the concepts to learners in a simple way, which is easy to understand. Digital children must learn to read critically, write effectively, listen intently, and speak fluently. They must be able to find information, understand the information they locate, evaluate the reliability of that information, and see how to apply it to answer a pressing question or to take advantage of a new opportunity. They must be able to communicate their ideas to diverse groups using a variety of media. They must also be able to understand the ideas of others and see how their own concepts might blend with those of their work-mates to solve problems and create new things.. The ability to identify similar and relevant features in varying situations yields better schema construction and enhances problems solving skills and knowledge transfer.

MOTIVATING

Attention can be gained and sustained through graphics, images, animation, applets, intersting facts and thought provoking questions to stimulate a sense of inquiry and curisoity. Relevance refers to the alignment of content with the learner's goal, learning styles, past experience and its application in real world situations. Confidence can be enhanced by helping students to experience success through understanding of the concepts and their ability to apply these concepts for problem solving. Satisfaction is necessary for learners to have positive feelings about their learning experience. The students satisfaction could be achieved by helping them perform better in their educational institutes while satisfying the quest for knowledge and spirit of inquiry.

INTERACTIVE

Collaboration and interaction among learners is a very important component of effective learning. Simulations, streamed video, project teams, chat rooms, bulletin boards, online references, personalized coaching and email are some techinques that could help create an intereactive online environment. Interactive learning can be stimulating and encourages critical thinking as it facilitates problem solving.

LEARNER – CENTRIC

Learning is an active process in which meaning is developed on the basis of experience. Learners actively construct their own knowledge by connecting new ideas to existing ideas on the basis of their experience while structuring and restructuring of ideas is an essential part of the learning process. Learner centric pedagogy gives primacy to learners interests, experience, preferred learning style and their active participation. The content design should enable learners to construct knowledge from their own experience in their own way and develop multiple perspectives. Learner centric approach also allows learners to learn at their own pace and to engage with concepts, reflect on the underlying cause and effect relations, patterns, simliarities, and interconnections to deepen understanding.

We need a learning strategy to implement SMILE and unify the initiatives by Government, industry, educationists and educational institutes, that extends the reach of quality education to all and prepare ourselves, through our educational system to cope with an ever-changing world. The strategy should help shape the vision of learning for future where in every student enjoys learning with smile, free from strees caused by learning without understanding.

Every student learns with smile to achieve his/her full

potential. We need to create and provide access for all to a learning environment that helps students learn how to learn and achieve their full potential.

STRATEGIC VISION

In the knowledge age creation of wealth will largely be determined by how one continuously acquires and applies knowledge to the changing needs of the society. So we need to work towards an educational system which prepares students for life long learning. This requires an environment in which students enjoy learning, develop curisoity, learn how to learn by learning to share and sharing to learn.

One important aspect of the Information Society is explosion of information available and an increased access to a variety of rich information sources. Another aspect is the increased possiblity of presenting, editing, organizing and mainpulating information.e.g, in multimedia format. The chances that a teacher will be able to compete with the entertainment industry concerning the presentation of information should not be overestimated.   The success of the virtual classroom model would obviously depend on active use of the communication technologies and the incorporation of real time communication into a strategy with a wider range of learning activities.

Desinging the self-learning content would require experts multidisciplinary in nature who have the knowledge of designing interactive contents for web like media and who have the knowledge and understanding of education delivery. These specialists who are known as 'Instructional Designers' would be very vital in supporting and developing teaching pedagogy for supported self-learning in virtual environment.

Teaching pedagogy and teachers' role changes as per the teaching environment and there is a noticable difference between traditional classroom setting and digital environment. While information and communication technologies are sophisticated enough to create the platform needed for virtual classes, self- learning and collaborative learning, the training programme can have a serious lacunae if the teaching pedagogy is not matched with the learning environment. Thus to sum up, the teacher assumes the roles of a facilitator and helps learner towards a managed learning environment where the learner utilizes the learning resources to its best possible ways to achieve the learning outcomes.

E-LEARNING INFRASTRUCTURE

A connected infrastructure is a requirement for remote e-learning. However for online e-learning, where rich content is downloaded a high-speed link is important and in some cases essential. The avilability and cost of high-speed broadband connections varies widely and coverage tends to be very patchy in rural areas. The important challenges is to increase the availablity of inexpensive high-speed connections. Where land-based connections are not avaiable some governments are using satallite links such as Edusat to overcome this barrier.

E-LEARNING STANDARDS

In order to achieve true sophistication in terms of understanding the obejctives of a learner and addressing those objectives with a highly customized program of learning, all of the components of a technology-based learning system must be speaking the same language. Accredited standards ensure that the investment in time and intellectual capital could move from one system to the next. The goal of standards is to provide fixed data structures and communication protocols for e-learning obejects and cross-system workflows.

CONTENT DESIGN

The effectiveness of technology enabled learning experience depends on the design of the content and the instructional methods including content structuring and sequencing. In its report, "The power of the internet for Learning", the US commission for Web-based Education identified "the lack of compelling content as a major constraint on the development of e-learning in educational institutes".

COLLABORATION

e-Learning can support educational institutes working together to raise standards by allowing collaboration between colleagues in different educational institutes, allowing pupils to take speical subjects offered by another educational institute without the need to travel. ICT should enable the development of teaching communities that can be used by teachers to share resources, including online libraries, discussion boards, and synchronous communication tools and help teachers to strengthen their curricular and teaching practices in professional collaboration to develop and reivew teaching materials. Networking of teachers working through an Educational Institute Net strengthens this form of collaboration.

ACCESS TO ICT

Access refers to the ability to access the information and knowledge with the help of ICT, which facilitates learning anywhere at any time, extending the classroom boundaries and the learning experience.

Broadband facilities, access to creative content such as simulations and game-based learning to explain learning points in interesting, absorbing and imaginative ways enhance inter-institutional collaboration with sharing of scarce teacher resource between educational institutes in a high-speed interactive video conferencing to encourage communication and cooperation. The distance education programs of ISRO such as EDUSAT are very successful by providing connectivity to remote areas through satellite link.

EDUSAT, India's dedicated education satellite carries the capability of providing audio, video and data services to India through its national and regional beams. This is a satellite operating in Ku band frequency facilitating the use of easy to handle small transmit/receive ground terminal. EDUSAT when it is fully operational in the third phase, will have the capacity of 30 uplinks and about 50000 remote terminals per uplink.

TECHNOLOGY

Technology transforms learning experiences by supporting the teaching and learning process with flexibility. Technology plays a very important role in offereing learning opportunities, which are relevant, compelling, and collaborative on a continuous basis. We need to use these technologies innovatively to take full advantage of the potential of global access to information, knowledge and experts. Technology can change the curriculum and students access to it and increase the ways in which learners can be assessed, so that more students have the opportunity to select the range of media to best demonstrate their knowledge and understanding. Blended learning environment facilitates competency development in learners and provides learning in context across diverse student groups.

TEACHERS ROLE IN THE NEW PARADIGM

Teacher is at the heart of this transformation in learning to facilitate every student to enjoy learning and achieve his/her full potential. The position of the teacher has been elevated and is expected to play a more important role as facilitator in the development of students.

Teachers can access the rich,shareable, learning objects available from a digital repository and customize them to meet the specific requirements of their students depending on the learner and the context by assembling and packaging them in innovative ways.

Teachers should be assisted by technical support staff to ensure that the networks and equipment are properly installed, operated, updated and maintained.

STRATEGIC CHOICE CRITERIA

Strategic options have to be evaluated and tested for internal and external consistency, feasibiilty, advantage, value creation and consonance before selecting the strategy. The role of the teacher as the centre of the learning transformation needs to be recognised and reinforced and teachers must be given every opportunity to enhance their own skills and knowledge in order to create conducive e-learning environments for learners.

LEARNING FLEXIBILITY

Students find more ways to develop the skills they need to participate fully in a technology –rich knowledge society through wide access to digital resources and information systems, combined with quality through shared tools and resources. Students will have more choice about where, when and how to study, learning through engaging, versatile and challenging activities and materials that adjust to the level and ease appropriate to them

NEW WAYS OF LEARNING

The new technologies share the new learning and in turn will shape the new educational system.

LEARNING TO SHARE AND SHARING TO LEARN

The collaborative e-learning brings learners, teachers, specialist communities and experts together to share ideas and good practice, contributing to new knowledge and learning. Collaborative online environments help students to learn from other students or groups of learners as well as tutors and develop the cognitive and social skills of communicating and collaborating.

INNOVATION IN TEACHING AND LEARNING

Teachers can access the digital content available on line and modify or adapt the same in innovative ways appropriate to the context and the learner to make learning enjoyable.

CONCLUSION

Learning environment plays an important role in transforming learning and helping students develop curiosity and enjoy learning. Students learn how to learn and apply what they learnt in new situations to find innovative solutions. SMILE enables students learn with smile and we need a strategic approcah to create such a learning environment. Key elements of such a strategy are content, technology, access and collaboration and teacher is at the heart of the strategy to develop a vision and realize it.

REFERENCES

* **Sharma, Lokesh.** *Information analysis in the libraries.* New Delhi : Shri Sai Printographers, 2007
* http://www.digitallibrary.com

B-07

Self Development of Library Professionals : Leadership Qualities

P. Clara Jeyaseeli

*Librarian (SS), V.V. Vanniaperumal College for Women,
Virudunagar – 626 001*

ABSTRACT

The library professionals until recently have concentrated more on management skills and technical skills than on leadership qualities. The same is the case with library education curricula also. Leadership quality has become a topic of concern in the contemporary society whatever the profession may be, especially in library and information science. These changes have made an impact in the increasing number of library professionals to include political, social and environmental trends in the planning stage itself. Over time, effectiveness became more important than efficiency. In the contemporary society of the knowledge era, the investments in libraries are more in order to have information rights for everyone in the society. If the library professionals acquire leadership qualities, maximum service can be provided to the society. The various ways to attain leadership qualities are discussed which in turn will help to enhance the leadership skills of the library professionals to the maximum.

INTRODUCTION

Library is the nerve center of any institution. Usually in all the institutions there will be less number of librarians or library professionals. Although they are less in number, they play a very vital role. Since libraries are the core centers for information, the library professionals should have acquired management skills, so that the interpersonal relationship will be maintained and the ethics of librarianship will be fulfilled.

James McGregor Burns, a Pulitzer Prize-winning figure in the field of leadership study, has concluded that leadership is "one of the most observed and least understood phenomena on earth" (Witherspoon, 1997, p. ix). Riggs found over 100 definitions of leadership, such as situational leadership, servant leadership, emotional intelligence or team leadership (Riggs, 2001).

During a presentation at the 2004 Florida Library Association Conference, Dr. Mark D. Winston, assistant professor at Rutgers University, pointed out the scarcity of scholarly research regarding libraries and leadership, which is in sharp contrast to the vast amount of news/opinion articles in the library press. Until recently, librarians have focused on management skills more than leadership concepts at professional events, in professional literature and in the library education curricula.

Leadership has surfaced as a topic of concern in the face of constant change. These changes, in turn, have caused an increasing number of librarians to examine broader political, social and environmental trends in their initial steps of the planning process. Over time, effectiveness has become more important than efficiency.

The library professionals have to play three roles in any institution. They are

- Relationship with clients
- Relationship with co-workers
- Relationship with Higher Authorities

Now the role and responsibilities are explained briefly.

RELATIONSHIP WITH CLIENTS

The users are the clients of the library profession. It is not necessary for every user to know about the techniques that are adopted in a library in order to gather information. As library professionals, the main responsibility is to educate the users and to make the users to visit the library regularly. The users should be made to trust the library professionals so that they can get the right information at the right time from the right source.

Unless the library professionals are kind, the library will become just a store house for preservation of information and not for client use. For the clients, the library professionals are the teachers who orient and teach them how to gather the correct information and how to use the various techniques to save their time.

RELATIONSHIP WITH CO-WORKERS

A leader is one who has to get the work done through other people. Every one differs psychologically and physically. As a librarian, he or she should get the work done by his or her co-workers, since he or she can't do all the work of all the sections of the library.

In order to get the work done by others, the first leadership quality is the ability to win the recognition from others. Unless there is recognition, the work place will not be a fruitful one and there will not be any peace of mind on both the sides. If there exists a very good relationship between the team leader and the team members, surely there will be a very good rapport and all the work will be finished at the stipulated time with accuracy and enthusiasm.

The second leadership quality needed is motivation. Motivation should be there in each and every member of the library. Since the tasks in a library are continuous processes, unless the library professionals are motivated, it will be very hard to provide the maximum service. As a result, all the work will go in vain and will fail to be highlighted, which will end in less use of the library.

RELATIONSHIP WITH HIGHER AUTHORITY

A librarian or a library professional should have management skills like leadership quality, communication skills, etc. No librarian can act according to his or her own attitude. Of course, one's attitude should be very positive and should have high regard for the profession, environment, etc. Then only the librarian can work peacefully, since most of the time the librarian has to act as a liaison officer. When moving with the higher authority autocratic or stubborn attitude must be eschewed. Anyway the library professional should not lose his authority in certain tasks and at must be expressed in a very polite manner.

Therefore, the first leadership quality needed is politeness with listening skill. If listening is there, then there will be free flow of ideas and a mutual understanding will emerge between the higher authority and the library professionals. If there exists no such relationship, then the services can not be provided to the maximum by the library professional and there will be stress. The next leadership quality is good communication. Good communication means the thoughts should be very clear enough and they should be expressed clearly.

As far as the relationships are concerned, the librarian or the library professionals should enrich and enhance their management skills to the maximum especially the leadership qualities. What follows is a brief sketch of the leadership qualities a library professional should possess.

QUALITIES OF LEADERSHIP

The leader should have very good rapport with everyone. The existence of such a relationship shows that the leader is recognized. If a leader is recognized, there will not be any difficulty in influencing the people to finish the task. In order to **gain recognition**, the following qualities are needed. They are

Positive Appreciation

On the positive side, give a sincere, hearty and generous appreciation. Always be optimistic and see the benefits and appreciate. Give positive appreciation in front of others. Then all the members will be motivated to perform the assigned tasks with delight.

Avoid criticizing others

Criticism gives very bad impact and on one fine day that will be repeated or returned. Truly speaking, there should not be any criticism in front of others. If the person gets wounded, it is hard to maintain a good relationship and also difficult to get the task done by that member.

Banish backbiting

It is an unhealthy practice especially for managers like library professionals to indulge in backbiting. In course of time, this will become a habit and can't be stopped at all. In due course, the professional will lose the image and recognition.

Be in other's shoes

In order to get willing cooperation, the leader should see at things from the other's point of view. The leader should see what the member wants and not what the leader wants.

Then the leader should go in the way of the member or make the member to realize the situation, so that the member will extend full cooperation.

Concentrate on others

The leader should concentrate on others needs and views. If the leader practices that, automatically the people will do things for the leader, without ever waiting for a command.

Show real interest

Always show real interest in the members. This can't be achieved by giving more money, or much effort or time. Cultivate the habit of playing down "I" and playing up "YOU". Just with warm smile and enthusiastic words, wonders can be done.

Point out positive points

Whenever a meeting occurs, always talk and appreciate the positive or good points of others. Then the leader's image will be elevated and the team members will also be motivated to see about good points among others. Stress level will be very much reduced and a harmonious environment will exist for maximum service.

Be a good listener

To be a very good leader, first of all the leader should be a very good listener. Most often, just listening to others and what they want to express without interference can solve many problems. Encourage the team members to talk about themselves and listen to them. If possible, in between appreciate them. Be an enthusiastic and encouraging listener and pay rapt attention to what others say. Ask them of the areas of doubts where they are very much interested. The more the leader knows about the team members, easier it is for the leader to achieve the task.

Communication skills

Good communication is what makes the leader wake up to buzzing opportunities and then every word and every action is the mission, the reason to remain the best, the choice, the heartbeat, and the future! The idea or the thought should be clear to the leader himself. Therefore, communicate with a very good, easy to understand, with out grammatical mistakes. Make sure that the content is audible and not submissive.

Impressive Personality

The leader should always have in mind the possession of impressive personality. Do not have complexes about the physical frame or look.

Mnemonic Devices

Use mental mnemonic devices and in depth knowledge about the views or tasks. Always avoid having notes in case of presentations. The members and the higher authority should have confidence and should be convinced by the knowledge and the readiness of the leader in every task.

Eye Contacts

Always have direct eye contacts so that there will be no deviation in the arguments.

Remain Open-minded

When the task is going to be assigned, then be open and let the members take opportunity to express their ideas and be motivated to involve in the task with full enthusiasm.

Be Patient and Prepared

Whenever an awkward question arises, be calm and prepared to tackle the situation in a very gentle manner. Otherwise, there will be lot of misunderstanding and the interpersonal relationships will be spoiled. But always express the suitable idea and that too in a very polite and polished way.

Effective Voice

Use effective and polite voice. Always share ideas with facts and figures and make others understand and accept the leader's aims.

Love the Task

There should be love for task. Whenever the task is given or to be given to others, smile and make others work smart. If the leader shows love and sincerity towards the task, then automatically the leader will make the team members to complete the task successfully.

Make others understand

Let the leader explain the task. Explanation means not only expressing how to do the task, but also explaining the purpose of the task, and why the task is to be done and the time allotted. If the required output is clearly explained, the members will finish the task without any difficult.

Equal Priority

The leader should not be biased. The priority should be distributed equally to all. If a priority is to be given to one, then the reason should be explained to others. This makes the environment cool and avoids scope for cold war among the members.

Humanity

A leader should always be humane. Although there will be some irritations, take the situation in a very cool manner and forgive them. Warn the people who do mistakes and be constructive.

Tackling Tough People

There will be tough people in the institutions. To make

the tough people work, give them the responsibility and make them leader for that particular task and ask them to report. These people usually have superiority complex and good intelligence. In such circumstances, they will become friendly and give their hands in difficult tasks.

Tackling Lethargic People

There will be lethargic people in the institutions. To make them work, these people should be put under the control of tough people. Then the tough people can understand the difficulties of the leader and also make the lethargic people to work. Usually these lethargic people will have inferiority complex with less intelligence quotient. But they will work and they won't bother about the complexities. These people will work under the tough people and finally the task will be completed successfully.

Rewards

Rewards should be given for the members if they deserve. The rewards may be promotion, incentive, leave, etc. If rewards are given, the members will be motivated to offer their best to complete the task when their turn comes.

Change is Permanent

A leader should always have in mind that change is permanent. Whenever the new technological improvements flourish, the leader especially the library professionals should make up their mind to inculcate the new trends and technology for their utility. The leader should have eagerness to learn about the technological developments and improvements.

CONCLUSION

Leadership is a long-term investment for library professionals, and it has its own long-term benefits. The leader needs to invest in the social, human and intellectual capital of the institutions and the country. Each library professional can be trained through the academic curriculum to become a better and transformational leader. After all, leadership must be a personal journey before it can become an organizational one. The library professionals should practice leadership qualities along with technical skills. The curriculum should be set in a way to enhance and enrich the leadership qualities, which plays a major role in the contemporary society.

REFERENCES

* **Australian Institute of Management.** *Heart and Soul of Leadership.* New Delhi:Tata McGraw Hill, 2004.

* **Dale Carnegie.** *The Leader in You: how to win friends, influence people and succeed in a changing world.* New York:Pocket Books, 1995.

* "Develop Your Communication Skills". *Competition Success Review,* (February 2007),pp 131-135.

* "Improve Your Personality: play down the I". *Competition Success Review,* (May 2006), pp.165, 208.

* "Improve Your Personality: keep smiling". *Competition Success Review,* (September 2006),pp. 202.

* http://www.pubmedcentral.nih.gov/articlerender.fcgi?artid

* http://www.ifla.org/IV/ifla68/papers/160-110e.pdf

* http://dlis.dos.state.fl.us/bld/Leadership/Florida_Library_ Leadership%20Plan_0405.doc

* http://www.dlib.org/dlib/september06/choi/09choi.html

* http://www.law.duke.edu/fac/danner/callweb.htm

* http://www.law.duke.edu/fac/danner/article.pdf

B-08

Career Advancements and Job Prospects for Librarians

M. Kannan

Plot No.28, Door No.3, I Cross Street, Vanamamali Nagar,
By-Pass Road, Madurai-625 016.

ABSTRACT

Every human being is attracted by monetary benefits and incentives. Being professionals, librarians are no exception to this phenomenon. Incentives and monetary benefits act as catalysts for the working personnel to be motivated and to perform in high esteem. Even though societal recognition and feeling of self-esteem play a great role in a professional's career, money and material things gain importance as motivating factors. Job opportunities are more in numbers for library professionals in this era of electronic revolution and digital innovations. There are certain apprehensions over recognition of personnel from various entities such as public, academic and special libraries among one another. The super system of the three entities discussed can flourish, only if the sub system namely the libraries concerned are taken care of. In the 11th five-year plan; the government of India has proposed to start 1500 universities to enhance the system of higher education. So the job prospects for graduates and professionals of library science seems to be a highly hopeful situation in the days to come. This paper will try to address the issues involved with the career advancements and job opportunities for the library professionals in the context of three types of libraries namely public, academic and special libraries.

INTRODUCTION

Every human being is attracted by monetary benefits and incentives. Being professionals, librarians are no exception to this phenomenon. Incentives and monetary benefits act as catalysts for the working personnel to be motivated and to perform in high esteem. Even though societal recognition and feeling of self-esteem play a great role in a professional's career, money and material things gain importance as motivating factors. Job opportunities are more in numbers for library professionals in this era of electronic revolution and digital innovations. There are certain apprehensions over recognition of personnel from various entities such as public, academic and special libraries among one another. This paper will try to address the issues involved with the career advancements and job opportunities for the library professionals in the context of three types of libraries namely public, academic and special libraries.

LIBRARIANS IN PUBLIC LIBRARIES

Public libraries were started with the aim of delivering information to all and even to the remote corners of our state. Initially the career of librarians in public libraries started with a cadre called 'Grade-3' librarian. But nowadays with the introduction of village libraries and part-time libraries, the appointments are made at the entry level only for part-time libraries and village libraries. Among these, librarians of part-time libraries receive a meager salary of Rs605/= (per month) and village librarians are paid a salary of Rs1500/= (per month). The salaries of part-time and village librarians have no time bound increment and they are not entitled for any kind of leave during their service in such designations. Job prospects for the village librarians were at a stake for the past eleven years from when they were appointed in the first instance (1995). Only recently (November' 2006), they were appointed in the time scale of pay pattern and are covered under contributory pension scheme.

For librarians in the cadre of 'Grade-3', the salary is in the time scale of Rs3200- 85-Rs4900/- (junior-assistant's scale). Regarding career advancements, an increment of Rs85/- (per month) is sanctioned for personnel who have acquired M.L.I.Sc (Master of Library and Information Science). Other than this, there is no increment for whatever educational qualification a personnel acquires such as M.Phil or Ph.D in library and information Science. This hinders the attitude of the personnel working in public libraries to enhance their qualification and enrich themselves on par with their academic counterparts.

LIBRARIANS IN ACADEMIC LIBRARIES

School Libraries

Barring certain matriculation schools, in almost all the schools there is no such post in the name of librarian. Even if it happens to be, a teacher or a clerical cadre person is entrusted with the responsibility of holding the stocks in a safe condition, without being used at all. Conditions of books and holdings of a school library are even worse in certain situations where books are dumped in storerooms. The scenario may change if the government authorities come forward to appoint librarians in schools. Such a move would create awareness among the school children on the need for reading materials other than the textbooks. This would pave way for providing job opportunities for the graduates of library science and helps for the enhancement of school education movement. The question of career advancement for school librarians does not even arise with almost no personnel being appointed in the designation of 'librarian' in a vast majority of schools.

COLLEEGE LIBRARIES

Appointment for the post of college librarians has not been made over a decade or so. Personnel working in clerical cadre and who have acquired B.L.I.Sc (Bachelor of Library and Information Science) and M.L.I.Sc (Master of Library and Information Science) degrees through distance education modes have gained appointments in certain government arts and science colleges as librarians. For the rest of the colleges the post of librarian is either kept vacant or entrusted with personnel of clerical cadre as a duty in additional charge. Career advancement for college librarians is on par with the UGC (University Grants Commission) norms laid down for university librarians. Leaving apart certain anomalies in revision of pay scales after putting in five or ten years of continuous service, the librarians in government arts and science colleges are paid with a decent salary along with their academic counterparts. Wage increments on acquiring higher qualifications are also too good when compared with public libraries. Job opportunities for college librarians are quite high in universities and deemed universities (which are now liberalized to name themselves as universities under the act (3) of UGC).

UNIVERSITY LIBRARIES

The most coveted designation for library science professionals would be the post of an university librarian. The pay scales and allowances for library science professionals in universities are on par with teaching community being envisaged by UGC. Baring certain anomalies in the promotion of personnel in the cadre of

'Technical Assistant' to that of 'Assistant University Librarian' and the difference in pay scales of such personnel among various universities of our state, the situation appears quite good for librarians in universities. The greatest injury to the system of university libraries lies in the non-happening of appointments for more than a decade and so. Due to these kinds of activities there are almost no person available for heading the post of university librarian in our state, since the UGC norms expect a deputy librarian to have ten years experience for the post. The authorities in the UGC should come forward to redress such anomalies by way of reducing the years of experience or providing weightage for higher qualifications such as 'Post Doctoral Fellowships' for the posts such as university librarian.

LIBRARIANS IN SPECIAL LIBRARIES

The librarians in special libraries are paid according to the institutions to which they are attached with. In earlier days special libraries were attached only with organizations and research and development establishments. But with the advent of information technology companies like TCS (Tata Consultancy Services) and INFOSYS have begun to establish libraries and are recruiting library professionals with decent perks. Central Government institutions such as CSIR (Council for Scientific and Industrial Research) and the like have time bound promotion or 'Assured Career Promotion' (ACP) for their professionals. In this era of electronic revolutions the job prospects for LIS (Library and Information Science) professionals are more in the context of special libraries.

NEED FOR SELF – MOTIVATION

For any professional the need for self-motivation and thirst for enhancement is a must for sustenance and well-being. The profession of a librarian, being that of non-target oriented as in the case of business organizations, is a routine one and so library professionals need to acquire more and more from the developments that happen in their fields and others too in order to keep them alive and active.

NEED FOR TRAINING PROGRMMES

With the introduction of digital technologies like barcode and RFID, (Radio Frequency Identification Devices) traditional modes of book lending and library routines are replaced by modern techniques such as OPAC (Online Public Access Catalogue) and computerized smart cards for members of the libraries. So the library professionals have to be trained in such innovations, in order to provide a better service for the users. Such trainings will enhance the mental mindset of the professionals and will help to overcome the feeling that librarians need not be treated as professionals of teaching category.

CONCLUSION

The whole nomenclature of 'Librarian' and their work culture has undergone a change in the context of information officer or information professional nowadays. The authorities concerned whether it be public, academic or special libraries should come forward to look into the appointment of the professionals without delay and be prepared enough at the minimum to listen to the pay anomalies. The super system of the three entities discussed can flourish, only if the sub system namely the libraries concerned are taken care of. In the 11th five-year plan; the government of India has proposed to start 1500 universities to enhance the system of higher education. So the job prospects for graduates and professionals of library science seems to be highly hopeful situation in the days to come.

REFERENCES

* **Bhagavam, GD.** *Librarian ship in India and Abroad.* New Delhi: Metropiliton Book Co.,1997

* Deshpande, KS. *University library system in India.* **New Delhi : Sterling Publishers, 1985.**

* Sharma, CDE. *Developing horizons in library and information science.* **Jaipus : Print Well Publishers, 1983**

* Goswami, Badri Prasad. *Personnel motivation and work efficiency in libraries.* **Varanasi : The Eureka Printin Works P Ltd, 1972**

* Monappa, Arun and Saiadin, **Mirza S.** *Personal management.* **New Delhi : Tata Mc Graw Hill Publishing Co., 1980**

B-09
The Role of Librarian in Improving Search Activities in a College : A Study

D. Revathi Selvi
Librarian, S.T.E.T. Women's College,
Sundarakkotai, Mannargudi – 614 061 Thanjavur Dt.

ABSTRACT

Research is one of the core activity in a college. At the same time, it is found that many colleges are not encouraging the research environment particularly in medium and small colleges due to various limitations. The role of librarian is one among the major factors that influences the research attitude of faculties and students in a college environment. This paper deals with research in library and information centers, importance of serials in research and particularly emphasises the know how and skill of librarian that is required to disseminate the research information to the faculty in a personal way.

INTRODUCTION

According to New Oxford Dictionary 'a library is a public institution or establishment charged with the care of collection of books and the duty of making them accessible to those who require the use of them'.

A glossary of library and information science has defined library as a collection of materials organized to provide physical, bibliographic and intellectual access to a target group, with a staff that is trained to provide service and programes related to the information needs of the target group.

In those days, a library was regarded as storehouse of books and the books were kept there for preservation only. The librarian was merely a caretaker or custodian of the books. A modern library acquires materials, processes and makes it available for use rather than preservation. To provide services to the users it allows open access to its collection. It converts potential users into habitual users, who has visited library regularly and use the library as a matter of habit.

RESEARCH IN LIBRARIES AND INFORMATION CENTRES

The Librarian guides the research scholars about systematic, painstaking investigation of a topic, or in a field of study, often employing techniques of hypothesis and experimentation, undertaken by a person of intent on revealing new facts, theories, or principles, or determining the current state of knowledge of the subject. The results are usually reported in a primary journal, in conference proceedings, or in a monograph by the researcher(s) who conducted the study. In the sciences, methodology is also reported to allow the results to be verified.

THE IMPORTANCE OF SERIALS IN RESEARCH

For many academics and researchers, the serials to which a library subscribes are the most important and useful elements of its stock. Articles in serials are published much more rapidly, than books and thus serials constitute, a vital flow of up-to-date information. This is particularly important in rapidly developing areas of science and technology. Furthermore articles in serials frequently discuss in depth highly specialized topics and include information that may never appear in book form.

LIBRARIANS ROLE IN PROVIDING INFORMATION ON RESEARCH

A higher level of dissemination of information service is achieved if the library or a related institution generates the relevant information itself, compiles it and forwards it to the clients. All relevant sources (Printed material, bibliographic and factual databases, hosts, internet resources) are scanned and evaluated for this purpose regularly by the library. The Profile – Corresponding selection and compression of relevant information is also done by the library.

The content of disseminated of information can include metadata and primary sources, hypothesis, validated information, should be detailed and include annotations and abstracts so that customers are enabled to judge whether, for example, the ordering of digital or printed material with resulting costs is worthwhile.

CONCLUSION

College library is a research unit which provides materials and facilities for research, a place where the scholar with a question can search for it wherever it leads, among both primary and secondary materials.

The library professionals help the research scholars to acquire information from universal collection both in print and electronic media. Digitization may further foster comprehensiveness, though no one knows to what extent the mass of millions of early printed materials will ever actually be available as an electronic research collection.

REFERENCES

*   **Siwatch, Ajith S. ed.** *Approches to modern librarian ship.* New Delhi : Sanjay Prakasam, 2006

*   **Gudia, Kundan.** *Electronic services in Library and Information Services.* New Delhi : Adhyayan Publications, 2007

B-10
Essential Skills for a Future Librarian

B. Jyothi

Manager, Library and Information Services,
Tata Consultancy Services Ltd, Chennai

S.K. Sundar

Executive, Library and Information Services,
Tata Consultancy Services Ltd, Chennai

ABSTRACT

No one can predict the future. The future will have lot of changes. Changes are the real challenges that the knowledge economy librarians are going to face with. Since we cannot predict the future changes, we all can challenge the future changes, we all can challenge the future by horing our skills, which are essential to survive as a librarian. Being in service, as our motto, we have to have some specific skills for the satisfaction of our customers. In this paper, we are going to analyze and understand various skills required for a librarian to be a librarian for the future.

INTRODUCTION

In today's world there are several angles to librarianship. Librarians are sometimes called information navigators, knowledge managers, information brokers etc.

The Librarian has to keep his traditional skills and acquire competencies in a changed environment – print as well as electronic -- today & for the future.

Complexities have increased multifold with the plethora of information available. In this context, the role of a librarian as handler and manager of information; as trainer of others to use information effectively and efficiently; as evaluator of information quality and information provision; as caretaker of user's needs, becomes critical.

We need people who are flexible and adaptable & those who can manage change innovatively, imaginatively and proactively, recognising new opportunities and grasping new challenges. This will require well-educated professionals, constantly developing through personal improvement and continuing education / training.

Comprehending our brave new world of search is a constant challenge for Librarians. In the early days, we talked about "information retrieval," which now has an archaic ring to it. Internet browsing and search is the current mantra and presents a different research environment that tests the research skills of information professionals. Today's researcher needs to be fluent both in traditional online search and in the nuances of precise finding, search engines, semantic clustering, automated indexing, and non-textual information. Collaborating with technology to effectively search and more importantly, to find requisite high quality information remains a significant component of the information professional's daily work life. The future lies in less searching and more finding.

DIVERSITY OF THE PROFESSION

Library and information Services have changed rapidly in recent years. The strategic and operational value of good information provision is recognized by a wide range of employers. Information handling and information management in all their various guises have increasingly been seen as crucial for survival in a burgeoning diversity of markets: health; financial; legal information; software development; publishing; multimedia; research; information broking and information consultancy. In addition the traditional areas of the academic, public, government and special library sectors have widened in terms of their definition of service delivery, with information specialists taking on an enhanced role of consultancy, learner support and information systems engineering.

But maybe herein lies the problem. The very diversity of demands on initial higher education and the broadening of markets into which information students move, means that initial professional education needs to be broad-based and cross-sectoral. As a result it cannot easily cater for the in-depth needs of specific markets or may not concentrate sufficiently on technology, if it is at the expense of other areas. It appears we are turning out highly educated, computer literate, people-oriented, highly employable individuals; but maybe only a very few information professionals who will have to fit into new and specific roles in the workplace. Any qualification is worth its weight only for about five years. Individuals need therefore to be flexible, adaptable to change and open minded to continue to educate themselves and be educated through life, personally and professionally. Lifelong learning has a professional as well as personal dimension.

EDUCATION AND TRAINING

Much training and awareness is left to post-LIS education. This poses a real problem. The experience is that such trainings are inadequately recognised by employers and managed piecemeal, if at all.

Skills may range from being a children's librarian, whose knowledge of children's reading and psychological needs allied to book knowledge (and more recently multimedia knowledge) allow him or her to find just the right book for the right child at the right time; to the medical librarian able to use Medline or other online sources to answer complex scientific or medical enquiries.

The key areas where the skill sets of the existing librarians will be most challenged in future and where new skill sets will be required are:

- they must know how to access electronic databases, texts, CDs, networks and also educate users on it
- in academia, they will essentially require to have subject knowledge to understand learning / teaching skills to fulfill para academic duties
- customer care and attitude towards service has to be applied. For sensitive delivery of services, focus must be on delivering a system highly responsive to user needs
- should build team commitment towards achievement of LIS goals

All the above challenges can be met only through creative and positive means of managing change

In order to be proactive rather than reactive, the following skills will be a must for any librarian who wants to be in the business in future!

INFORMATION HANDLING SKILLS

Cataloguing, indexing, general management and organisation of information & organisation of knowledge.

TRAINING AND FACILITATING

Helping people, of any age, background, specialty or need, to use libraries and information resources in any media, user support and user instruction.

EVALUATION SKILLS

Selection, critical evaluation and review, quality assurance of information, fitness for purpose, as needed in both traditional and digital library environments, and concern for the customer!

All these incorporate an understanding of information technology, as well as our personal transferable skills.

COMMUNICATION / MARKTING SKILLS

The ability to communicate what we do, what we've done and what else we can do for our customers is very important. Librarians need to sell their competencies to their customers, whether it's storytelling for children, research methods for students or online resources for busy managers. The only way this can be done is if we learn to speak the language of our external and internal customers.

INFORMATION TECHNOLOGY SKILLS

The IT skills required for a future librarian could be mind blowing. Starting from learning to access blogs, RSS, IM, wikis, and audio ebooks. The following skills will be essential - Word Processing, Spreadsheets, Database, Electronic Presentation, Web Navigation, Web Site Design, E-Mail Management, Digital Cameras, Computer Network, Knowledge Application, File Management, Downloading Software from the Web (including eBooks), Installing Computer Software onto a Computer System, WebCT or Blackboard Teaching, Videoconferencing, Computer-Related Storage Devices (Knowledge: disks, CDs, USB drives, zip disks, DVDs, etc.), knowledge to use Scanners & PDAs, Educational Copyright Knowledge, Computer Security detects.

KNOWLEDGE MANAGEMENT SKILLS

There is definitely a role for us as autonomous

information professionals in evaluating, filtering and managing information, including the skills of cataloguing and classification, indexing and abstracting. These are applicable in new information contexts, such as the management of metadata, the design and application of search engines or the creation of organisational thesauri. Other skills can also be useful in making the knowledge more accessible, including their knowledge of the organisation, customer service orientation, and their training skills.

If we are to have a place in knowledge management, many of us will need a mind shift; we will need to become more proactive, think more strategically, and align our work more closely with the goals of the organisation. We need to understand that KM is more than information and technology and that tacit knowledge may be of critical relevance. Its collection, distribution and management are critical; if we are to play a significant role in this process, then how we relate to the organisational context and those at all levels within it will determine the extent of our success or failure. To do this, we will need to start thinking outside our box and align everything we do with the broader objectives of our context. To do this we will need to work together to promote ourselves and to start working more closely with areas such as HR, IT and senior management. A team approach is essential.

TEAM WORKING SKILLS

In today's context team working becomes a major concept for the librarians which will help them to analyse, plan and implement the required changes that are going to happen in future. Since librarian is a service provider, he/she needs to have a good network among the librarians and other academicians as well as be able to work and help within their team and with other teams as well. Team members possess a variety of technical/management skills and encourage other team members to develop new ones to increase their versatility, flexibility and add value to the team. Apart from this, each team members or librarian should be capable of giving a solution when there is a crisis or problem in their team to achieve a common goal of an organization or institution.

Also, the library of the future will need a team where each member is specialized in a particular skill & the skills in total complement each other. To be specific, each member should be an expert in classification / web page development / specific subjects required by the institution or corporate / information retrieval from the internet (including expertise in using wikis / RSS) to name a few.

BEHAVIORAL SKILLS

In the Knowledge era, the behaviors of a librarian help him/her to support the marketing skills. Because of your behavior market your products to the end user or customers. But in turn they will bring more customers and add value to your work. To achieve this a librarian must have capabilities like:

1. Approachability
2. Flexibility-Ability to respond to pressure and change
3. Capacity to learn quickly and constantly based on the requirement
4. Innate Skepticism
5. Risk taking capacity
6. Good interpersonal skills
7. Ability to deal with a range of users

If a librarian has or develops the above skills then the future will not be a challenge but in turn he/she will get more opportunities.

PROBLEM SOLVING SKILLS

In the context of library the problem is how we are going to solve the information needs of the users. We can use the six skills approach to solve any type of problem including the information-seeking problem.

The Six skills are:

1. Define the task (the information problem) and identify the needed information to complete the task

2. Brainstorm all possible sources of information seeking strategies and select the best source among them.

3. Locate required sources and find information within that source.

4. Read, hear, view or touch the sources to get the relevant information.

5. Synthesis the information from multiple sources to present it.

6. Evaluate the efficiency and effectiveness of the information product.

SELF MANAGEMENT SKILLS

As an individual each librarian has different type of responsibilities that will relate to a final product or an ongoing process. So there is a necessity to have a self-management skill to achieve the organization goals on time. There is need for all information professionals to plan, organize and prioritize their work and implement on time for a common goal.

To hone and encourage creative skills & innovation, librarians should be rewarded for their best practices & good practices and innovative experiences can be shared across librarians.

To bring about the above changes, there needs to be a marked improvement / change in the LIS curriculum starting from the undergraduate level.

Librarians are people-oriented; content oriented; customer-oriented people. Their role is critical in creating and maintaining awareness of issues such as data quality, timeliness and reliability. They should value their end user's time & help them against information overload by navigating through information.

We need to merge the two cultures of information managers with librarians. They should sharpen the traditional skills & acquire new skills to become analysts of information instead of just being collectors of information, thereby complementing their own skills.

Continuing professional education is key to resolve the upsurge in skills required by the librarian in the new era. Lifelong learning is a must. The characteristics of lifelong learning are – Learning to do (acquiring and applying skills); Learning to be (promote creativity); Learning to know (flexible, critical, capable); Learning to Live together (collaboration / tolerance)

CONCLUSION

To quote the great...

"Today's advanced knowledge is tomorrow's ignorance!" (Drucker; 1997)

"The illiterate of the 21st century will not be those who cannot read and write, but those who cannot learn, unlearn and relearn" (Toffler; 1971)

The information world of the next generation will depend on a literate and skilled workforce with collaborating skills. There is an urgent need to equip our librarians with information handling skills to make them more productive as individuals and effective as citizens. Librarians are at the entrance of a new era where they need to play new roles – as an interpreter, a navigator, a mediator and guide.

REFERENCES

* 1999 Dunn & Wilson Scholarship Project: Skills transfer for library technicians, ALIA, 28 January 2004.

* ALIA, The Library and information sector: core knowledge, skills and attributes, 8 June 2005.

* Chales B Lorry, Dean of Libraries, University of Maryland: Working Paper #1 on Team Management, The Vision of a Team-Based Learning Organization, June 26, 2000.

* David Ward & Maria I. Liriano, Reference User Services Association (RUSA) RSS Management Committee Members and Authors; Guidelines for Behavioral Performance of Reference and Information Service Providers, June 2004.

* Eisenberg, Michael B. -Johnson, Doug: Computer Skills for Information Problem-Solving: Learning and Teaching Technology in Context. ERIC Digest, ERIC Clearinghouse on Information and Technology Syracuse, New York, 1996-03-00.

* Jenny Aitchison, Editor-Editorial: What are they looking for? UNP Library bulletin, No. 341 April 2002.

* Julie Todaro, Attention New Librarians and Career Changes: Identifying and Conveying Transferable Skills, ALA-APA, V4, Special Issue, April 2007.

* Linda Ashcroft: Developing competencies, critical analysis and personal transferable skills in future information professionals, Library review, 53 (2) 2004.

* Linda Marion: Digital Librarian, Cyberarian, or Librarian with Specialized Skills: Who Will Staff Digital Libraries?, ACRL Tenth National Conference, March 15-18, 2001, Denver, Colorado.

* Meredith Farkas: Skills for the 21st Century Librarian, Wolf Waters, July 17, 2006.

* The Regional Environment Reconstruction Programme for South Eastern Europe (RERep): Tools and Skills of Today's and Tomorrow's Information Manager-A Keynote lecture, Sofia, Bulgaria, 20 June 2003.

* Youngok Choi & Edie Rasmussen: What is Needed to Educate Future Digital Librarians, D-Lib Magazine, September 2006.

B-11
Coping with Challenges of Youth and Libraries

T. Stephen
Librarian, Malankara Catholic College,
Mariagiri, Kanniyakumari Dt. 629 153

Dr. A. Lawrence Mary
Librarian, T.D.M.N.S.College, Kallikulam, Tuticorin Dt

ABSTRACT

Kids and curiosity go together. Children and teenagers have an unquenchable thirst for knowledge that usually pleases but sometimes overwhelms their parents. Fortunately, there are libraries and librarians to help answer these unending questions, send kids on wondrous adventures and provide them with the resources they need to learn and grow. And parents can relax knowing it is a friendly place for all families. Here are answers to some commonly asked questions, along with suggestions for helping children become lifelong learners and library users. Libraries are often challenged by individuals and groups concerned about the availability of a wide variety of library materials to everyone. Addressing these challenges requires a balance of carefully crafted library policy, knowledge and understanding of intellectual freedom principles and sensitivity to community needs and concerns. It also requires effective communication.

INTRODUCTION

Kids and curiosity go together. Children and teenagers have an unquenchable thirst for knowledge that usually pleases but sometimes overwhelms their parents. Fortunately, there are libraries and librarians to help answer these unending questions, send kids on wondrous adventures and provide them with the resources they need to learn and grow. And parents can relax knowing it is a friendly place for all families.

Here are answers to some commonly asked questions, along with suggestions for helping children become lifelong learners and library users.

What is the role of libraries and librarians in serving children?

Libraries are family-oriented public institutions charged with making a broad selection of materials available for everyone, including children and teenagers.

Most public libraries have special areas for children and teens with materials that appeal to various ages and interests. Libraries also offer summer reading programs, storytelling, book discussions and other special programs for young people. Programs such as these help kids learn to enjoy libraries and use them for their information and entertainment needs.

School libraries have a responsibility to support their school's curriculum and to provide materials that serve the diverse backgrounds, interests, maturity levels and reading levels of the entire student body.

HOW ARE LIBRARIES DIFFERENT FROM MOVIE THEATERS, BOOK OR VIDEO STORES, WHICH OFTEN HAVE RESTRICTIONS FOR CHILDREN AND TEENS?

As public institutions, libraries cannot discriminate based on age, sex, race or any other characteristic. Movie theaters are privately owned businesses that can choose to show only children's movies or westerns. Similarly, video stores can decide not to rent certain movies to anyone under the age of 18.

Libraries must meet the diverse needs of everyone in their communities. They cannot overrule the rights and responsibilities of individuals by deciding who does or doesn't have access to library materials. Most libraries provide movie reviews and ratings for parents to use these in guiding their children's library use.

Can't parents tell the librarian what material they don't think children should have?

Decisions about what materials are suitable for particular children should be made by the people who know them best—their parents or guardians.

Children mature at different rates. They have different backgrounds and interests. And they have different reading levels and abilities. For instance, a video that one 10-year-old likes may not interest another. Or parents may feel a particular library book is inappropriate for their daughter, while the same book may be a favorite of her classmate's family. These factors make it impossible for librarians to set any criteria for restricting use based on age alone. To do so would keep others who want and need materials from having access to them.

Like adults, children and teenagers have the right to seek and receive the information that they choose. It is the right and responsibility of parents to guide their own family's library use while allowing other parents to do the same.

Librarians are not authorized to act as parents. But they are happy to provide suggestions and guidance to parents and youngsters at any time.

Sample questions and answers

The following questions provide sample language to use when answering questions from the media and other members of the public. You will want to personalize your remarks for your library and community. Remember, keep it simple. Keep it human.

WHAT IS THE ROLE OF LIBRARIES IN SERVING CHILDREN?

The same as it is for adults. Libraries provide books and other materials that will meet the needs of a wide range of ages and interests. Many libraries have special areas for children and teenagers. They also have many special programs, such as preschool story hour, movies, puppet shows, term paper clinics. In fact, more children participate in summer reading programs at libraries than play Little League baseball!

WHY DON'T LIBRARIES RESTRICT CERTAIN MATERIALS BASED ON AGE LIKE MOVIE THEATERS OR VIDEO STORES?

Movie theaters and video stores are private businesses and can make their own policies. Libraries are public institutions. They cannot limit access on the basis of age or other characteristics. Our library does provide copies of movie reviews and ratings, and we encourage parents to use them in guiding their children's library use.

HOW DO LIBRARIES DECIDE WHAT TO BUY?

Every library has its own policies, which are approved by its board. Our library has adopted the *Library Bill of*

Rights. We also have a mission statement that says our goal is to serve a broad range of community needs. Librarians are taught as part of their professional education to evaluate books and other materials and to select materials based on library policies.

DOES THAT MEAN A CHILD CAN CHECK OUT PLAYBOY OR OTHER MATERIALS INTENDED FOR ADULTS?

We believe in freedom of choice for all people but we also believe in common sense. It would be extremely unusual for a young child to check out that type of adult material. Most libraries are designed with special areas for children and teenagers. And there are librarians to provide assistance. We also provide suggested reading lists to help them make proper choices. Our goal is to provide the best possible service for young people, and we are very proud of what we offer. If you haven't been to our library recently, we encourage you to come and see for yourself!

WHAT SHOULD I DO IF I FIND SOMETHING I DON'T AOPPROVE OF IN THE LIBRARY?

Libraries offer a wide range of materials and not everyone is going to like or approve of everything. If you have a concern, simply ask or speak to the librarian. We do want to know your concerns, and we're confident we have or can get materials that meet your needs. The library also has a formal review process. If you wish put your concern in writing.

WHAT DOES THE LIBRARY DO IF SOMEONE COMPLAINTS ABOUT SOMETHING IN ITS COLLECTION?

We take such concerns very seriously. First, we listen. We also have a formal review process in which we ask you to fill out a special form designed to help us understand your concerns. Anyone who makes a written complaint will receive a response in writing.

WHAT CAN PARENTS DO TO PROTECT THEIR CHILDREN FROM MATERIALS THEY CONSIDER OFFENSIVE?

Visit the library with your children. If that's not possible, ask to see the materials your children bring home. Set aside a special shelf for library materials. If there are materials on it you don't approve of, talk with your children about why you would rather not read or view them. Most libraries provide suggested reading lists for various ages. And librarians are always glad to advise children and parents on selecting materials they think they would enjoy and find helpful.

KEY MESSAGES

When responding to a challenge, you will want to focus on three key points:

- Libraries provide ideas and information across the spectrum of social and political views.
- Libraries are one of our great democratic institutions. They provide freedom of choice for all people.
- Parents are responsible for supervising their own children's library use.

These simple, but sometimes overlooked essentials are the bulwark against challenges.

TIPS FOR CHILDREN'S AND YOUNG ADULT LIBRARIANS

- Make sure you and your staff are familiar with the library's collection policy and can explain it in a clear, easily understandable way.

- Take time to listen to and empathize with a parent's concern. Explain in a non-defensive way the need to protect the right of all parents to determine their own children's reading.

- Keep your director informed of any concerns expressed, whether you feel they have been successfully resolved or not.

- Join professional organizations to keep abreast of issues and trends in library service to children and families.

- Encourage parents or guardians to participate in choosing library materials for their young people and to make reading aloud a family activity. Host storytelling, book discussion groups and other activities that involve adults and youth, must be encouraged.

- Offer "parent education" programs/workshops throughout the year National Library Week in April, Teen Read Week in October and Children's Book Week in November, provide timely opportunities. Suggested topics: how to select books and other materials for youth, how to raise a reader, how books and other materials can help children and teens cope with troubling situations, the importance of parents being involved in their children's reading and library use; concepts of intellectual freedom.

- Reach out to the media. Offer to write a newspaper column or host a radio or TV program discussing good books and other materials for children and teens. Give tips for helping families get the most from libraries.

- Build bridges. Offer to speak to parents and other groups on what's new at the library, good reading for youth, how to motivate children and teens to read, how to make effective use of the library and other topics of special interest.

SCHOOL LIBRARIES

School librarians play a key role in making sure that students have the broad range of resources and ideas they need to develop critical thinking skills. Challenges to materials provide a "teachable moment" that can help you build understanding and support for the principles of intellectual freedom, including First Amendment rights, student rights of access and professional ethics.

APPLYING THE PRINCIPLES OF INTELLECTUAL FREEDOM

- Connect academic freedom with intellectual freedom. Academic freedom guarantees the teacher's right to teach and to select classroom and library resources for instruction.

- Make sure that everyone involved understands the right of people in a democratic society to express their concerns.

- Explain the obligation of the school to provide intellectual and physical access to resources that provide for a wide range of abilities and differing points of view.

- Define intellectual and physical access when appropriate. Intellectual access includes the right to read, receive and express ideas and the right to acquire skills to seek out, explore and examine ideas. Physical access includes being able to locate and retrieve information unimpeded by fees, age limits, separate collections or other restrictions.

- Emphasize the need to place the principles of intellectual and academic freedom above personal opinion and reason above prejudice, when selecting resources.

- Connect intellectual freedom and access. The freedom

to express your beliefs or ideas becomes meaningless when others are not allowed to receive or have access to those beliefs or ideas.

- Stress the need for teachers and librarians to be free to present students with alternatives and choices if students are to learn and use critical thinking and decision-making skills.

PREPARING FOR CHALLENGES

- Develop rationales for the use of required materials in each department and/or grade.
- Introduce the rationale at Parent's Night or open houses or through the school newsletter to help parents understand what materials are being bought and why.
- Work with administrators, teachers and librarians to prepare a list of alternative materials for instructional activities.
- Prepare a packet of materials, including the school's educational goals and materials selection policy, to give to those registering concerns.
- Review all policies dealing with access to ensure that school rules are conducive to free and open access to the library.
- Prepare an audiocassette that explains principles of intellectual and academic freedom contained in the materials selection policy and reconsideration process for staff members to listen to at home or in their car.
- Inform staff and board members that complaints and requests for reconsideration made by them will get the same due process as from a parent or community member.
- Engage students in discussions and activities related to intellectual freedom. An educated and informed student body can provide a strong support group for

the school when educational resources are challenged.

- Remind school administrators that to ignore or override a board-approved materials selection policy can place them in legal jeopardy.

- Unite with other groups in your community that are concerned with intellectual freedom issues. Make them aware of the rights of children and young adults.

- Educate administrators, teachers and other school personnel about the importance of the school library and the role it plays in the education of the student as part of in-service training.

CONCLUSION

Libraries are often challenged by individuals and groups concerned about the availability of a wide variety of library materials to everyone. Addressing these challenges requires a balance of carefully crafted library policy, knowledge and understanding of intellectual freedom principles, and sensitivity to community needs and concerns. It also requires effective communication.

REFERENCES

* **Verma, Kusur.** *The Electronic library.* New Delhi : Akansha, 2004

* Balakrishnan, Shyama and Paliwal, PK.

* **Nath, Mahendra.** *Handbook of library services.* Jaipur : Pointer, 2001

B-12
Librarianship Today : Challenges and Changes in the Age of Technology

G. Pandi Selvi
Librarian, ICFAI National College, Madurai

P. Umarani
Faculty ICFAI National College, Madurai

ABSTRACT

In recent years technology has made tremendous impact on every profession including librarian ship. Technology has brought dramatic changes in every sphere of library activity. The library professionals, as intermediaries, have to cope with the "knowledge explosion" which is the result of the information technology and high expectations of the users. New skills and knowledge will have to be acquired and the existing skills have to be enhanced to survive and face the challenges in this dynamic information society. This paper focuses on some of the skills, personal traits and attitudes and knowledge that are necessary for the library professionals of this millennium.

INTRODUCTION

Library is a LIGHT HOUSE , which is a knowledge disseminating center.

A Wiseman's Den , where the ring of WISDOM is glowing and sprouting to feed the quest of Knowledge.

A lighted match to the trail of gunpowder , which ignites the thought process, invokes the action process to produce Key Result Areas.

Matching the Classical, Neo – classical, Modern and Futuristic information for a Materialistic Productive Changing Technology, the sky is the limit, where The LIBRARY is the sky and the LIBRARIAN is the Father and the equipment are the TOOLS.

Libraries are riding the currents of rapidly changing technology. While continuing to provide many traditional information services, librarians are developing new skill sets and growing into the new roles that are necessary to support technology-based services. Technology has impacted nearly every facet of library work. Selectors must now deal with providing user-access to digitized resources without "owning" the resources. Catalogers must make these new resources accessible. Reference librarians still assist patrons in the library, but most , now have an additional clientele of remote-access users.

The mission of the librarian — Providing excellent information service to patrons — has not changed, but technology has added several new dimensions to this task. Fulfilling this enhanced mission can be difficult. Most libraries are not positioned for rapid change. In many libraries, staff turnout is low and does not facilitate towards rapid changing directions. Adding technology-based services usually increases, rather than decreases, the number of staff hours required to develop and maintain effective patron services.

THE NEW ROLES

Librarians are moving into dramatically different roles as new services are implemented. The rate of change is breathtaking, especially for libraries that have been accustomed to stability. Technology is driving change across the entire range of library responsibilities.

Librarians cannot and should not function as attorneys, but the analysis provided by a librarian is essential in ensuring that electronic product license agreements are appropriate for local circumstances and anticipated patron use patterns.

SCROLLING CATALOGUING SYSTEM

Scrolling Cataloguing System is also moving into new roles as they attempt to provide enhanced access to the new resources. They now process not only books, but also CD-ROMs, computer discs, and multi-format items. Library automation systems have grown in sophistication. Catalogers must make informed decisions on matters such as linking to electronic journals and managing holdings "hooks" to various databases. Catalogers today create records that accommodate multiple means of accessing a particular resource. Patrons are coming to expect records that include print holdings, microforms, and direct links to an electronic version of the item. Records must be successfully linked with not only the library, but also with a growing variety of indexes, full-text services and browsers.

TOUCH SCREEN CATALOGUING SYSTEM

Touch Screen Cataloging is a task that has fallen to librarians. "It's not a metadata element set that is going to replace MARC. Digital library (a term still being defined) initiatives generate many local-content information resources that require different bibliographic control schemes.

LIBRARY IS EDUCATION RESOURCE INFORMATION CENTER

ERIC stands for Education Resource Information Center, has an Internet-based digital library of education research information sponsored by the Institute of Education Sciences(IES) of US Department of Education. Users can access bibliographic information related to journals and non-journals indexed from 1966 to date. ERIC repository includes bibliographic records, and important data, with more than 1.2 million items indexed since 1966 that includes journals, articles, conference papers and technical reports.

The Website offers services to instructors and students in teacher-preparation programs, education researchers, librarians, teachers, administrators, media, business community and general public. ERIC provides information about journals indexed in it. Offering free online tools and resources the site suits well to the requirements of the users and proves very useful with its digital library where information is readily available.

Along with a very general note on contribution to ERIC collection, the section is further divided into three sections: 'contributors', 'publishers' and 'Microfiche Digitization'. The contributors section contains conference papers, research reports, dissertations of individuals, who are not associated with any publisher or organization. While the publisher section offers excellent opportunity for the government agencies, commercial publishers and educational institutions upload their research works in ERIC, Microfiche Digitization, makes full text available online.

E-LEARNING – EMERGING OPPORTUNITY IN THE LIBRARY

E-Learning has become a global phenomenon, which can be termed as technology-driven learning. E-learning is becoming a strategically important component of education and training in the new millennium. E-learning can be defined as a methodology in teaching, supporting, managing and assessing students on their respective subjects using online technologies which has been provided in the library. E-learning will be in terms of time, geographical distances, and technology-driven teaching. "E-learning has the potential to revolutionize the way we teach and how we learn". In 21st century e-learning should develop skills needed for enriched life. They are,

- Raising standards for readers knowledge
- Improving quality in learning process
- Potential feasibilities –removing distance barrier
- Preparing for employment and placement
- Upgrading the skills in the workplace
- Pedagogical skills and In-depth focus on curriculum coverage
- Apt communication skills and Adoptability
- Maintaining a good rapport with learners

CURRENT AWARENESS

It means "Knowledge about recent development in a specific field". Current awareness service involves the following four categories:

1. New theoretical ideas and hypothesis
2. New problems to be solved
3. New methods and techniques for studying old and new problems
4. New circumstances offering plans and procedure of what people can do.

RESPONSIBILITIES IN NEW ERA

Student Empowerment

- Conduct Library Orientation Programme to all students about library management, of various sources and services that are available in the library.

- Conduct oral quiz and two written quiz (MCQ pattern) competitions during the Library Session and encourage the students by giving prizes for the top performers.

- In connection with placements, e-mail ID of various companies and address collected from various sources can be given to the students

- Encouraging the students to develop the reading habits through paper cutting edge.

- Motivating the students to collect the Annual reports from all leading companies.

- Encouraging the students to collect Corporate House Magazines.

- To organize the students themselves in various groups like IT, Marketing, HR club etc., to familiarize them to various subject knowledge.

- Similarly a club can be formed to collect current news from Newspapers/Magazines & Journals and watching T.V from various channels.

- To give periodical assignment for group of students, evaluate and suggest suitable further readings for every library session.

- To help the students to get the appropriate books and journals for doing their Live Project and Operation workout for various subjects.

- Collect the current news from various magazines & newspapers and give to students to equip them for updated knowledge

- Display the list of current arrivals of magazines, journals & books in the notice board to create awareness of new arrivals among the students.
- Encourage the students to make book review of their interested area.
- Organize a guest lecture, workshop, annual conference meeting about the Automation of Library Management.
- Motivate the students to visit other College/University libraries to collect their requirements.

FACULTY DEVELOPMENT

- Exchange of resources and information
- Learning from Papers and Presentation
- Data Base Centers

PUBLIC AWARENESS

- Contemporary news shared in the market in a practical background
- Rare collections for references
- Reading habit as one of the morning duties is inculcated by the Library.

CONCLUSION

Technology is moving librarians into new roles — some welcome, some uncomfortable, but nearly all benefit the library patrons. In most cases these new roles are an addition to, not a replacement for traditional duties. New services will continue to develop, but many traditional library services will continue in some form for the foreseeable future. Libraries are challenged to meet the increasing demand for service with limited staff and budget, but change can be managed by making use of several elements common to most libraries.

Flexibility is the key to success, and professional

(information access and management) and personal (skills, attitudes, beliefs) competencies will be critical in maintaining the flexibility needed for continuing success into the future. By acknowledging technology, combining appropriate change management elements and preparing for continuing change, libraries will be well positioned to meet the technology-driven patron service challenges of the future. They should be involved as a Research Tool for Scholars in their future technology expedition.

" Without Library, No Knowledge

Without Librarian, No Academics"

REFERENCES

* *E-Business,* ICFAI Publication, November 2007 and May 2006

* *The ICFAI Journal of Higher Education,*August 2006, February, May, August 2007

* **Brudvig, Glenn L.** "Managing the sea change in science and technology libraries", *Science and technology libraries,* 12 (Summer 1992), p.35-50

* **Chepesuiak, Ron,** "Organizing the internet : The core of the challenge (Dublin Core Metadata Set)". *American Libraries,* 30 January, 1999. p.60-64

* **Grodzins-Lipow, Ann,** "Who will give reference service in the digital environment?", *Reference and user services quarterly,* 37 (Winter 1997), P.:25-129

* Library of congress, 1999, Reference service in a digital era, (Online) Available : http://www.leweb.loc.gov./rr/digiref/. (September 25, 1999)

* **Osorio, Nestor.** 1997, "In distance learning, Is there a role?", *Issues in science and technology librarianship,* Spring 1997. Available: http://www.library.ucsb.edu/istl/97-spring/article3.html (September 25, 1999.)

* **Spiegleman, Barbara M (ed.), 1997.** "Competencies for special librarians of the 21st century", *Special libraries association,* Washington D.C.

B-13
Self Development of Library Professionals: Team Building

P. Clara Jeyaseeli
*Librarian (SS), V.V. Vanniaperumal College
for Women, Virudunagar – 626 001*

ABSTRACT

In the contemporary society, libraries are the central processing units of this knowledge era. Being library professionals, management skills have to be motivated and enhanced to fit the changing scenario. The team building in libraries motivates the library professionals to be innovative, creative, ask what and why, with long range perspective, committed with vision, trust, etc. The characteristics of traditional management (groups) and contemporary management (teams) are explained. The term "TEAM" is defined. The need for team building is also discussed. The various ways are suggested to achieve team building.

INTRODUCTION

Libraries play a vital role in all walks of life from infancy till death. As far as libraries are concerned, the staff members are the pillars of the effective service provided. A team comprises of involvement and combination of human beings. If the team is effective, then the service provided and received will also be effective. Since, the information seekers of the libraries are from various back ground seeking various information the team of library staff should be able to provide the right information at the right time to the right user.

The library and information science professionals should enhance and manage the skills needed to serve the contemporary society. One such skill, which is mainly needed for the Total Quality Management (TQM), is Team Building. In this millennium, especially in the contemporary society, the users and the learned community look for TQM in all areas and in all services provided.

CHARACTERISTICS OF TRADITIONAL ADMINISTRATION (GROUPS)

In traditional organizational behavior and administration, groups existed. The boss and subordinate level of management existed. Among the subordinate level, lots of groups were there and the whole process of task was divided among the groups. The groups also had boss and subordinate relationships.

The boss was mainly concerned about the task of the group and the subordinates also worked only for that particular group. Some groups achieved their particular task with high motivation while others did not. Moreover each group did not care for others. There was no support and little communication existed along with lack of vision.

The subordinates were not given chance to involve in the decision making process and one-way communication was there. If new subordinates entered, there was no openness and they had to find their own way to achieve the task but conformity was insisted. The commitment, inclusion and trust were group oriented. Therefore the team concept came into existence and the team building also emerged. This works well in service-oriented institutions like libraries.

TEAM – DEFINITIONS

"The moment you start doing anything at all with another person, you've established a team. Begin a conversation; pick up the phone, brainstorm an idea and you're in teamwork"

One more electronic articles states that "A team is group organized to work together to accomplish a set of objectives that cannot be achieved effectively by individuals".

CHARACTERISTICS OF CONTEMPORY MANAGEMENT (TEAMS)

As library professionals in this contemporary society, the librarians and library professionals should be very good team leader/team member. There is not much difference between a team leader and a team worker unless the organizational climate is involved. The basic difference is that the team leader is one who stands in a place where the team worker cannot stand to the level of management.

In teams, there exists lot of support and every member is given equal opportunity in decision-making process. The new entrant is always welcomed by being shown existing norms and there is openness to change. Two-way communication exists and lot of enthusiasm and involvement from all the member teams occur. If needed, all the teams can be merged into one to have a single team. Each team shares with other teams and helps other teams also in their achievements.

NEED FOR TEAM BUILDING IN LIBRARIES

The library professionals should have self motivation and enhance themselves to acquire management skills to fit for the changing scenario. The management skills, especially soft skills include leadership qualities, interpersonal relations, communication skills, motivation, decision-making, team building, etc. Since libraries involve society, the team building should be enriched to achieve TQM, which the society is mainly concerned about.

The team building in libraries motivates the library professionals to be innovative, creative, ask what and why, with long range perspective, committed with vision, etc.

The library professionals at all cost should know how to relate with their ability to promote other's ability. Productive team in a library improves motivation in their service, which in turn enhances enthusiasm and apparent service to the contemporary society, which is needed for TQM. This ability can be achieved only by learning and practice. To achieve this soft skill of team building, the library professional should mainly depend upon common sense, communicate with people, team members and follow certain principles.

WAY TO ACHIEVE TEAM BUILDING

Every library has a team of members (library professionals) and this team has to be motivated in order to promote team building to achieve TQM in all the services whatever the library provides. Therefore, the following ways are suggested to achieve team building in libraries and every library professional should follow them.

1. Unity
2. Vision
3. Priorities
4. Commitment and Inclusion
5. Interpersonal Communication
6. Contribution and Learning
7. Trust
8. Responsibility

9. Continuous Process

10. Results Oriented

11. Goals and Decision Making

12. Personal Issues

13. Enjoyable

14. Critical Feedback

15. Sharing of Data.

UNITY

The team leader and the team members should be united about the task, vision and mission and no personal conflicts should enter to achieve the goal that is set.

VISION

The vision should not be vague or confusing. The team leader should correctly set the vision as per the future requirements and this vision should be clearly clarified to make the team members understand the vision according to the mission of the task.

PRIORITIES

The tasks should be given due importance as per the priority and should be intimated to the members and the task should be handed over to the correct member motivating him to complete at the right time.

COMMITMENT AND INCLUSION

Inclusion means getting others to commit to the team effort, helping others to genuine commitment. Since leaders now understand this process first hand, need arises only to communicate with the potential team members to complete inclusion.

The team leader should follow three steps to achieve inclusion. They are

Non-assumptive Questions

The team members should not be left with assumptive questions. Every question whatever the member(s) raise(s) should be cleared in order to make him remain committed to achieve the task.

Direct Response

The task should be handed over to the member directly without passing with non-assumptive questions. In such cases clear statements should be provided.

Good Listening

Must be patient to the queries of the members and all possible queries should be answered after proper listening so that the task may not be reiterated.

Interpersonal Communication

Interpersonal communication should be maintained. Communications should be made open among all team members. There should be no preference to anyone and each one should be given equal preference.

Contribution And Learning

Everyone should contribute his/her effective skill to achieve the task and should be sportive to learn from the tasks and mistakes of other members. It is not only doing service but also learning and helping others.

Trust

Trust means confidence in team leadership and vision. When trust prevails, team members are more willing to go through a difficult process, supported through ups and downs, risk and potential loss. Trust is most efficiently established when leadership commits to vision first and everyone knows those commitments are genuine.

Responsibility

Members should know their role and responsibility in achieving the task. In all organization there exist difficult and non-committed people. For the difficult people, the responsibility should be given, while they are made to achieve the task. The non-committed people must be made to support some other committed people.

Continuous Process

This teamwork should be made so clear, that it is a continuous process especially in libraries. It is not spasmodic confined to a short-term task.

Result Oriented

Although it is a continuous process, every task should be result oriented. There should not be any contradicting intentions. The results should be recorded and if possible relevant reports should be generated to study the process for future reference and further improvements.

Goals And Decision Making

Plenty of opportunity should be given for discussion. The team leader and team members should make the goals and decisions jointly.

Personal Issues

Concern should be shown to members' personal issues. Stubbornness should not always be there. Simple rewards should be provided for the team members to promote motivation showing proper appreciation enlightens the members and the team.

Enjoyable

Every one should be motivated in such a way that work becomes enjoyable and if time permits others are also made to involve, achieving the task in stipulated time. Team building is a way of life and it should be made enjoyable.

Critical Feedback

The critical feedback and due training if necessary should be provided. The critical feedback should be regarded important to the improvement and not to provoke the members.

Sharing of Data

All relevant data should be shared for achieving the task and no data should be shared as per the choice of the team leader alone.

CONCLUSION

It is concluded that a team of library professionals with complementary skills ought to remain committed to a common purpose, performance goals, and approach for which they hold themselves mutually accountable.

REFERNCES

* http://www.learningcenter.net/library/building.shtml
* http://www.nsba.org/sbot/toolkit/LeadTeams.html
* http://www.learningcenter.net
* http://wumanresources.about.com/od/involvemntteams/a/twelve_ip_team.html
* http://mail.asis.org/pipermail/asis-1/2002-September/00295.html
* http://library.priceton.edu/hr/training/ExcellenceTeambuilding TechniquesHandout.doc

Technical Session – III
Applications of ICT in LIS

C-01
RFID In Libraries

R. Nagarathinam
*Assistant. Librarian, Cherraan's Institute of
Health Science, Coimbatore.*

J. Santhi
*Librarian, Cherraan's Institute of
Health Science, Coimbatore.*

ABSTRACT

*Advances in the technology have changed virtually
every aspect of our lives. New Technologies have
always been of interest for libraries, both for the
potential of increasing the quality of services and for
improving the efficiency of operations. At the present
time, when libraries of all kinds (public, research,
special) are facing economic hardships the
overwhelming reason for considering new
technologies is the potential for cost savings in the
operations and the management of material flows.
RFID (Radio Frequency Identification) is the latest
technology to be used in library theft detection
systems. Unlike EM (Electro-Mechanical) and RF
(Radio Frequency) systems, which have been used in
libraries for decades, RFID-based systems move
beyond security to become tracking systems that
combine security with more efficient tracking of
materials throughout the library including easier and
faster charge and discharge, inventorying, and
materials handling Libraries began using RFID*

systems to replace their electromagnetic and bar code systems. RFID is an inevitable technology in libraries, both for financial and humane reasons. This paper addresses many of the specific issues and privacy concerns associated with RFID technology in libraries and suggest best RFID implementation practices for librarians.

INTRODUCTION

RFID in libraries is a hot topic. Radio Frequency Identification is a means of capturing data about an object without using a human to read the data. Radio Frequency Identification (RFID) is the technology that is stated to replace barcodes in library applications. It is a form of identification that is contact-less and does not require line of sight.. The RFID tags are placed in books and generally covered with a property sticker. Antennas of different sizes, based on application, are used to read the tags and manage the various library functions[1]. The RFID solution is a revolutionary application of automatic identification and data capture (AIDC) technology.

HISTORY OF DEVELOPMENT

The Decades Of RFID

Decade	Event
1940 - 1950	Radar refined and used, major World War II development effort. RFID invented in 1948.
1950 - 1960	Early explorations of RFID technology, laboratory experiments.
1960 - 1970	Development of the theory of RFID. Start of applications - field trials.
1970 - 1980	Explosion of RFID development. Tests of RFID accelerate. Very early adoption and implementations of RFID.
1980 - 1990	Commercial applications of RFID enter mainstream.
1990 - 2000	Emergence of standards. RFID widely deployed. RFID becomes a part of everyday life.

What is RFID?

Radio frequency identification, is a generic term for technologies that use radio waves to automatically identify people or objects. RFID tags/transponders that can be attached to or incorporated into a product and the antenna enables the chip to transmit the identification information to a reader. The reader converts the radio waves reflected back from the RFID tag into digital information that can be passed on to computers that can make use of it.

COMPONENTS OF AN RFID SYSTEM

A comprehensive RFID system has four components:

1. RFID tags that are electronically programmed with unique information
2. Readers or sensors to query the tags
3. Antenna
4. Server on which the software that interfaces with the integrated library software is loaded.

RFID TAGS

The heart of the system is the RFID tag, which can be fixed inside a book's back cover or directly onto CDs and videos. Each RFID tag contains a tiny chip, which is both readable and writable and can store information to identify items in your collection.[2]. This tag is equipped with a programmable chip and an antenna with a capacity of at least 64 bits. RFID tags come in three general varieties:

* Passive
* Active
* Semi passive

Passive : Passive tags require no internal power source Passive RFID tags have no internal power supply. The minute electrical current induced in the antenna by the incoming radio frequency signal provides just enough power for the

CMOS integrated circuit in the tag to power up and transmit a response. Passive tags have practical read distances ranging from about 10 cm (4 in.)up to a few meters (*Electronic Product Code* (EPC) and depending on the chosen radio frequency and antenna design/size.

Active : active tags require a power source, usually a small battery Unlike passive RFID tags, active RFID tags have their own internal power source, which is used to power the *integrated circuits* and broadcast the signal to the reader. Active tags typically have much longer range (approximately 500 m/1500 feet) and larger memories than passive tags, as well as the ability to store additional information sent by the transceiver.

Semi-passive : Semi-passive tags are similar to active tags as they have their own power source, but the battery is used just to power the microchip and not broadcast a signal. The RF energy is reflected back to the reader like a passive tag.

ANTENNA

A connection between RFID tags and the coupler. RFID antennas emit radio waves that activate RFID tags and read and write data to it as they pass through the activation field. After a tag is activated, it can send information to or receive information from the coupler. Antennas are the channels between the tag and the reader, which controls the system's data acquisition and communication. Antennas can be built into a doorframe to receive tag data from person's things passing through the door.

PC / SERVER

The server is the heart of any comprehensive RFID systems[4]. It is the communication gateway among the various components .It receives the information from one or more of the readers and exchanges information with the circulation database. The server typically includes a transaction database so that reports can be produced

COUPLER

The link between RFID tags and the PC. The coupler can send information in two directions: It can read information from a tag and send it to the PC (read mode) or it can read information from the PC and send it to an RFID tag (write mode).

READERS

The reader is a handheld or fixed unit that can interrogate nearby RFID tags and obtain their ID numbers using radio frequency (RF) communication (i.e. the process does not require contact). When a passive tag is within range of a reader, the tag's antenna absorbs the energy being emitted from the reader, directs the energy to 'fire up' the integrated circuit on the tag, which then uses the energy to beam back the ID number and any other associated information.

There are two main classes of RFID readers:

* read-only,
* read/write,

Readers in RFID library are used in the following ways

- Conversion station: where library data is written to the tag
- Staff workstation at circulation: used to charge and discharge library materials
- Self check-out station: used to check out library materials without staff assistance
- Self check-in station: used to check in library materials without staff assistance
- Exit sensors: to verify that all material leaving the library has been checked out

- Book-drop reader: used to automatically discharge library materials and reactivate security
- Sorter and conveyor: automated system for returning material to proper area of library
- Hand-held reader: used for inventorying and verifying that material is shelved correctly.
- Search for books, which are miss shelved
- Search for individual book requested.

HOW DOES RFID WORK IN A LIBRARY?

In the library context, RFID works by placing a one-inch passive tag, without power supply, in each library item (book, CD, DVD, etc.). Each tag contains only barcode information for that item. When library patrons place items to be checked out on or near a receiver pad and insert their library card, the items are checked out to them. This occurs when the minute electrical current induced in the antenna by the incoming radio frequency scan (from the transmitter/receiver) provides enough power for the tag to send a response to the receiver. Items can also be checked back in easily, saving time and energy, and simplifying up-to-date inventory tasks[3].

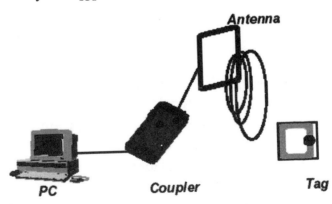

STEPS INVOLVED IN RFID TECHNOLOGY ARE

1. Tag enters RF field created by the antenna.
2. Antenna's RF signal activates the tag.
3. Coupler sends a modulated signal.
4. Tag demodulates the signal and returns its data to the reader.
5. Coupler sends data to the computer.
6. Computer transmits new data through the coupler to the tag.

COST OF IMPLEMENTATION

The cost of an RFID implementation is not low. The tags still cost around rupees forty each depending on the capabilities required. Readers are key tools and cost over a rupees forty thousand each. The redesign of circulation areas adds significant costs to the system. The labeling and encoding of each item in the library's collection is also a time-consuming and costly one-time step.

RFID – THE FREQUENCIES

RFID operates in several frequency bands. The generic frequencies for RFID are:

- 125 - 134 kHz
- 13.56 MHz
- UHF (400 – 930 MHz)
- 2.45 GHz
- 5.8 GHz

Although there are other frequencies used, these are the main ones.

ADVANTAGES OF RFID

1. Self-charging/Discharging
2. Reliability

3. High-Speed Inventorying
4. Automated Materials Handling
5. Tag Life

DISADVANTAGES OF RFID SYSTEMS

1. High cost.
2. Accessibility to compromise.
3. Removal of exposed tags.
4. Exit gate sensor (Reader) problems.
5. User Privacy Concerns.
6. Reader collision.
7. Tag collision.
8. Lack of Standard.

CONCLUSION

It is quite clear from the above analysis that an RFID system may be a comprehensive system that addresses both the security and materials tracking needs of a library. The technology saves money too and quickly gives a return on investment. RFID technology promises to change our world. It has the capability of making our personal lives and our experience in the library more convenient. The reliability of the system, its ease of operation and the flexibility of tagging all kinds of media easily are important criteria in choosing an RFID system. The main aim for today's libraries in adopting RFID is the need to increase efficiency and reduce cost. RFID technology uses waves to automatically identify individual items. In the long run, the RFID technology, when perfected, would eventually be a big help to human beings.

REFERENCES

* **Boss, RW.** "RFID technology for libraries [Monograph]", *Library Technology Reports*, November-December 2003.
* **Flagg, G.** "Should libraries play tag with RFID?", *American*

Libraries, 34(11),December, 2004. pp *69-71*

* R. Moroz Ltd. (2004, July). Understanding Radio Frequency Identification (RFID) (Passive RFID). Markham, Ontario: R. Moroz Ltd. Retrieved August 4, 2004

* **Ward, D.M.** "RFID Systems". *Computers in Libraries,* March, 2004, pp.*19-24.*

C-02

Usage of Information and Communiction Technology (ICT), Information Seeking and Use Pattern of the Industrial Information System with Reference to Small Scale Industries

Dr. J. Abraham

Deputy Librarian, Gandhigram Rural University,
Gandhigram – 624 302, Dindigul Dist., Tamilnadu.

Dr. B. Ramesh Babu

Professor, Department of Information Science,
University of Madras, Chennai – 600 005

ABSTRACT

The New Economic Policy has opened altogether a

different industrial scenario. Industry being a very dynamic and complex system has to be managed on scientific lines for development in the face of competition, tremendous technological changes and innovations that are taking place. Management of industry entails planning, directing, controlling, decision making, motivating and forecasting, all of which require harnessing and utilization of information. In the present industrial environment, the application of right information at right time and at right place is one of the major needs of all the industries. As the small scale entrepreneurs need a variety of information covering an exhaustive range, proper information and guidance are required for all sorts of work and for development and diversification. Such information has to be obtained from a large number of sources. The paper describes information needs, information seeking and usage of Information and Communication Technology (ICT) for information retrieval and support system for the entrepreneurs of Small Scale Industries and also discusses the information needs, information seeking and the problem of access to the rapidly expanding volume of information and the Infomediary Services of National Small Industries Corporation, New Delhi – to strengthen Small and Medium Enterprises (SME) and to face the challenges of the new economic policy initiatives in view of globalization, liberalization and investment of foreign capital in the industrial activities in India.

INTRODUCTION

Information is one of the basic vital resources that are needed and utilized for the nation's well being. The use of information, whether in the form of empirical data or in the developed form called knowledge, has become essential phenomena for the growth and development. The world has now moved from the industrial revolution into information revolution. The need for information in every sphere of intellectual activity has increased day-by-day. Information is an aggregation or processing of data to provide knowledge and intelligence. The progress of the modern society depends a great deal upon the provision of the right kind of information in the right form at the right time. As the information whether it may be abstract or concrete is valuable, it must be put to proper use. Information is the recorded or communicated knowledge gained by the man through experience, observation and experiments. It has been growing in ever increasing volume and rate. It is therefore necessary that the information generated at any point be procured, organized and disseminated expeditiously to its users for its optimum use. There is no field of human activity wherein the information is not required – whether it is research and development, business and industry, government affaires, education and training. Hence the information has to be acquired, processed, stored, retrieved and disseminated for communication. The Library and Information professionals are expected to function as an intermediary between information sources and information seekers in order to serve the information users / seekers efficiently and effectively.

INFORMATION SOURCES AND USE PATTERN

Traditionally speaking, information sources would not only include primarily books, periodicals and newspapers but also the information resources consisting of documents such as the audio and video materials and the units of information or data that can be processed and organized by a computer. The number and forms of information sources are continuously increasing. As the knowledge grows and the number of the records increases, our dependence upon them also increases proportionally and the need to gain access to them becomes more essential and even crucial. Further the information is required by the user without pre-condition about the form of document. The information or knowledge resources, if unsupported and uncoordinated in growth and usage, would certainly be in danger of being wasted and inefficiently utilized.

INFORMATION

Information can be broadly defined as "knowledge concerning some particular fact, subject or event in any communicable form". Information is fundamental to communication process both intra-personal and interpersonal communication for the development, growth and prosperity. Effective and continuous use of information has been the causative factor in the history and development of science, culture and civilization in the universe.

INFORMATION MARKETING AND INFORMATION USE

The world today saw a dramatic increase in the amount of information that is freely available resulting in the characterization of the situation as an information explosion. The Library collects, stores, preserves and disseminates information. As such the Library can be called as an information market and the library user, a consumer of information.

It was Dr.S.R. Ranganathan who first publicized the term 'use' in his book 'Five Laws of Library Science' as early in 1931. Though the term suffered initially for acceptance, it achieved wider recognition gradually by the scholars and working librarians and based on the concept 'use', the term "user" came to be accepted as an equivalent to "reader/ clientele".

Till World War II was over, librarians concentrated more on documents/information resources rather than on users. In the course of time, identification of user needs became pivotal for any decision making in libraries and the user studies became popular during 1970's. The traditional document retrieval tools pave a way to the development of mechanized information retrieval system in the Library and Information Centres in order to make the library and information services and activities more efficient and effective.

NEED FOR INFORMATION

Modern Society produces and uses information. All technical activity must be based on specially acquired information and gives rise to the fund of knowledge and the recorded knowledge grows apace. The information needs of a user depend on such factors like his work activity, discipline and availability of facilities. They also depend on his hierarchical position in the organization where he works.

The user needs a great variety of information to solve the problem or to take appropriate action in the day to day activity. No matter how well versed he is in his field, information that is new to him is continually being recorded and he needs selective service to keep him aware of current developments. When he is faced with a specific problem, as his fund of knowledge may not be adequate, he wishes to find data, a technique, a process, a method, a theory, to aid his solution.

INFORMATION NEEDS

Information needs of a user vary according to the category he belongs to and the assignment on which he is working. It is well known that users make use of different communication media in accessing their information. The information system has the task of organizing the mass of documentary information/knowledge available for everyone to use - wherever it may be recorded and located and/or whenever it is needed. Nevertheless it is becoming difficult to provide accessibility and maintain the availability in the mass of information and is getting too large to handle by traditional means.

INFORMATION COMMUNICATION AND INFORMATION RETRIEVAL SYSTEM

Information is for use. Information is an essential resource for all economic and social change. It is capable of converting natural resources into artifacts and consumable products. There is a general acceptance of significant and important aspect of information that there should be free flow of information and exchange of scientific and technical information with out any barriers. Library is a communication centre consisting of published materials either print or non-print media. Modern communication, according to Shalini and Khan, "includes the twin activities of information transfer and information use; publishing of research results in the form of an article/paper is an act of information transfer. On the other hand the sources of information consulted/ used while writing a paper are demonstrating an act of information use".

It is well known that users make use of different communication media in accessing the information. Information diffuses through society in many ways and at many stages oral communication is the most important channel. Bringing people with similar interest together - whether permanently in an organization or association or temporarily at a meeting or conference, by personal visit, by letter / correspondence and by telephone - is a potent way of organizing the flow of information.

Even though a particular user may acquire information by oral personal communication, in most cases there is some where a documentary record of information communicated. If it is so, it is likely that the user can obtain his knowledge, at first or second hand, from source document. The librarians

/ Information professionals try to collect, digitize and collate existing information, hoping to ease the task of the user. The information retrieval tools serve the user to identify documents and to cope up with the growth of literature. The information retrieval system is a device interposed between a potential user of information and information itself to capture the wanted items and to filter out the unwanted items for a given information problem.

INFORMATION AND COMMUNICATION TECHNOLOGY (ICT) IN INFORMATION ACCESS AND RETRIEVAL

All the human activities result in the creation of information. Information generation, dissemination, transfer and communication take place between people through diverse channels and media in variety of contexts and environments. The effective performance in all the spheres of activity depends largely upon the availability of right information at the right time in adequate quality and quantity. Information handling activities are to be based entirely on the needs of the users. The user needs for information vary distinctly among the categories of users depending upon their functions, responsibilities and duties. So it is absolutely necessary for an information system to respond to the user needs and to acquire information to meet the requirements of users' interest. The matching of information needs to the sources of information has to be based on the careful assessment of information needs of users. Hence the assessment of information needs forms the primary basis for all information activities and for effective provision of information service, meeting their needs. In order to serve the users efficiently and effectively, the Library and Information professionals are expected to function as an intermediary between the information sources and information system and services or as a Information Provider wherein the finding of information matters but not the sources of information.

The Scientists and Technologists feel a pressing need to keep up-to-date, to know not only what appeared in print, but also what has not yet appeared in print, at the moment. The growing demand for systematic access to the recorded knowledge must be satisfied by providing rapidly, conveniently, economically and with precision that portion of the current or retrospective literature. The information needs and urgency in acquiring the needed information has made the Libraries and Information Centres to change rapidly. The Library and Information Centres use the Information and Communication Technologies(ICTs).

INFORMATION SEEKING BEHAVIOUR (ISB)

Information Seeking Behaviour is often construed based upon on the use of information by users. The "Information Seeking Behaviour" concept stands interlinked to denote the process occurring in the individual who seeks information in a variety of circumstances and from a variety of sources. As there is no definite pattern or methods for information seeking or for search of information, the procedure for finding information will vary from person to person depending upon various factors. However the success of finding information would greatly depend upon the kind of experience that matters.

Information seeking is a behaviour, a human activity such as writing a memo, driving a car or talking on the phone. Since it is a behaviour it is logical to propose that it stems from sources common to all behaviours. In a library/ information system, where the users with the specific information needs, undertake the document search / information search, they are exposed to a number of problems in searching for information.

As such, Information Seeking Behaviour comprises of

the following aspects namely,

1. Motivating factors for use or not-use of information.
2. Psychological attitudes affecting the preference to source materials even though a set of information may be available in various sources.
3. Access to sources
4. Evaluation of information
5. Selecting and putting the specific set of information to the use.

TYPES OF INFORMATION SEEKING BEHAVIOUR (ISB)

The ISB falls into two types, namely

1. Compulsory Information Seeking
2. Non-Compulsory or discretionary Information Seeking.

Compelling situations persuade to seek information necessarily, lest in many cases a person risks a penalty for not finding that which is known to be in a source; for e.g., a lawyer has to obtain legal information regarding his case within next hearing, failing to do so, he may not win the case. Information Seeking becomes a compulsory activity. In this case, a lawyer can not afford to miss or fail to locate the needed information.

In some cases, where searching for information may not be essential or whose source is not known with certainty, not locating the information may not lead to serious consequences. Hence a user can do away with the seeking of such information.

Whatever be the type of information seeking, the environmental factors play a vital role in motivating a user either to seek or not to seek information. A motivated person goes to seek his information from various sources including those in a library.

SMALL SCALE INDUSTRIES (SSI)

The Small Scale Industrial (SSI) Sector is a vital, dynamic and vibrant sector of the Indian Industrial Economy. The sector acts as a nursery for the development of entrepreneurial talent and has been contributing significantly to the National Gross Domestic Product, besides meeting the social objectives of providing employment opportunities to millions of people across the country. The SSI sector plays an important role for policy formulation on credit, marketing, technology, entrepreneurial development and infrastructure development. The growth and development of SSI depend very much on the diffusion of technological know-how, the availability of current information on raw materials, adoption of new technological ideas, market area, prices of the product etc. Identification of information needs and sources of information of Small Scale Industries at the rural areas have been increasingly felt in different sectors of industrial economy of India.

Small Scale Industries require comparatively a smaller investment and are generally within the means of entrepreneur with the support offered by various financial institutions / government agencies. The Small Scale Industries can lead to a decentralised mode of production and therefore remove the regional imbalances. Small Scale Industries create more avenues of employment and lead to an equitable distribution of wealth usually based on local resources. The Small Scale Industries Sector is one of the most important features of our planned economy that fulfills socio-economic objectives and the structural transformation of our economy by bringing about integration with the rural economy and the industries that produce essential commodities and consumption goods.

INDUSTIRAL INFORMATION SYSTEM FOR SSI SECTOR

Entrepreneurs of the Indian Small Scale Industries (SSIs) constitute an important and crucial segment of the industry sector in the country. A Small Scale Industrial unit is defined in terms of investment ceilings on the original value of the installed plant and machinery. An industrial undertaking in which the investment in fixed assets in plant and machinery, whether held on ownership terms or lease or on hire purchase basis does not exceed Rupees one crore (Rs. 10 million), will be deemed as small scale industrial unit.

Information plays a vital role in the success of any business. Information propels productivity, development and innovation. Small Scale Industry, being a very dynamic and complex system, has to be managed on scientific lines for development in the face of competition and tremendous technological changes and innovations that are taking place. Management of industry requires recognition of economic, psychological and sociological factors affecting it. It entails planning, directing, controlling, decision-making, motivating and forecasting, using variety of statistical techniques. All these require harnessing and utilisation of information. Industrial enterprise requires various types of information for the establishment of a new unit, production of new item, import of certain materials, export of some products and so on. Identification of information needs and the sources of information are important for the development of such industries at the rural areas. The Small Scale Industry (SSI) sector in India is vast and diverse covering different type of industries. Hence the type of information required varies and includes socio economic data and statistics, information on current plans and projects, financial data, information on technologies, equipment, management practices, technological research, technology tie-ups, reports, studies, policies etc. Such information has to be obtained from a large number of sources within the country and even at the global level. In this information age, the rapidly expanding volume of information presents problem of access to right information at right time and at the right place to the entrepreneurs of SSI sector in India where there is a constraint of resources and manpower. Hence the distributed Industrial Information System particularly in different sectors of Small and Medium Enterprises has been increasingly felt.

INFORMATION SUPPORT/DELIVERY SYSTEM FOR SSIs

In the present environment the identification of information needs and requirements of Small Scale Entrepreneurs and the access to the right source of information are important for the design and development of Industrial Information System especially in the Small and Medium Enterprise (SME) sector. In the present era of borderless and market-oriented economy with the increase in competition and due to the process of globalization and other connected developments the demand for information is reaching new heights. The government has established Small Industries Development Organisation, National Small Industries Corporation, Small Industries Service Institutes and a network of subunits in many major cities and towns in order to provide timely, accurate and pertinent information in the organized manner and make it available at reasonable price. Apart from these, the other organizations which cater to various information needs of the small and medium industries at different stages include the State Small Industries Development Corporation, State Financial/ Industrial Investment Corporation, District Industrial Centres etc.

INFOMEDIARY SERVICES OF NSIC

Information plays a vital role in the success of any

business. Recognizing the importance of information and its relevance to SSI units, NSIC provides Infomediary Services to small units. Besides hosting a web site (www.nsicindia.com), NSIC hosts sector specific portals for focused information dissemination. Under this scheme, small units can become members and avail a number of value added services. Some important services are:

- Supplier database
- Market intelligence
- Technology providers
- Information providers
- Linkages with relevant institutions
- B2B services
- Value additions like directories, bulletin boards, discussion forums, virtual exhibitions, etc

Infomediary services provide information on business, technology and finance to develop the core competence of Indian SMEs in terms of price and quality – internationally as well as domestically. Infomediary services disseminate vital information through websites, sector-specific newsletters (both print and electronic) and e-mails. Salient features of Infomediary services of NSIC are as follows:

- Sector based information focus, Internet-related support and access to wide range of technologies from India and abroad
- Access to national and international business, joint venture opportunities and trade information
- Comprehensive information on Government policies, rules and regulations, schemes and incentives
- Access to industrial databases and directories
- Access to wide range of assistance for participation in business delegations, exhibitions/fairs

- Availability of a wide range of escort services such as product design, credit and support rating, developing catalogues and product literature, energy and environment audit, introduction of Information Technology solution in business operations
- Skill up gradation, training, mentoring services and market surveys

DECENTRALISED DISTRIBUTED SECTORAL INFORMATION SYSTEM FOR SSIS

The industrial establishments of all sizes are in need of information support and delivery system, but the need is greater in the case of small scale industry. It is not only because of the special handicaps arising out of smallness of the enterprises, but also neither they have the capacity to own the information unit nor the infrastructure to access the required information. Hence in the present global economy scenario it is necessary to strengthen the Small and Medium Enterprises (SME) sector suitably so that it could adopt itself to the changed environment and face the challenges effectively. In view of the various and heterogeneous industries spread over the vast area, it may not be possible to provide effective information service with speed and efficiency with a Centralised Industrial Information System. Therefore a few centres at different regions with specialization to serve different trade and industries like chemical engineering, mechanical engineering and machine tools, textile & other fiber industries, electronics & electrical industries, and leather and allied industries etc. should be organized.

CONCLUSION

The information system essentially concerns with the documents and other media of information sources, the problem of storage, retrieval and access to, and the use of information in the most effective and efficient manner. For this purpose the information needs, resources and the information access and use must be user – oriented and the Information System must assist the users in the best use of information collection, and the availability of relevant information. Providing Access to right information is a difficult task due to the very fact that information is abundant and scattered far and wide in various forms and format. The problem that often comes in the way of their effective use of information is that the user does not know whether it is available and if it does where to locate it.

As the information is recorded in innumerable separately published documents, emerging from hundreds of thousands of sources all over the world, the prospective user needs the tools to guide him through the flood of documents with the information he needs. Therefore it is necessary to assess the information needs of various small and medium industries so that a well designed Industrial Information System can be thought of. In the development of the nation, Small and Medium Scale Industries occupy an important place. The people should be encouraged to come forward to invest in starting new industrial units. All sorts of assistance need to be extended and the procedures be simplified. The industrial cluster areas should be well connected with other parts of the country by road, rail, sea and air transports enabling the producers to market their products quickly. The small-scale entrepreneurs need a variety of information covering an exhaustive range, proper information and guidance for development and diversification of SSIs.

REFERENCES

* **Prasher, RG.** *Developing Library Collection.* New Delhi: Medallion Press, 1993.

* **Surendra Singh and Sonal Singh.** *Trends in Library and*

Information Science (Essays in Honour of Professor G.D. Bhargava). New Delhi: Gyan Publishing House, 2000.

* **Dhawan, KS.** *Readings in Library Science : Principles of Information Retrieval.* Vol 4. New Delhi : Commonwealth Publishers, 2001,

* **Veketesh, S.** *ICTs and economic development.* New Delhi : Authors, 2001.

* **Sinha, Arun Kumar.** "Information handling in Industries". **Sharma (C.D) and Kailash Vyas, Eds.** *Developing Horizons in Library and Information Science: Ranganathan's Tenth Death Anniversary Commemoration Volumes.* Vol. 2. Jaipur: Printwell Publishers, 1983, pp.245 - 253.

C-03
Impact of Library Automation in the Present Scenario

P. Pounraj

*Librarian, Victory Teacher Training Institute and
College of Education, Kambiliyampatty (PO),
Dindigul Dt – 624 306*

P. Ganesan

*Assistant Librarian, Central Library,
Alagappa University, Karaikudi-3.*

INTRODUCTION

Prior to 1970's, library automated systems were dedicated to a single function designed for a single purpose operation. The circulation function was the first library operation to be automated due to its repetitive, routine and time consuming, multifaceted tasks. In the late 1970's and early 1980's, vendors of automated systems introduced the Online Public Access Catalogue (OPAC) function to existing circulation systems. By the late 1980s, integrated automation systems, those that combine circulation, OPACs and cataloguing, had become widely accepted in large libraries. These systems operated on mainframe and miniframe computers. The high cost of these computers and the automation software were beyond the reach of many college libraries.

The proliferation of microcomputers in the early 1980s provided an incentive to automate the small collection libraries like school and college libraries. Computer Cat, an Apple II microcomputer based online catalogue, was the first automated system to be introduced in small sized libraries.

In 1985, school libraries had implemented stand-alone circulation and cataloguing systems. In the next few years, microcomputer processing and storage capacity increased while the price of hardware plummeted. This provided a unique opportunity for automation vendors to develop automation software to operate on microcomputers.

Integrated microcomputer-based automated systems that support single and multi user configurations and that combine multiple functions were introduced before the end of the decade.

The introduction of Online Public Access Catalogue (OPACs) into libraries has had a marked impact on the way users access and retrieve information. This powerful function tool has allowed the information professional to provide more effective and efficient information services.

The microcomputer-based systems have been widely accepted in small size libraries. The popularity of these systems is on the decline due to the cost of the hardware and software, the integration of a seamless "web" of information resources and services, the continues augmentation of software search features and capabilities, the increased migration to windows ™ and WWW interfaces, software capability with the PC and Macintosh platform and the use of powerful operating systems.

REASONS FOR AUTOMATION OF THE LIBRARIES

The major factors which forced to automate the library functions are explained in the ongoing paragraphs.

OVERGROWTH OF INFORMATION / INFORMATION EXPLOSION

Last few decades have witnessed a chaotic situation in the information field; it is the result of so called information explosion. The amount of information being published increases exponentially. The growth rate of information is quite high in the field of science, technology and medicine, as compared to other fields.

LACK OF SPACE

One of the problems faced by all the libraries is that of shortage of space. The computer application would reduce the pressure on this front. Most of the documents are now available in CD-ROM. The CD-ROM occupies only a fraction of the space occupied by its hard copy. This results in the saving of public catalogue and its availability at different locations as well as on LAN, WAN and on the Net will also results into considerable saving of space.

TO SAVE THE TIME OF THE READER

If the information is made available in computer readable form and particularly if it is made available on LAN, WAN and on the Net, information can be retrieved by any number of users from any place at any time. Thus it saves the time of the reader.

EXPLOSION OF ELECTRONIC DOCUMENTS

Due to growth of information technology, the quality of information produced in electronic form has been increased. In recent years, the Internet revolutionized the information field. Many of the journals are available only in electronic form. It has necessitated the use of computers for information handling. Due to the development in the telecommunication system, we are now able to access any information/database/bibliographic records from any part of the world.

COST EFFECTIVENESS

Automation of library results in saving of money in long range: saving in the sense, it reduces the cost of library operations and recurring expenditures.

DATA MANIPULATION

The information entered for one function can be used for other functions like citation analysis, alphabetical, or subject wise order etc. the same data can be used any number of times with same speed and accuracy.

EXPLOITATION OF COMPUTER READABLE DATABASES

The application of information technology can exploit for better advantage the computer based database services and internet resources.

MODULES AND THEIR FUNCTIONS

The basic modules of automated system are Cataloguing, Circulation, Acquisition, Serial Control and Online Public Access Catalogue.

ONLINE PUBLIC ACCESS CATALOGUE (OPAC)

OPAC is what users consult to find and retrieve information of interest. Generally, the OPAC is equivalent to the card catalogue, but it provides advanced search features. The OPAC function allows searching by author, title, subject or keyword; search using Boolean operators (AND, OR, NOT) hyperlink searching, wild character searching and combined search strategy options. The OPAC module is the only one that is inseparable from cataloguing. A library cannot have the OPAC without the cataloguing module, because cataloguing module is the heart of the automated systems.

CATALOGUING MODULE

The module performs various cataloguing tasks, such as original cataloguing using the Machine Readable Cataloguing (MARC) Protocol, editing, copying, saving, and retrieving catalogues records. When a record is saved in the cataloguing database, the record automatically appears in the OPAC, and a brief copy of the record is also generated automatically for the circulation module.

CIRCULATION MODULE

The circulation module performs the task, involved in the circulation function, such as material check-in, check-out, inventory, overdue notices, holds and reserves, fines, and statistical reports.

ACQUISITION MODULE

The acquisition module enables library staff to handle the following major functions related to acquisition of library material.

- Suggestions management.
- Ordering, cancellation and reminders.
- Receiving.
- Payment including fund control.
- Master file management such as currency, budget, vendors, publishers etc.

Through this module library staff can search the entire database of library holdings for the purpose of duplicate checking etc. Using various combinations, number of reports could be generated.

SERIAL CONTROL

The complex job of keeping track of serials can easily and effectively be handled using SOUL through its Serial Control module. This module broadly handles following functions.

- Suggestions.
- Subscription (renewal and new subscription).
- Payment including fund control etc.
- Check in of issues including prediction of issues arrival.
- Reminder generation.
- Binding management.
- Search status of every item.
- Master database management.
- Reports generation etc.

INTEGRATED LIBRARY SYSTEM

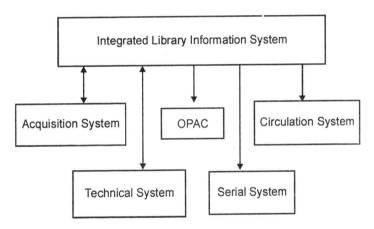

Fig. 1. Integrated Library Information System

IMPORTANCE OF LIBRARY AUTOMATION

Automation saves the effort, time and resources involved in the manual operation of libraries. In the automated system the information can be altered and updated without the repetition involved in the manual system. Other reasons for library automation are:

- To achieve a new level of library management

- To improve the existing services and to introduce new services
- To avoid the duplication of the work
- To use the services of the existing staff effectively
- To facilitate the sharing of the resources

CONCLUSION

Though the Library Automation concept is old one, still in India, most of the Universities and Colleges have not yet started the automation process and still Library staff has not acquired the adequate skill for automating the libraries. The major reason for not automating the college libraries may be due to the reluctance of the management. These constraints may prevail in almost all the institutions. It will be library professionals' job to convince the management authority by explaining all the features of library automation.

REFERENCES

* **Bass, RW.** *Library Manager's Guide to Automation.* 2nd ed. New York: Knowledge Industry, 1984.

* **Kumar, PSG.** *Computerisation of Indian Libraries*, New Delhi: B.R. Publishing, 1987.

* **Mahapatra, PK and Chakrabarti, C.** *Redesigning the Library*, New Delhi:Ess Ess Publications, 1996.

* **Singh, S.** "Selection of Library Software for Library Automation: A critical study and evaluation", *Lucknow Librarian.* 29 (1-4) 1997, pp.33-35.

* **Vashishth, C.P. (ed.).** *Computerization of Library Networks*, New Delhi: ILA, 1991.

C-04
Digital Library:
An Overview

M. Ravichandran
Librarian, Mohamed Sathak Engineering
College, Kilakarai – 623 806

ABSTRACT

The Internet and the World Wide Web (WWW) have enabled seamless access to these sources from any corner of the globe. In a networked environment, the challenges and opportunities for the information professionals are manifold. Internet needs to be exploited as an information source. Information sources residing on the Internet need to be taken into account in the collection development strategy and in rendering information services. Digital Libraries are expected to bring about a significant improvement over current models of information publishing and access methods. Educators, researchers and students will be among the first to benefit from Digital Libraries. Digital Libraries Motivation is anytime, anywhere access to large document collections. Building digital libraries begins with creating digital content and collections. Digital content may be created in the following two ways Born digital and Digitisation.

INTRODUCTION

Digital Library is an organized collection of digitized material deployed over intranets and internet via web. A digital library is an organized and focused collection of digital objects, including text, images, video and audio, along with methods for access and retrieval and for selection, creation, organization, and maintenance of the collection. Digital Libraries provide an infrastructure for publishing and managing content so it is discovered easily and effectively. Internet provides a variety of Digital Information Resources. Librarian can make use of the Internet to provide various services to their users. WEB is now being used as a preferable media to disseminate Library and Information services. Goals of DL are improved access, preservation, application environment in library: school, college, university, public, R&D, corporate, etc. KM, publishing, preservation, E-Governance, etc.

WHAT IS DIGITAL LIBRARY?

"Digital libraries are organizations that provide the resources, including the specialized staff, to select, structure, offer intellectual access to, interpret, distribute, preserve the integrity of and ensure the existence over time of collections of digital works so that they are readily and economically available for use by a defined community or set of communities."

- Full text (e.g. books, journals)
- Images (e.g. photographs, scanned pages)
- Graphics (e.g. charts, drawings)
- Animations (e.g. cartoons)
- Audio (e.g. music)
- Video (e.g. movies, lectures)
- Digital Library contains materials in digital form
- Conventional materials cannot be given in the DL

- Digitization brings together materials available in various formats and in various locations
- Digital resources are widely scattered

WHY DIGITAL LIBRARY?

The Growing impact of Information and Communication technologies, Web technologies, and Database technologies has compelled Library and Information Centres to use these technologies effectively to provide information services.

- Go beyond library catalogue, bibliographic, surrogate
- Deal with content
- Full text documents with associated images, audio and video (e-documents)
- New forms of access
- Improved information
- Improved access sharing
- Wider access
- Improved preservation.

DIGITAL LIBRARY FEATURES

A digital library is expected to support the following features,

- Provide access to very large information collection(s)
- Focus on providing access to primary (or complete) information, not merely surrogates or indexes
- Support multi-media content
- Network accessibility
- Provide user friendly interface
- Unique referencing of digital objects
- Enable 'link' representation to local/external objects (hypertext)

- Support advanced search and retrieval
- Integrate personal, group, enterprise, public digital libraries
- Open communication protocols (client-server, e.g., Z39.50 for IR)
- Information access tools (browse, display and search tools)
- Meta databases (databases that describe and provide links to other databases/information sources)
- Electronic publishing tools (personal, institutional, publisher)
- Data compression
- Digital storage
- Scanning and conversion technologies
- Media integration technologies (multi-media)
- Advanced retrieval, indexing, natural language processing, routing and filtering
- Document description and representation standards (e.g. SGML)
- Inter-operability (how do multiple digital libraries interact?)
- Privacy, authentication and security
- Location independent naming of digital sources.

DIGITAL LIBRARY ADVANTAGES

Digital libraries are expected to provide several advantages, including,

- It can be stored digitally
- Resources can be used simultaneously by more than one user
- Provide timely access
- Save physical storage space

- Contains multimedia information
- Resource Sharing among Libraries
- Supports searching facilities
- Immediate access to highly demanded and frequently used items
- Easy access to individual components with in the items (Articles with in journals)
- Rapid access to remote materials

DIGITAL LIBRARY DISADVANTAGES

- Initial H/W and S/W cost
- Scanning the original documents of entire collections
- Required special skills and training to set up and maintain Digital Library
- Librarians are vary of new technologies
- IPR issues
- Users has to accept data

BUILDING DIGITAL LIBRARY

- Creating databases of library collections
- Providing links to many organizations
- Providing links to Reference Sources
- Providing links to important libraries
- Subscribing / procuring bibliographical databases available on CD
- Accessing bibliographical databases through Online / Web
- Subscribing / Accessing Contents Pages through e-mail / Web
- Subscribing Full Text e-journals
- Accessing Full Text e-journals

DIGITIZING RESOURCES PRODUCED / PUBLISHED INTERNALLY

- In-house R & D journals
- Articles published in National / International Journals
- Newsletter of the Institutions
- Annual Reports
- Technical Reports
- Regular course materials
- Thesis / Dissertation submitted by Staff / Students
- Video / Audio Clippings
- Information on Specific Subject Area
- Newspaper Clippings
- Publications / Services from Libraries
- Internally created files and databases

DIGITAL LIBRARY PROJECTS

- IEEE Computer Society Digital Library (*www.computer.org/publications/dlib/*)
- ACM Digital Library (*www.portal.acm.org*)
- The Berkaley Digital Library (*www.sunsite.berkeley.edu*)
- Networked Computer Science Technical Reference Library (NCSTRL) (*www.ncstrl.org*)
- Networked digital Library of Thesis and Dissertations (*www.thesis.org*)
- California Digital Library (*www.cdlib.org*)

DIGITAL LIBRARY PROJECTS IN INDIA

- Digital Library of Indian Institute of Management, Kozhikode
- Digital Library of Library and Information Science,

DRTC, Bangalore
- ETD at Indian Institute of Science, Bangalore
- Indira Gandhi National Centre for Arts (IGNCA) Digital Library
- Nalanda Digital Library, National Institute of Technology, Calicut Library.
- Vidyanidhi Digital Library and E-Scholarship Portal, Dept of Library and Information Science, Mysore University, Mysore,

DIGITAL LIBRARY S/WS

E - PRINTS

Primary goal of EPrints is to set up an open archive for research papers.

EPrints provide a web interface for managing, submitting, discovering and downloading documents, evolved from the practice of authors emailing pre-prints of their papers to peers for informal feedback, popularized through arXiv.org, started at Los Alamos in 1991 – granddaddy of Eprints servers.

EPrints is a free GNU General Purpose license (GPL) archive software developed at the E&C Dept. of the Univ. of Southampton

Available at: www.eprints.org

GREEN STORE

Comprehensive open-source software for constructing and distributing digital library collections Developed by the New Zealand Digital Library Project (www.nzdl.org) Distributed in co-operation with UNESCO and Humanities Library Project, Romania Available at: www.greenstone.org

Binaries: Linux, Windows

Source: available, under GNU GPL

SITE SEARCH

The OCLC SiteSearch software provides a comprehensive solution for managing distributed library information resources in a World Wide Web environment. www.sitesearch.oclc.org/

CDS WARE

CERN Document Server Software is the software developed by, maintained by and used at the CERN Document Server.

D SPACE

Dspace has been developed jointly by MIT Libraries and Hewlett-Packard (HP).

JAKE

Jointly Administered Knowledge Environment - jake.med.yale.edu Open source software for libraries - www.oss4lib.org (lists several softwares)

CONCLUSION

It is possible to initiate interesting and useful projects on institutional/campus local area networks by innovative use of Internet and WWW technologies, to provide network access to in-house collections, can be expanded for external connectivity and usage. But what is important is to plan and design systems in a way that they can be integrated easily later into the emerging national and international digital library architectures.

REFERENCES

* http://www.computer.org/publications/
* http://www.thesis.org
* http://www.library.yale.edu/
* http://www.portal.acm.org
* http://www.cdlib.org

* http://www.ifla.org
* http://www.ncstrl.org
* http://www.eprints.org
* http://www.infolibrarian.com
* http://www.sunsite.berkeley.edu
* http://www.nzdl.org
* http://www.dml.indiana.edu/
* http://www-diglib.stanford.edu/
* http://www.infoloom.com
* http//:www.cnri.reston.va.us/ home/dlib
* http://dspace.iimk.ac.in/
* http://www.drtc.isibang.ac.in/
* http://www.etd.ncsi.iisc.ernet.in/
* http://www.ildc.gov.in
* http://www.nalanda.nitc.ac.in
* http://www.vidyanidhi.org.in

C-05
Metadata in Libraries

N. Santhi
Librarian, N.S. College of Arts and Science,
P.B. No.55, Theni.

ABSTRACTS

Metadata is simply described as data about data which contains a set of information. In general, metadata is considered as the machine readable information for WEB resources. This paper deals with various types, needs, their applications and benefits of metadata in libraries. It also discusses the World Wide Web and the creation of metadata using different tools.

INTROUDUCTION: DEFINITIONS OF METADATA

Metadata refers to a set of information. It is the internet term or information that Libraries traditionally have put into catalogue and it mostly refers to descriptive information about web resources. World Wide Web Consortium (W3C) defines metadata as the machine understandable information for the web. Metadata is the structured data to describe resources systematically. A user might be a person or a program. Metadata allows finding, managing, controlling, understanding or preserving information over time.

NEED OF METADATA

Meta data is an eminent intermediary for the control and access to digitized sources Metadata creation, standards and practices have been evolved because of

- Lack of bibliographic control tools/aids for managing digital networked information resources
- Absence of elaborate rules for managing multiple forms of digital information including text, image, video, audio etc
- Demand for content analysis and organization of digital resources
- Failure of search mechanisms, for effective information retrieval
- Changes of information handling methodologies for information generation, distribution and access
- Information overload in terms of quality and quantity
- Problems with preservation of content and context of digitized sources

APPLICATIONS IN METADATA

With the changing trends in information handling, metadata has wide applications in digital collections. Metadata could well document both preservation and dissemination activities.

In objectives are to

- Organise and maintain the organization investment in data
- Provide information to data catalogues
- Provide information to aid data transfer
- Assist effective discovery and retrieval of information
- Control restricted access information and prevent unauthentic persons from accessing data

- Give information that affects the use of data, such as legal conditions on use, in size and age
- Give information about the owner or creator of the next

TYPES OF METADATA

Categorization of metadata based on certain parameters is more or less a difficult task. According to one viewpoint, metadata are of three types ;

i. **Descriptive metadata :** Identification and collection of information contained with in by the resource. It is ideally meant for resource discovery and identification. e.g. data contained within a bibliographic record

ii. **Structural metadata:** The information includes the structural divisions of a resource. e.g. chapter, sections, paragraphs

iii. **Administrative metadata :** A variety of data related to viewing, interpretation use and management of digital resources. It deals with the rights, permissions and ownership information. E.g. information such as who created, when or who can access.

BENEFITS OF METADATA IN LIBRARIES

Metadata applications in modern information management environment offer many inherent benefits for professionals and users.

i.   Search for effectiveness
ii. Preserving the context
iii. Version control
iv. Rights management

INFORMATION AVAILABILITY

Researchers in developing world are often experience difficulties to access journals and books from international publishers leading to unnecessary duplication of research in developing countries. The Open Access movement is gaining ground in which the proponents of this movement propose that though authors publish in popular journals, there is a possibility for authors and institutions for enhanced access and better visibility of their research output, with the availability of free software tools like e-print and D-space. Indian Institute of Science, Bangalore setting up an archive for Institute publications using the former and DRTC configuring a Digital Library of Library and Information Science using the latter. Open Archives Initiative Protocol for Metadata Harvesting (OAI-PMH) can play a crucial role in harvesting the metadata. Metadata harvesting services can definitely free scholarly information from the clutches of vested and commercial interests leading to better research output and more fruitful solutions.

WORLD WIDE WEB AND METADATA

Internet is a huge repository of information. Web search engines attempt to harvest and index a major share of information and provide low cost access to it. However the metadata creation is a labour intensive activity requiring knowledge of the principles and practices of Knowledge Management. Metadata could accomplish a different approach by ensuring specific control and access to networked and distributed digital sources.

METADATA CREATION

Metadata creation is basically an art of cataloguing digital resources, performed mainly by a human agent identified differently as Creators, Owners, Knowledge Managers, Information Scientists, Librarians and so on. The creation and maintenance of metadata in networked digital information systems are a complex mix of manual and automatic processes. Creation of Metadata in two methods are cataloguing method and matter of concern in metadata practices. Many formats enable the creator of the documents to supply the metadata with the object within the HTML headers. In many cases the responsibility is attributed to Creators. Other than this group, publishers, information professionals, librarians, would be the other communities to influence creation and the maintenance of metadata.

TRADITIONAL LIBRARIAN VS METADATA LIBRARIAN

Traditional librarian is identified as a person located in the library building, dealing with printed materials.

Metadata Librarian is identified as a person dealing with electronic resources.

CONCLUSION

The use of metadata for resources discovery in networked digital environment is being increasingly implemented all over the world. Since digital libraries and electronic resources are gaining more ground in the country, perhaps this is the right time for libraries and librarians to shed their inhibitions in adopting metadata tools and standards to carry forward cataloguing, classification and indexing to efficiently control and effectively track electronic information in the digital age.

REFERENCES

* **Upadhaya, JL.** *Information resources in modern libraries.* New Delhi : Shree Publications, 2004

* **Khanna, JK.** *Handbook of library administration.* New Delhi : Crest, 2001

* **Sharma, SK.** *Information technology and library services.* New Delhi : Shree Publications, 2007

C-06

Role of Push Technology in Information Management

M. Gangatharan

*Librarian, Sardar Vallabhbhai Patel Institute of
Textile Management, Coimbatore*

ABSTRACT

Push technology is nothing but "A set of technologies collectively referred to as PUSH". This means there is no need for us to find information. Information finds you after your registration. The main aim of this technology is "providing reliable and authentic information", from the sites or their own collection. Also it provides current awareness service and information about companies. The best example of push technology is television. If you switch on the TV, you can get more channels without your request. In the push technology also, you can get any information such as movies, current information, news and information about companies, etc. This paper deals with Role of Push Technology in Current Awareness Service and its usage in Information Management.

PUSH TECHNOLOGY: INTRODUCTION

In recent years the internet has become important in business education and government. The most publicized and fastest growing aspect of the internet is the World Wide Web. Typically the web user "pulls" information by requesting specific pages, where a "page" is a file formatted for display on a web browser such as Metscape Navigator. A new approach instead depends on an information provider "push" news, announcements and so on to the user without a specific request for each item, after the user has registered with the provider and indicated the types of information desired for future delivery.

WHAT IS PUSH TECHNOLOGY

Push technology is nothing but "A set of technologies collectively referred to as Push". Push technology may help by delivering or pushing information directly to your desktop. This means there is no need for the user to find information. Information finds you. The best example of push technology is television. You turn it on to view content that others send you. You can make broad choices such as the channel and whether you want to see news or movie but the content is got and sent by others. You make yourself available to watch and broadcasters push their selection of programs to you.

HOW DOES PUSH TECHNOLOGY WORK

Simply download and install the push vendor's software from a website such as www.pointcast .com and www. Marimba.com. There is a profile available. Users fill out a profile specifying what types of information they want. The profile acts as a filter and is stored on the push vendor's server (server based filter). Based on the users profile the vendor's server searches across a variety of websites or its own channel- a collection of web based content that it has rights to distribute. The filter then retrieves relevant information and sends it to the user's desktop.

WHO PUSHES

As a result of the growing market for push a wealth of push technology companies have emerged each offering a variation on the technology.

POINT CAST

Pointcast (www.Pointcast.com) was the first free news net work to deliver current event news and information directly to a viewer's computer screen via the internet. Pointcast partners with content providers such as USA.TODAY, CNN inorder to supply their users with a broad scope of current information.

MARIMBA

Marimba's castanet offering designed to be used in conjunction with a web browser automatically distributes and maintains software applications and content with in a company or across the internet.

INCOMMON

While not one of the big names, Incommon has developed a product called Downtown that delivers updated information to users from any www site.

The Backweb company offers a product that is generally similar to Pointcast, and also provides software for Intranets and "extranets". The product may be used to distribute software updated online.

Microsoft is a famous company, which has proposed a standard for push technology called Channel Definition Format (CDF), that has not been widely accepted. In short CDF defines a specific set of instructions to be included on web pages in order to turn them into "channels" for receipt and display by compatible client software. (that is a client software that understands CDF)

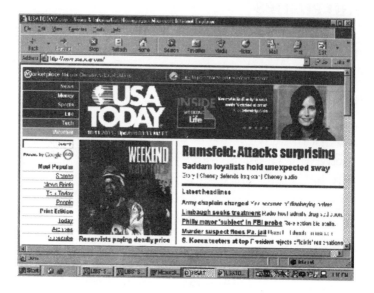

Fig. 9. CAS Service of USA TODAY

BENEFITS OF IMPLEMENTING THE IRM STRATEGY

If we follow the above strategies we can get the following benefits.

a. identifies gaps and duplication of information

b. clarifies roles and responsibilities of owners and users of information.

c. provides costs saving in the procurement and handling of information

d. identifies cost/benefits of different information resources

e. actively supports management decision process with quality information.

CONCLUSION

In this information era, because of the information

overload, two thirds of managers believed information overload had caused loss of job satisfaction, two thirds believed it had damaged their personal relationship, one third believed it had damaged their health, nearly half believed important decisions were delayed and adversely affected as a result of having too much information. For solving all these problems we have to implement the IRM strategy.

REFERENCES

* **Garai, Hugh.** *Managing information.* Ed.1.New Delhi : Gower, 1997, pp.181-211

* **Pedley, Paul.** *Intranets and push technology.* Ed.1. London : Aslib, 1999, pp.47-61

* **Rowley, Jennifer.** *Organizing knowledge.* Ed.3. London Gower, 2000, pp.3-37

* **Malanchuk, Maureen.** *Info relief.*Ed.1.New York : Jossy Boss, 1996,pp.49.79

* **Earl, Michael J.** *Information management.*Ed.1.New York : Oxford,1996, pp.136-171

* **Bryson, Jo.** *Managing information services.*Ed.1. England : Gower, 1997, pp.263-305

* **Mason, Richard O.** *Ethics of information management.*Ed.1.New Delhi : Sage,1995. pp.35-47

C-07
Digital Library Initiatives

G. Amudha
Librarian, V.H.N.S.N.College, Virudhunagar.

Mr. N. Baskaran
Librarian, Kamaraj College of Engg.& Tech., Virudhunagar.

Dr. A. Lawarence Mary
Research Guide & Librarian(SGL),
TDMNS College, Kallikulam, Valliyoor,
Tirunelveli District.

ABSTRACT

This paper deals with how information technology and emerging computer technology play an important role in building digital library. This article also discusses the need, design, hardware and software requirements for digital library development.

INTRODUCTION

The subject of electronic superhighways has been the focus of intense media attention in recent years, because of the dramatic impacts these are expected to have on people, business, scientific research and structure and organization of economic society. Electronic technology, electronic communications and electronic networks have transformed it into an information and communications society.

Traditional Libraries' budgets are devoting an ever increasing share of their funds to electronic services – CD-ROMs, Online access and OPACS. This trend will continue as digital storage costs go down relative to the cost of library shelf-space and as electronic services become more user friendly, affordable and available. The government of India has recognized the potential of information Technology for rapid and all-round national development.

AREAS OF INFORMATION TECHNOLOGY

Information Technology is most commonly used to mean computer technology. The technologies of optical / video systems like CD-ROMs are also included in the computers group by the books and periodicals on computer technology. In the field of journalism, IT is generally meant as technology used for information dissemination, which includes systems like telex, fax, teleprinter and so on. For a Librarian, IT has a wider connotation, which includes the technologies and systems like microfilm, microfiches, CD-ROM, Computers, information networks, etc., It includes all those technologies which the libraries and information centres use for collection, processing storage, retrieval and dissemination of recorded information.

COMPUTER TECHNOLOGIES

With the continuing advancements in microprocessor technology, the personal computer systems are undergoing substantial changes. On the one hand, emphasis is being placed on network capabilities in the Personal computers and on the other hand emphasis is on powerful computing capabilities in the PCs. Accordingly, two classes of computers viz, nctwork computers and multimedia personal computers are emerging.

DIGITAL LIBRARY

Digital Library is a library that maintains all or a substantial part of its collection in computer – processible form as an alternative, supplement or complement to the conventional printed material that currently dominates the Library collections.

HARD WARE REQUIREMENTS

Personal computers with multimedia applications on a network with a server dedicated to the library, CD writer, DVD writer, HP scanner & Laser printers.

SOFTWARE

Library Management software package for various library functions like acquisition, cataloguing, circulation, serials management etc., Reports from each module can be taken to assist in managing the various functions of the library.

DIGITAL LIBRARY INFRASTRUCTURE

It requires

- Global network accessibility.
- Network accessibility
- User friendly interface
- Advanced search and retrieval
- Supporting multimedia content
- Accessibility from anywhere, home, school, libraries etc.,
- Greater opportunities of access.
- Equal opportunities of access
- Searching & retrieval facilities.

DIGITAL LIBRARY SYSTEM DESIGN

Conceptually, a digital library system has certain kinds of interactions among people and computing systems. To help clarify the interactions occurring in these relationships, the computing resources are partitioned into server resources and client resources.

CONCLUSION

Digital Libraries are using information technology to build their services. With the emergence of CD-ROM & DVD technology and Internet technology, electronic resources enter the area through the use of digital technologies. (But mostly electronic resources fulfill all the needs of the users now a days.)

However, the digital libraries help the readers to get the information quickly at the national and international level without delay and with limited cost.

REFERENCES

* http://www.si-umich.edu/
* http://www.dir.org/pubs/abstract/pub92
* http://www.dlib.org/dlib/march00/moore

C-08
Application of RFID in Libraries

L. Uma

Assistant University Librarian, Anna University, Chennai.

ABSTRACT

RFID has become one of the latest emerging technologies in the field of library science. The adoption of Radio frequency identification technology by libraries promises a solution that could make it possible to inventory hundreds and thousands of items in their collections in days instead of months. In addition it would allow users to check out and return library property automatically at any time of the day. Besides speeding up check ups, keeping collections in better order, RFID promises to provide a better control on thefts and non return and misfiling of libraries assets. With estimated 35 million-library items tagged worldwide in more than 300 libraries this technology is generating interest.

RFID technology has slowly begun to replace the traditional barcodes on library items (books, CDs, DVDs, etc.). However, the RFID tag can contain identifying information, such as a book's title or material type, without having to be pointed to a separate database . The information is read by an RFID reader, which replaces the standard barcode reader commonly found at a library's circulation desk. The RFID tag can also act as a security device, taking the place of the more traditional electromagnetic security strip.

Even though RFID tags cost anywhere between four to five times as much as barcode and magnetic strip combined, the increase in efficiency and functionality provided by the technology is persuasive enough for an increasing number of libraries to implement or consider this technology. The number of RFID enabled library system is constantly increasing.

INTRODUCTION

RFID (Radio Frequency IDentification) is the latest technology to be used in library theft detection systems. Unlike EM (Electro-Mechanical) and RF (Radio Frequency) systems, which have been used in libraries for decades, RFID-based systems move beyond security to become tracking systems that combine security with more efficient tracking of materials throughout the library, including easier and faster charge and discharge, inventorying and materials handling.

RFID is a combination of radio-frequency-based technology and microchip technology. The information contained on microchips in the tags affixed to library materials is read using radio frequency technology regardless of item orientation or alignment (i.e., the technology does not require line-of-sight or a fixed plane to read tags as do traditional theft detection systems) and distance from the item is not a critical factor except in the case of extra-wide exit gates. The corridors at the building exit(s) can be as wide as four feet because the tags can be read at a distance of up to two feet by each of two parallel exit sensors.

Briefly, the RF in RFID stands for "radio frequency"; the "ID" means "identifier." The tag itself consists of a computer chip and an antenna, often printed on paper or some other flexible medium. The shortest metaphor is that RFID is like a barcode but is read with an electro-magnetic field rather than by a laser beam. The similarity ends there. RFID is an advanced technology compared to barcodes. The RFID tag does not have to be visible to be read; instead, it can be read even when it is embedded in an item, such as in the cardboard cover of a book or the packaging of a product. It can also carry a more complex message than a barcode, which is limited to an identification number. The chip that is part of the RFID tag can carry many bytes of information, which means that it has the potential to carry not only the item number used by a library but also information such as the title of the book and/or its call number. The size of the information payload of RFID chips is one of the features that will undoubtedly expand as future technology advances, allowing the creation of smaller and more powerful chips.

Library RFID Management System

The above figure shows how RFID functions in a library.

RFID AND LIBRARY FUNCTIONS

RFID as an identifier, is particularly suited to inventory functions and a library has a strong inventory component. There is, however, a key difference to the library's inventory as compared to that of a warehouse or retail outlet. In the warehouse and retail supply chain, goods come in and then they leave. Only occasionally do they return. The retail sector is looking at RFID as a "throw-away" technology that gets an item to a customer and then is discarded. Yet the cost per item of including an RFID tag is much more than the cost of printing a barcode on a package. In libraries, items are taken out and returned many times. This makes the library function an even better use of RFID than retail because the same RFID tag is re-used many times.

Second for circulation, libraries look to RFID as a security mechanism. The RFID tags can facilitate security in a variety of ways. In one method, the tag that is used has a special "security bit" that can be switched from "checked-in" to "checked-out." The exit gates at the library read each tag as the user passes out of the library and sounds an alarm if the bit is not in the "checked-out" state. The check-in function resets the bit. Another method is for the tags themselves to remain the same; as the user passes through the exit gate the system reads the tags in the books in the user's arms or bag and queries the library database to be sure that the items have been checked out.

Although RFID can be used in library anti-theft systems, this doesn't mean that it is a highly secure technology. What libraries don't tell their users, and none of us should probably say very loudly, is that RFID tags can be shielded by a thick layer of Mylar, a few sheets of aluminum foil, or even an aluminum gum wrapper, so they won't be detected by the reading device. In addition, today's tags are not hidden in the spine of the book, like security tape, but are often found on the inside of the book cover, barely concealed by a library label, and can be removed. This is not a condemnation of the technology nor even a reason not to use it in the library security system; the reality is that library security has never provided more than a modicum of security for library items. The gates and their alarms are as much social deterrent as they are actual prevention. The reason to use RFID for security is not because it is especially good for it, but because it is no worse than other security technologies. There is, however, some potential savings because a single tag serves many different functions. The library saves some time in processing new items because it only has to affix one technology to the item. It may also save some money due to the integration of circulation and security with a single vendor and into a single system. Some future-positive thinkers in the library world see the potential to have a combined exit-gate/check-out station that allows patrons to walk about the library with their books in hand and their library card in their pocket. That brings up other questions, especially privacy ones, but the notion is intriguing.

As well as being an inventory technology, barcodes also serve the point of sale (or lending). The need to have a direct line of sight on the barcode makes it difficult, however, to perform functions on more than one item at a time. RFID systems can read multiple tags at once, allowing you to check out a stack of books with a single transaction. Barcodes also have some disadvantages when taking an inventory of the library. The line of sight requirement means that each book must be tipped out far enough to read the barcode if it is on an outside cover or removed entirely from the shelf if the book or item must be opened to see the barcode. This is an area where RFID can provide great advantages because the tags can be read while the books sit on the shelf. Not only does the cost of doing an inventory of the library goes down, the odds of actually completing regular inventories goes up. This is one of those areas where a new technology will allow the library to do more rather than just doing the same functions with greater efficiency. Library experience with RFID is still in its early stages, but already some librarians are getting ideas for additional uses of this technology. RFID could be used to gather statistics on the re-shelving of books in the stacks area, by equipping shelves with hand-held readers. Vendors of RFID systems for libraries are already offering automated sorting of returned books into a handful of bins that facilitate the re-shelving of books that are checked in. A fully automated library could potentially know exactly where an item is, down to the very book truck or bin, during the return process. In theory, a library could "know" when a book leaves the shelf and could trace the progress of the book through the library to check-out. In reality, it is already possible to find a requested video in a jumbled browsing section that gets out of order due to high use.

SHOULD LIBRARIES USE RFID?

Because of the privacy issues, some librarians and library users question whether libraries should consider using RFID at all. While we can ask this question today, we may be facing RFID in our future, especially if RFID becomes the successor technology to barcodes. Should barcodes and barcode readers go the way of vinyl records and turntables, libraries needing new or replacement technology will have little choice but to purchase RFID-based systems. Because of this possibility, we cannot afford to ignore this new technology, even if we do not embrace it today.

In considering the introduction of any technology into the library we need to ask ourselves "why?" What is the motivation for libraries to embrace new technologies? The answer to this question may be fairly simple: libraries use new technologies because the conditions in the general environment that led to the development of the technology are also the conditions in which the library operates. In the case of RFID, anyone managing an inventory of physical objects needs to do item-level functions, such as sales or lending, more efficiently and with less human intervention.

RFID is a highly advantageous technology for a wide variety of inventory tracking situations. It is also coming into its own for payment systems, including the ever elusive "micro-payment," the holy grail of non-cash transactions. Whether or not libraries embrace RFID, they will probably continue to replace barcodes in the retail supply chain. And it will contribute to the general speeding up of our world, which affects libraries as well as other institutions. A key fact is that library circulation, the primary function where RFID can be used, is increasing while library budgets and purchasing power are losing ground.

JUSTIFICATION AND RETURN ON INVESTMENT

In the commercial world, all things are measured by "return on investment" or ROI. A company invests in a new technology that speeds up its delivery of widgets and cuts warehousing costs. The cost of the new technology is compared to the increase in profits and in the best of cases profits rise enough to pay for the new technology. This is the return on investment. When libraries measure their success, profit isn't part of the equation. Like other institutions that provide services, such as schools and city governments, the bottom line is less quantitative than the business case. Libraries "spend" their ROI on new services or on beefing up existing services. They also spend their ROI to respond to budget cuts or to loss of buying power when budgets do not keep up with inflation. This makes it hard to demonstrate that an investment in technology is worth the cost.

Laura Smart's Library Journal article on RFID lists fourteen areas of library operations where one might measure gains in time and materials costs. The obvious gains are in checking out and checking in books, although the gains vary by the degree of automation. Additional investment can be made on a book return system that automatically checks in items as they pass along a conveyor attached to a book drop. This system can be attached to an automated sorting machine that sorts the items into bins based on their call numbers. All of this saves time, but there is one thing to remember about this efficiency: the items still need to be shelved. The increase in circulation, which is often one of the few quantitative measures that libraries have to show that RFID has made their operations more efficient, has to be balanced against the cost of re-shelving more items.

It is generally agreed that the greatest return on investment depends on turning over the check-out functions to patrons, in essence, practically eliminating the need for circulation staff. Some libraries intend to become 100% self-check-out. Others are content to allow patrons to choose between the staffed check-out desk (which should operate more quickly) and the self-check stations. There are arguments for and against these approaches. On one hand, for many people who frequent libraries the circulation desk staff is the only staff with whom they have any interaction. Some librarians fear that self-check could eliminate what little human factor that libraries have for these patrons. On the other hand, the act of running patron cards and library items through a check-out station for hours at a time is mind-numbingly dull and probably not the best use of staff time. It's also the source of many staff repetitive stress injuries.

What the ROI statements fail to take into account is user satisfaction. In a service business like that of the library, satisfying your users is one of the few measures of success that you have. You can intuit satisfaction from an increase in use statistics, but an actual survey of users, ideally both before and after a change is made in library operations, would be the best evidence the library has that it is fulfilling its mission. Self-checkout could be seen by users as a mere shifting of the burden of check-out from the library to the users themselves, who will feel that they are being asked to do the work of the library. Or it could become the "ATM" of the library world, the fast service with few lines that users come to prefer to old way of doing things. Just adding self-check stations will not be enough; libraries must be sure that the stations serve the needs of the users and perhaps even provide additional services to win over their hearts.

SOME PROBLEMS REMAIN

It seems clear, at this moment in time, that RFID will become a widespread technology, replacing bar-coding for a variety of industries. It is also already leading to entirely new functionality, such as the "touchless" payment systems for debit cards and highway toll payments. But this is a very new technology and there are "gotchas" and limitations that we need to recognize. For libraries, RFID is very promising for items with a certain physical "substance," such as books and media in cases and boxes. But as we move to less sturdy items, RFID tags pose problems. Libraries must decide if they need to attach RFID tags to magazines, pamphlets, sheet music and a host of other items that may not have a good location for a somewhat bulky two-inch square tag and that are so numerous that the tag cost is significant. If it is determined that RFID will not work for these items, then an alternative check-out system needs to be maintained, which has real costs as well as a certain nuisance factor both for patrons and the library. It also may not be possible to accurately check out a stack of items that are particularly thin, such as journals or even children's books. The RFID tags on these materials can be so close together physically that the signals essentially cancel each other out.

Items with odd shapes and metal components, such as CDs and DVDs, are stretching the creativity of vendors of

RFID systems for libraries. RFID tags for optical discs have been developed that fit around the hole of the disc. This requires a reduction in the size of the antenna and thus reduces the read distance of the tag. But discs with an extra thick metal layer can still block the reading of the tags.

Another concern for libraries is that there are two main directions for the RFID industry at this time: one is toward the use of tags in the retail chain, the other is toward higher end tags for payment systems. In the retail environment, tags are only needed up to the point that the item is sold. This means that there will be some emphasis on inexpensive and not entirely durable tags and ones that can be written at the time of manufacture. For the payment systems, tags carry more information but are more durable and more secure. Libraries need a slightly different technology from either of these. Libraries need tags that are durable, since they be placed on an item that will be used repeatedly. The library function will probably have the longest-lived tags of any other sector, since books can remain on shelves and circulate over decades, while retail products have a short shelf life and even debit cards rarely are issued for more than four or five years. Libraries may also need tags that, although inexpensive, can be reprogrammed and may even need to have more than one "lifetime," for example in the case of an item that is moved into storage or is sent to another library through interlibrary loan. These functions may be available, but perhaps not at the rock-bottom prices that libraries want to pay for the tags and the related technology.

CONCLUSION

RFID technology has several advantages of the current bar code systems being used at libraries worldwide. For the libraries that use it, RFID promises to save time and operate more efficiently and effectively than the barcode systems. Some of the compensations of RFID over a barcode system are that RFID tags can be used for security as well as for status control, thereby eliminating the need to attach security strips to library items; RFID systems make self check out faster and easier for the library patrons and RFID portable scanners can take inventory by just being passed slowly along the library shelves without having to handle each item individually. RFID vendors, however, need to resolve some issues before libraries feel confident in adopting them. In the forefront are the issues such as cost, lack of standardization amongst vendors and privacy.

REFERENCES

* **Boss, Richard W.** "RFID Technology for Libraries", *ALA Tech Notes,* May 14, 2004

* **Margulius, David L.** "The Rush to RFID", *Infoworld*, April 12, 2004. pp. 36-41

* **Want, Roy."**A Key to Automating Everything", *Scientific American*, January, 2004. pp 56-65.

* "RFID Journal Frequently Asked Questions", located at http://www.rfidjournal.com

* "RFID Gazette", located at http://www.rfidgazette.org

C-09
Internet for Library Automation and Management

M. Ravichandran
Librarian, Mohamed Sathak Engineering College,
Kilakarai - 623 806

V.P. Ramesh Babu
Librarian, Rev. Jacob Memorial Christian College,
Ambilikkai – 624 612

ABSTRACT

Libraries have the major responsibility of managing information resources enabling their users quick and convenient access to these resources and to provide variety of on-demand and in-anticipation information services. Increasing use of information technology in the production of information has resulted in an explosion of electronic information sources. The Internet and the World Wide Web (WWW) have enabled seamless access to these sources from any corner of the globe. Internet needs to be exploited as an information source. Information sources residing on the Internet need to be taken into account in the collection development strategy and in rendering information services. These sources also need to be reflected in the catalogues and indices prepared by the library. The collection and services of the library need to be made available on the Internet and intranet, through the library web site. Information may be delivered using e-mail and web browsers, which have emerged as the preferred information access mechanisms. Internet can also be used for information resource sharing among libraries in a city or region.

INTRODUCTION

Library is a storehouse of collection of reading materials to preserve them and make them available for use. Computerization of library activities and applications of various technologies is known as Library Automation. Computerization of library in-house operations is known as library automation. The library in-house operations are Acquisition, Cataloguing, Circulation, Serial Control, OPAC & WEBOPAC and Reports. Most of the libraries maintain their catalogues in Machine Readable Form and claim that they have done library automation. It is not true. Library automation involves total computerization of library activities starting from acquisition to management and circulation to reference service. The library technology involves the use of Xerox machine to Microfilm machine and Bar-code reader to electronic security gate. Planning for library automation should not be taken lightly and may be one of the biggest projects a librarian will ever undertake.

WHY LIBRARY AUTOMATION

There are two main features of Library Automation:

- Library Services
- Operation in Library

Operation in Library is labor intensive & costly due to salaries, support facilities, increase in cost of library materials.

The advantages of Library Automation are,

- To avoid maintenance of registers such as Issue register, Return register, Membership register, Journals register, Articles register, Serials register.
- To provide search facilities to the users in a network environment.
- For better management of library resources.
- For use of various modules based on authentication.

BARRIERS OF LIBRARY AUTOMATION

Following could be the few possible barriers of library automation:

- Fear of adverse impact on employment. (Manpower)
- Apprehension that the technology could be too expensive. (Infrastructure)
- The library staff has to undergo extensive training. (IT Skills)
- Lack of support from the management, may be owing to budget constraints. (Budget)
- Retrospective conversion of data.

AREAS OF LIBRARY AUTOMATION

Computerization of library in-house operations is known as library automation. The library in-house operations are Acquisition, Cataloguing, Circulation, Serial Control, OPAC & WEBOPAC and Reports.

ACQUISITIONS: MAJOR ACTIVITIES

- Handling of Library and Department funds
- Receive and follow up of recommendations from faculty and staff
- Select books and other materials to be procured
- Verify bibliographic details

- Place orders with vendors
- Process payments
- Maintain on-order files on the automated system
- Process books for accessioning
- Books to be sent to technical processing section for classifying and cataloguing

ACQUISITIONS: INTERNET USE

- Book order requests can be placed through web by faculty and students
- Use online catalog for searching to identify duplicates before placing order
- Web-based ordering for books by Acquisition staff with vendors
- Lists of booksellers, publishers and booksellers indexes, book metasites, lists of libraries and book fair, reviews, awards
- Lists which are available on the Web aid in book selection
- Use paperless electronic transactions to handle routine book ordering with all major vendors
- Users can enquire about ordering status or availability of a title in the Online Catalog, or to be notified when the title has been received, to suggest other titles by filling out the Request Form.
- Maintain and provide Web access to On-order and In-process files
- Exchange information, ideas and to find solutions to any problem pertaining to acquisition

TECHNICAL PROCESSING: MAJOR ACTIVITIES

- Classifying documents by assigning class numbers

using standard classification system

- Cataloguing documents using standard cataloguing manual, by assigning subject headings, preparing required added entries for the documents depending on library users needs

- Book processing - preparing charging cards for circulation, stamping, entering call nos. on the book

- Inputting classification numbers and cataloging information and all other bibliographic details into the automated system

- Weekly display of latest books received

TECHNICAL PROCESSING: INTERNET USE

- Web access to the latest authoritative tools related to classification and cataloguing help in better processing of the documents.

- Documenting the technical processing procedures will guide the staff in their work, bringing uniformity in their efforts.

- Providing web access to union catalogue of books subscribed by leading libraries help in better resource sharing

- Lists of books received can be sent to all users by e-mail or maintained on the library web site.

SERIALS CONTROL: MAJOR ACTIVITIES

- Budget allocation of funds from Library grants for Journal subscriptions

- List of existing journals to be sent to Library committee for approval, along with latest publisher's catalogue for inclusion of any new journal titles

- Receive and follow up recommendations from Library committee and faculty

- Select Journals and Conference proceedings to be procured
- Verify bibliographic details and pricing from latest publisher's catalogue
- Place orders with vendors/publishers
- Process payment - raise indent against invoice, certify bills for payment
- Maintain on-order files
- Accessioning of Journal issues on receipt
- Provide access to serials holdings information through library's OPAC
- Periodically generate reminders for missing/ incomplete issues
- Weekly display of journal titles - alphabetical, subjectwise

SERIALS: INTERNET USE

- Journal procurement recommendations can be placed through web by faculty and students
- Web-based ordering of Journals by serial staff with vendors
- Lists of publishers and their indexes, journal metasites, which are available on the Web help in journal selection process
- Web access to journals subscribed will increase better usage among staff and students
- Handle routine journal ordering and journal claiming with vendors who are on the Web

CIRCULATION

The Circulation module provides a complete set of circulation transaction functions.

Circulation Module Features Include:

- Checking items out to a patron
- Checking items in from a patron
- Renewing items that have been checked out
- Placing an item on hold for a specific patron
- Setting a temporary due date for specific items
- Automatically assigning fines on check-in
- A full range of circulation reports and statistics

REFERENCE AND INFORMATION SERVICE: MAJOR ACTIVITIES

- Getting familiar with the printed/electronic reference sources available at the reference section
- Identify the sources which provide the right information for user's queries
- Depending on the type of queries answered, suggest new reference sources to be procured
- Compile bibliographies
- Access electronic databases (CD-ROM, Online)
- Provide services like SDI, CAS

REFERENCE & INFORMATION SERVICE: INTERNET USE

- Identify and collect Internet sources, which are likely to be of interest to users, providing links to the same.
- Extensive Internet sources with subject guides and search engines help in locating the right information for the queries posted by users.
- Reference staff can access these sources to answer reference queries posted by the users.
- Users themselves can access the links to reference sources from their desktop to get quicker information.

REPORTS

The Reports module provides a wide range of reports for all the modules.

Reports include:

- Catalog Holding Reports by title, author, and subject
- Brief and Full Patron record reports with current transactions
- Overdue notices, lists and letters
- Items on hold, overdue and fines outstanding reports
- Circulation activity reports for various time frames
- Library Status reports with counts of each type of material
- Report customization features

OPAC & WEBOPAC

OPAC is a database of books holding of library. An OPAC is an electronic resource that provides a record for each item that a library owns. Within each catalogue record you can find out where an item is located within the library as well as if it is available or checked out. OPAC includes record for books, periodicals, newspapers, videos, audios, maps and more. There are also links within some catalogue records that allow you to access the contents of certain e-journals and other electronic resources.Web OPAC is a simple yet sophisticated searching module that provides access to your library's Online Public Access Catalog over the Internet

CONCLUSION

Information professionals should adapt themselves to this transition and should attempt to experiment and explore on their own, to identify and use the information available on the Web, to provide better service to their users.

REFERENCES

* http://www.libraryworld.net/cgi-bin/home.pl
* http://www.infosciencetoday.org/index.html
* http://lcweb.loc.gov/catdir/cpso/dcmb19_4.html
* http://www.industrialautomationguide.com/industrial-automation.html
* http://www.l4u.com/
* http://www.ncsi.iisc.ernet.in/raja/netlis/iirml/iirml.html
* http://www.datavillage.com
* http://www.libsys.co.in
* http://www.netls.org/ATHCGI/athweb.pl
* http://www.ibiblio.org/librariesfaq/index.html
* http://www.purl.org/oclc/cataloging-internet/
* http://www.ncsi\WISE\WISE - Technological environment.htm

C-10
A Study of Digital Library

S. Kalimuthu Kumaran
B. Rajaseelan
M.L.I.Sc Students, Department of Library and Information Science,
AVVM Sri Pushpam College, Autonomous, Poondi, Thanjavur Dt.

ABSTRACT

The world's biggest digital library is INTERNET. To day digitization has become one of the main activities in the library & information centres which is an excellent way of providing open access to library resources. This paper discusses the basic concepts about digital libraries objectives, characteristics, function, scope, services, digital library skills & future in digital library. Its main aim is the right information to right user at the right time.

INTRODUCTION

The digital library has been used to characterize a large storehouse of digital information accessible through computer. Digital library services as an archive of knowledge that spans many topics, provides information that changes quickly, also provides access to events as they occur. Digital libraries basically store materials in the electronic format and manipulate large collection of those materials effectively. The major objective of library is to provide information or reading materials for its users. A library should help its clients to satisfy their information requirements by providing efficient service. Digital technologies and their applications have also come in to every part of our daily life. It is accepted that we are now living in a digital world.

MEANING

A digital library is, collections stored in digital formats as opposed to print, or microform or other media & accessible by computers. The digital content may be stored locally or accessed remotely via computer networks.

DEFINITION

According to digital library federation (DLF) digital libraries are *"organizations that provide the resource including the specialized staff, to select, structure, offer intellectual access to interpret, distribute, preserve the integrity and ensure the persistence over time of collections of digital works so that they are readily and economically available for use by a defined community or set of communities ".*

CHARACTERISTICS OF DIGITAL LIBRARY

There are special characteristics in digital library

- User friendly interface
- Searching and retrieval facilities
- Usage of electronic information will steadily increase and usage of printed material will decrease.
- Equal opportunities of access
- Access to the digital library is not bounded in space or time. It can be accessed from any where in any time.
- Jobs, training and recruitment will be re-profiled.
- Net work accessibility.

OBJECTIVES OF THE DIGITAL LIBRARY

The main objectives of the digital library are

- To introduce and produce new services
- To provide facility for networking and resource sharing
- To have large number of databases in CD.
- To access national and international journals which are being published only in machine – readable form.
- To improve the cost effectiveness of library operations.

FUNCTIONS OF DIGITAL LIBRARY

- Require talented and highly trained man power.
- Information is available round the clock.
- High speed internet connectivity maintains other routine office works and develop in house database.
- Electronic Mgt systems that supports overall Mgt of digital searches.
- Digitized documents for presentation and for space saving.

SCOPE OF DIGITAL LIBRARY

Now a days users of the library utilization have increased because the scientific technologies have increased. To reduce the physical strain to maintain status, with in the durable time, minimum expenses, accuracy & storage capacity etc., the users utilize the digital library. These up-to-date information and innovations are obtained from the computer not only at national level but also at the international level.

TOOLS OF DIGITIZATION

- Scanners
- Vector Scanners
- Raster Scanners

- Flatbed Scanners
- Sheet Feed Scanners
- Drum Scanners
- Digital Cameras
- Slide Scanners
- Micro Film Scanners
- Video Frame Grabber or Radio Digitizer

BUILDING DIGITAL LIBRARY

- Know your content
- Expect change
- Involve the right people
- Design usable systems
- Ensure open access
- Automate wherever possible
- Adopt & adhere to standards.
- Be concerned about persistence.

SERVICES

- Current awareness services
- Selective dissemination of information services
- Online public access catalogue
- Types of information exchange that happen in the digital library.
- E mail- services.
- Browsing the world wide web
- CD-ROM databases
- Getting the latest news from around the world.

USES OF DIGITAL LIBRARIES

- Online library catalogue through internet gives access to bibliographic records of millions of books & details of holdings of academic and research libraries, electronic journals & news letters.

- Electronic publications provide aids for connectivity, audio- visualization, customizability, creation and revision of documents, interactivity and rapid information retrieval. Electronic publications may help in overcoming the restrictions on the length of the paper imposed by many scholarly journals.
- Helps to reach information of their users at faster rate through on – line communication.
- Save the library manpower and funds.
- Access to more information than possible through physical acquisition and maintenance

DEVELOPING OF DIGITAL LIBRARY

Digital library development is mainly three steps.

- Planning
- Implementation
- Promotion & provision of services.

LIBRARIES IN FUTURE

Future libraries may not require a vast area for housing the shelves & books, as the internet facilities grow by leap & bounds. One can have any amount of information from any library any where in the world , right from his table. The modern digital library will be a sleek array of computer based information systems and will be gauged by the number of access mode rather than by the number of titles it holds. The modern digital library will be tested for collecting quantitative statistics that will ultimately decide the quality & worth of information that the library processes.

CONCLUSION

The priority of a library , digital or any other, is to serve the research needs of its clientele. The development, maintenance and extension of its collection and its technologies must be supportive as well as subordinate to the objective. Digital libraries promise us a wide range of information services & universal access to information.

REFERENCES

* **Borgom, CA.**(1999) *what are digital libraries completing vision information processing & management ,1999*

* http://www.diglib.org/preserve/giteria.ntm

C-11
Self Development of Professionals in Modern Libraries

S. Paramasivam
Librarian, GGR College of Engineering,
Pillaiyarkulam, Perumugai, Vellore-9.

A. Rajinikanth
Library Assistant, PSNA College of Engineering
and Technology, Muthanampatty, Dindigul Dt.

ABSTRACT

Modern Libraries are providing the information function services. Due to the development of communication technology contemporary society is moving towards knowledge based society for which information is considered as primary source. Libraries began developing web pages to organize and publicize internal links to information. Web based information; CD-ROM databases are increasing and play a vital role in the libraries to satisfy the user's requirements as quickly as possible effectively and efficiently. So the self development of professionals in modern libraries is an essential one and its includes various form of skills like administrative skills, communication skills, developing personality qualities, leadership, appropriate technical training, developing library websites and non-web technologies including MS-office software, time management, evaluation skills, developing network between the libraries and information centers.

INTRODUCTION

Emergence of computers and communication technology has great impact in every facet of library activities and services. In this area new technologies are replacing the old method of collection, storage and retrieval. Developments in information technology have played a crucial role and will continue to a play a central role in restructuring of the libraries. Library is an extremely important entity in an ever changing society and it must be responsive to the needs of society. Due to the revolution of information communication technology library and information science professional must develop themselves in various categories and work effectively and efficiently.

COMPETENCIES FOR LIBRARIANS

Competencies have been defined as the interplay of knowledge, understanding, skills and attitudes on the part of so called information persons required to execute their job effectively from the viewpoint of both the performer and observer.

ADMINISTRATIVE SKILLS

Librarian must be able to analyze and solve problems, to demonstrate organizational ability, to demonstrate team building skills and manage fiscal resources/budgets.

COMMUNICATION SKILLS

Communication skill is an essential part of library and information centers. Without communication one can't solve the user's requirements. Librarian should be able to communicate effectively with staff/public (good interpersonal/people skills) with oral and written presentation skills.

CREATIVITY

Librarian should have creativity skills to solve the problems (web creation, web services)   .

KNOWLEDGE BASE

Knowledge managers or Information officers have broad knowledge of issues like (1) Scholarly communication (2) Financial management (3) Planning (4) Digital libraries (5) IT collection management and development (6) Out come assessment (7) User expectations (8) Information needs (9)Intellectual Property Rights (10) Fund raising (11) Public relations (12) Service Quality measurement (13) Goal setting (14) Information Delivery system and publishing.

LEADERSHIP

Leadership is an integral part of management and plays a vital role in managerial operations.

MOTIVATING EMPLOYEES

Motivating is an important factor for achieving goal.

To create an environment that fosters accountability.

To develop various sources of funds (Grants. Gifts)

PERSONAL QUALITIES

Librarian must develop the following personal qualities

(i)   To treat people with dignity and respect.

(ii)   To be diplomatic

(iii)   To be a good listener and good facilitator.

(iv)   To be an open minded person, work effectively in groups (appropriate timing)

(v)   To be persuasive and committed to a set of values

(vi)   Self awareness of strength and weakness

(vii)   Should have a sense of perspective and commitment

IT SKILLS

Librarian should have the following skills, Creating library website skills, skills in HTML, XML, SMIL, PERL, PHP, ASP, SQL, JSP, JAVASCRIPT, COLD FUSION, JAVA, DREAMWEAVER, FLASH AND VISUVAL BASIC and Non-web technologies, including MSWORD, EXCEL, ACCESS, POWERPOINT.

PROFESSIONAL COMPETENICIES

1. Knowledge of content of information resources available both in print and non-print formats.

2. Systematic and scientific organization of different formats of collection.

3. Appropriate information technology for information management and retrieval capabilities.

4. Management techniques.

5. Conducting user studies and imparting user education.

RELATIONSHIP AND NETWORK BUILDING

Build relationship with customers, internal colleagues, external colleagues, vendors and others, to help others do their work better, to assist other colleagues and for personal development.

EVALUATION

Evaluation shows the progress of institution and individual activity

Clear, realistic objectives

Shared sense of purpose

Best use of resources

TIME MANAGEMENT

Time management is an essential part of library and information centers. It includes the following points (1) To set goals (2) To make daily priority list (3) Dignity and self-respect (4) To handle every piece of paper only once. (5) Use prime time for doing top priorities and (6) Should have protected time.

CONCLUSION

The professional librarian will have to ascertain the impact of information technology on the library and will have to monitor and acquire skills to cope intelligently and objectively for effectiveness and efficient function of a library. Librarians must prepare themselves to meet the changing scenario and update the latest skills. Library and information science people must be well equipped with up-do-date skills, knowledge on the computer and networking with other libraries and be flexible. Librarian should take positive approach to provide better services and continue to prove their usefulness before the non-professionals take over their roles.

REFERENCES

* **Peter Heron, Ronald R Powell, Arthur P Young.** *The Next Library Leadership*. London:London Libraries unlimited, 1995.

* **Karl Bridges.** *Expectations of libraries in the 21st century*. London: Greenwood press, 2000

* **Kaul, HK and Baby, MD.** *Library and Information Networking NACLIN 2002*. New Delhi : Delnet, 2003.

* **Vijayraghavan, GK and Sivakumar, P.** *Principles of Management*. Chennai : Lakshmi Publications, 2005.

* **Raju, AAN ...etal,** *New vitas in Library and information science*. New Delhi : Vikas Publishing House Pvt ltd, 1995.

C-12
Digital Resources: Internet & The Google

N. Vasanthakumar

Assistant Librarian, Thiagarajar School of Management (TSM),
Centre for Higher Learning, Thirupparankundram,
Madurai – 625 005

ABSTRACT

Authors of this paper intend to present digital resources (Internet and the Google) in detail. History of the Internet, definition, users, availability, WWW, URL, E-Mail, advantages the art of googling, facts, search methods, tools services are discussed in this paper.

INTRODUCTION

The Internet is a computer network made up of thousands of networks worldwide. No one knows how many computers are connected to the Internet, or how many people use it, though it is certain that both are expanding at a rapid rate. No one is in charge of the Internet. There are organizations which develop technical aspects of this network, but there is no governing body in control.

HISTORY OF THE INTERNET

The internet was conceived in 1969 when the Defense Advanced Research Projects Agency (DARPA), a United

States defense department, found a need for a way of exchanging military research information between researchers based at different sites. A network of four computers was established and was called DARPANET. By 1972 there were 37 computers or nodes on the network which had become known by now as ARPANET due to a change in the name of the agency responsible for it. By this time it was no longer being used for the exchange of research data but its users were talking to each other through private electronic mailboxes.

INTERNET : DEFINITION

The internet is not restricted to any particular section of users like librarians, engineers, doctors, advocates, and others. In general the Internet can be defined as below:

"The Internet is the network of networks of numerous computers spread all over the world."

"The internet is world wide network of networks. It is a conglomeration of smaller networks and other connected machines spanning the entire globe."

"The internet is a composite creature made up of lakhs of computer systems scattered across the world."

"The Internet is a global system of public and private computer networks that allow desktop computers to exchange data, messages and files with any of the millions of other computers connected to the Internet."

WHO USES THE INTERET?

It seems like everyone uses the Internet these days. Actually, Internet users come from every age and income bracket. Users connect from home, school, and work place. Ask your friends and colleagues if they've used the Internet. You'll probably be surprised at how many people you know are happily using the Internet right now.

WHAT IS AVAILABE ON THE INTERNET?

On the Internet, a user has access to a wide variety of services:

- Send electronic mail to friends, academic and business colleagues
- Take part in group discussions
- Pursue an interest or hobby through one of the many newsgroups
- Download files & look up reference information.
- Perform key word searches
- Watch video clips - view exhibitions or look through remote cameras
- Get the latest national and international stock, financial and weather news.
- Book a journey or do your shopping

WHAT CAN YOU DO WITH INTERNET?

- Information Systems
- Information Exchange
- Advertisement
- Education
- Research
- Employment
- Entertainment
- Publications
- Electronic Commerce

WORLD WIDE WEB (WWW)

The World Wide Web (abbreviated as the Web, WWW, or W3) is an information retrieval system that allows users on computer networks a consistent means of access to a variety of media through the Internet. Almost every protocol type available on the Internet is accessible on the Web. This includes e-mail, FTP, Telnet and News Groups. In addition to these, the World Wide Web has its own protocol: Hyper Text Transfer Protocol, or HTTP. The World Wide Web provides a single interface for accessing all these protocols. Because of this feature and because of the Web's ability to work with multimedia, the World Wide Web is the fastest-growing component of the Internet. The operation of the Web relies primarily on hypertext as a means of information retrieval. Hypertext is a document containing words that connect to other documents. These words are called links and are selectable by the user. A single hypertext document can contain links to many documents.

HOW DOES THE WWW WORK?

The WWW system is based on the client/server architecture. A web client is used to send request for information to any web server that store the requested information. A web server is a program that, upon receipt of a request, sends the document requested, back to the requesting client.

Typically the client program runs on a separate machine from that of the server. The server takes care of all the issues related to document storage, whereas the task of presenting the information to the user is left to the client program.

THE UNIFORM RESOURCE LOCATOR (URL)

The URL specifies the Internet address of the electronic document. Every file on the Internet, no matter what ever be its access protocol, has a unique URL. Web software programs use the URL to retrieve the file from the source computer and the directory in which it resides. This file is then displayed on the user's computer monitor.

FORMAT OF THE URL

Protocol://host/path/filename

For example:

http://www.bell.ac.uk/computer/dipsad.htm

- a hypertext file *ftp://ftp.wwa.com/pub/Scarecrow/ Misc/Flowers*

- a file at an ftp site

Anatomy of a URL

This is a URL at the CNN home page http:// www.cnn.com/feedback/comments.html

Structure of the URL

1. Protocol: http
2. Host computer name: www
3. Second-level domain name: cnn (i.e. the organization name)
4. Top-level domain name: com
5. Directory name: feedback
6. File name: comments.html

E-MAIL

One of the most popular and important functions of WWW is free E-Mail Service. It is a mailing facility based on hyperlink technology and can be accessed with the help of browser. A few web based free E-mail services are: Hotmail, Yahoo, Rediffmail, Gmail.

E-mail is common for business organizations and academic institutions in almost all developed and developing countries mainly because of its falling cost. A large number of people use e-mail in their professional and personal activities. In fact number of users of e-mail are more than those of entire Internet itself.

DESCRIPTION OF FUNCTIONALITY

Electronic mail was originally designed to allow a pair of individuals to communicate via computer. The first electronic mail software provided only a basic facility: it allowed a person using one computer to type a message and send it across the Internet to a person using another computer.

Current electronic mail systems provide services that permit complex communication and interaction. For example, electronic mail can be used to:

- Send a single message to many recipients.
- Send a message that includes text, audio, video, or graphics.
- Send a message to a user on a network outside the Internet.
- Send a message to which a computer program responds.

ADVANTAGES

Every organization or professional worker who has started to use e-mail will have their own view of its benefits to their work, but following uses will certainly influence Library and Information Science (LIS) professionals:

- System is capable of sending text files, programmes, graphics, word processed files, audio and video files.
- The freedom to communicate swiftly over great distance, overcoming the barriers such as separation of correspondent by time zones, working and non-working days and slow speed of conventional mail services.
- Internet ever widens with its miraculous devices and novelty.

SEARCH ENGINES

List of some useful search engines

i.e.   *www.rediff.com,*   *www.yahoo.com,* *www.msn.com, www.dogpile.com, www.askjeevs.com, www.angelfire.com,*   *www.altavista.com*   and *www.google.com*

GOOGLE

Google is an American public corporation, specializing in internet search and online advertising. The company is based in *Mountain View, California* and has 13,748 full time employees (as of 30 June 2007) Google mission statement is *"to organize the world's information and make it universally accessible and useful"*. Google's corporate philosophy includes statements such as *"**Don't be evil**"* and "work should be challenging and the challenge should be fun" illustrating a some what relaxed corporate culture.

FOUNDERS

Google was co-founded by Larry Page and Sergey Brin while they were Ph.D students at Stanford University and the company was first incorporated as a privately held company on September 7, 1998. Google's initial public offering took place on August 19, 2004, raising $1.67 billion, making it worth $23 billion.

KEY PEOPLE

Eric. E. Schmidt	- CEO/Director
Sergey Brin	- Co-founder, Technology President
Larry E. Page	- Co-founder, Products President
George Reyes	- CFO

WORD "GOOGLE"

The name "Google" originated from a misspelling of *"googol"* which refers to 10^{100} (the number represented by a

1 followed by one hundred zeros). Having found its way increasingly into every day language, the verb "*google*" was added to the Merriam Webster collegiate dictionary and the oxford English dictionary in 2006, meaning the use of the google search engine to obtain information on the internet.

LIFE OF A GOOGLE QUERY

The life span of a Google query normally lasts less than half a second, yet involves a number of different steps that must be completed before results can be delivered to a person seeking information.

Google User

Google Web Server

3. The search results are returned to the user in a fraction of a second.

1. The web server sends the query to the index servers. The content inside the index servers is similar to the index in the back of a book - it tells which pages contain the words that match the query.

2. The query travels to the doc servers, which actually retrieve the stored documents. Snippets are generated to describe each search result.

Index Servers

Doc Servers

HOW TO SEARCH GOOGLE?

- Log on to *http://www.google.com*
- Preferences
  - Interface Language
  - Search Language
  - Number of results.

IMPORTANT POINTS FOR SEARCHING

- Choose words carefully
- Case sensitivity
- Use multiple search terms
- Use 32 words or less
- Phrase searching
- Language tools.
- Boolean operators (AND, OR, NOT)
- Word operators [Inclusion(+), Exclusion(-), Wildcard (*)]

SEARCHING METHODS

There are two different kind of advanced searching methods on Google.

- The first would be using the Advanced Search page, which is located at *http://www.google.com/ advanced_search.*
- The second way to conduct an advanced search is through the use of search operators or words that have a special meaning to Google.

GOOGLE TOOLS OR SERVICES

- Desktop (http://Blogger.com)
- Earth (http://earth.google.com)
- Gmail (http://gmail.google.com)

- Orkut (http://www.orkut.com)
- Picasa (http://pocasa.google.com)
- Talk (http://www.google.com/talk)
- Toolbar (http://toolbar.google.com)
- Deskbar (http://deskbar.google.com)
- Alerts (http://google.com/alerts)
- Answers (http://google.com/answers)
- Catalogs (http://catalogs.google.com)
- Directory (http://directory.google.com)
- Groups (http://groups.google.com)
- Images (http://images.google.com)
- Maps (http://maps.google.com)
- Mobile(*http://mobile.google.com*)

GOOGLE FEATURES

- More relevant results
- Highlighting terms
- Restricting your research by date
- Advanced search and Search operators
- Preferences
- Advertisement
- Links.

GOOGLE WEBSITES

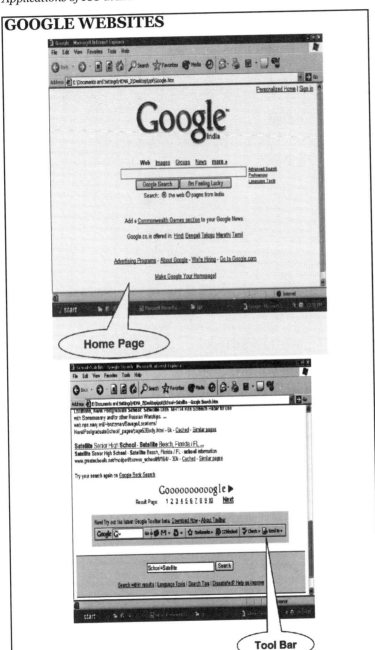

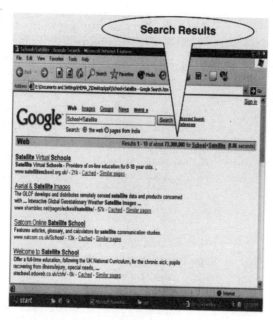

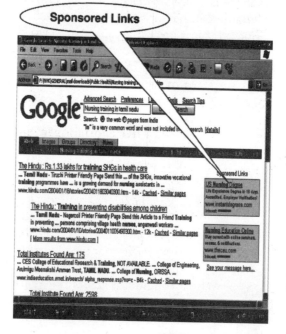

REFERENCES

* **Kailash Narain Vyas,** *Information Technology for e-Libraries.* Jaipur : Raj Publishing House, 2005. pp.1-9.

* **Jain, Nirmal K.** *Internet and Library Services (in 50 Years of Library Information Services in India),* **Ed. By M.K. Jain,** New Delhi : Shipra Publications, 1998. pp.240-248).

* **CIStems,** Tata McGraw-Hill Series, Internet an Introduction (2002), New Delhi TMH, 2002. pp.21-25

* **Alexis Leon and Mathews Leon** "E-Mail in a NutShell", *Leon Tech World,* Chennai,1997. pp.4-42

* **James, KL.** *The Internet: A User's Guide.* New Delhi : Prentice-Hall of India Private Limited, 2003.pp.70-88 and 101-108.

* **Comer, Douglas. E.** *The Internet Book.* Ed.3. New Delhi : Pearson Education, LPE, 2003 pp.157-169.

* http://*www.google.com*, visited on 12 July, 2007

* http://*http://en.wikipedia.org/wiki/google.* visited on 13 July, 2007

* http://*www.googleguide.com* visited on 13 July, 2007

C-13
Internet Based Library and Information Services: A Study on Bharathiar University Library Coimbatore

M. Mariraj

Assistant Technical Officer, School of Management,
Bharathiar University, Coimbatore-46.

ABSTRACT

The current and future applications and implications of the Internet within and far away libraries are indicated. Aspects of the internet based library and information service are considered, followed by the impact of the Internet on aspects of library holdings. Features of online access, including search engine performance are noted and collection development effects pointed out. Finally future implications of the Internet for libraries, through home versus library use and discussion groups and influences of library science in the internet are discussed.

INTRODUCTION

The emerging information and communication technologies have offered potential solutions to the problem created by the ever–growing literature publication. Information Technology has its impact on all disciplines and areas of operations including libraries and information centers. The future generation is going to witness, what is called "Digital libraries" instead of conventional libraries. There are many activities associated with information processing and retrieval, like production, location, modification, and manipulation of information. Computers are the best tools for performing all such activities. Computer is the best available tool for the library and information science professionals for quicker processing, storing and dissemination of information. Libraries and Librarians have come a long way since the days of chained books and closed stacks. We are in an era of scientific development at its peak and a consequent information explosion. Their number is also increasing in recent years and many of them are available on INTERNET and on CD.

INTERNET

Internet has made information, any bit of knowledge recorded at any time, kept at any time, kept at any part of the world if it is available in digital media just a click away, and lakhs of libraries are now on the side of information super Highway and millions of people are joining the rush in the superhighway seeking information from the net.

The Internet revolution arrived faster and with more complications, than many academic institutions expected. The rapid development of search engines and the expanded use of the web by all types of organizations increased the demand for Internet – related services on college campuses.

PURPOSE OF INTERNET

Information / Data, Research work ,E-journals, E-books, Downloaded software, Downloaded text ,Chatting ,Discussion, E Mail and Reference.

It was not any single invention or event that led to the web taking off in such a dramatic way. But numerous related events, including the following ones have resulted from it.

Easy availability of Internet connections.

Removal of restrictions to commercial development of the Internet.

Access to powerful graphical browsers such as Mosaic and Netscape.

Adoption of many important standards.

SEARCH ENGINES

In 1991 Tim Berners-Lee developed a network of files connected by hypertext links; this network to day is referred to as World Wide Web. The popularity of the web exploded when user-friendly browser applications are created to enable people to view text and graphics and jump quickly from page to page. The next thing that was needed was a way for users to find what they wanted and that is why search engines are created. Image search is a kind of *search engine* specialised on finding pictures, *images, animations* etc. Like the text search, image search is an information retrieval system designed to find information on the Internet and it allows the user to ask for images etc. using *keywords* or search phrases and to receive a set of thumbnail images, sorted by relevancy.

OBJECTIVES

The following are the objectives of the study

- To identify the contribution of internet in the dissemination of information in the library.

- To compare the use of online information resources in the Bharathir University library
- To observe the impact of electronic resources over the traditional ones.
- To suggest suitable recommendations to improve the electronic resources and services for the benefit of faculty members.

METHODOLOGY

The present survey has used questionnaire method. First the problems were identified and the survey questionnaire was developed. The advantages of the questionnaire method lie in its more complete coverage of users interests and analysis of replies, which is a relatively simple procedure.

For the convenience of analysis the users data are categorized among the major groups viz. Professor, Reader, Lecturer, Research Scholar and Post Graduate Students. Efforts are also made to assimilate users from different fields of study to make the sample representative and to contribute to the success of study.

75 copies of questionnaire have been circulated among the sample representatives and the response is 100%.

BHARATHIAR UNIVERSITY – SCENARIO

The Government of Tamilnadu established the Bharathiar University at Coimbatore in February 1982 under the provision of the Bharathiar University Act, 1981 (Act 1 of 1982), with jurisdiction over the districts of Coimbatore, Erode and the Nilgiris. The Postgraduate Centre of the University of Madras, which was functioning in Coimbatore till 1982, formed the nucleus of Bharathiar University. The University Grants Commission (UGC), New Delhi recognized the University in 1985.

The University is situated at the foothills of Maruthamalai, a mountain that forms the part of Western Ghat, in a sprawling campus of one thousand acres, at a distance of 15 KM from the city of Coimbatore. As of now, the University has 85 affiliated institutions (73 Arts and Science Colleges, 2 Colleges of Education, 8 Management Institutions, 1 Air Force Administration College and 1 College of Physical Education). Also, there are 19 Research Institutes of the State and Central Governments, which are recognized by this University for research purposes. All these Institutions cater to the educational needs of about 1,50,000 Students and Research Scholars.

The Library of Bharathiar University was established in the year 1981 at the Madras University Autonomous Postgraduate Centre of the University in an area of 11,750 sq.feet. The seating capacity currently is about 300 and has over 1,20,000 volumes covering all disciplines. The library subscribes to 163 National and International journals and seven leading newspapers. 150 journals, magazines and periodicals are received as gratis. Back issues of journals are available some dating back to 1880's. Photocopying facility is also available inside the library.

ANALYSIS AND FINDINGS

Background Information of Respondents

The researcher was able to get general information from the respondents being surveyed:

- 57 percent respondents are male
- 43 percent respondents are female.
- 10% of respondents are Professors
- 12 % of respondents are Readers
- 13% of respondents are Lecturers
- 21 % of respondents are Research Scholars
- 19% of respondents are P.G Students..

ACCESS TO THE INTERNET

Respondents are asked to state whether they used the internet or not, aiming at determining their level of access to it. Among the respondents, 8 percent of respondents replied that they are not using the internet, while 92 percent responded that they are using the internet.

Those who replied that they did not use the internet are asked to give reasons for their non-use. The reasons given include:

- Computers are few, 2 percent of the respondents;
- Little or no skills, 3 percent of the respondents;
- Computers are slow, 2 percent of the respondents;
- Shortage of time, 1 percent of the respondents.

The Bharathiar University had plans to increase the ratio of computers as one computer per five respondents and to give training to all faculty and students.

POINTS OF ACCESS

The findings of the study revealed that

- Most respondents (71 percent) accessed the internet from computer center and department
- The university library (22 percent)

All the internet access points observed (Computer center and Department) did not charge the students any fee, but would normally require a computer occupant to vacate after a specified period of time had elapsed if there are other students waiting to access the internet

EXPERIENCE OF INTERNET USE

The findings of the study revealed:

- 18 percent of the respondents had been using it for more than two years.
- 25 percent of the respondents who reported using it

for less than two years.

- 22 percent of the respondents for one year.
- 10 percent of the respondents for less than one year.

TIME SPENT ON ONE INTERNET SESSION

The findings of the study revealed:

41% of the respondents spend 1 hour for internet, 26% more than one hour, 13% more than two hours, 9% more than 4 hours, 7% more than three hours and 5% more than 5 hours.

MODE OF IMPARTING SKILLS

Skills are a pre-requisite to effectively use the internet and therefore students are required to state how they acquired their internet skills. The findings revealed:

- That most respondents acquired their Internet skills through teaching by friends and self-teaching
- Only 5 percent of the respondents had acquired their skills through library orientation
- 23 percent through reading of journals
- 18 percent through attending a course

USE OF INTERNET FACILITIES

The findings of the study revealed:

- 32 percent, used the Internet for communication purposes, e-mail;
- 18 percent reported using it to browse the World Wide Web (WWW);
- 25 percent reported using it to access online journals.

Their use of it for information retrieval was thus very limited. This finding is supported by studies conducted by a number of respondents, who found out that respondents used the internet mainly for communication purposes, that is e-mail, than for information retrieval. The possible reason for this could be respondents lack of relevant search skills. Respondents are also required to elaborate on their use of e-mail and the WWW to determine whether their use of these facilities are for academic purposes or not. The findings of the study on their use of the WWW revealed:

- 21 percent of the respondents used the WWW to gather academic materials
- 19 percent of the respondents used the WWW for general browsing
- 19 percent of the respondents reported using the WWW for entertainment and sports
- 17 percent to access news
- 24 percent for e-mail

METHODS USED TO LOCATE INFORMATION

Findings of the study revealed that most of the respondents used search engines more than subject gateways or web directories in order to locate information on the internet. Further elaboration about their favourite search engines revealed that most students preferred using Google (56 percent) and Yahoo! (44 percent) in locating information on the web.

FACTORS THAT HAMPER EFFECTIVE USE OF THE INTERNET AND REMEDIAL MEASURES

Regarding factors that hamper effective use of the internet, the majority of respondents listed:

- inadequate computers with internet facilities (65 percent);
- slow internet connection (18 percent);
- lack of skills (12 percent)
- frequent power cuts (5 percent).

The inadequacy of computers with internet facilities is attributable to budgetary constraints, as stated earlier. Slow internet connection has also been reported by a number of scholars.

CONCLUSIONS

Findings of the study have revealed that many respondents are using the internet, and the reasons given for this study are, teaching purpose, research purpose, communication (e-mail) and other purpose. Many students have opportunity to avail themselves of the many resources on the Internet that could benefit them academically, such as up-to-dating information.

It was also revealed that most respondents used the internet for academic purposes. There is need therefore to make arrangements so that respondents may have more opportunities to learn about the internet. They should be made more aware of the many resources on the internet that can benefit them academically. Lecturers should also encourage their respondents to use internet.

Respondents also listed factors that hampered their effective use of the internet and these included, inadequate computers with internet facilities, slow internet connection, lack of skills and frequent power cuts. Suggestions and comments from respondents are also given, and some of them are increasing the number of computers connected to the internet, increasing the number of access points, as well as provision of training in internet use.

RECOMMENDATIONS

Recommendations by Most Respondents Include

- increasing the number of computers connected to the internet (62 percent);

- increasing the number of access points (12 percent);
- increasing speed of the internet (26 percent);

Based on the findings, a number of issues have to be addressed so that students may avail themselves of the benefits of the internet. To start with, more computers with internet facilities should be provided in order to increase students' level of access. The computers provided should be up-to-date models recognizing that they will perform better and faster. Increasing connectivity and speed will drive usage to higher levels. The speed of the internet should be increased. Higher bandwidth should be sought so as to provide faster access that will save much of the users' time and be a source of motivation to use the internet. Maintenance of computers should also be done more regularly.

Students should be provided with more chances of formal training in order to acquire skills on effective internet use. Training should also be provided to academic and other members of staff. Constant availability of power should be guaranteed. Standby generators, as well as Uninterrupted Power Supply (UPSs) should be provided to those access points that do not have these facilities.

Negative attitudes as well as conservatism act as barriers to effective internet use. These should be changed through awareness raising programmes that will impart an understanding of the internet's role in learning.

REFERENCES

* **DELNET:** Developing library network – 2002
* **Jawahar and Varatharj,** "Use of the internet for reference services in Indian academic libraries", *Online information review*, Vol.23,No.5,2001, pp.380-387.
* **Kaliammal, A and SARASVADY, S.** "Significance of information and communication Technologies in the New NAAC standards for University libraries", *University news*, March 19 - 25, 2007.

- http://*www.b-u.ac.in*
- http://www. Google.com
- http://www. Emeraldinsight.com
- http://www. Ebsco.com

C-14
Digital Libraries:
An Overview

S. Mathurajothi
Assistant Librarian(Sl.Gr), Dr. Ramachandra Library, Ganhigram Rural University, Gandhigram- 624 302 Dindigul Dt

ABSTRACT

Digital libraries are heterogeneous nature with hardcopies to online data bases. DL calls for advanced information technology. The paper deals with components, characteristics, technical requirements and practical difficulties of digitization process and issues related with digitization

INTRODUCTION

The digital revolution has altered the way societies function at the global, local and personal level. In this revolution, we have seen certain changes in information field, especially in relation to collection, storing processing and transmitting of information. These changes have resulted into the evolution of libraries into digital. Digital library involves the applications such as content development, technology management, indexing and linking in an integral way. It has changed the way we perceive and disseminate information and has even threatened the traditional library approaches. The impact of such technologies has led to a paperless society. It is possible now to digitize and store information in the form of high quality graphics, network texts, color images, voice signals and video clips at a relatively affordable cost.

DIGITAL LIBRARY : DEFINITION

The term "Digital Library" in a broad sense is a computerized system that allows obtaining a coherent means of access to an organized, electronically stored repository of information and data. The information resources available in the form of digital or electronic format are known as digital resources.

There are many definitions of digital library concept. Terms such as electronic library and virtual library are often used synonymously. The elements that have been identified as common to these definitions are:

- The Digital library is not a single entity.
- The digital library requires technology to link the resources of many.
- The linkage between many digital libraries and information services are transparent to the end users.
- Universal access to digital libraries and information services is a goal.
- Digital library collections are not limited to document surrogates, they extend to digital artifacts that cannot be represented or distributed by printed formats.

CHARACTERISTICS OF DIGITAL LIBRARY

Digital library resources are in electronic formats. They may include:

- Converted materials from printed works.
- Original electronic publications.
- Resources in a wide variety of types such as reference works, visual materials, sound recordings, moving pictures

FUNCTIONS OF DIGITAL LIBRARY

The most important functions of digital libraries are:

- To provide friendly interface to users.
- To avail network facilities.
- To enhance advanced search, access and retrieval of information.
- To improve the library operations.

REQUIREMENTS OF DIGITAL LIBRARIES

Digital library requires well tested and proven information technologies including the multimedia kit. Much of the work in digital libraries is achieved through e-mail service, by participating in usernet(s), by accessing the databases or servers through networks, like Internet. Locally developed databases will contribute a lot to develop digital libraries. In other words, the components of digital libraries are:

- Local library system, with adequate PCs having LAN, local databases in machine-readable form. CD-ROMs etc,
- provision to provide – mail service, access to servers, and to remote databases etc.
- Networks, including the network of networks.
- A variety of system functions to coordinate, manage the entry and to retrieve data.
- Well- trained manpower.

NETWORK

Digital libraries operate and evolve in an electronic network environment. They can provide the hyperlinks. It also shares different libraries' information together. The networked communication enables the library to provide universal access, so that library users do not need to be physically presented in the library.

DIGITIZATION – DIFFICULTIES

There are several difficulties to be overcome by digitization programs. There is a vast amount of hard – copy material in existence. It is very difficult to scan all of them at a stroke. So strategic decisions must be made about what will and will not be digitized. It is a more time- consuming and resource intensive process to scan the selected materials. The scanned materials are often quite large computer files, which places heavy demands on technology capabilities and data storage requirements.

It is difficult to solve copyright problems. Even when permission can be obtained, licensing fees can be prohibitive, and the limitations placed on usage can be too restrictive to be practical. To convert the existing library and information systems into digital library system it is essential to plan it before a switch over.

CONVERSION OF EXISTING DATA AND DATABASE

The existing data in the form of text or reference material, back volumes of journals etc. need to be digitized with the help of digital scanners so that it could form a part of digital library collection This is not an easy job. So care should be taken to see the quantum of time and labour involved. It is therefore suggested that we must be very much selective in converting the existing data after assessing its value and obsolescence.

ISSUES

The dramatic growth of the Internet in recent years has accelerated the pace of change and the debate over the role and future of the information is intensified.

There are five areas that need addressing before the

electronic library can become a reality. They are:

a) Technical issues.

b) Legal issues

c) Economic issues

d) Psychological issues

e) Educational issues.

CONCLUSION

We need to understand how to preserve and safeguard digital material, so it doesn't become obsolete simply because we didn't pay attention. Finally, we need to strive for continued open access to all knowledge. Care should be taken while digitizing the materials because we have to overcome many issues and difficulties.

REFERENCES

* **T.Ashok Babu, T ....etal.** *Vision of future library and information systems,* Chennai : Viva Books private Ltd.,2000

* **Anandan, C and Gangatharan, M.** *Digital Libraries: From technology to culture,* New Delhi, Kaniska publishers distributors, 2006

* **Siddique, JA.** *Classification and cataloguing in Digital Libraries.* New Delhi : cyper Tech Publications, 2007

C-15
RFID: An Introduction to Rural LIS Professionals

N. Vasanthakumar
*Assistant Librarian, Thiagarajar School of Management (TSM),
Centre for Higher Learning, Thirupparankundram,
Madurai – 625 005*

P. Karuppusamy
*Assistant Librarian, The Standard Fireworks Raharatnam
College for Women, Sivakasi- 626 123*

ABSTRACT

The new technological development has occupied the libraries and information centers. In this technological revolution libraries have no other way than to adopt new technology in one form to other form. So we are in the position to implement the Radio Frequency Identifier (RFID) technology in libraries. RFID is a tool to help trace the materials, charging and discharging of library materials and mainly to prevent theft. Urban area LIS professionals are briefed about the RFID concepts through internet and other resources. Hence authors of this paper has given an outline of RFID like history, components, applications, advantages and disadvantages in implementing RFID in libraries to rural LIS professionals.

INTRODUCTION

RFID is describing a system that transmits the identity of an object wirelessly, using radio waves, short for Radio Frequency Identification, a technology similar in theory to bar code identification. With RFID, the electromagnetic or electrostatic coupling in the RF portion of the electromagnetic spectrum is used to transmit signals. An RFID system consists of an antenna and a transceiver, which read the radio frequency and transfer the information to a processing device and a transponder or tag, which is an integrated circuit containing the RF circuitry and information to be transmitted.

Now a day libraries do adopt RFID to increase efficiency and reduce cost. This technology helps librarians to reduce precious staff time spent on scanning barcodes while charging and discharging items. RFID is also called Dedicated Short Range Communication (DSRC)

WHAT IS RFID?

Radio Frequency IDentification (RFID) is a method of remotely storing and retrieving data using devices called RFID tags. An RFID tag is a small object, such as an adhesive sticker, that can be attached to or incorporated into a product. RFID tags contain antennae to enable them to receive and respond to radio-frequency queries from an RFID transceiver.

RFID TAG

(*Source*: Electronic Product Code RFID Tag used for Walmart)

HISTORY OF RFID

Although some people think that the first known device may have been invented by Leon Theremin as an espionage tool for the Russian Government in 1945, the first real usage of RFID devices predates that. During World War II the United Kingdom used RFID devices to distinguish returning English airplanes from inbound German ones. RADAR was only able to signal the presence of a plane, not the kind of plane it was.

COMPONENTS OF RFID

An RFID system consists of 3 components: *The tags, the reader/sensor gates and application/server/docking station*. In addition to that three optional components are available. i.e. Label printer, Handheld reader, External book return.

TAGS

It is also known as transponder. It consists of an antenna and silicon chip encapsulated in glass or plastic. It contains a very small amount of information. The heart of the system is the RFID tag, which can be fixed inside a book back or front cover or directly on CDs and other library materials. Tags range in size from the size of a grain of rice to 2 -inch square, depending on the application. Passive and active tags are available.

THE READER OR SENSOR GATES

Reader/Sensor gates are composed of radio frequency module, a control unit and an antenna to interrogate electronic tags via frequency communication. Readers can be handheld or mounted in strategic locations to ensure they can read the tags as the tags pass through an "interrogation zone". The interrogation zone is the area within which a reader can read the tag. The size of the interrogation zone varies depending on the type of tag and power of the reader. Passive tags with shorter read ranges tend to operate within a smaller interrogation zone. Reader system is normally installed in library exits. These are radio frequency devices designed to detect and read tags to obtain the information stored there in.

APPLICATION / SERVER / DOCKING STATION

This is the communication gateway among various components. It receives the information from one or more of the readers and exchange information with the circulation database. RFID exit sensor at exit look much like those installed in libraries for the last several decades however the insides are very different. One type reads the information on the tags going by and communicate that information to the server. The server after checking against the circulation database activates an alarm if the materials/documents are not properly checked out.

LIBRARY WITH RFID

A library uses RFID in various ways to manage the library resources and utilizes, this technology to streamline their inventory, check out and shelving process as well as for the document protection.

RFID technology is extremely useful for libraries in the following two ways. They are easy and accurate in circulation functions and security of library materials preventing them from leaving library premises in any unauthorized way.

RFID LIBRARY – READER'S USAGE

Conversion station, staff workstation at circulation, self-check in/out station, exit sensors, book-drop reader, sorter & conveyor and hand-held reader/portable reader.

RFID ADVANTAGES IN LIBRARY

- Better Reader/User service
- Misplaced documents can be traced
- Self charging or discharging, reliability, long life tags
- Labels can be applied easily to different types of library collections
- Automated book return system allowed
- Prevents media thefts and losses
- Easy integration into existing library circulation software.
- Simultaneous check in / check out of more than one document is possible.
- Increased operational efficiency
- Not necessary to continue barcode.

DISADVANTAGES

- High Cost
- Chances of removal of exposed tags
- Exit gate sensor problems
- Reader collision
- Tag collision
- Lack of standard

CONCLUSION

Libraries started using RFID systems to replace bar code systems in late 1990's. Today more than 130 libraries are using RFID systems in North America alone. The Cost of passive type RFID tags is tumbling day by day. Currently the low end RFID tag is costing about ~13 cents (~Rs. 6.00) only. Hence large number of libraries around the world is looking for RFID deployment.

In a nutshell, to enhance the work flow of a complete

management of any reasonably big libraries, one has to deploy RFID based systems. The full RFID deployment will increase the efficiency and customer satisfaction. Even though the investment is huge, it is likely to become reality soon. RFID is emerging as a good way to improve automation and security in library.

REFERENCES

* http://en.wikipedia.org/wiki/Radio-frequency_identification Visited on 24/8/07

* http://www.webopedia.com visited on 24/8/07

* http://www.manh.com visited on 27/8/07

C-16
Use of Online Public Access Catalogue (OPAC) in School of Management Library, Bharathiar University: A Case Study

M. Mariraj
Assistant Technical Officer, School of Management,
Bharathiar University, Coimbatore-46.

A. Robert William
M. Phil Research Scholar, Alagappa University, Karaikudi.

ABSTRACT

*OPAC stands for **online public access catalogue**. It is a library catalogue accessed via a computer terminal for the benefit of library users. A OPAC provides users on line access to the library's catalogue allowing them to search and retrieve records from the online catalogue and depending on the underlying library management software it also offers other facilities such as online reservation, borrower status checking and so on. With the advent* *of the Internet and more recently with the World Wide Web (www) many library OPACs can now be searched by remote users anywhere in the world, who have an access to the Internet. This paper makes an attempt to survey the utility of the OPAC in the school.*

INTRODUCTION

The introduction of OPACs has created enormous changes in the library practices. Further more, it has made the library files easily accessible to everyone by breaking the physical boundaries of the library itself.

The present study focuses on the use of online public access catalogue in School of Management Library, Bharathiar University by the MBA Students, in which attempts have been made to know the information requirements of students and how these are met satisfactorily. The main focus of this study is to describe the needs and requirements in general and analyse the use of Online Public Access Catalogue (OPAC) in School of Management Library, Bharathiar University by the MBA Students in particular.

PROFILE OF BSMED

BSMED has started its operations form October 24, 1984 MBA was started by admitting 35 students into the pogramme. During the year the department received a donation of Rs. 15 lakhs from LMW for the purpose of research. In 1985 the department., started offering Ph.D programme Specialized Management programmes for the practicing managers were also offered by the department. M.Phil course was introduced in the year 1989 – 90. During the year of 1987 BSMED received a grant of Rs. 1.75 crors from UGC under the special Assistance Programme.

A seminar hall with state of the art facilities such as video conferencing and two class rooms (Smart classrooms) with the provision of advanced electronic teaching aids to provide the best possible management education were made available.

A separate department library hosting more than 5000 books and 30 journals, magazines, reports and video is available. This is in addition to the books (10000 numbers) available in the university main library. The library is also offering some of the advanced search facilities like INFLIBNET and online database like CMIE provide the services to the researchers and students. Printing facility is also available inside the library.

OPAC

OPAC facilitates retrieval of books' details and availability of books and users details. OPAC facilities are also included in the homepage. For the security purpose, OPAC has been developed in Java and VB with options such as search, User ID and User History. The resource 'search' means to search 'document' from the selected resources namely books, CDs, periodicals and also search by author, title, etc. User ID searches help to know the resources taken by the user. User history shows details of borrowed books and other resources from the library with full details.

OBJECTIVES OF THE STUDY

The study was designed mainly to identify and evaluate the users'

- Frequency of visit to School of Management Library, instruction received and the sources of such instruction in the use of OPAC;
- Students approaches to and the purpose of consulting the OPAC;
- Use of OPAC and the difficulties faced in using them;
- Usefulness of library staff in providing the assistance for the use of OPAC

- Opinion(s) of students regarding the up-to-date ness, the location, need for user orientation and lectures.

METHODOLOGY

The primary aim of any research is to discover the methods and principles that are universal in their application. A survey of the use of OPAC in School of Management, Bharathiar University by the MBA Students, was carried out during the 2007 – 2008s academic sessions using a questionnaire. Specially designed questionnaire, was randomly distributed to 50 MBA students of the library, Out of 50 questionnaires, 35 were received back from the respondents. The questionnaire sought information on the state of automation, use of the OPAC, problems identified by users militating against the use of OPAC and comments on ways of improving the use of OPAC as an information retrieval tool.

The profile of the respondents is shown in the table

DISTRIBUTION OF GENDER OF RESPONDENTS

Sl.No.	Gender	No. of Respondents	Percentage
1	Male	20	57
2	Female	15	43
	Total	35	100

It is found that 57 percent of the respondents were male and 43 percent of the respondents were female.

FREQUENCY OF USE IN OPAC

Frequency of use	No. of Respondents	Percentage
a. Daily	10	29
b. Once in two days	10	29
c. Once in three days	6	17

d.	Once in Four days	5	14
e.	Once in a week	4	11
Total		35	100

The above table shows that 29 percent of the respondents use the OPAC daily, 29 percent of the respondents once in two days, 17 percent of the respondents once in three days, 14 percent of the respondents use at once in four days and 11 percent of the respondents use it once in a week.

THE RESPONDENTS APPROACHES TO OPAC

Sl.No	Access Points	No. of Respondents	Percentage
1	By author	12	34
2	By title	15	43
3	By subject	8	23
	Total	35	100

Whenever the students want to confirm about the existence of a required document in the stock of the library, they can approach the OPAC through author, title, and subject.

The above table shows that 34 percent of the respondents approach the OPAC by author, 43 percent of the users approach the OPAC under the title and 23 percent of the respondents approach the OPAC by subject wise.

THE PURPOSE OF CONSULTING THE OPAC

Sl.No	Purpose	No. of Respondents	Percentage
1	To check whether the required book is available in the library or not.	8	23
2	To check the number of copies of the required book in the stock	7	20

3	To locate the book in the library	9	26
4	To find the bibliographical detail.	5	14
5	To compile bibliography of books on a particular subject	4	11
6	Any other	2	6
	Total	35	100

Another specific question raised was to know the purposes of consulting the OPAC. Results are given in table 4. 26 percent of the respondents to locate the books in the library, 23 percent of the respondents to check whether the required book is available in the library or not, 20 percent of the respondents to check the number of copies of the required book in the stock, 14 percent of the respondents to find the bibliographical details, 11 percent of the respondents to compile bibliography of books on a particular subject and 6 percent of the respondents for others purposes.

OPINION OF THE RESPONDENTS

Some of the open questions were asked to know the opinion of the respondents to obtain much more information from the students related to use of OPAC for various other purposes. The respondents are making use of the OPAC for the following purposes

- To find out particular articles in journals.
- To check the copies of available reading materials.
- To collect literature for seminars, thesis, etc.
- For review of literature.
- To know the arrival of new journals and other reading materials.

In this modern world there is no human activity where the computers are not playing their role. The libraries are not an exception to this where the role of computers in collecting, organizing, storing, retrieving and disseminating the great volume and the varied form of information with great speed and accuracy, is indispensable. A lively functioning computer in the library gives the modern look to the library itself. Most of the activities in the libraries can be computerized, including the OPAC.

The School of Management Library acquired a OPAC, in view of this. The students were asked to give their opinions.

- It saves the time and gives quick accurate and efficient information.
- It is easy to search.
- It is easy to locate
- Retrieving of required information is at a much faster rate.
- Without wasting much time we can find the required book.

The respondents in favour of it have suggested the authorities to provide training in the use of OPAC.

The students' opinion about their use of OPAC are:

"It is very good, fully satisfying well organized.

The students were also asked to give their suggestions for the improvement of the OPAC."

CONCLUSION

A key characteristics of the information age today is the growth of information services of various kinds, the advent of the computing age, as well as increasing awareness of the value of information in personal, organisational and national activities, to promote the development and growth of diverse new information services based on modern information and communication technologies.

The online catalogue is not only an instrument of change in today's libraries, it is also ever changeable. Automated library systems in general and specifically on line catalogues will continue to be produced and enhanced from a variety of sources; in-house development, library consortia and commercial firms. This will result in a diversity of online catalogues for some time to come.

Librarians must continue to play the role as an agent of change for the online catalogue. But this will require that they make efforts to learn about the potential of online retrieval, catalogue access issues that cannot be couched in the familiar terms of card catalogue use and user-system interface problems.

The use of OPAC by students has increased their information retrieval rate especially in the location of books and other reading materials in the library. This is evident from the fact that all the respondents are satisfied with their search outputs.

The study also reveals that the major access point used in retrieval of information on the OPAC is the author, it can be said that the non satisfaction of some students may not be unconnected with their inability to use the appropriate search terms on the OPAC.

In order to meet the challenges of the new millennium, without wasting further time, it is recommended that all the academic libraries in the country must reintroduce and upgrade their information technology and computerized systems to render better services to the library clientele.

REFERENCES

* Varghese, M, "Subject search and Retrieval in online public access catalogues: A review of literature", *Kelpro Bulletin*, vol.1(1), June 1997, pp. 54 - 68.

* Oduwole, AA, Oyesiku, FA and Labulo, AA. "Online Public Access Catalogue (OPAC) use in Nigerian Academic Libraries: A case Study from the University of Agriculture, Abeskuta". *Library Herald*, 40(1), 2002, pp. 20 - 28.

* http://www.bsmed.net

* **http://www.emeraldinsight.com**

C-17

Role of Digital Libraries in Open and Distance Education in Agriculture

M. Sankar
Assistant Librarian, Tamil Nadu Agricultural
University AC & RI, Madurai-625 104

V.T. Mani
Library, Tamil Nadu Agricultural University,
AC & RI, Madurai -625 104

ABSTRACT

The improvements in communications and information networks have made remarkable progress over the last two decades and has now gained widespread acceptance as a viable alternative delivery system and alternative to the conventional system. Information Technology can be used both for instruction and document delivery. Distance Education in Agriculture is gaining momentum to cater to the needs of the vast majority of the farmers and other rural people who constitute about 75 per cent of the total population in India. Digital Libraries with various technologies namely audio, video, computer, internet, multimedia, satellites, TV, Cable

TV, interactive video, electronic transmissions via telephone lines, postal service etc. greatly support the Distance Education.

INTRODUCTION

Learning nowadays is becoming a life long process. Teaching and learning are no longer confined to the classroom or the school day. Distance education (DE) has been in existence for more than a century. Until recently, many people regarded DE as unconventional and a peripheral function and the sheer distance between teachers and students, rendered teaching and learning not only inefficient but also ineffective. The improvements in communications and information networks have demolished the barriers of physical distance and other inherent shortcomings affiliated with DE. DE has made remarkable progress over the last two decades and has now gained widespread acceptance as a viable alternative delivery system and alternative to the conventional system. Further, the use of information technology (IT) is giving this system an edge over the conventional system. Information technology can be used both for instruction and document delivery and libraries play a vital role in this context. The rapid expansion of IT, computer literacy and access to the internet offers immense opportunities for online delivery of DE and training. The real-time web-based courses are a matter of reality on the internet and the virtual university is no longer a fiction. The objective of the paper is to provide an overview of the Role of Digital Libraries in Open Learning and Distance Education in Agriculture.

ROLE OF DIGITAL LIBRARIES

Distance education can be defined broadly as: Any educational or learning process or system in that the teacher and instructor are separated geographically or in time from his or her students; or in that students are separated from other students or educational resources; the learning is effected through the implementation of information and communication technologies to connect teacher and student in either real or delayed time or on need basis; and the content delivery may be achieved by integrating various technologies, including audio, video, computer, internet, multimedia, satellites, TV, cable TV, interactive video, electronic transmissions via telephone lines, postal service, etc. DE is a modality consisting of a broad, mixed, category of methods to deliver learning.

A digital library can link e-learners to library catalogues, licensed journal databases, electronic book collections, selected internet resources, electronic course reserves tutorials and to forums for communication and interaction with others. The digital library permits e-learners to access library and networked resources and services anytime and anywhere, where an Internet connection and computing equipment are available.

The digital library serves mainly as a facilitator in organizing and providing knowledge and resources to its users. Sharing knowledge and information among library staff, researchers, faculty, students and other departments within the institution encourage them to work together, develop their skills and form strong and trusting relationships. A focus on collaboration between the library and the faculty promotes a responsive approach to course design and supports teaching and learning objectives, particularly when this collaboration incorporates student contributions and feedback. All parties must have a common vision in which each one participates actively by contributing their skills and perspectives to the building of a genuine partnership. This new approach considers the library as an active partner of the learning community, helping learners to become "information literates" by integrating information literacy skills into the curriculum.(Sharifabadi, 2006)

SPECTRUM OF DIGITAL LIBRARIES

Technology	Characteristics	Notable features
Print	Readily available, materials in expensive, portable and for high comfort level	Requires reading skills, nointeractions, limited sensory involvement and time delay
Audio tape	Audio learning tool, very mobile, easily accessible and duplicated and inexpensive when compared with print materials	Useful in language learning and practice as well as literature. Linear format with no visual cues and interaction
Video tape	Visual and audio tool, easily accessible and duplicated	Multi-sensory tool with linear delivery format. Complex to record with no interaction and requires hardware
Laptop computer checkout	Versatile approach to provide a wide range of learning activities from skill and drill to simulations	Hardware is expensive and being replaced by less expensive internet delivery
Mobile van/ lab	Resources taken to the learners, useful for work site learning	Useful way to distribute videos, audio tapes and other learning tools
Radio course	A low cost way to reach learners and should be used by more learning providers	Model must include ways for learners to interact with the instructor. Phone call during or after air time could be integrated into the programming
Telecourse	Delivery over TV, usually a cable public access channel or school owned channel	Model must include ways for learners to interact with the instructor. Print materials accompany on-air Instruction
Audio conference	Inexpensive and easy to set up	No visual cues and interaction; requires hardware
Teleconference- two way inter- active video	Electronic communications among people at separate locations. It can be audio, audio graphic, video or computer based	Often uses proprietary software and consequently expensive. Internet models, broadband communications will make it more affordable and accessible
Satellite video conference	High realism	Expensive hardware and must be scheduled. Usually one-

		way only
Microwave videoconference	High realism, may be interactive and relatively inexpensive	Limited coverage and must be scheduled
Cable / broadcast TV	Easy to use and accessible; may be video taped and includes audio and visual	High production costs and must be scheduled; requires hardware and no interaction
E-mail	Asynchronous text files and attachments; flexible, interactive and convenient	Good tool to stimulate learning, writing and communications skills. Requires hardware and software variations
Voice mail	Low cost, easy to use and increases interactions	Length may be limited, no visual cues and may involve toll charges
Internet/ web based	Instruction delivery over the internet, either learning modules or entire courses; incorporates multimedia, worldwide access and interactive	Improved broadband communications will enable the effective use of video and communications. Requires computer and web access
Online chat	Real-time interactions and instant feedback	Requires similar software and must be scheduled; requires hardware

(**Source**: Rao 2001)

OPEN AND DISTANCE LEARNING IN AGRICULTURE

The Tamil Nadu Agricultural University, Coimbatore started Open and Distance Learning which is first of its kind in India, among State Agricultural Universities. This Directorate concentrates its efforts on Distance Education in addition to non-formal and continuing education. The Directorate of Open and Distance Learning, one of the constituent units of the TNAU was started during April, 2005 by renaming the Directorate of Publications. This Directorate has started offering certificate courses, PG Diploma and PG Degree courses through Distance Learning Mode with following objectives

- To promote entrepreneurial skills among learners

- To offer continuing Professional Education
- To offer Development Extension Education to farming community, unemployment youths, school dropouts etc.
- To provide opportunities through Open and Distance Learning for Life Learning among the clients.

CONCLUSION

Digital library services are an essential component of a quality e-learning system in Agriculture. As access to internet-based courses grows, an increasing number of e-learners are dispersed around the globe, often in parts of the world where physical access to the collections of large academic and research libraries is impossible. These learners are largely dependent on the quality and academic usefulness of services in Agriculture that the digital library can offer electronically. The strength of digital libraries and digital collections depends on the relationships libraries develop and maintain with the creators, publishers and aggregators of e-resources in agriculture as well as with those who use, learn from and evaluate these resources. Providing ongoing technical, reference and instructional support to e-learners requires that libraries redefine their values and services, collaborate with their users and approach their tasks creatively.

REFERENCES

* **Siriginidi Subba Rao**. " Distance Education and the Role of IT in India" , *The Electronic Library,* Vol.24(2) 2006. pp.225-236

* **Sharifabadi, Saeed Rezaei.** " How digital libraries can support e- learning". *The Electronic Library*, Vol.24 (3), 2006. pp.389-401

* **Rao, S.S.** " Networking of Libraries and Information Centre: Challenges in India", *Library Hi Tech*, Vol.19 (2), 2001 pp. 167-178

* http://www.tnau.ac.in

C-18
Web Archiving

M. Dorairajan
Librarian, St.Joseph's College, Tiruchirappalli-2

P. Raghavan
Librarian, National College, Tiruchirappalli

M. Kodeeswari
*Librarian, Swami Dayananda College of
Arts & Science, Thiruvarur*

ABSTRACT

*Web archiving is the process of collecting the Web or
particular portions of the Web and ensuring that the
collection is preserved in an archive, such as an
archive site, for future researchers, historians and
the public. Due to the massive size of the Web, web
archivists typically employ web crawlers for
automated collection.*

INTRODUCTION

Web archiving is the process of collecting the Web or
particular portions of the Web and ensuring that the
collection is preserved in an archive, such as an archive site,
for future researchers, historians, and the public. Due to the
massive size of the Web, web archivists typically employ web
crawlers for automated collection. The largest web archiving
organization based on a crawling approach is the Internet
Archive which strives to maintain an archive of the entire
Web. National libraries, national archives and various

consortia of organizations are also involved in archiving culturally important Web content.

COLLECTING THE WEB

Web archivists generally archive all types of web content including HTML web pages, style sheets, JavaScript, images, and video. They also archive metadata about the collected resources such as access time, MIME type and content length. This metadata is useful in establishing authenticity and permanence of the archived collection.

METHODS OF COLLECTION REMOTE HARVESTING

The most common web archiving technique uses web crawlers to automate the process of collecting web pages. Web crawlers typically view web pages in the same manner that users with a browser see the Web and therefore provide a comparatively simple method of remotely harvesting web content.

Examples of web crawlers frequently used for web archiving include:

- Heritrix
- HTTrack
- Offline Explorer

On-demand

There are numerous services that may be used to archive web resources "on-demand", using web crawling techniques:

- WebCite, a service specifically for scholarly authors, journal editors and publishers to permanently archive and retrieve cited Internet references (Eysenbach and Trudel, 2005).
- Archive-It, a subscription service, allows institutions

    to build, manage and search their own web archive

- hanzo:web is a personal web archiving service created by Hanzo Archives that can archive a single web resource, a cluster of web resources or an entire website, as a one-off collection, scheduled/repeated collection, an RSS/Atom feed collection or collect on-demand via Hanzo's open API.

- Spurl.net is a free on-line bookmarking service and search engine that allows users to save important web resources.

DATABASE ARCHIVING

Database archiving refers to methods for archiving the underlying content of database-driven websites. It typically requires the extraction of the database content into a standard schema, often using XML. Once stored in that standard format, the archived content of multiple databases can then be made available using a single access system.

This approach is exemplified by the DeepArc and Xinq tools developed by the Bibliothèque nationale de France and the National Library of Australia respectively. DeepArc enables the structure of a relational database to be mapped to an XML schema, and the content exported into an XML document. Xinq then allows that content to be delivered online. Although the original layout and behavior of the website cannot be preserved exactly, Xinq does allow the basic querying and retrieval functionality to be replicated.

TRANSACTIONAL ARCHIVING

Transactional archiving is an event-driven approach, which collects the actual transactions which take place between a web server and a web browser. It is primarily used as a means of preserving evidence of the content which was actually viewed on a particular website, on a given date. This may be particularly important for organizations which need to comply with legal or regulatory requirements for disclosing and retaining information.

A transactional archiving system typically operates by intercepting every HTTP request to and response from the web server, filtering each response to eliminate duplicate content and permanently storing the responses as bitstreams. A transactional archiving system requires the installation of software on the web server and cannot therefore be used to collect content from a remote website.

Examples of commercial transactional archiving software include:

- PageVault
- Vignette WebCapture

DIFFICULTIES AND LIMITATIONS OF CRAWLERS

Web archives which rely on web crawling as their primary means of collecting the Web are influenced by the difficulties of web crawling:

- The robots exclusion protocol may request crawlers not to access portions of a website. Some web archivists may ignore the request and crawl those portions anyway.

- Large portions of a web site may be hidden in the Deep Web. For example, the results page behind a web form lies in the deep web because a crawler cannot follow a link to the results page.

- Some web servers may return a different page for a web crawler than it would for a regular browser request. This is typically done to fool search engines into sending more traffic to a website.

- Crawler traps (e.g., calendars) may cause a crawler to download an infinite number of pages, so crawlers are usually configured to limit the number of dynamic pages they crawl.

The Web is so large that crawling a significant portion of it takes a large amount of technical resources. The Web is changing so fast that portions of a website may change before a crawler has even finished crawling it.

GENERAL LIMITATIONS

Not only must web archivists deal with the technical challenges of web archiving, they must also contend with intellectual property laws. Peter Lyman (2002) states that "although the Web is popularly regarded as a public domain resource, it is copyrighted; thus, archivists have no legal right to copy the Web." Some web archives that are made publicly accessible like WebCite's or the Internet Archive's allow content owners to hide or remove archived content that they do not want the public to have access to. Other web archives are only accessible from certain locations or have regulated usage. WebCite also cites on its FAQ a recent lawsuit against the caching mechanism, which Google won.

REFERENCES

* Brown, A. (2006). Archiving Websites: a practical guide for information management professionals. Facet Publishing. ISBN 1-85604-553-6.

* Brügger, N. (2005). Archiving Websites. General Considerations and Strategies. The Centre for Internet Research. ISBN 87-990507-0-6.

* Day, M. (2003). "Preserving the Fabric of Our Lives: A Survey of Web Preservation Initiatives". Research and Advanced Technology for Digital Libraries: Proceedings of the 7th European Conference (ECDL): 461-472.

* Eysenbach, G. and Trudel, M. (2005). "Going, going, still there: using the WebCite service to permanently archive cited web pages". Journal of Medical Internet Research 7 (5).

* Fitch, Kent (2003). "Web site archiving - an approach to recording every materially different response produced by a website". Ausweb 03.

C-19
Computer Application in College Libraries

P. Muthumari
Librarian, G.S.A. College, Rajagambeeram,
Manamaduari – 630 606

ABSTRACT

The technique of making an apparatus or a process of a system automatically is called as automation. Automating all the libraries house keeping operations with the use of soft ware application in networked environment with many computers for effective information processing and retrieval is library automation. In modern times, the face of library automation has drastically changed by incorporating more services and web based applications. The author discusses the need, customization and various modules of library automation.

INTRODUCTION

The publication of information sources are very high and are increasing day by day. Manually maintaining these sources is a very difficult task for librarian and library staff. So we need a system to maintain this source successfully. Manual maintenance involving all routines in library consume more time.

AUTOMATION

Definition of Automation

(According to Webster's dictionary)

1. "The technique of making an apparatus of a process or a system automatically"
2. "Automatic control of an apparatus process / or system by mechanical and electronic devices that take place in the human organs of observation / effort or decision".

NEED FOR AUTOMATION

Libraries or information centers serve their users for their requirement. In college libraries various information sources are available. So librarian or library staff carry all the routine work in library manually which is not possible. Hence computer is essential to support their work.

AREAS OF APPLICATION

In library we can use computer for all the functional areas. E.g. acquisition, circulation, stock, budget, library staffs details and so on.

ACQUISITION

Acquisition includes purchase of books, journals, serials and non-book materials like CD, microfilm, microfiche and so on. Before purchasing any materials for library we consider the quality and necessity of the source. Suppose the materials are not available in library they may or may not be purchased depending upon the requirement of sources. Manually finding out whether the source in available or not available in library is not easy, it takes some hours. If we entered all the books and other sources in a computer, we will get the result within few seconds.

FILES

In this area we maintain some files for our purpose.

ORDER FILE

It contains details of vendor or book seller, ordering date, ordering items and so on.

RENEWAL FILE

It contains information about the particulars of serials and journals, vendor, journal / serial ordered data, title, price and subscription date.

REMAINDER FILE

It contains the details about the received issues of serials / journals. When we do not receive serials / journals a remainder is sent to vendor. So we keep the remainder data. These files support the acquisition work.

STOCK FILE

It contains details about updated sources in the library.

CIRCULATION

Circulation is a very important work in all libraries. Librarian or library staff give careful attention in this work, because issue and return of books or any other sources from library is an important job. When we do circulation work we may wrongly enter the accession number that will create some confusion.

FILES

Some files are maintained to do the circulation work easily.

STUDENT FILE

It contains details about student name, branch, year, date of joining and token number.

ISSUE FILE

It contains details of token number, student or staff name, title, author, accession number and data of issue

RETURN / RENEWAL FILE

It contains details about token number, student / staff name, title, accession number, author, date of issue, and date of renewal or date of return. These files support the circulation work easily.

CONCLUSION

Now a days information sources are published in various forms like CD, video, audio material films, microfiches and so on. Handling these kinds of sources is a difficult task for librarian and library staff. Because not only there is increase of sources but also increase in the number of users. Librarian or library staff must have the potential for administration of sources and users simultaneously.

REFERENCES

* **Balakrishnan, Shyama and Paliwal, PK.** Automated libraries. New Delhi : Anmol, 2001

* **Balakrishnan, Shyama and Paliwal, PK.** Library automation, New Delhi : Anmol, 2001

* **Chauhan, Sachin.** *Administration of libraries.* New Delhi : Mohit Publications, 2004

C-20
Digital Library : An Overview

K. Sekar
Librarina, Tamil Nadu College of Engineering, Coimbatore.

S. Venkatesh
Assistant Librarian, PSG College of Technology, Coimbatore.

R. Radha
Librarina, Tamil Nadu College of Engineering, Coimbatore.

ABSTRACT

In the modern complex and corporate world everyone need quality information within the shortest time. Digital Library provides almost all information required by the user. This paper gives an over view of digital library. The author explains about the component and technical requirements for the digital library. And also this paper explains the definition, objectives, needs, features, hardware and software requirements, digital publication, advantages, limitations of the digital library and so on.

INTRODUCTION

The term digital library is vast, covers many and different applications and has been used interchangeably for systems, like digitized collections, e-journals platforms, network databases, library websites, etc. Moreover the current electronic publishing business models enrich the DL technology aiming to provide powerful information access options to the users.

Nowadays it is possible to get required information (text, images, reports, graphics) from anywhere in the world at any time through internet and computers. Number of books, Journals, articles and lots of information are available on the net free of cost. We can download and modify the information as per the needs and requirements. We need not go to information center. We can get information in our place through Internet. Digital Library is the outcome of information explosion.

DEFINITION

Digital Library could be referred to as computerized network system where all the information is stored in electronic format, which can be accessed and transmitted through networks enabling retrieval of desired information by a large number of users.

Digital Library is an organization containing electronic documents, computers, networks, Internet connection, Scanner and Digital camera, collection of information that is stored and accessed electronically. The user is able to consult materials that are stored on computers around the world. Digital Libraries are heterogeneous, multimedia and data retrievable and are aided by hypermedia and hypertext programs and experimental expert systems.

There are number of terms to represent the concept of digital library as Polyglot Library, electronic library, desktop library, online library, library without walls, virtual library, etc. Of these, the digital library is the commonly used terminology by majority of authors.

Digital Libraries are heterogeneous in nature. These include work related to information and how to digitize, store, find, link, visualise, use, manage and share information.

OBJECTIVES

To promote the facilities for all (multi-users), to access library collection.

To provide new means of exploring and accessing reading materials created and produced in variety of fields of knowledge and from different places, but will be accessed as a single entity. The digitised information will be organised, categorised, or indexed for easier access to user. The information should be stored and maintained to ensure its availability after a long period.

NEED

The trend of globalization and free marketing increases global competition in all fields and also it increases fast development in the knowledge industry and human resource development.

Within the next decade, most of the information output created in our society will be made and communicated only electronically. For e.g. more than 90% of newsletters, 15% of reports, 10% books and 10% journals are available only in web. If we fail in exploiting the digital contents, we will be left out in the information world.

COMPONENTS OF DIGITAL LIBRARY

The following components are required for digital Library:

Local Library system with adequate PCs having LAN, local database in machine-readable form, CD-ROM, provision to provide e-mail services, access to services and to remote database.

Networks including the network of networks

Digital Scanner

A variety of system functions to co-ordinate, manage the entry and to retrieve data and well – trained manpower.

THE FEATURES OF DIGITAL LIBRARY

- Access to very large information collection
- Network accessibility
- Provide user friendly interface
- Unique referencing of digital objects
- Use declarative representation of documents (e.g. tagged SGML,text), in addition or as against image, post scripts, etc. forms.
- Clearly separate the digital library and the user interface by employing client-server architecture.
- Support advanced search and retrieval
- Available for a long time
- Support traditional library missions of collection development, organisation, access and preservation.
- Integrate personal, group, enterprise, and public digital libraries.
- Support publishing, annotation and integration of new information.

HARDWARE AND SOFTWARE REQUIREMENTS

- High bandwidth computer networks supporting efficient multimedia document transfer.
- Open communication protocols (client-server, e.g. 39,50 for IR)
- Information access tools (browse, display and search tools).
- Meta databases (databases that describe and provide links to other databases /Information Sources)

- Electronic publishing tools (personal, institutional, publisher)

  Digital storage

  Data compression

The digital library users adopts various technologies for data capture or context creation, data storage and management, searching and accessing digital data, publishing and distributing contents over networks and rights management.

CONTENT CREATION

Content creation is the process of converting non-digitised data such as printed documents, photographs, video and audio recording into a digital format using scanners, authoring tools and digital camera.

DATA AND METADATA

Data is a general term used to describe information that is encoded in digital form. Metadata is data about the other data. Common categories of metadata include descriptive metadata (e.g. bibliographic information), structured metadata (information about formats and structures), and administrative metadata (which includes, rights, permissions and other information used to manage access).

STANDARDS OF DIGITAL LIBRARY

Data structures such as Dublin core (DC), MARC 21, MAB, Text Encoding Initiative (TEI), and Electronic Achieve Description (EAD),

Data context of Pages in TIFF, GIF, JPEG, or PDF formats; text in SGML, HTML or XML formats.

Data interchange via 239.50, SQL, HTTP, Dienst, and open Archive Initiative

Information industry syntaxes (SGML, HTML, XML, AND Resource Description Framework (RDF).

DIGITAL RESOURCES : STORAGE AND MANAGEMENT

Server Machines store and retrieve digital data, RDBMS like SYBASE, ORACLE and DB2 are being used popularly for organising and managing the digital data using the software 'ADSTAR' using distributed storage management 'ADSM' developed by IBM, the data can be automatically transferred to various storage media such as tape and optical disc.

DIGITAL PUBLICATION/DISTRIBUTION

Most of the digital library use Internet for electronic publication, Electronic environment enables editors to send the manuscript of scholarly articles to reviewers, to receive responses more quickly and to publish the journals expediouly. The scribers elsewhere can retrieve them from the network.

KEY FEATURES OF DIGITAL LIBRARY

a. The digital library brings the library and the user-information to the user desk.

b. Computer power is used for searching and browsing.

c. Information can be shared

d. Information is easier to keep current

e. The information is always available

f. New forms of information become possible through teleconferencing, video conferencing

g. Cost of digital library

h. Technical developments – share catalogue records, meddling service

i. Electronic storage is cheaper than paper

j. Personal computer displays are becoming more pleasant to use

k. High speed networks are becoming widespread

l. With the help of PC and internet connection access is possible any where at any time.

m. Obviously many users can simultaneously access a single electronic copy from many locations and it would be possible to reformat the material as per the readers preference.

ADVANTAGES OF DIGITAL LIBRARY

1. Combines diverse collection

2. Accessing information of expensive and rare materials from remote places

3. Provides access to more information than possible by physically acquiring and maintaining

4. Extracting information from digital video quickly & automatically

5. Creating interfaces that allow user to search for and retrieve digitised information based on extracted information

6. Information interface – provides users with quick access to relevant information in the digital video library.

7. Supports both formal and informal learning

8. Media integration

9. Finds right integration of traditional library facilities and current web based approach.

LIMITATIONS OF DIGITAL LIBRARY

The "human factors" of a printed book are superb; it is portable, it can be annotated, it can be read anywhere, it can be spread out on a desktop or carried in the hand, no special equipment is needed to read it.

Developing countries like India face the following problems in materialising the concept of digital libraries:

1. The developed countries are the major producers of digitalised information sources which lack coverage of literature produced from thirdworld countries

2. Fiscal allocation in libraries is not always in tune with the inflation

3. Imbalance between the manpower produced in library science schools and the manpower requirements in libraries.

4. Lack of indigenous, efficient and effective library software packages.

5. Lack of information policy and information culture.

6. Lack of information audit in libraries and information centres.

7. Problems relating to the conversion of the existing manual databases into computer-readable databases.

DIGITAL LIBRARY SOFTWARE

The digital library software available are the VTLS, Voyanger, SIRLIS, Green Stone, D Space etc.

Some of the digital sources in medical and health sciences are

AIDSLINE, BIOSIS, CANCERLIT, AGELINE, TOXLINE, PUBMED, PSYINFO, POPLINE, Nursing Journal collection, (OVID), CINAHL, MEDLINE etc.

CONCLUSION

The modern technologies like computer & communication and internet development are changing types of libraries to redefine their skills and attitude towards information management. There is no doubt that the digital revolution is leading to great changes in libraries all over the world. Digital library plays an important role in promoting the use of information. Due to information explosion, technological development, increasing cost, globalization etc., there is a need for Global library with all modern facilities. Global library will be made available for use by all citizens of the world everywhere at any time free of cost.

REFERENCES

* ALA American Library Association (http://www.benedict.com/index.html)

* Amazon.com books (http://www.amazene.com)

* American Memory Project (http://lcWeb2.loc.gov/ammen/ammemhome.html)

* Berkeley Public Library online Reference (http://www.ci.berkeley.ca.us/bpl/bkmk/ref.html)

* Chicago public library (http://cpl.lib.uic.edul)

* IPL the Internet public library (http://ipl.sils.umich.edu/)

* Innovative Internet Applications in libraries (http://ipl.sisls.umich.edu.ref/)

* Internet public Library's Reference centre (http://ipl.sils.umich.edu.ref/)

* Library Information servers via www (http://sunsite.berkeley.edu/libweb/)

* Library of congress (http://www.loc.gov)

* Michigan Electronic Library (http://mlink.hh.lib.umich.edu/)

* Public service librarian's Guide to INTERNET Resources (http://kiz.oit.umass.edu/rref.html)

* Ready Reference using the INTERNET (http://k12.oit.umass.edu/rref.html)

* Reference source on the Net: our questions answered – here – (http://www.san.edu/CWIS/INTERNET/Wild/Refdesk/refidex.html)

* University of Virginia INTERNET Library (http://www.lib.virginia.edu)

* Surya (www.jiva.org)

* www.virtual library (http://www.w3.org/pub/datasources/

bysubject/http://overview.html)

*   National library of Australia (http://www.nlagov.qu/web.pac/)
*   Online computer library centre (OCLC) (http://www.ock.org)
*   OPAC 97 (http://www.opac97,bl.uk/)
*   National Information services and systems (NISS) (http://www.niss.ac.uk/referecnce/opacs.html)
*   Aarward university library (http://www.harvard.edu/museuns/)
*   Libraries on the Internet (http.//www.jsr.cc.va.us/lrc/library.html)

C21
Library 2. 0 : Sixty Two Views and Seven Definitions

R. Muthukrishnan
Librarian (SG), Aditanar College, Tiruchendur.
Thirunavukkarasu
Assistant Librarian, Bharathiar University, Coimbatore
R.Thiruppathi
Librarian, SRM College of Arts and Science, Kattankulathur, Kanchipuram Dt.

ABSTRACT

Library 2.0 is a model for library service that reflects a transition within the library world in the way that services are delivered to library users. This redirection will be especially evident in electronic offerings such as OPAC configuration, online library services and an increased flow of information from the user back to the library. The concept of Library 2.0 borrows from that of Web 2.0, and follows some of the same philosophies underpinning that concept. Proponents of this concept expect that ultimately the Library 2.0 model for service will replace outdated, one-directional service offerings that have characterized libraries for centuries.

SIXTY TWO VIEWS ABOUT LIB 2.0

- Library 2.0 is disruptive.
- Library 2.0 is a path toward improvement of services.
- Library 2.0 means abandoning services that serve small or unimportant groups.
- Library 2.0 means never having stable production-quality systems.
- Library 2.0 is not about replacing 1.0 technology.
- Library 2.0 will replace existing library services.
- Library 2.0 is about adding additional functionality— and that's threatening to some people.
- Library 2.0 is revolutionary.
- Library 2.0 is about improving services to patrons— not a revolution.
- Library 2.0 is not about technology.
- Library 2.0 is all about technology.
- Library 2.0 is a way of thinking and operating.
- Library 2.0 is a matter of survival.
- Library 2.0 is too much, too soon for many libraries; most would be served better by trying one or two new ideas.
- Library 2.0 discussions must take place in your library!
- Library 2.0 is a new name for ideas, librarians have been discussing for quite some time.
- Library 2.0 is so urgent that every state and national library association needs to plan a Library 2.0 conference
- Library 2.0 is sloganeering, signifying very little.
- Library 2.0 will offer services people want; current libraries offer services most people don't want.
- Library 2.0 is the wrong message at the wrong time.

- Library 2.0 means massive change in every library, since all existing libraries are restrictive places with rigid boundaries underpinned by change-avoidance.

- Library 2.0 features may not be feasible or useful for all communities and libraries.

- Library 2.0 is the only way libraries will remain viable.

- Library 2.0 lumps desparate things with a contrived term that detracts from the real ideas.

- Library 2.0 means libraries that fill your emotional needs.

- Library 2.0 encompasses every library that doesn't want to be a relic.

- Library 2.0 as a doctrine is too universal for the needs of real libraries.

- Library 2.0 means constant change.

- Library 2.0 puts the librarian anywhere a user's heart takes them.

- Library 2.0 is needed if the library is to continue to matter.

- Library 2.0 is a paradigm shift that changes almost everything in a library.

- Library 2.0 is hype that can interfere with the sound ideals involved.

- Library 2.0 means the user can modify library services.

- Library 2.0 builds OPACS without local databases.

- Library 2.0 is about rock bands in the library and gaming nights as library services.

- Library 2.0 services will primarily serve the minority who are always connected.

- Library 2.0 requires that libraries have more rights with regard to their systems.

- Library 2.0 won't even require systems knowledge within libraries; you'll just run a black box.
- Library 2.0 is "L2" when you're in the In Crowd.
- Library 2.0 doesn't (or shouldn't) allow for a concise definition.
- Library 2.0 should reach critical mass within two years.
- Library 2.0 won't even require hardware, databases, or application servers!
- Library 2.0 will, for the first time, deliver meaningful service to end users.
- Library 2.0 principles sound vaguely familiar—like the things academic librarians have been doing for some time.
- Library 2.0 is too important to leave to librarians and users; vendors must also help to shape it.
- Library 2.0 is World Cat with an API.
- Library 2.0 is library-centric rather than user-centric.
- Library 2.0 is confrontational: You're with us or you're against us.
- Library 2.0 could disenfranchise those who need libraries the most.
- Library 2.0 focuses on the technology end of customer service without any discussion of the other aspects of library work.
- Library 2.0 trivializes exciting and useful work that isn't "Web 2.0" enough.
- Library 2.0 gives us new tools to carry out the best practices libraries have had for many years.
- Library 2.0 will allow libraries to serve community needs; otherwise, they're only symbols of wealth and refinement.
- Library 2.0 adds even mre layers of obfuscation

between librarians and the public.

- Library 2.0 means making your library's space (virtual and physical) more interactive, collaborative and driven by community needs.
- Library 2.0 is first and foremost an effort to reach out to those people who, for whatever reason, are not using the services, libraries offer.
- Library 2.0 is anything that challenges the traditional approach to conducting library business.
- Library 2.0 is nothing different than what librarians have been striving for decades.
- Library 2.0 is just a faddish catchphrase.
- Library 2.0 is an attempt to bring libraries' electronic services in par with what people expect in a Web 2.0 environment.
- Library 2.0 is a new sense of ownership over library services and a new set of relationships with both vendors and others in the library community.
- Library 2.0 is a more intensive way of sharing all the resources that the library already offers.

SEVEN DEFINITION OF LIBRARY 2.0

Library 2.0 is a model for library service that reflects a transition within the library world in the way that services are delivered to library users. This redirection will be especially evident in electronic offerings such as OPAC configuration, online library services and an increased flow of information from the user back to the library. The concept of Library 2.0 borrows from that of Web 2.0 and follows some of the same philosophies underpinning that concept. Proponents of this concept expect that ultimately the Library 2.0 model for service will replace outdated, one-directional service offerings that have characterized libraries for centuries.[3]" [Wikipedia—or Michael Casey]

Library 2.0 sees the reality of our current user-base and says, "not good enough, we can reach more people." It seeks to do this through a three-part approach—reaching out to new users, inviting customer participation and relying on constant change. Much of this is made possible thanks to new technologies, but the services will only be partially tech-based." [Michael Casey take 2]

L2 is, to me, a service philosophy built upon three things; a willingness to change and try new things; a willingness to constantly re-evaluate our service offerings; and finally, a willingness to look outside our own world for solutions, be they technology-driven or not (this is where Web 2.0 fits in)." [Michael Casey take 3]

"Library 2.0 is not about technology[4]. Library 2.0 seeks to harvest good ideas from outside and use them to deliver improved and new services, often times in an effort to reach a new target population. Library 2.0 is, at its core, a way of thinking, a way of operating[5]. It's a framework for integrating change into all levels of library operations. It's in our effort to reach this new level of service that we will utilize these new, often times Web 2.0, technologies." [Casey Bisson]

"The whole 2.0 thing in general seems to be about using the hive mind and the affordances of technology to synthesize newer, better and more useful systems which will become available for everyone." [Jessamyn West]

"The idea of Library 2.0 represents a significant paradigm shift in the way we view library services. It's about a seamless user experience, where usability, interoperability and flexibility of library systems is key. It's about the library being more present in the community through programming, community building (both online and physical) and outreach via technology (IM, screencasting, blogs, wikis, etc.). It's about allowing user participation through writing reviews and tagging in the catalog and making their voice heard through blogs and wikis. It's about making the library more transparent through its Web presence and its physical design. We need to make the library human, ubiquitous and user-centered. This involves a change in our systems, our Web presence and our very attitudes. It will take a lot of work for a library to be completely 2.0, but the idea should influence every decision made at the library[37]." [Meredith Farkas]

"Library 2.0 simply means making your library's space (virtual and physical) more interactive, collaborative, and driven by community needs[55]. examples of where to start include blogs, gaming nights for teens, and collaborative photo sites. The basic drive is to get people back into the library by making the library relevant to what they want and need in their daily lives...to make the library a destination and not an afterthought." [Sarah Houghton]

CONCLUSION

Quality is the concern today. Service quality is most important to satisfy the users needs in libraries. Hence, Web 2.0, Lib 2.0 are the tools to sharpen the service perfection by understanding the perception of the users towards these services.

REFERENCES

* http://www.phoenix,orhost.org
* http://ispecies.org
* http://www.smpl.org
* http://www.chicagocrime.org
* http://www.acrlblog.org/2005/12/05/what-do-you-know-abou-weblib-20
* http://www.orweblog.oclc.org
* http://www.ariadne.ac.uk.issue45/miller/#16

C-22
Role of ICT in Public Libraries of Tamil Nadu

R.R. Saravanakumar

5/1546, Subathra Street, Sadhasiva Nagar, Maduri-625 020.

ABSTRACT

Impact of ICT (Information Communication and Technology) is felt in every walks of our daily life. Public libraries too are in the forefront of absorbing technological innovations and modern inventions. Public libraries were initiated with the objective of providing information to all masses of people in the remote areas of the state of TamilNadu. The services of the public libraries can be modernized with the help of ICT and the like. Modern tools such as Internet and institutional networks replace traditional methods of dissemination of information. Communication technology has encroached our day-to-day life in the form of mobile phones, I-POD, personal digital assistants and laptops. Multimedia resources such as DVD players, Home Theatres have become accessible for common man at an affordable cost. The life style of every Indian is being changed dramatically with such inventions. Public libraries being providers of up to date information for a common man are supposed to make use of ICT in every possible way and deliver the information needed for the users. This paper examines the use and applications of ICT in public libraries of TamilNadu.

INTRODUCTION

Impact of ICT (Information Communication and Technology) is felt in every walks of our daily life. Public libraries too are in the forefront of absorbing technological innovations and modern inventions. Public libraries were initiated with the objective of providing information to all masses of people without any racial discrimination and in the remote areas of the state of TamilNadu. The services of the public libraries can be modernized with the help of ICT and the like. Modern tools such as Internet and World Wide Web replace traditional methods of dissemination of information.

ICT IN DAY-TO-DAY LIFE

Communication technology has encroached our day-to-day life in the form of mobile phones, I-POD, personal digital assistants and laptops. Multimedia resources such as DVD players, Home Theatres have become accessible for common man at an affordable cost. The life style of every Indian is being changed dramatically with such inventions. Public libraries being providers of up to date information for a common man are supposed to make use of ICT in every possible way and deliver the information needed for the users.

SERVICES OFFERED IN PUBLIC LIBRARIES

REPROGRAPHY

Reprography/Xerox service is already being offered in the district central libraries. The same may be extended through Taluk Centre libraries and branch libraries in rural areas too.

SCANNING

Scanning of manuscripts, rare and costly book collections service shall be provided through public libraries at a nominal cost for the users.

VOICE OVER INTERNET PROTOCOL

VOIP (Voice Over Internet Protocol) facility shall be utilized to help the users reduce the cost of making overseas calls to talk to their dearer ones.

PRINT OUTS OF E-NEWS PAPERS

Electronic pages of newspapers that are available in Internet for cost shall be made available to users at an additional nominal cost. This service might be of great help for the unemployed youth to benefit from it, since certain advertisements appear only on Chennai editions of the respective newspapers.

RENEWAL THROUGH E-MAILS

Books that are lent for members shall be allowed to renew through e-mail alert options. This helps the user to renew the books even while at far away places and in case of emergencies.

COMPUTERIZATION OF PUBLIC LIBRARIES

Computerization activities started in the first phase with district central libraries being provided with computers for book accessioning and lending. Later on, with the aid of social service organizations such as RRRLF (Raja Ram Mohan Roy Library Foundation, Calcutta), three branch libraries in a district were selected and are supplied with three computer terminals with printers, barcode scanners, UPS (Uninterrupted Power Supply) and the necessary peripherals. With the help of these computer gadgets, public libraries can generate certain income to meet their establishment and maintenance needs by providing services such as Internet browsing, print outs of downloads, CD writing, and so.

NETWORKING OF PUBLIC LIBRARIES

Public libraries in each district shall have a separate web page of their own and the same can be hosted on NICNET (National Informatics Center Network) free of cost, since being a government organization. A separate network for public libraries can be created, so that public libraries of the state can share their digitized catalogues for the benefit of the users. Such a network may also help in smooth functioning of the administration, since information can be shared at any moment through such networks. Networking will also lead to bringing public libraries under one roof as a single entity of higher order. OPAC (Online Public Access Catalogue) of public libraries if provided shall help the users to browse the titles available by sitting in their home itself.

KNOWLLEDGE MANAGEMENT

Experiences that are gained from what previously happened could be stored and used for future purpose by a process termed as knowledge management. Public libraries have a wealthy bunch of such information by providing services to a vast variety of users or customers. Creating, storing, processing and disseminating such knowledge assets using ICT can be done through public libraries at a minimal cost, since they are located already at almost all the districts and rural suburbs.

INTERNET BASED SERVICES

Apart from providing Internet browsing and voice chat services, computers with Internet connectivity at public libraries can be utilized for fee based services such as train ticket reservation, distribution of ration cards and free services such as alerts about natural calamities and traffic congestions. Income generated through such activities can be used to enhance the services, which are offered presently. This may pave way for changing the status of public libraries from 'spending organizations' to 'revenue fetching organizations'.

DIGITAL INITIATIVES

Innovations in digital inventions such as barcode technology and RFID (Radio Frequency Identification Devices) have come to a stay. Libraries are the first to adopt such technologies in a larger scale and magnitude. The cost involved with RFID technology makes it difficult for all kinds of libraries to use them. In future with increased usage and mass production the cost may come down and RFID technology, shall become viable for all kinds of libraries to use with.

VIDEO CONFERENCING

With the help of satellite communication and its advancements public libraries have been able to make use of such facility for interacting with the staff cadre throughout the state. A group of higher officials, from the Madras 'Block Resource Centre' of EDUSAT (Educational Satellite Programme) programmes, use to chat with staff about the developments and hardships faced in the day-to-day routines at predetermined timings. This helps the staff to share and gather ideas of their counterparts in various districts of TamilNadu. Such a conference shall be arranged in future for users also to benefit from it.

CONCLUSION

Life comes to a standstill when power is off or a cable connection is gone off. The impact of technology is such that it has become inevitable in our common life. Public libraries have begun to shed their passive role as providers of continuing education for the general public, to become modern storehouses of information using ICT products and services. The use of ICT has shown the signs of improvement in speedy disposal of user's requirements from public libraries at the district level. Days are not far beyond for public libraries to replicate the same scenario in the rural suburbs through its networks.

REFERENCES

* http://pondicherry.nic.in/
* http://nic.merit.edu/statistics/nsfnet/nets.by.country
* http://www.webpages.uidaho.edu
* http://www.cs.berkeley.edu~dmolnar/library.
* http://www.bibliotheca-rfid.com
* http://www.rfidjournal.com/article/articleview/207

C- 23
Digital Reference Services

R.U. Ramasamy
Librarian, SACS M.A.V.M.M. Engg. College,
Kidaripatty (PO), Madurai – 625 301.

Dr. S. Srinivasa Raghavan
Librarian, Bharathidhasan University, Trichy.

ABSTRACT

The paper highlights how the new face of services is evolving as a natural solution to keep pace with the multifaceted technological environment. The Library and information profession is also facing the challenges of electronic age and been transformed by technology. Advancements result in incredible changes in almost every aspect of information services. Reference Services are also not an exception. Easily accessible digital information has rapidly become the hallmark of Internet. The paper discusses about the basic concepts and essential elements of reference service and the technology base of the various established and emerging forms of digital reference.

INTRODUCTION

Internet has also proved as a cost effective and efficient alternative to traditional communication methods. All these developments gave way to new range of reference services. In this series of developments digital reference is the latest trend of the digital era.

CONCEPT OF REFERENCE SERVICE

According to Dr.S.R.RANGANATHAN reference service is "Personal Service to each reader in helping him to find the documents answering his interest at the moment pin-pointedly, exhaustively and expeditiously".

ELEMENTS OF REFERENCE SERVICE

The following are the three basic elements of reference service

- Information or Knowledge base
- User or client-now likely to be a member of the new cyber-community in which the library operates
- Information professional or librarian, who plays the role of intermediary assisting and advising the user in their information seeking.

Out of these basic elements of reference service listed above the first is the information or knowledge base. Reference material of information, which is used for answering enquiries in a library, witnessed a complete change in their structure. A complete new range of tools, techniques and information products are available in electronic and digital form to work.

The most important element of the reference service is user. Essence of the five laws of library science is that user and his information need are the prime factor in designing a reference service. Reference service is user centered. It means the emphasis is not on the book, the reference tool or the format of the information sought, but on the users, their needs, the service that can be offered to meet these needs.

With the technological advancements, user

information seeking behavior has also changed. User does not want to visit physically an information center or library rather he expects the required information right on his computer screen at his seat sitting at some remote location. This means no face-to-face discussion. i.e., No reference interview. Keeping in view all the above factors it is useful for us as information professionals to see where we have come from and to use that knowledge to guide the path for the future. The connections between the three basic elements of reference service are made in a triad of individual relationships between the three, as in the reference interview, the translation of the users query into the structures of knowledge through the reference sources themselves and the information professional's knowledge of those information sources.

DIGITAL REFERENCE SERVICE

Technically speaking digital reference refers to a network of expertise, human intermediation and resources placed at the disposal of users in an online environment. Digital reference service is only an advancement of the same traditional services, which is emerging as natural solution to meet the users information needs in the changing technological environment. Digital libraries provide efficient and speedy services to its users.

Internet, which is an indispensable valuable source of information and efficient information delivery medium, offers a platform for a wide range of existing and future reference services. In this context the new emerging terms like digital reference service and virtual reference service can really make use of the prevailing technologies and may become the preferred and prevalent services of the digital era.

DIGITAL REFERENCE SERVICE: FORMS

Some forms of digital reference services available through Internet.

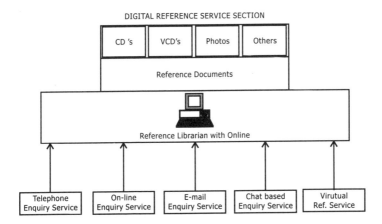

DIGITAL REFERENCE SERVICES

E-Mail

E-mail is the earliest and perhaps the most prevalent medium of virtual reference. With the proliferation of the Internet in the past decade and the availability of an email account to almost everyone in R&D organization, email reference service becomes a popular service in large research and academic organizations. Many libraries and information centers are extensively using email facility to provide online reference service. Now a days more and more users are inclined to use email reference than some other traditional reference service.

Many academic libraries and information centers are extensively using e-mail facility to provide online reference service to the students. E-Mail reference has the advantage of providing more complete answers than what could be possibly be given at a busy reference desk. When answering a question through e-mail, the reference librarian usually has more time to think about the question, the users information needs and if necessary he consults with other colleagues who have more related expertise or knowledge.

TELEPHONE OR ONLINE ENQUIRY SERVICE

The users ask a question to the reference Librarian through telephone, at that time that information is readily available that is ready reference service. That is other wise called as online enquiry services. The students directly come and get the relevant documents for the reference section that is called face-to-face method service. There are many Ask a services available on the web. Some of the important and well-known services are listed below,

(a) Ask ERIC *http://aseric.org*

Perhaps the one most well known earliest Ask a service on Internet in academic circles is Ask ERIC. This is provided by non-profit educational organization

(b) Ask A Question *http://talonline.ca/askaquestion*

This service is hosted by albeta Library. It is a cooperative venture among post secondary libraries.

(c) Ask Me *www.askme.* Com

It is a free service where a user simply asks a question and gets answers from the experts. Users enter their questions and their email addresses, though they can choose not to reveal their name and thus remain anonymous.

CHAT BASED REFERENCE

Chat, sometime referred to as instant messaging, is real-time communication between two or more computer users over the Internet. Every keystroke a chat user makes is instantly transmitted and appears on the monitors of all other users in the same chat session. Chat is a very popular means of communication over the Internet.

VIRTUAL REFERENCE

Real-time reference line on the web is the latest trend in virtual reference. Already some librarians are providing live web reference services to their students. Ex:

1. *http://www.247ref.org*
2. *http://www.public.iastate.edu/~cyberstaks/live.ref.htm.*
3. *http://www.cpi.org*
4. *http://www.libraryspot.com/spotlight/cdrs.htm*
5. *http://www.vrd.org*

The librarian and information professionals are required to cope up with the new technological changes, but at the same time one should not fear that the new emerging technology based services will replace the traditional services completely. Rather these are emerging as supplementary services to improve the information dissemination amongst the student community.

Some of the Digital Libraries having collection of CD'S, VCD's, Scanned Photos, Scanned Slides and other kind of digital materials, are very useful for digital Library users and Library Science professionals.

DIGITIZATION OF SPECIAL COLLECTIONS

Special collection forms the core of the primary research collection of a library. Whatever may be the format, the common features of special collection are that they are unique, rare, require special handling and in limited availability or just some thing that cannot be located in the open stacks. Equally important is that the material is valued as an artifact. Special collection may use digitization as a preservation technique but its real value is related to the increased access to special collections. Almost all major libraries of the world are having digitization programmed to provide greater access to its special collections through the digitization of material including Photographs, Maps, Printed Music, Pictures, Cartoons, etc.,

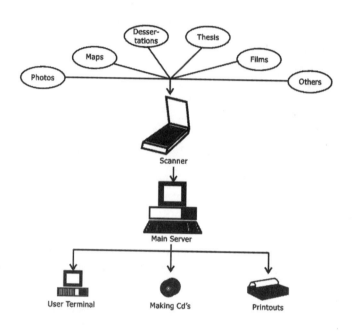

Digitization of Special Collections

Ex: a. The British Library

There is a growing number of collaborative digitization initiatives within the British Library and the library already has an estimated four terabytes of digitized information. Special collection of the British Library are digitized to maximize their use by facilitating a greater volume of net worked access and by providing the enhanced functionality intrinsic to the digitized items.

Ex: b. National Library of Australia:

A number of digitization projects have been undertaken by the National Library of Australia for long term preservation of traditional documentary materials.

Digitization provides access to electronic information resources such as image, database, recordings, theses, manuscripts and full text of periodical articles index by the library.

Special collection (including Photos, cartoons, drawings, negatives, postcards, maps, printed music, etc.,) of the National Library of Australia has been digitized under a major digitization programme aiming at providing greater access to its collection.

CONCLUSION

All of the digital reference forms discussed above have different technological nature, and hence they differ in their capabilities and how they are actually used. E-mail is the most prevalent and primary communication medium for communication services. Though the information professionals are required to cope up with the new technological changes, they should not fear that the new emerging technology based services will replace the traditional services completely rather these are emerging as supplementary services to improve the information dissemination amongst the user community.

REFERENCES

* **Rao,M** , *Leading with knowledge.* New Delhi : TMG, 2001.

* **Vijaya Lakshmi.** *Digital Libraries.* New Delhi : Isha Books, 2004.

* **Shan Hong.** *Knowledge management in libraries in the 21ˢᵗ century.-* Beijing – China

* **Rusbrindg,** "Towards the hybrid library", *D-Lib Magazine,* July – August, 1998 *http://www.google.com, http://www.infolibrarian,com*

* **Sumati Sharma, Ashok Kumar and Mohinder Singh.** "Digital Reference Services", *DESIDOC Bulletin of Information Technology,*24(6), 2004. pp.11-18.

* **Satija.** "Digital information system and services", *IASLIC Bulletin,* 48(1), 2003, pp.11-15.

C-24
RFID Technologies in Libraries: An Over View

M.S. Amanulla
Librarian, The New College (EVE), Chennai.14.

ABSTRACT

Radio Frequency Identification is one of the most exciting technologies, which helps in increasing the efficiency of the library management. This emerging technology helps to reduce the valuable staff time spent on scanning the barcode while charging and discharging the library documents. The RFID tags are placed in books and generally covered with a property sticker. Antennas of different sizes, based on application, are used to read the tags and manage the various library functions. Library users can enjoy self-charging and discharging of documents. It is highly useful for shelf rectification and stock verification. Therefore RFID helps the library materials processing in a very speedy way which will in turn increase the user's satisfaction. This paper discusses the growing importance of RFID technologies in libraries and its major components, applications, drawbacks and so on.

INTRODUCTION

Radio Frequency Identification is one of the most exciting technologies and fastest growing technologies for increasing the efficiency in the library work environment. This technology helps to reduce the valuable staff time spent on scanning the barcode while charging and discharging the library materials. The RFID tags are placed in books and generally covered with a property sticker. Antennas of different sizes, based on application are used to read the tags and manage the various library functions. Thus RFID helps the library materials processing in a very speedy way, which will in turn increase the user satisfaction.

RFID SYSTEM COMPONENTS

RFID system consists of the following main parts.

RFID TAGS

Flexible, paper-thin smart labels that are applied directly to items. Each RFID tags contain tiny chip which is both readable and writable and can store information to identify items in your collection. In library applications, it also stores a security bit and if needed, information to support sorting systems.

ANTENNA

A conduit between RFID tags and the coupler. RFID antennas emit radio waves that activate RFID tags as they pass through the activation field. After a tag is activated, it can send information or receive information from the computer.

COUPLER

The coupler can send information in two directions It can read information from a tag and send it to the PC (read mode) or it can read information from the PC and send it to an RFID tag (write mode).

READERS

RFID readers or receivers are composed of a radio frequency module, a control unit and an antenna to interrogate electronic tags via radio frequency communication.

SERVER

The server is the heart of some comprehensive RFID systems. It is the communications gateway among the various components. It receives the information from one or more of the readers and exchange information with the circulation database.

PC

The link between the computer and your library automation system. VTLS has developed software that runs on your PC to provide an interface between the RFID hardware and your library automation system.

USES

RFID readers at checkout counters usually are flat back pads. A librarian simply sets stacks of books on the pad and the reader picks up the signals from all of the books, marks them as checked out in the library system. RFID based system move beyond security to become tracking systems that combine security with more efficient tracking of materials through the library, including easier and faster charge and discharge, inventorying, and materials handling.

APPLICATION OF RFID IN LIBRARIES

Application of RFID in libraries will increase the efficiency and reduce cost. It can relieve the library professionals from routine and repetitive works and operational task.

CHARGING AND DISCHARGING STATIONS

It can be used for charging and discharging of documents. This facility will allow users to borrow, return and renew documents. Users can charge and discharge documents through the user self-service charging and discharging stations. This facility will relieve library professionals from routine and repetitive works and allow them to spend more time for value added personalized information service to their users.

ANTI- THEFT GATE

It has an advanced security component that may alert library staff when documents are removed from the library without authorization. It can use the alarm from sound and flashing lights for detecting tags. It can also trigger a camera to record users who trigger the alarm.

RFID SELF MEMBERSHIP REGISTRATION STATION

RFID, can also be used to allow users to register and collect library membership cards through a self-membership registration station. This facility can also be used for replacement of lost cards. It can enhance the speed of enrolment process, generate more library loan and return transactions from users.

STOCK VERIFICATION AND SHELF RECTIFICATION

Library staff can use portable hand held readers for electronic inventorying by passing them rapidly along the shelves to read all the documents. There is no need of handling each document individually. They can report the lost hidden or unordered documents more easily by using their portable readers.

RFID CIRCULATION AND GROUPING STATIONS

This facility will make the back room processing of the RFID systems more simple, productive and efficient, allowing better management and lesser manpower item processing. It can be used for tag issuing, sorting, weak tag recovery etc.

Advantage of RFID system

1. Self charging and discharging : The use of RFID reduces the amount of time required to perform circulation operations. This technology helps libraries eliminate valuable staff time spent scanning barcode while checking out and checking in borrowed items.

2. Reliability : The readers are highly reliable that some RFID system have an interface between the exist sensors and the circulation software to identify the items moving out of the library and not be caught in library or would at least know what have been stolen. If the user could also use an RFID tag, the library will also be aided to determine who removed the items without properly charging them.

3. High-speed inventorying : A unique advantage of RFID systems is their ability to scan books on the shelves without tipping them out or removing them. A hand –held inventory reader can be moved rapidly across a shelf of books to read all the unique identification information.

4. Automated material handling : Another application of RFID technology is automated material handling. This includes conveyor and sorting system that can move library material and sort them by category into separate bits or onto separate carts. This significantly reduces the amount of staff time required to read material for shelving.

5. Long tag life of file : RFID tags last longer than barcodes because the technology does not require line- of-sight.

DISADVANTAGE OF RFID SYSTEM

HIGH COST

The major disadvantage of RFID technology is its cost. The readers and gate sensors used to read the information are very costly. A substantial amount is needed for maintaining RFID systems.

READER'S COLLISION

The signal from one reader can interfere with the signal from another where coverage overlaps. This is called reader collision.

TAG COLLISION

Tag clash occurs when more than one chip reflects bad signal at the same time, confusing the reader

LACK OF STANDARDS

Lack of standard is another problem in RFID system. A uniform standard is necessary to bring inter-operability of libraries using RFID. More staff training is necessary for the library staff to handle the RFID system .The tags are easily removable, so it is difficult to identify when the tag is removed.

CONCLUSION

RFID systems are advantageous because of their non-line -of-sight property. Tags can be read through a variety of substances such as snow, ice and paints crusted and other environmentally challenging conditions. RFID technology is more effective, convenient, and cost effective and provides efficient result in libraries. It is high time that the library users are to be educated about the importance and use of RFID technologies. Rigorous hands on training may be organized by the implementing libraries to its patrons. Once the idea of RFID takes place it will surely convert the most of the libraries into RFID libraries. This will significantly improve the patrons' satisfaction.

REFERENCES

* **Jones Peter, etal.** "Radio Frequency Identification in the U.K. : Opportunities and Challenges", *International journal of Retail& Distribution Management*, 32(3), 2004, pp.164-171.

* **Kern Christian.** "RFID for security and Media Circulation in libraries", *The Electronic library*, 22(4), 2005, pp.317-324.

* **Korero, Indira.** "RFID Technology: A Revolution in library management", *Proceedings of the Second International CALIBER 2004*, Feb.11-13, 2004, New Delhi.Ed.T.A.V. Murthy and others. Ahmedabad:INFLIBNET Centre,pp.412-418.

* **Mohamed Haneefa.** "Application of Radio Frequency Identification in libraries", *KELPRO BULLETIN*, Vol. 10(1), 2006, pp.56-59.

Globalization, Knowledge Industry and Management and Other Related Topics in LIS

D-01
A Comparative Study on Buyer's Attitude Towards Performance of E-Marketing

J. Ramesh
Librarian, Park's College, Chinnakkarai,
Tirupur – 641 605

P. Eps
Librarian, All India Radio, Tirunelveli

G. Sudha
No.789, 5th North Street, Thiagaraja Nagar, Tirunelveli.

ABSTRACT

This study is an attempt to analyse the buyer's attitude towards e-marketing. It shows the current trends in the online business and also predicts the future of the online marketing. It will help the e-marketers to know the buyer's attitude on online shopping.

INTRODUCTION

Over 100 million connected users worldwide are doing more than $80 billion of commerce. Thus the Internet is significantly impacting the economy. Technology advances of the early 1990's have expanded the economy to operate on a global scale, requiring that the rules of business and competition change. These changes are part of the new economic model called the Net economy, an environment based on the use of the Internet as a worldwide business delivery channel. This channel, along with traditional channels such as EDI, is now conducting e-Commerce on a massive scale. Over 80 percent of CEOs believe that e-Commerce will completely reshape how they compete.

Electronic commerce is buying and selling online. In general, e-Commerce is the term for any type of business or commercial transactions that involves the transfer of information across the Internet. For business, e-Commerce means any transaction that involves an online commitment to purchase or to sell goods or services.

Electronic commerce is the process of using digital technology as the medium for transmitting information between organizations. Digital technology replaces paper-based processes, resulting in lower costs, greater accuracy, higher speed and larger scale inter-company collaboration.

It also nurtures the relationship between consumers and organization, between government and people it serves and between industry and society.

OBJECTIVES

- To review the business trends in online.
- To analyse the buyer's attitude towards e-marketing.
- To predict the future of online marketing.

HISTORY OF E-COMMERCE

Computers first made their way into commercial applications in 1990's, with ERMA (Electronic Recording Machine Accounting). Banks were swamped with growing volume of checks that needed to be processed. By automated ERMA Bank of America nine employees could do a job that previously took 50 people. Also in this period, many companies were looking at ways of exchanging data between trading partners. Clearly what was needed was a common language that computers could use to share data. In 1969, American's Department of Defence commissioned the ARPANET for researching on networking. However it was purely used for military purpose for more than 20 years. Then Tim Berners-Lee at CERN developed WWW which was officially released in 1991. In 1970's and 1980's, business extended their computing power beyond the company's walls, sending and receiving information with business partners and suppliers electronically via EDI (Electronic Data Interchanging).

EDI often occurred over private communication networks called Value Added Networks (VAN). The cost of installation and maintenance of VAN put electronic communication out of the reach of many small and medium sized businesses. But now it is available at very low cost. In 1991, America's National Science Foundation (ANSF) discontinued its restriction on communication and use of internet business started to taking place. In 1993, the first graphics Web browser, Mosaic was introduced. The combination of a WWW with pictures, a graphic web browser to appreciate it and no commercial restrictions on the Internet, provided the necessary ingredients for Internet e-Commerce.

TYPES OF E-COMMERCE

1. Business to Business (B2B)
2. Business to Consumers(B2C)
3. Consumer to Consumer(C2C)
4. Consumer to Business(C2B)
5. Business to Government(B2G)

CHANNEL OF E-COMMERCE

Commercial channels

The Internet.

COMMERCIAL CHANNELS

Commercial channels means that various companies setup on-line Information and marketing services that can be accessed by those who have signed up for the service and pay monthly fee.

INTER NET

Internet means connection of networks of networks. A network which connect users to an amazingly large information highway is called internet

COMPONENTS OF E-COMMERCE

E-Commerce covers the range of on-line business activities for products and services, through the internet. E-Commerce breaks into two components

Online shopping and

Online purchasing.

THE DIFFERENCE BETWEEN E-BUSINESS AND E-COMMERCE

E-Business is a super-set of e-Commerce. E-Commerce is the online selling component of a web site. E-Business is the integration of a company's activities including products, procedures and services with the internet . You turn your company from a business into an e-Business when you integrate your sales, marketing, accounting, manufacturing, operations with your web site activities. An e-Business uses the Internet as fully integrated channel for all business activities.

E-MARKETING

E-Marketing is promoting a product, company, service or website online. It can include a variety of activities from online advertising, to search engine optimization to online networking and much more.

- Build loyalty among existing customers.
- Improve customer services.
- Streamline business processes.
- Incremental sales to existing customers.
- Growing market share.
- Enhance communication among customers.
- Enhance communication among employees.

APPLICATION OF E-MARKETING

- E-Mail marketing.
- Online information for sales representative.
- Cyber branding
- White paper
- E-Learning
- Virtual marketing.
- E-signature

DELIVERY OF PHYSICAL GOODS BOUGHT ON THE INTERNET

Physical goods bought via the internet are delivered by the same means as goods bought by mail order:

1. Regular post.
2. Private courier service such as Federal Express, UPS, etc.
3. Hand delivery by business.
4. Customer collects at a pick-up point.

PAYMENT IN E-MARKETING

In e-Marketing transactions, payments should be of both direct and electronic payments. Direct payment refers the case transaction between the buyer and seller, after delivery of goods. Electronic payments refers to the cash transaction through any other medium electronically e.g.,

1. Credit Cards,
2. Debit Cards,
3. E-Checks,
4. Smart Cards etc.,

LIMITATION OF E-COMMERCE – FOR A SMALL BUSINESS

The main limitation of e-commerce for small businesses is budget. Small businesses generally do not have substantial budget for investment nor are they easily able to get funding. A second limitation is sometimes human resources. Some small companies have set up e-commerce sites and have been explosively successful. Unfortunately, they do not have the human resources or budget to handle the huge number of orders.

REASON FOR FAILURE OF E-BUSINESS

Every major initiative has its obstacles and e-Business is not an exception to it.

- Lack of training.
- Lack of technology.
- Security problem.
- Lack of management support.
- Participation of digital market place.
- Back office service
- Business to consumer focus.
- New business product lines.

- Serving global markets.

ADVANTAGES

- Ability to reach a wider market
- Ability to source product from a wider supplier-base
- Ability to automate and cut costs in repetitive processes
- Ability to give the impression that you are a bigger business than you really are
- Ability to respond to customer queries quickly and cheaply.

THE BENEFITS OF B2B E-COMMERCE

- Reduced costs
- Inventory
- Productivity
- Procurement and payment
- Increased reliability
- Reduced shipping costs
- Human resources
- Reduced systems maintenance.
- Improved customer satisfaction
- Convenience
- Information available
- Customization
- Management
- Improved reporting/decision making
- Maintenance of control
- Raise the cost of switching
- Sales and marketing
- Extend sales territory

DISADVANTAGES

- Expense of setting up or purchasing e-commerce systems.
- Finding staff with appropriate internet experience.
- Risk of fraud and inability to grow quickly if business is very successful.
- Marketing expense.

REFERENCES

- G.winfield freese and Lawrence C Stewrence. *Designing system for internet commerce.*
- Kamelesh K Bajaj and Dehjani Nag. *E-Commerce the cutting edge of business.*
- Ravi Kalakota and Whinston. *The Frontiers of E-Commerce.*
- Ravi Kalakota and Marcia Robinson. *E-Business road map for success.*

WEBSITES

- http://www.DrE_Commerce.com.
- http://www.pweglobal.com
- http://www.onlineservice.com
- http://www.indianmarketing.inc

D-02
Total Quality Management in Library Activites

M. Santhi
Librarian, Erode Sengunthar Engineering College,
Thudupathi – 638 057 Erode Dt

P. Ilangumaran
Librarian, Erode Sengunthar Engineering College,
Thudupathi – 638 057 Erode Dt

ABSTRACT

Total Quality Management (TQM) is a systems approach for the continuous improvement of service and abilities to meet and exceed internal and external customer expectations and organizational objectives. TQM has evolved over the past five decades by incorporating and synthesizing ideas from many sources. By implementing TQM principles, many countries have experienced dramatic economic growth. TQM is now practiced not only in organizations and industries but also in government, military, education and in non-profit organizations including libraries.

Key components of TQM are employee involvement in training, problem solving teams, statistical methods, long – term goals and thinking and recognition of that system. Libraries can attain benefit from TQM by breaking down interdepartmental barriers, redefining the beneficiaries of library services as internal customers and external customers, constant attainment of customer satisfaction through the continuous improvement of all processes in the library.

This paper outlines various steps that a library administrator can implement through a TQM programme in libraries. Suggestions to enhance library services by using TQM principles have also been attempted. A library administrator's attention should focus on catering best services possible and be willing to meet the needs of the customers. He should determine the type of niche markets, the type of consumers, service to be rendered and so on. TQM involves the question of whether services do correspond to customer's expectations and needs and whether both are congruent with each other. This work formulates the implementation of TQM in a library in a useful way to evaluate the quality of library services and provide goals for improvement.

INTRODUCTION

Total Quality Management (TQM) is a systems approach and application of quantitative methods and human resources for the continuous improvement to meet and exceed internal and external customers expectations and organizational objectives. TQM is a long-range never-ending process and takes time to make the changes necessary to achieve super quality.

TQM has evolved over the past five decades by incorporating and synthesizing ideas from many sources. With the implementation of TQM principles, many countries have experienced dramatic economic growth. TQM is practiced not only in organizations and industries, but also in government, military, education and in non-profit organizations including libraries. The implementation of TQM in the library is a useful way to evaluate the quality of library services and provide goals for improvement. The beneficial aspect of TQM is its emphasis on continuous improvement.

Libraries are both master and servant of society. A library has as its learner a set of customers. A client enters into the library, with the hope that he will get the material or information he needs. The library administrator trusts that the library will satisfy the customers as well as staff. TQM is achieved by involving all the employees throughout the organization in satisfying all the requirements of every reader, who ever the reader may be either external or internal.

TOTAL QUALITY MANAGEMENT

Quality management is the basis for library management. General principles of TQM should meet the customer needs, exact assessment, continuous improvement, teamwork and enthusiasm of the library administrator for effective library service.

BASIC TOOLS FOR QUALITY MANAGEMENT

Management tools that can be used for measuring and documenting quality of the products, processes and services: (Jaafar, 1998)

- Control Charts
- Pareto chart
- Flow charts
- Cause and effect diagram
- Run charts
- Histogram
- Scattered diagram

It is very important to satisfy today's customer demands immediately, than preparing for tomorrow's customer needs. TQM tools help in giving personal service and efficient backroom preparation. This manages the moment's transaction and the whole experience for the customer thereby provides value and maintains a distinction. To achieve all of this dynamically, Library administrator needs data and mechanisms to provide it. He needs minimum of four channels of information, one to keep him in touch with customer's changing requirements, a second to monitor his output against those requirements and a third to feedback his performance in matching the two. But these are also reactive so he needs a fourth channel to anticipate his customers' need and help in keeping him one step ahead. This data applies at the macro level of the whole organization and at all levels down to one individual.

WHY SHOULDLIBARIES ADOPT TQM?

Libraries are the most ancient social and cultural agencies. To provide "Right information to the right user at the right time in right form" the library administrator requires good organizational ability. The basic concern is to create a structure of the organization where desired information is retrieved and made accessible efficiently in a timely manner to the users. Creation and maintenance of such a structure requires an effective management which facilitates to work toward that goal. Since library management is management of vast amount of information stored in different formats-printed, electronic, audio and video it requires the use of most if the modern management techniques.

Modern technologies have changed our social and economic life in workplace. Methodologies change — people work at home or on the web with flexible timetables and more and more virtual communities are emerging in different fields. The most important stockholders in the library are customers, the providers of subsidies, staff and other libraries. These stockholders for various reasons are interested in introducing TQM in libraries. The introduction of TQM makes great demands on the staff. To introduce TQM the following factors should be taken in account:

1. TQM involves a process of change and therefore requires staff to be ready to play a constructive role in that process.

2. TQM requires a basic re orientation from the media stock towards customers and markets. TQM is a result oriented approach.

3. A strongly hierarchical organization with fragmented responsibilities is not well suited to the introduction of TQM since all staff needs to feel responsibility for influencing quality.

4. The effort necessary for implementing TQM is at the same time rewarding for both staff and the institution. Improvement of the institution in which they work gives more opportunity to staff to influence their own work (Klaassen &Wiersma)

STEPS TO TOTAL QUALITY MANAGEMENT

Based on his work with Japanese managers and others, Deming (1986: Walton 1986) outlined 14 steps that managers in any type of organization can take to implement a total quality management program.

1. Create constancy of purpose for improvement of product and service. Constancy of purpose requires innovation, investment in research and education, continuous improvement of product and service maintenance of equipment, furniture and fixtures and new aids to production.

2. Adopt the new philosophy, Management must undergo a transformation and begin to believe in quality products and services.

3. Cease dependence on mass inspection. Inspect products and services only enough to be able to identify a way to improve the process.

4. End the practice of awarding business on price tag alone. The lowest priced goods are not always the highest quality: choose a supplier based on its record of improvement and then make a long term commitment to it.

5. Improve constantly and forever the system of product and service. Improvement is not a one time effort: management is responsible for leading the organization in to the practice of continual improvement in quality and productivity.

6. Institute training and retraining. Workers need to know how to do their jobs correctly even if they need to learn new skills.

7. Institute leadership. Leadership is the job management. Managers have the responsibility to discover the barriers that prevent staff form taking pride in what they do. The staff will know what those barriers are.

8. Drive out fear. People often fear reprisal if they" make waves " at work. Managers need to create an environment where workers can express concerns with confidence.

9. Break down barriers between staff areas. Managers should promote team work by helping staff in different areas/departments work together. Fostering interrelationships among departments encourages higher quality decision-making.

10. Eliminate slogans, exhortations and targets for the workforce. Using slogans alone, without an investigation into the processes of the workplace, can be offensive to workers because they imply that a better

job could be done. Managers need to learn real ways of motivating people in their organizations.

11. Eliminate numerical quotas. Quotas impede quality more than any other working condition; they leave no room for improvement. Workers need the flexibility to give customers the level of service they need.

12. Remove barriers to pride of workmanship. Give workers respect and feedback about how they are doing their jobs.

13. Institute a vigorous program of education and retaining. With continuous improvement, job descriptions will change. As a result, employees need to be educated and retrained so they will be successful at new job responsibilities.

14. Take action to accomplish the transformation. Management must work as a team to carry out the previous thirteen steps.

TQM IN LIBRARY SERVICES

Sirkin (1993) suggests some ways a library might use the principles of TQM to enhance library services

- Create service brochures and information kits
- Conduct a user survey about library services
- Change hours of operation
- Provide a more convenient material return
- Simplify checkout of materials
- Use flexibility in staff assignments
- Co-operate with local government
- Ask vendors to give product demonstrations
- Give new staff a through orientation
- Create interdepartmental library advisory groups
- Improve the physical layout of the library

- Track complaints
- Develop an active outreach program
- Open satellite offices
- Publicize new or changed services.
- Develop user and staff training materials
- Target services to specific groups
- Offer electronic document delivery
- Follow the mission statement
- Smile.

POTENTIAL CHALLENGES

While TQM clearly has positive aspects, implementing it can have potential challenges as well Jurow and Barnard(1993) identify four barriers to the adoption of TQM in libraries:

1. Vocabulary : objections to terms such as "Total" Quality" and "Management" which imply that high standards are not already being met (2) commitment: TQM takes several years to implement and requires a long term commitment by library mangers (3) process: our culture tends to be impatient and we try to solve problems quickly, contrary to TQM s careful process analysis; and (4) Professionalization: professional staff can be resistant to turning over their practice and services to what they perceive as the "uninformed whims of the customer" Sirkin(1993) also notes that it is not possible to satisfy everyone's demands ; choices need to be made.

CONCLUSION

Libraries are ideal place to implement TQM. They are service organizations dedicated to their customers, the patrons. By formulating a strategic plan, and following it with a commitment to continuous quality improvement, library managers can transform and improve their organizations .Riggs(1992) summarizes the notable principles of TQM;(1) manage by fact: make library decisions after careful analysis of data gathered with tools such as check sheets, histograms and Pareto charts(2) eliminate rework :library work is often labor intensive-simplify it and make sure it is done properly the first time(3)respect people and ideas: staff are the library's most valuable resources and they should be encouraged to point out problems without fear of management (4) empower people: trust library staff to act responsibly and give them the appropriate authority to make decisions that can improve the quality of work they do .Finally, remember that TQM is not a "quick fix" It needs to be implemented gradually over a two –to three-year period.

REFERENCES

* Butcher, K.S. "**Total quality management :the Oregon State University Library's experience. ",** *Journal of Library Administration*,18(1/2),1993, pp.45-56.(EJ469 102).

* **Deming,W.E.(1986).**"Out of the crisis." Cambridge, MA:Massachustts Institute of technology, Center for Advanced Engineering Study.

* **Jurow,S and Barnard,S.B** (Eds)(1993)"Integrating total quality management in a library setting." Binghamton,NY:Haworth press.

* **Jurow .S and Barnard S.B**(1993) Introduction TQM Fundamentals and overview of contents", *Journal of Library Administration*, 18(1/2),1-13

* **Mackey.T and Mackey,K**. (1992).Think quality the Deming approach does work in libraries. "*Library Journal*,"117(9), pp.57-61.(EJ 446234)

* **O'Neil R M.** (1994)"Total quality management in libraries: A Source book." Englewood, CO: Libraries Unlimited(ED 377868)

* **Riggs,D.E.**(1992) "TQM: quality improvement in new clothes." *College& Research Libraries*, 53(6),pp.481-483(EJ 454 720)

* **Riggs.A.F.** (1993). "Managing quality: TQM in Libraries", *Library Administration & Managemnt*,"7(2),pp.73-78.(EJ461 627)

*   **Sirkin,A.F.**(1993). "Customer service : Another side of TQM", *Journal of Library Administration*,18(1/2),pp.71-83(EJ469 104)

*   **Walton,M.***The Deming management method.*New York : New York : Perigee, 1986

D-03
Globalization and Marketing of Information

T. Thilagavathi
Faculty of Education, Avinashilingam University for Women, Coimbatore, 641 108.

ABSTRACT

Information revolution and communication technology brings about enormous changes and impacts in our daily lives. Information centers play a vital role in disseminating information to its users. Today's library professionals are facing a number of challenges such as technologies adopted for the dissemination of information, diversification of networking organizations and marketing of information . Globalization is the process of integrating economy, culture, technology and governance. Marketing of information requires effective planning, skilled manpower, knowledge of user's information demand and money.

INTRODUCTION

We are living in a technology oriented world. Technology increases, maintains and improves the potential of an individual. Technology influences our day-to-day lives.

Library and information centres are also being transformed by technology. This transformation is due to rapid development and diffusion of information technology, resulting in innovations in generation, collection, storage, processing and dissemination of information and knowledge.

Information is a commodity. Today a lot of information is generated through printed media, mass media and electronic media. Twentieth century has witnessed an "Information Explosion" owing to the exponential growth of publications. The growth of knowledge in science and technology is greater than that of social sciences. The phenomenal growth of publications has created a number of problems in the administration of libraries in the areas of acquisition, collection, organisation, maintenance and dissemination of information.

Information management by traditional methods is already overburdened and is now unable to cope up with the rising tide of exponential growth of publications. Information management is done efficiently and effectively by utilizing the information technology.

Information revolution and communication technology brings enormous changes and impacts in our routine life. Information centres play a vital role in disseminating information among its end users. Today's library professionals are facing a number of challenges due to technologies adopted for the dissemination of information, diversification of networking organizations and marketing of information. To overcome all these problems, globalization came into existence.

Globalization is the buzz word, gaining momentum in world's economy. The distinctive features of globalization as stated by the United Nations Development Report (UNDP), and Human Development Report (1999) are Shrinking Space, Minimized Time and Disappearing Borders. These unique features of globalization are linking people's lives more profoundly, more intensively and more immediately. It is the process of growing interdependence of the people across the globe, integrating economy, technology, culture and governance. Further, globalization is opening new and diverse opportunities for millions of people around the world.

Lancaster has forecasted that 21st century will be a "Paperless Society" because of the boom in electronic revolution. This dream has come true. Now the physical form of document is changed drastically as a result of recent developments in micrographic technology. Microforms such as microfische, ultrafische, microfilm, magnetic disks, magnetic tape, CD-ROM etc are means to miniaturise and substitute for the large bulk of conventional documents. Acquisition of microform is a method of solving space problem in the libraries. The invention of INTERNET, a global information network with the Information Highways and "Super Highways", librarians may be compelled to learn a new range of skills. Today's Librarian has the urge to design, construct and maintain value added databases to hold information that is immediately pertinent to the user community. Librarian will be a marketing manager who keeps the library on a desktop and retrieves information and disseminate to the users by using in-house databases.

CONCEPT OF MARKETING

Libraries and Information centres are the social institutions which transfer knowledge and content to the society. The current society is knowledge society and the users with specific needs are the customers of the library. Speedy access and relevant information are the demands of the user and they are ready to pay for that. User satisfaction is the main motto of the library. So we are in a position to market our library resources and services to the users.

Marketing is an essential component of any organization's work plan. Even the products and services of organizations are noteworthy and if the consumers do not know them, the product would not reach the target groups. Majaro defines "marketing is the management process responsible for identifying, anticipating and satisfying customer requirements profitably".

Kotler's definition of marketing is the one most often encountered in the library literature on marketing: "the analysis, planning, implementation and control of carefully formulated programs designed to bring about voluntary exchanges of values with target markets for the purpose of achieving organizational objectives. It relies heavily on designing the organization's offering in terms of the target markets' needs and desires and on using effective pricing, communication and distribution to inform, motivate and service the markets.

NEED FOR MARKETING LIBRARY SERVICES

Planning for effective and efficient operations are the key challenges faced by the library managers in terms of

- Limited Financial resources and Information Explosion
- Greater demand of the user
- Effect of free economy
- Less usage of the available resources
- Changing concept of library and information services
- The present information services which are not user friendly
- More efforts and imagination required in marketing and selling of information.

PROFESSIONAL SKILLS FOR MARKETING INFORMATION

Information management requires the ability to synthesize and shape information into forms appropriate for each individual or groups. The library personnel should acquire the following professional knowledge and skills for marketing of information:

1. Perception of the information requirement of users
2. Knowledge of the ways of accessing information
3. Acquire skills of marketing strategies, distribution, advertising and user satisfaction
4. Skills of obtaining feedback from the users of information
5. Coupling of new information with the already existing information source
6. User interest analysis
7. Understanding the reasons for potential users of information not seeking service from the system meant for them.

The Information Specialist must be a critical thinker and decision maker, being able to solve the information problem within seconds. He/She should act as a crisis manager at times. He/She must have highly-developed communication skills and be able to work with individuals. Knowing how to work with people and understanding the art of negotiation are imperative.

Survey is a marketing research technique that provides a systematic way to gather and analyze useful information about users' attitudes, interests and activities. The information needs assessment process is a planned, systematic approach to determine the information needs of each distinct clientele group. The information manager should possess up-to-date knowledge about the resources within the organization and external to it. Keep on top information products and services being offered from traditional information suppliers as well as new entrants in to the market. Use information gathered in the needs assessment process to position the library at the center of information activity within the organization.

AWARENESS CREATION OF LIBRARY RESOURCES

To create awareness among the users about the information availability, the information professionals should perform certain awareness creation functions. It will be helpful to the information managers to market their products and services in an efficient manner. The awareness on the resources can be made through

- Creation of an information centre web site – highlighting services responsive to user requirements
- Broadcasting e-mail messages to targeted groups
- Highlighting new services, new acquisition, products in the Bulletin Boards
- Preparation of newsletter, pamphlets, posters and send it to the library clientele
- Sending notification to the end-users based on user profile
- Displaying flowcharts related with resources and collections in the library.
- Displaying of arrangement guides
- Provision of special material guides
- Preparation of special subject guides
- Classification of schemes adopted
- Publicity of library resources
- Attractive arrangements of the collection

LIBRARY PRODUCTS AND SERVICES

The Library's success depends upon the quality and excellence of its products. According to Weingand, "there is simply no substitute for a topnotch product; inferior or inadequate design will scuttle the most meritorious planning and marketing strategies." The products that libraries provide are varied, ever changing and consist of core, tangible and augmented products. It includes all of the goods and services made available through the library. Products might be electronic information or access to information actually held by other libraries. Further, products consist of both existing and potential services and materials.

Library products may include:

- Library catalogues
- Bibliographies
- Indexing services
- Abstracting services
- Translation services
- Reprography services
- Document backup services
- Selective dissemination of information services
- Current awareness services
- Digest services

PROMOTION ACTIVITIES

The following promotional activities can be easily implemented:

- Personal contacts : conduct seminars, workshops to attract the user
- Advertising
- Brochure, Fact sheets, Catalogues
- Newsletters
- Articles in newspapers and journals
- Demonstrations
- Exhibitions
- Evaluation

- Feedback

PRICING STRATEGIES

Fixing the price for information products and services is a new concept.

- COST-ORIENTED : Estimate the cost for the information, work out the price
- COMPETITOR-ORIENTED : The centre should look at, what other information centres are charging, and act accordingly, decide to charge the same, to undercut, or to provide better service with higher charges.
- DEMAND-ORIENTED: In fixing the price one can look at "what the users will bear" the perceived value of service.

BENEFITS OF MARKETING

The marketing of information products and services shall be beneficial in the following ways:

- Increase visibility of the library and information centres
- Improve the quality of library services
- Gain management support and commitment
- Expand the professional role of the librarians and information scientists
- Manage the affairs more effectively
- Gives general information to the users about the library, the information services and products
- Encourages a general awareness and appreciation of services of the library and information centre
- Ensures economic use of major resources.

Libraries are providing effective services to its users and improve the country's economy. The seekers of information are living in a golden era because the world is at their fingertips! Implementations of marketing principles in the library and information centres bring better future for the library as well as the clientele of the globalized world. The cost of getting information is very low and it is efficient, enjoyable and enduring.

REFERENCES

* **Bushing, Mary C.** "The Library's Product and Excellence", *Library Trends*, Winter 1995, 43(3), pp.384-400.

* **Keiser, Barbie E. and Carol K Galvin.** "Marketing Library Services: A Nuts-and-Bolts approach". *Hague, FID*, 1995.pp.139 (FID Occasional Paper 9).

* **Perumalsamy, K.** "Marketing of Library Services", *University News*, 36(25), June22, 1998, pp.11-13.

* **Saxena, Sudha.** "Marketing of Library and Information Services", *ILA Bulletin.* Vol.XXX, No.1-2,April-July,1994,pp 8-12.

* **Weigand, Darlene.** "E,Issue Editor.Introduction", *Library Trends*,Vol.43,No.3, Winter 1995,pp 289-94.

* **Kotler, P.** *Marketing for nonprofit organizations.*Englewood Cliffs : New Jersey:Prentice-Hall,1975,p.165.

D-04
Virtual Library Real – Time Software in Reference Services

K. Thilahavathi
A. Rekha
II M.L.I.Sc. Students, Department of Library and
Information Science, AVVM Sri Pushpam College,
Poondi, Thanjavur Dt

ABSTRACT

Library is a store house of knowledge. The world today is in the midst of a major social, economic technological and information revolution by means of retrieval and calculation machines. As computer electronic communication systems like satellite internet, intranet etc, has brought significant changes, so is the usage of real time software in reference services. This paper discusses the characteristic and virtue of each class of software you may wish to revisit because they introduce the wide assortment of programs that enable communication on the internet in real time

INTRODUCTION

There are many types of more advanced software programs than IRC, MOO, or instant messaging (IM) that hold promise for Real- Time Reference for online library users. In addition to simple text-based chat, they offer sophisticated features, such as escorting, pursuing or sending web pages to users, while boarding powerful knowledge bases. Selecting the software for a real time reference service is difficult because there are so many programs and variables within each program to consider.

VIRTUAL LIBRARY

According to Alan Powell, *"virtual library is a library with little but no books, periodicals, reading space or support staff but one that disseminates selective information directly to library customers usually electronically "*.

CHARACTERISTICS

- It is not related with any physical documents like books, periodicals, etc.
- Mode of information is in electronic form
- It does not exist in a particular place
- Information can be accessed from any where
- It provides effective searching and browsing facility.

REAL – TIME REFERENCE INDICATORS

Your Library

- Has a large percentage of users who regularly use the internet at home or work
- Serves users like real – time online communication such as chat or instant messaging
- Supports distant learners
- Provides access to a sizeable number of online databases and information stores.
- Has a popular e-mail reference service

If some of these statements describe your library

audience, you probably have a base of users who would benefit from real-time Reference.

SOFTWARE SELECTION CRITERIA

One of the most difficult part of software selection is balancing a desire for special features of frequently used sayings, with the realities of price, operating system compatibilities and administrative features. The software needs to be easy to use for both patrons and librarians. Using a criteria list to run a software will help to compare and contrast features in a logical fashion. Features can be divided into the following areas for purposes of comparison.

- User interface
- General and administrative features
- Librarian interface
- Cost and Licensing
- System

USER INTERFACE

The most important issue to consider is usability, starting with the user interface. Perhaps the most important user interface consideration is whether the chosen software in their computer reach the service. Many synchronous software packages require nothing more than a web browser to log on.

Another aspect of the user interface is to evaluate real reference uses. Will answers be displayed in a window as with conference room or is it an accompanying web browser incorporated into the programs interface along with the chat window.

USER INTERFACE FACTORS

- Attractive, friendly
- Minimum instructions needed

- Help feature
- Alert feature
- Ability to customize interface
- Java applet or otherwise accessible form of web page
- Client installation required
- Single or multiplatform support.

GENERAL AND ADMINISTRATIVE FEATURES

Now that we have discussed the user interface, it is time to turn to more general features that help librarians deliver answers effectively, as well as manage the day- to-day operations of the service. Listed below are the few features that are useful to compare.

- Ability to control number of users
- Ability to disconnect or ban users
- Environment: number of rooms / channels, privacy
- Private messaging
- Clickable URLS
- Push Page
- Escorting (Co-browsing)
- Productivity features
- Site restrictions based on IP address
- Statistical reporting

USER MANAGEMENT

User management features vary widely across real-time software and are important in establishing "Crowd control". Crowd control the number of users that can be connected at one time, to restrict connections, and to disconnect or ban user, as well as communication or navigation commands.

LIBRARIAN INTER FACE

First, consider whether the system you are evaluating offers the librarian and the user the same interface or an enhanced one as in web based chat and call center software.

- Easy to navigate, find features
- Integrated with web browsers or requires multitasking
- Help feature
- Spell checker
- Alert feature
- Productivity features
- E-mail Support

PRICE AND SYSTEM FEATURES

The factors summarized next concerning cost, licensing system software and hardware should be helpful whether you are evaluating all features or a fuller-feature selection such as that used in web- based corporate call centers.

- Cost per user
- User expense
- Advertising
- Software trial or demonstrations available
- Technical support and documentation
- Training

SKILLS FOR EFFECTIVE VIRTUAL REFERENCE

- Ability to derive professional satisfaction from virtual reference transactions.
- Keyboarding proficiency
- Online communication skills and etiquette, for chat, e-mail and other online communication.
- Internet searching skills, in particular, the ability to

choose the best starting points for online searches

- Ability to assist online users in developing critical thinking, skills in locating, using and evaluating information

CONCLUSION

Several factors have been introduced that typically play a role in selection of real-time reference software. This paper has discussed the features as a reproducible checklist to assist in decision making.

REFERENCES

* http://www.yahoogroups.com
* http://www/chat.Yahoo.com.

D-05
Effectiveness Standards of Autonomous College Libraries

J. Franklin
Librarian, Evening Session, Bishop Heber College, Trichy

Dr. S. Ally Sornam
Head, Department of Library and Information Science,
Bishop Heber College, Trichy

ABSTRACT

The higher education system in India is one of the largest systems in the world. Autonomy to the colleges is one of the ways to enhance the quality of higher education. This paper discusses the various standards like collection, personnel, services, ICT and physical facilities that are used to measure the effectiveness of libraries in autonomous colleges.

INTRODUCTION

The higher education system in India is one of the largest systems in the world. Autonomy to the colleges is one of the ways to enhance the quality of higher education The UGC had taken steps during the 5th plan period to promote autonomous colleges, with a view to introduce innovation at all levels. Autonomous colleges in India have been functioning for about 20 years now, particularly in Tamil Nadu which can be rightly called the pioneer state in establishing autonomous colleges, carving them out of traditional university system. This paper discusses the various standards like collection, personnel, services, ICT and physical facilities that are used to measure the effectiveness of libraries in autonomous colleges.

AUTONOMY

The term 'autonomy' in the Random House Dictionary is defined as, " the right of self-government" which inter alia means 'no outside interference'. The word 'autonomy' is used in the learning process, teaching methods, curriculum construction and evaluation. It is said that true learning happens in a non-threatening environment which indicates that the learning environment should be free from barriers both physical and psychological. Autonomy refers to the status conferred on an institute for its unique identity and outstanding work.

AUTONOMOUS COLLEGES

Autonomy for a college implies that the college and its teachers assume full responsibility and accountability for the academic programmes they provide for the content and quality of their teaching and for the admission and assessment of their students.

AUTONOMOUS COLLEGE LIBRARIES

The reputation of Autonomous College Library in general is much greater than affiliated and government college libraries in terms of quality of collection and services. Autonomous College Library is expected to buy reading materials which match the standard and current developments of the curriculum and to satisfy the demands of the community. The facilities offered by an autonomous college library is generally on par with the other facilities offered by the college. Autonomous colleges are forced to achieve higher standards and greater creativity.

COLLECTION

The effective functioning and maintaining of quality in the library mainly depends on two factors

(i) the quality in the collection which serves as main source of information

(ii) efficient trained personnel who serve the readers

Therefore the collection of the library being intended for use must be evaluated from time to time with certain criterion, such as

a) Does the library has adequate collection of books and reference books?

b) Does the library has adequate collection of journals?

c) Does the library consider the users needs while acquiring new documents?

d) Does the library display the documents in an attractive manner?

e) Does the library offer open access to all the documents?

f) Does the library provide the required documents, at the very first time?

PERSONNEL

Among the three constituents of a library namely, books, readers and staff, it is the staff that occupies the position of the base upon which the structure of the library stands and which plays a pivotal role in the smooth running of a library. The quality and performance of library staff can thus make or mar the reputation of a library. The criteria used to measure the effectiveness standards of library personnel are;

a) Does the library staff are adequately qualified?

b) Does the staff have adequate training in giving modern services to users?

c) Are they equipped with soft skills to work as team?

d) Does the library staff help the user, when they fail to locate a needed document?

e) Does the library staff perform their work in time?

f) Does the library staff inform about the availability of the document requested?

g) Does the library staff immediately respond to the user's queries?

h) Does the library staff give personal attention to the users?

i) Does the library staff organise users' education programmes?

j) Does the librarian regularly interact with the users?

SERVICES

Library service is a social service which aims at self-development and improvement of skill and efficiency of the people of all walks of life. It is a vital input for research and national development. Obviously, the very purpose of library service will be defeated unless a minimum quality or standard is maintained by adopting some quality control methods. They are;

a) Does the library issue sufficient number of books to the users?

b) Does the library regularly exhibit a list of new books?

c) Does the library have convenient working hours?

d) Does the library provide all the basic services?

Today's library collection goes beyond print resources.

Hence quality of collection also depends on the subscription of e-resources. This poses additional questions like

e) Does the library have adequate number of systems?

f) Does the library have subscription to e-resources database?

g) Does the library have e-resources policy?

h) Is the library member of any consortia?

INFORMATION COMMUNICATION TECHNOLOGY (ICT)

Computer "technology provides a larger leap forward in inter-library communications than anything before, and thus it is certain to accelerate the development of resource sharing programmes among libraries and speedup the inter connection of data banks, reference centres, and information networks".

The various parameters used to measure the effectiveness and standards of ICT are;

a) Are the library services automated?

b) Does the library have OPAC / WEB OPACE service?

c) Does the circulation services of the library computerized?

d) Does the library provide, free internet services?

e) Does the library have a digital library unit?

f) Does the library have a website?

g) Does the library have a Xerox facility?

h) Does the library have printing/CD/DVD writing facility?

PHYSICAL FACILITIES

The physical facilities provided in a library are a very effective factor for the use of the library resources. The following are the standards used to measure the physical facilities

a) Does the library have a separate building ?

b) Does the library have well equipped furniture?

c) Does the library have better ventilation and lighting facilities?

d) Does the library have a separate reference section?

e) Does the library have adequate basic amenities?

CONCLUSION

The quality aspect is often not seriously considered in Indian libraries. This is evident from the fact that very rarely any attempt is made to evaluate the performance of a library in the context of its objectives. Any neglect of the quality aspect is self-inflicting since unsatisfactory service or deterioration in the quality of service lowers the image of the library in the eyes of the users as well as authorities. And without any objective evaluation of the performance and analysis of the causes behind deterioration neither it is possible to convince the authorities about the financial and other requirements for quality improvement, nor it is possible to take up any permanent remedial measure. In fact, there should be a regular mechanism for quality control in every library, as in every industry, if it has to succeed in its mission. Ofcourse the UGC/NAAC and NBA of AICTE have made impact on measuring and sustenance of the quality of L.I.Sc., particularly the NAAC have been giving more emphasis on the quality of autonomous college libraries while accreditation.

REFERENCES

* **Sushantha Kumar Roul.** *Effectiveness of Autonomous & Non-Autonomous College Teachers*, New Delhi : Gagan Deep Publications, 2004.

* **Vashishth, CP, Ed.** *Quality in Libraries,* New Delhi : ILA,1987.

* **Xavier Alphonse, SJ and Mani Jacob, Ed.** *Autonomous Colleges in India,2000,*New Delhi : Lokabodhan Kendra Publications, 2002.

D-06

Observations on LIS Education Through Distance Education

P. Clara Jeyaseeli

Librarian (SS), V.V. Vanniaperumal College for Women, Virudunagar.1.

ABSTRACT

In this paper, the transformation of libraries and library professionals are discussed. Since Library and Information Science education has to deal not only with printed but also with digital materials, it involves a lot of ICT (Information and Computer Technology) skills, interpersonal relationships and communicative skills. The various qualities that are expected from the LIS students are scrutinized. The credits and disadvantages of LIS education through distance education are also explored.

INTRODUCTION

Libraries are memories of mankind. With the growth of human civilization, knowledge increased in geometrical progression and reached beyond the capacity of man's memory. Hence, ways and means were developed to cope with the unprecedented growth.

Information explosion is one of the impacts of invention of printing technology and the emergence of democratic governments. With the invention and usage of Information and Communication Technologies, information is processed into knowledge and is made available enormously all over the world and is gaining maximum momentum both in developed countries and in developing countries.

Therefore, the library professionals are in a position to update and know why and how to manage the technologies. They should play their role dynamically as educator, mentor, facilitator and above all as social worker. In order to become an excellent LIS professional, the education and experience they acquire in the curriculum should be reflected when they practice as professionals. While undergoing the LIS course itself, the students of LIS should gain expertise in the art of management of knowledge, information, people, technology, etc.

LIBRARY AND INFORAMTION SCIENCE EDUCATION

Dr. Krishan Gopal rightly states that the Information Science programs should be framed keeping in view of the new challenges so that the future information professionals can do justice to an extremely demanding profession.

Also he states in his work "Library Collections" that the function of the library school is not to impart narrowly defined skills, but to provide students with sets of criteria needed to perform their duties and to screen candidates who do not meet the requirements of the profession.

Walker says that for many of our library and information service workers, their foundations in Library and Information Science and Information and Communication Technological skills are often inadequate or learnt on the job.

Shane Godbolt defines the different layers of knowledge as

Data	-	raw numbers/text or both.
Information	-	interpreted or analyzed data.
Explicit knowledge	-	published, transmittable and systematic. Adds value and assists action.
Tacit knowledge	-	resides in people's heads
Wisdom	-	combines all categories of knowledge into learning and experience.

The literature review of Library and Information Science states that the libraries are changing tremendously and in one fine day there will be only virtual libraries; it envisions libraries and librarians to exist in a different organizational structure and play a tremendously changed role depending upon the changes in Information and Communication Technologies. The Library and Information Science course also should be evaluated and changes should be adopted in the curriculum in order to cope with the challenging race of digital era.

The Library and Information Science course through Distance Education is really a boon to the professionals who are practising as well as the people who want to acquire and update knowledge apart from mere experience.

QUALITIES EXPECTED FROM A LIS CANDIDATE IN VIRTUAL LEARNING ENVIRONMENT

The following qualities are expected, should be gathered and acquired by the LIS candidate in order to cope with fast changing modes in this competitive knowledge era.

1. Leadership Quality.
2. Managerial Skills.

3. Communicative Skills.

4. Interpersonal relationships.

5. Communication Technological Skills.

6. Professional Skills.

7. Professional Ethics.

8. Application of power, authority and influence in the appropriate places.

9. Knowledge of the areas of development which leads to personal growth as well as professional growth.

10. Adaptation and preparedness to work up to the expectation of organizational values and priorities.

11. An awareness of issues related to diversity, including ethnicity, gender and generational difference.

12. Envision possibilities for a role in future organizational development.

13. Enlist others in supporting a common vision for the future.

14. Recognize and communicate key messages that frame organizational meaning and demonstrate presentation skills.

15. Understand how to manage change, define issues and seek innovative solutions.

16. Describe the role of the library director as a community leader, see a customer-centered view of library service and understand how to collaborate and establish partnership.

17. Develop team-building skills with awareness of facilitation techniques and conflict management.

18. Understand the importance of staff development in recruitment, coaching, delegation, trust and recognition activities.

19. Become familiar with the services of the agency and

aware of current statewide and professional issues affecting library services.

20. Should have a mindset to change according to the current technological changes and should self motivate.

CREDITS OF LIS THROUGH DISTANCE EDUCATION

- Professional degree certificates can be obtained.
- For the professionals, the degree can be got without losing the profession.
- Can apply the theoretical concepts practically.
- The computer professionals who want to acquire knowledge regarding library science also will also be able to study LIS course.
- Since it is mostly self learning, the candidates find more time for reference.
- No formal permission letters needed to visit other libraries or other meetings related to LIS.
- Can incorporate information skills in profession.
- Can visit many libraries out of self motivation.
- Practicing Library Professionals' experiences can be gathered out of self interest.
- Can schedule their own time and explore many concepts of LIS.
- Self motivation can be acquired by reading books as well as through practicing professionals.
- Can improve communicative skills.
- Spare more time to train themselves in computer skills through virtual learning.
- Can join as a trainee (salary should not be expected) to improve the interpersonal skills.

DISADVANTAGES OF LIS THROUGH DISTANCE EDUCATION

- Many students gather only theoretical knowledge.
- Academically the students are not given wide opportunities to visit digitized libraries.
- The students are not made aware of the basic skills that are required and practiced in ITC libraries.
- Owing to lack of motivation, the students find no opportunities to gather the updated and the current technological advancements in the fields.
- The basic need for a library professional is communicative skills. But it is not practised and not included in the curriculum also.
- Virtual Learning Environment and computer training are not provided even in seminar classes.
- The syllabus focuses on the traditional libraries and the practices of traditional librarians with introduction to digital library and virtual library concepts.
- Not exposed to social and cultural gatherings since interpersonal skills are very much essential for a library professional.
- The organizational behavior, the rights of the profession, the various professional bodies, and training centers are not focused.
- Equal weightage for the degree under DDE when compared with regular stream is not given socially.
- Appointed for low scale of pay when compared with other courses.
- The world has become a small village and it is marching towards digital and virtual world with communication and information technological skills but the curriculum does not provide practical sessions in such technological libraries.

- The curriculum deals only with the basics of computers, online catalogs and its applications in various centers theoretically but has no real time exposure to such centers.

- The exposure of digital libraries, the methods to be adopted for creating digital and virtual libraries is not focused in depth.

- Should have tie-up with virtual libraries and digital library agencies to get hands on experience.

- The teaching faculty should be exposed to the current technological developments and financial assistance should be provided to acquire knowledge about virtual learning, which in turn will reflect in the students.

CONCLUSION

The curriculum of LIS in virtual learning environment should be strengthened with the provision for practical sessions for communication and information technologies. Organizations like INFLIBNET, NCSI, NISSAT, digital society forums, etc. have to conduct extensive in-house training programmes for the students along with practicing professionals so that the future professionals are able to cope with new technological and managerial changes when they are expected to provide effective and efficient information services.

The practising librarians should also give a hand in training to the future generation. The essential qualifications required for library assistants should be made as Degree in Library Science along with Computer knowledge.

The distance schools of Library and Information Science should also sign MOUs with the libraries so that the practising library professionals can guide the students of LIS. During the contact classes, the students should be provided with virtual learning sources, computer training and communicative skills. A study tour should be arranged once so that the students will be oriented to visit a library and gather knowledge about the skills that are needed.

Unless the students participate in such practical sessions the certificates should not be issued. In order to accommodate these recommendations, the duration of the course can be changed from 1 year to 2 years course of study. Then only the LIBRARY AND INFORMATION SCIENCE students and professionals can take part in the rapidly changing environment.

REFERENCES

* **Krishan Gopal.** *Digital Libraries: in Electronic Information Era.* New Delhi:Authorspress, 2005.

* **Krishan Gopal.** *Library Collections: conundrums and contradictions.* New Delhi:Authorspress, 2005.

* **Walker, CM.** 2001. Janus in South Africa: Building for the future while keeping an eye on the past. In: *Delivering lifelong continuing professional education across space and time. The Fourth World Conference on Continuing Professional Education for the Library and Information Science Professions*; edited by Blanche Woolls and Brooke Sheldon. Munchen: KG Saur, p. 230-241. (IFLA Publications 98)

* http://www.dlib.org.

* http://www.londonlinks.ac.uk

D-07

Quality Assignment of Higher Educational Library Services

G. Ramadas

Librarian, Noorul Islam College of Arts and Science,
Kumaracoil, - 629 180

ABSTRACT

Quality enhancement in higher education is a deliberate process of chance which leads to improvement. Quality in higher education has become the prime concern world over. Establishing National External Quality Assurance to maintain and improve the standards of education is considered to be the best way of responding to the quality of higher education. In this context Indian Government has established NAAC and NBA as external quality assurance agencies to have a quality check in the Indian higher education system. This paper elucidates the concepts, methods and implementation of parameters of NAAC and LIBQUAL in improving the quality of LIS in higher academic institutions.

QUALITY ASSIGNMENT OF HIGHER EDUCATIONAL LIBRARY SERVICES

Quality enhancement [QE] in higher education is a

deliberate process of change that leads to improvement. The word 'quality' has been borrowed from the industry. In educational aspect of academic parlance, two terms are often used, namely 'Quality Assessment' and 'Quality Assurance'. They are like two sides to a coin .The former refers to the internal and external evaluations used to assess the overall teaching and research performance of the institution. The latter refers to the concern of different stakeholders regarding the continuous process of adopting various mechanisms and procedure to monitor performance and to take up remedial measures to improve academic standards and to increase the quality. Quality in higher education has become the prime concern the world over. Establishing National External Quality Assurance (NEQA) medium to maintain and improve the standards of education is considered to be the best way of responding to the quality of higher education. This is a relatively new concept to be adopted perhaps during the last decade even in countries like UK, Canada and Australia. By establishing the National Assessment and Accreditation Council (NAAC), India joined this International trend in 1994.

In recent decade, the University Grant Commission (UGC) the National Assessment Accreditation Council (NAAC), All India Council of Technical Education (AICTE), and National Board of Accreditation (NBC) have succeeded in promoting and encouraging quality in all elements of higher education in higher educational institutions in the country.

Higher education in India is one of the largest and oldest systems and now NAAC has assessed the quality of 140 Universities and 3492 higher institutions and AICTE has assessed the quality of 329 institutions in India up to May 2006. 48 universities and 234 colleges are getting Autonomous status in 2007.

There are 347 universities including deemed

universities and 16,500 colleges, in India. Of these122 universities and deemed universities and 2486 colleges are granted status of accreditation by the NAAC. The gap between accredited and non-accredited institutions will affect the quality of education.

As per the National Knowledge Commission [N K C] report submitted, one of the major recommendations is the element of infrastructure that supports the teaching-learning process, such as libraries, laboratories and connectivity, which needs to be monitored and upgraded on a regular basis.

The assessment bodies use many criteria for evaluating the quality of the educational institutions. The NAAC is adopting its new methodology of assessment for accreditation from April 2007. The major criteria used by them are

* Curricular Aspects
* Teaching, Learning and Evaluation
* Infrastructure and Learning Resources
* Organizational Governance
* Research, Consultancy and healthy practices.
* Student progress

Among these criteria library plays an important role in Teaching, Learning, Infra-structure & Resource, Research activities etc.

Recently the NAAC has issued a set of 'Guide Lines on Quality Indicators in LIS' to improve the quality of the learning resource center in affiliated and constituent colleges and universities in India. All these show that the quality of library and information services offered in higher education institution is a serious matter and the authorities and the library and information professionals in higher education institution must consider its seriousness.

In order to improve the quality, the institutions should

provide good library facilities, collection of documents and services. They should provide necessary facilities to promote effective current and accurate access to use latest information sources available.

Accessing the needs and requirements as well as the satisfaction of the user with regard to the library and information services is highly necessary. The NAAC has viewed that the main objective of the higher educational institutions should always be 'total user satisfaction.' It is opined that the functioning of the library should be user focused and the librarian should be the interpreter of thought and content and user satisfaction should guide the libraries. It shows that there should be a user-based assessment of the quality LIS offered in higher education institutions in India. There are certain reliable tools such as SERVQUAL; LibQUAL; WebQUAL; etc for understanding the expectations and perceptions of user with regard to higher educational institutions and the library information services and thereby assess its quality. The Association of Research Libraries (ARL) is using LibQUAL to measure the service quality of its member libraries. The LIS professional understand what the user actually expect from the library. What do they actually receive from the library and what is the level of quality of these services? It will also help the LIS professionals to improve, or switch over the library. It will also help to improve the quality of services.

SERVQUAL is an international tool used in marketing research to assess the quality of products and services. It contains 22 items grouped under five-quality dimensions namely Reliability, Access, Tangible, Empathy and Responsiveness. These 22 items are used to assess user or customer expectations, perceptions and the quality of products and services. This tool can be modified customized and enlarged to suit any service organization and service, including library and information services.

LibQUAL is a web-based service quality measurement tool developed by the Association of Research Libraries (ARL) to assess the user expectations, perceptions and the quality of library and information services offered in their member libraries. It contains 25 items grouped under four quality dimensions. The academic and research libraries in western countries like USA, UK, Germany etc. access the quality of Library Information Services regularly with the help of **LibQUAL**.

Now there are tools for measuring the quality of library websites, digital library, e-learning portal etc. called WebQUAl. Maximum higher education institutions offer these facilities, which can be accessed remotely. Compared to traditional libraries, the items of quality related to digital libraries and the websites are different. The visual medias are regularly assessing the quality of their program.

These facts indicate that the quality of the higher educational institutional library services can very well be assessed. The higher education is not possible without quality information services. Therefore this is the apt time to access the quality information services offered in traditional, computerized, digital, remote access, or online set up and improve the quality for satisfying the students and teacher community in higher education institutions in India.

REFERENCES

* **Bavakutty. M and Abdul Majeed. K.C.** *Methods for Measuring Quality of Libraries.* New Delhi : ESS Publications,2003
* **Abdul Majeed. K.C and Bavakutty. M,.**"Quality Assessment of College and University Library Services", *University News,* Vol.45, No.11,28
* http://www.libqual.org
* http://www.webqual.co.uk
* http://www.ugc.ac.in
* http://www.aicte.ac.in
* http://www.aiu.ac.in

D-08
Measuring the Library Quality Using Servqual, Libqual and Webqual

M. Dorairajan
Librarian, St. Joseph's College, Tiruchirappalli

Dr. S. Srinivasa Raghavan
Librarian, Bharathidasan University, Tiruchirappalli

R.T. Vijaya
Librarian, Pope John Paul II College of Education, Pondicherry

ABSTRACT

There are several methods or tools or techniques to measure, control and improve the quality of a library. The quality can be perceived from the organizational level or user level or both, but the perceptions of the library users is most important as the quality of a library has been defined as the gap between the expectations and perceptions of users about the library. SERVQUAL, LIBQUAL and WEBQUAL are the important tools to measure the standard and quality of the library services provided to the users for their satisfaction.

INTRODUCTION

The term quality is used to refer to the desirability of properties or characteristics of a person, object, or process. In the case of a person this is considered in a particular context, such as worker, student, sports person etc,. The term is often used in opposition to quantity. In science, the work of Aristotle focused on measuring quality whereas, the work of Galileo resulted in a shift towards the study of quantity.

It also describes that in manufacturing, the notion of quality relates to making a product fit for a purpose with the fewest possible defects. Finally, quality can historically have four different interpretations: conformance to specifications, fitness for use, must-be attractive and of value to some person.

The traditional orientation of measuring the quality is quantifiable terms of its collection and use or does it adequately address the campus community's demands for information. New ways to conceive of and measure quality in service industry is needed—and alternate approaches emerge in the business sector where organizations are increasingly evaluated in terms of their service quality.

The primary focus of a service industry is service, and service quality is the most studied topic in marketing research during the past decade. A repeated theme in the marketing literature is service quality, as perceived by consumers, which is a function of what customers expect and how well the firm performs in providing the service. Among the most popular assessments tools of service quality is SERVQUAL, an instrument designed by the marketing research team of Berry, Parasuraman, and Zeithaml (PB&Z). Through numerous qualitative studies, they evolved a set of five dimensions which have been consistently ranked by customers to be most important for service quality, regardless of service industry.

THESE DIMENSIONS ARE DEFINED AS FOLLOWS

Tangibles appearance of physical facilities, equipment, personnel and communication materials;

Reliability ability to perform the promised service dependably and accurately;

Responsiveness willingness to help customers and provide prompt service;

Access : knowledge and courtesy of employees and their ability to convey trust and confidence

Empathy the caring, individualized attention the firm provides its customers.

SERVE QUAL METHODOLOGY

Measuring customer satisfaction is a critical requirement for many organizations, but it does not need to be a painful one. T.S.P.G. offers a very useful process for measuring the overall customer satisfaction of an organization through the ServQual Methodology. Originally developed by leading customer satisfaction researchers Valarie Zeithaml, A. Parasuraman and Leonard Berry (Delivering Quality Service, Free Press: 1990), the ServQual Methodology is an invaluable tool for organizations to better understand what customers value and how well their current organizations are meeting the needs and expectations of customers.

ServQual provides a benchmark based on customer opinions of an excellent company, on the importance ranking of key attributes and on a comparison to what the employees believe customers feel.

It provides detailed information about:

- customer perceptions of service (a benchmark established by customers);

- your performance levels as perceived by customers;
- customer comments and suggestions;
- impressions from employees with respect to customers expectations and satisfaction. ServQual has proven to be a simple yet effective tool for many organizations.

LibQUAL+(TM) is a suite of services that libraries use to solicit, track, understand and act upon users' opinions of service quality. These services are offered to the library community by the Association of Research Libraries (ARL). The program's centerpiece is a rigorously tested Web-based survey bundled with training that helps libraries assess and improve library services, change organizational culture and market the library. The goals of LibQUAL+(TM) are to:

- Foster a culture of excellence in providing library service
- Help libraries better understand user perceptions of library service quality
- Collect and interpret library user feedback systematically over time
- Provide libraries with comparable assessment information from peer institutions
- Identify best practices in library service
- Enhance library staff members' analytical skills for interpreting and acting on data

Library administrators have successfully used LibQUAL+(TM) survey data to identify best practices, analyze deficits and effectively allocate resources. Benefits to participating institutions include:

- Institutional data and reports that enable you to assess whether your library services are meeting user expectations
- Aggregate data and reports that allow you to compare your library's performance with that of peer institutions

- Workshops designed specifically for LibQUAL+(TM) participants
- Access to an online library of LibQUAL+(TM) research articles
- The opportunity to become part of a community interested in developing excellence in library services

LibQUAL+(TM) gives your library users a chance to tell you where your services need improvement so you can respond to and better manage their expectations. You can develop services that better meet your users' expectations by comparing your library's data with that of peer institutions and examining the practices of those libraries that are evaluated highly by their users.

WebQual™ WebQual™consulting services use a statistically validated and reliable measure for determining Web site quality. A research method of instrument development served as the guiding process of development. In addition, newer statistical techniques (i.e. structural equation modeling) were used to confirm the reliability and discriminant validity of the measure. Three steps of qualitative data collection were used in the initial phases of research. First, consumer perceptions of Web site quality were captured in an open-ended questionnaire. Second, interviews were conducted with Web site designers to understand their definition of a quality site. Lastly, a Fortune 500 company's criteria for determining a Web site's quality were included. Then, two rounds of data collection were used to purify the measure and test its validity and reliability.

Revealed in this research are twelve essential components of Web site quality: informational fit-to-task, interactivity, trust, response time, design, intuitiveness, visual appearance, innovativeness, flow, integrated communications, business process relationship and substitutability.

MEASURING THE QUALITY IN LIBRARIES

The libraries have transformed drastically from the storehouses of books to the powerhouses of knowledge and information since the middle of twentieth century. The information and communication technology, which is responsible for this revolution has drastically changed the organization, management and functioning of modern libraries. The very existence of library is fully dependent on the satisfaction of users. Therefore, libraries are now more concerned about the library customers, their satisfaction, the quality of libraries and information products, services, their proper marketing.

A user is satisfied when the library is able to rise to his/her expectations or meet the actual needs. The library and information professionals have to properly understand the customers, what they want, how they want it and when they want the documents or information from a library. So the library has to consider the individuality of the customers, responsiveness of staff and the relationship of the customer with the library very seriously as it effects the quality of library products and services heavily. There are several methods or tools or techniques to measure, control and improve the quality of a library. The quality can be perceived from the organizational level or user level or both, but the perception of the library users is most important as the quality of a library has been defined as the gap between the expectations and perceptions of users about the library.

Every library exists to satisfy the needs of the customers and aims to achieve hundred percent customer satisfaction, however, there may be some discrepancy between what libraries provide and what the customers actually need. This mismatch results from the failure of the library to meet customer needs and from the unrealistic expectations of customers. Therefore, it is necessary to have some system through which the customer needs are heard and these must be used to improve the quality of the libraries.

REFERENCES

* **Dadzie, PS.** "Quality management initiatives in Balme library: possibilities, challenges and constraints for top management commitment", *Library Management*, Vol. 25 No.1/2, 2004, pp.56-61.

* **Fitzsimmons, JA and Fitzsimmons, MJ.** *Service Management: Operations, Strategy, and Information Technology*, 3rd Ed., Boston : McGraw-Hill, 2000,pp.43-67

* **Nitecki, DA.** "Changing the concept and measure of service quality in academic libraries", *Journal of Academic Librarianship*, Vol. 22, No.3, 1996, pp.181-90

D–09
A Study on Customer Relationship Management Towards Online Marketing

V.P. Ramesh Babu
Librarian, Rev. Jacob Memorial Christian College,
Santhipuram, Ambilikkai – 624 612 Dindigul Dt.

C.P.S. Balamurugan
Librarian, Kendira Vidhyalaya, CECRI Campus, Karaikudi

R. Maheswari
Plot No.4, 2/166A 5th North Street, Viraiya Koil Street,
Rajakambadi, Palkalai Nagar, Maduai-21

ABSTRACT

This study is an attempt to analyse the buyer's attitude towards online marketing. It also shows the recent trends in the online business and also predicts the future of online marketing. It also shows the buyers attitude on online shopping.

INTRODUCTION

Relationship marketing is now gaining wide acceptance among the business world. Customer retention has become more important. It is a big challenge for the marketers how to retain customers, as there is certain amount of customer migration at different stages of the customer life cycle due to various reasons. Sometimes even fully satisfied customers switch over to another brand without having any perfect reasons, hence there is a great need to put efforts to minimise the same.

The cost of retaining is just one tenth, the cost of acquiring a new one, is the core philosophy of relationship marketing. In today's business environment developing and maintaining an ongoing relationship with the customer is more important than the success of any product or service. Customer relationships are now at the forefront of the business. These days marketing is moving from being broad based to a one-to-one relationship with the customer. Hence more attention to detail is required. Indian companies need call centers to boost marketing efforts as the Indian consumer starts becoming more aware of the choice available.

The term relationship was first coined in America in the early 1980s. Relationship marketing is marketing with the conscious aim to develop and manage long term and /or trusting relationship with customers, distributors, suppliers or other parties in the marketing environment.

Pathmarajah defines "relationship marketing as the process whereby the seller and the buyer join in a strong personal, professional and mutually profitable relationship over a time". He characterised relationship as having the following properties: Effective, Efficient, Enjoyable, Enthusiastic, Ethical.

NEED FOR THE STUDY

Richheld concluded that there are some underlying reasons why retained customers are more profitable.

- Customer acquisition costs may be high, so customers may not become profitable unless they are retained for more years.

- There will be a stream of profiles from the customer in each year after acquisition costs are covered.
- Companies become more efficient at serving customers, so costs go down.
- Retained and satisfied customers may refer other potential customers.
- Relationship has a value to the customers too, so retained customers tend to become less price sensitive.

OBJECTIVES OF THE STUDY

To study the factors that helps online marketers to retain their customers.

To analyse the benefits derived by a customer and his supplier on online marketing.

To analyse the importance of CRM building blocks.

HISTORY OF ONLINE MARKETING

The concept of relationship is as old as human being, and the barter system as there was direct interaction between farm producers and their customers. However the modern marketer started realising the same only recently.

To understand the relationship marketing concept properly we have to see the periodical development of the marketing concept as the marketing concept leads to the relationship marketing concept. In1950's,the consumer goods companies were recognized as the most sophisticated marketers. In 1960's, considerable attention was paid to the industrial market. In 1970's the marketing of non-profit organisations and associated areas of public sector and social marketing received attention. In 1980's the service marketing sector started attracting attention. In the early 1990's, the concept of relationship marketing was formally introduced into the field of service marketing. And further the concept was also found applicable in the case of industrial as well as consumer products.

As the concept of relationship marketing has emerged the focus has been shifted from transaction marketing to relationship marketing.

BENEFITS

Benefits which are associated with the customer are

- Customers remain loyal and receive more value compared to the competitors.
- Customers have the sense of well being and quality of life as they have long term relationship with the service provider.
- Customers think that the service provider knows their preferences and have tailored service to suit their needs over a period of time and they do not want to change this arrangement thus they remain loyal.

BENEFITS FOR THE SERVICE PRODUCERS

- Due to good relationship, the service provider gets committed to loyal customers, thus increasing the purchases, which in turn increases the profits of the company.
- Training the current customers costs much lower than making new customers as new customers attract advertising cost and other promotion costs, operating costs of setting up accounts and systems and costs of getting to know the customers.
- Free advertising through word of mouth.
- It's easier for the firm to retain the employees when the company has stable base of satisfied customers.

USAGE OF SHOPPING CARDS IN ONLINE MARKETING

Business Features

- Indian Gypsy e-business platform offers a rich set of features supporting key functionality including configurable information access to collaboration and publishing. Its robust feature set includes :

- Customer service search upon various options like state, city, category, price by name.

- Real time availability check-automatically checks number of products available and allows webmasters to control number of packages available.

- Automatic tax calculation-calculates taxes automatically in real time through a tax open adapter.

- Site management tools and wizards enable non technical managers to manage contracts, develop contract and define the business rules that are crucial to business e-commerce system.

- Purchase lists allow business customers to save lists of frequently ordered items for efficient purchasing.

- Search capabilities includes powerful text, category and parametric search capabilities that allow keyword, product category or product features.

- Lock-in quotes(wish list) allow users to lock in the price of items and save the quotation for a later purchase.

- Real time pricing supports real-time, dynamic pricing with an internal pricing engine or by working with an external business system.

- Security authenticates, authorizes and ensures the confidentiality of all transactions and supports required login ID and password, users access control, SSL for secure connection from browser to web browser and X.509 based digital certificates for strong authentication

- Order processing supports comprehensive order workflow, including order pricing, order capture, payment authorization, order fulfillment, payment settlement and order status. Also includes configurable order processing using javascripts.

E-CUSTOMER FEATURE

Book marks make it easy to access most used content and information channels. Navigation filters present a selection of information channels based on users roles, profiles and preferences.

Access control determines which users can read, write or edit documents. Role based application access affords the convenience of single sign-on access to a pre-set group of applications based on the users role.

CUSTOMER NEEDS

- Delivery conformity
- Punctuality of delivery
- Short delivery times
- After sale care with expertise support
- Quick response to unexpected orders
- Quality/reliability
- The best value for money
- Quick and correct answers to requests
- Simple buying process.

To satisfy the needs of the customer, sellers follow some rules regarding their marketing activities to retain their customers.

IMPROVED CUSTOMER SATISFACTION

The customers are in control. They can find

information whenever they need it, regardless of the time or location. There is round the clock service, everyday of the year. Customer can find product information, pricing information and even technical support, there is no waiting for service.

And like employees, customer also have a low learning curve because of the common user interface, making it easy for them to use, reducing errors and thus helping to win loyalty.

SUGGESTIONS

- Suppliers should make available quality products at affordable prices that are accessible to the maximum number of places.
- The company must be selective in tailoring its appropriate customers for individual marketing programs.
- To built up enduring relationship marketers should offer special services, discounts, increased communications and attention beyond the care product or service without expecting an immediate payback to loyal customers.
- It is suggested that the supplier must provide well and good securities to their customers.
- It is suggested that if they increase their features, there will be more no of sales.
- It is suggested that if each and every family will have one PC in their house, online marketing will be more popular among people.
- Customer should be managed as important assets; customer profitability varies, desirable customers vary in their needs, preferences and buying behavior and price sensitivity.

By understanding customer drivers and customer

profitability, companies can tailor their offerings to maximise the overall value of their customer portfolio.

CONCLUSION

It is concluded that the surveyed customers seem to consider brand name and price as important elements in buying any type of product. They seem to buy any product without waiting for any other or festive season. By increasing the usage period and rendering quality goods and services future expectations of online marketing can be achieved.

REFERENCES

* http://www.en.wikipedia.org/wiki/online_marketing
* http://www.analogik.com/article_principles_of_emarketing
* http://www.optimizedmarketing.com/emarketing/index.htm
* http://www.emarketingassociation.com/

Technical Session – V
Collection Development Management in Electronic Environment

E-01
A Bibliometric Study on IEEE Transaction on Control System Technology

J. Santhi
Librarian, Cherraan's Institute of Health Science, Coimbatore.
Dr. N. Murugesa Pandian
Librarian, Ganesar College of Arts & Science, Melasivapuri.

ABSTRACT

A Bibliometric Examination of all the journal articles published in the IEEE Transactions on Control System Technology from 2002-2006 was carried out. The aim of this study was to identify country, year wise distribution, authorship pattern and ranking of authors. The study reveals that, the range of articles published per volume is between 93 and 115; average number of references per article is 22; the average length per article is 10 pages; the percentage of multi authored papers is slightly higher at 93.73%; the most prolific author contributed 6 articles; 37.92% of authors are geographically affiliated to USA.

INTRODUCTION

Bibliometrics is a type of research method used in

library and information science. It utilizes quantitative analysis and statistics to describe patterns of publication within a given field or body of literature. The researchers may use bibliometric method of evaluation to determine the influence of a single writer or to describe the relationship between two or more writers or workers. The term 'Bibliometrics' implies the use of quantitative or statistical methods to study the behavior of information. Allan Pritchard was the first man who coined the term Bibliometrics in 1968 but it became more popular during 1980s. According to him, it is an "application of mathematical and statistical methods to book and other media of communication". More recently Sengupta had defined this term as the "organization, classification and quantitative evolution of publication patterns of all macro and micro communications along with their authorship by mathematical and statistical calculus".

OBJECTIVES OF THE STUDY

The objectives of the study are as follows:

1. To know the overall distribution pattern of contributions
2. Distribution of Reference by Volume
3. To know the Year-Wise Distribution of Total Number of pages
4. To know the Year wise Distribution of Length of Articles
5. Year wise Distribution of Total number of Contributions Vs Total Number of Pages
6. Authorship pattern of Contribution
7. Analysis of Authors and their contribution
8. Country wise Distribution of Authors
9. Ranked List of Most prolific Contributor.

SOURCE OF JOURNAL

The IEEE, a non-profit Organization, is the world's leading professional association for the advancement of technology. The full name of the IEEE is "Institute of Electrical and Electronics

Engineers, Inc.", although the organization is referred to by the letters I-E-E-E and pronounced Eye-triple- E .The IEEE was formed in 1963 with the merger of

- The AIEE (American Institute of electrical Engineers, Formed in 1884) and
- The IRE (Institute of Radio Engineers, Formed in 1912) From its earliest origin, the IEEE has
- Advanced the theory and application of electro technology and allied sciences
- Served as a catalyst for technological innovations
- Supported the needs of its members through a wide variety of programs and services.

The mission of IEEE is to promote the engineering process of creating, developing, integrating, sharing and applying knowledge about electro and information technologies and sciences for the benefit of humanity and profession. The volumes of IEEE Transaction on Control System Technology published from 2002 - 2006 have been chosen as the source document.

METHODOLOGY

The data has been compiled from online journal articles. For each article following data has been noted: Name of authors, Number of authorship, Number of references, Authors geographically affiliated, Length (pages) of article and other data required for the study. All the necessary information were compiled, recorded, tabulated and analysed for making observations as indicated in the objectives of the study. The study covers the journal issues from 2002-2004.

FINDINGS-OVERALL   DISTRIBUTION PATTERN OF CONTRIBUTIONS

Table 1 shows the total number of articles published from 2002 to 2006.On the whole from the 5 volumes and 30 issues of the journal under study, the total number of articles published is 510. The distribution of articles by volume shows that the number of articles was highest in 2006, with 115 articles. It was noted that there is an increasing trend in the quantum of publications from 2004.

Table 1: Overall Distribution Pattern of Contributions

Year	Vol. No	No. of Issues	No. of the articles/contributions						Total No. of Articles	%age of articles
			I	*II*	*III*	*IV*	*V*	*VI*		
2002	10	6	17	15	15	15	16	15	93	18.24
2003	11	6	19	15	13	17	15	16	95	18.63
2004	12	6	21	8	16	16	16	17	94	18.43
2005	13	6	15	16	18	20	19	25	113	22.15
2006	14	6	18	21	21	18	19	18	115	22.55
Total			90	75	83	86	85	91	510	100

DISTRIBUTION OF REFERENCE BY VOLUME

Overall distribution pattern of citation in the IEEE Transaction on Control System Technology during the period 2002-2006 contained 11139 references in 510 articles and each article has an average of 22 references as shown in the table 2.

Table 2: Distribution of Reference by Volume

Year	No. of Contributions	No. of citations	Average citations per contribution	Cumulative reference	%
2002	93	1799	19	1799	16.15
2003	95	2075	22	2075	18.63
2004	94	2142	23	2142	19.23
2005	113	2610	23	2610	23.43
2006	115	2513	22	2513	22.56
Total	510	11139	22	11139	100

YEAR-WISE DISTRIBUTION OF TOTAL NUMBER OF PAGES

Table 3 shows the analysis of the number of pages of publication which is one of the most important factor in bibliometric analysis. From the table it is observed that there is an increasing trend in the quantum of publications from 2002-2006. From 2002 all the issues cover pages above 700. Year 2006 has the first place in terms of publication pages

Table 3 : Year-Wise Distribution of Total Number of Pages

S.No	Year	Number of Pages						Total	%age	Cum. %age
		I	II	III	IV	V	VI			
1	2002	164	139	172	153	122	153	903	17.87	17.87
2	2003	157	122	137	177	170	174	937	18.55	36.42
3	2004	215	103	163	152	151	195	979	19.38	55.8
4	2005	166	170	162	173	165	254	1090	21.58	77.38
5	2006	177	195	197	199	189	186	1143	22.62	100
Total		879	729	831	854	797	962	5052	100	

YEAR WISE DISTRIBUTION OF LENGTH OF ARTICLES

Table 4 indicates the length of articles in term of pages.

Out of 510 articles, 76.07% of the articles are above seven pages in length. Only 23.93% of the articles are between 1-6 pages in length

Table 4: Year wise Distribution of Length of Articles

Number of Pages	2002	2003	2004	2005	2006	Total	%
Two	0	1	0	0	0	1	0.2
Three	0	1	0	0	0	1	0.2
Four	0	1	0	1	2	4	0.8
Five	3	3	4	3	4	17	3.33
Six	8	5	10	11	8	42	8.23
Seven	10	7	6	21	13	57	11.17
Above Seven	72	77	74	77	88	388	76.07
Total	93	95	94	113	115	510	100

YEAR WISE DISTRIBUTION OF TOTAL NUMBER OF CONTRIBUIONS VS TOTAL NUMBER OF PAGES

An attempt is made to compare the total contributions and their pages. For more understanding the total number of journal articles is also compared with their pages. the comparative data are presented with average in table 5. It is observed from table 5, there is a fluctuation in the number of contributions. While analyzing the average number of pages on total contribution from 2002 to 2006 it has an increasing trend. From 2001-2006 the average number of pages is 10.

Table 5: Year wise Distribution of Total number of contributions vs Total Number of Pages

Year	Quantum of Contribution	Quantum of Total Pages	Average number of pages per Contribution
2002	93	903	10
2003	95	937	10

2004	94	979	10
2005	113	1090	10
2006	115	1143	10
Total	**510**	**5052**	10

AUTHORSHIP PATTERN OF CONTRIBUTION

The authorship pattern of contribution indicated that multi authored articles (93.73%) outnumbered single-authored articles (6.27 %) which have been shown in table 6.

Table 6: Authorship Pattern of Contributions

Pattern	2002	2003	2004	2005	2006	Total	%
Single	10	5	6	5	6	32	6.27
Two	34	38	29	39	45	185	36.28
Three	32	26	34	34	36	162	31.76
Four	11	17	17	23	21	89	17.45
Five & above	6	9	8	12	7	42	8.24
Total	93	95	94	113	115	510	100

ANALYSIS OF AUTHORS AND THEIR CONTRIBUTION

Table 7 : Analysis of Authors & Their Contribution

S. No	No. of Authors	No. of Contribution	Percentage
1	1116	1	87.6
2	129	2	10.1
3	19	3	1.5
4	8	4	0.6
5	1	5	0.1
6	1	6	0.1
	1274		100

An analysis of the number of contributions given by every individual author is indicated in table -7. The analysis by percentage indicates that relatively 87.6%(1116) of authors have written only 1 paper. 12.2% of authors have written 2 to 4 articles. 0.1 of authors have written 5 & 6 articles

COUNTRY WISE DISTRIBUTION OF AUTHORS

Table 8 shows that 559(37.92%) of the authors are geographically affiliated to USA, followed by Canada with 90(6.11%) and Italy with 85(5.77%). 261(17.71%) of authors are from France, U.K Taiwan and Korea. The remaining 479 (32.49 %) authors are from 48 countries

Table 8 :Country -wise Distribution of Authors

S.No	Country	No. of Authors	%
1	USA	559	37.92
2	Canada	90	6.11
3	Italy	85	5.77
4	France	66	4.48
5	U.K	65	4.41
6	Taiwan	65	4.41
7	Korea	65	4.41
8	Other Countries	479	32.49
		1474	100

RANKED LIST OF MOST PROLIFIC CONTRIBUTOR

Table 9 shows the most prolific contributor. On the whole, a total of 2350 authors contributed 827 articles over a period of 5 years between 2002-2006. The most prolific authors, are S. O. Reza Moheimani, who contributed 6 articles. and S. N. Balakrishnan occupies the second place who has published 5 articles and eight authors have contributed 4 articles each, 19 authors have contributed 3 articles each and 129 authors have contributed 2 articles each and 1116 authors have contributed 1 article each..

CONCLUSION

1. The range of articles published per volume during the

Table 9 : Ranked List of Most Prolific Contributor

S.No	Author	Contribution
1	S. O. Reza Moheimani, Senior Member, IEEE	6
2	S. N. Balakrishnan	5
3	8 authors	4
11	19 authors	3
12	129 authors	2
13	1116 authors	1

period under study is between 93 and 115. The increasing trend is from the year 2002.The study has examined totally 510 articles published over a span of 5 years.

2. The growth of Total contributions is increasing from 2004. The number of contributions gets maximum with 1143 pages in 2006.

3. The findings reveal that the average number of pages per article is 10. This value is attained in all the years of study from 2002 - 2006

4. Out of 510 articles, 76.07 % of the articles are above seven pages in length. Only 23.93% of the articles are between 1-6 pages in Length

5. The number of multi-authored papers is very high about 93.73% or 478 papers out of a total of 510.

6. Out of 1274 authors who contributed a total of 510 articles, 559 (37.92%) are geographically affiliated to USA

7. Out of 1274, 87.6 %(1116) authors have published single paper and 12.2%(156) authors have published 2 to 4 articles and 0.1%(1) authors have published 5 or 6 articles.

8. The most prolific author is S. O. Reza Moheimani, who contributed 6 articles & S. N. Balakrishnan occupies the second place with 5 articles.

REFERENCES

* **Arora,J and Kaur, S.** "Bibliometric: A Study Based on the Annual Review of Immunology". *Annals of Library Science and Documentation*. Vol. 141 (3), 1994, pp84-94.

* **Sudhir,KG.** "Output Science research in Kerala : A Bibliometric Analysis". *Annals of Library Science and Documentation*. Vol. 44 (4), 1997, p113-126.

* **Pritchard, Alan.** "Statistical Bibliography or Bibliometrics". *Journal of Documentation*. Vol.25; 1988, pp.179-191.

* **Howkins,DT.**"Unvocational Used of online Information Retrieval Systems: Online Bibliometric Study", *Journal of American Society for Information Science*. Vol. 28 (1); 1981,pp13-18.

E-02

Delivering Internet Health Resources to an Underserved Health Care Profession : Paramedical Students

B. E. Rajkumar
Librarian, Institute of Ophthalmology,
Joseph Eye Hospital, Trichy

R. Daniel Prince
Assistant Librarian, Institute of Ophthalmology,
Joseph Eye Hospital, Trichy

ABSTRACT

Purpose

This paper reports on a course developed for paramedical students. The students are trained on locating reliable and high quality information resources on the internet

Description

As paramedical students have to know current information, the internet helps them to locate the current information and update their knowledge within a few minutes. They are the main key persons to provide information and assist doctors in the field of clinical and also operation theatres. Now a days students know very well about how to use the computer and also they can use some packages to do their work. But most of them (75%) are not using internet for academic use, only 20% do so. Most of them use the internet for chatting , mailing and so on. This article tries a new approach to catch the 75% of students to use the internet for their subject and guide them in easy way.

INTRODUCTION

The word paramedic is restricted by law and the person claiming the title must have passed a specific set of examinations and clinical placements and holds a valid registration with the governing body. Even in countries where the law restricts the title, popular media has created a culture where lay persons may refer to all emergency medical personnel as 'paramedics', even if they hold a lower qualificiation, such as *emergency medical technician.*

The definition of paramedical students is extensive in scope. The role of the paramedical students is given as "a specialized practice of professional nursing that advances the well being; academic success and life long achievement of students". The American Academy of Pediatrics Committee on School Health describes how paramedical students provide acute, chronic, episodic and emergency health care along with education, counseling and advocacy for students with disabilities. The continuous expansion of the health care industry brings with it a growing demand for trained paramedical professionals. They are mainly trained in the following areas with their studies.

- Health care features
- Leadership development
- Nursing excellence

- Clinical education and clinical investigator training
- Quality Management
- Adapting to managed care environment
- Organizational strategic planning and development
- IT strategies and provider network development
- Faculty development and leadership programs
- Quality management and accreditation of systems

METHODOLOGY

Paramedical Students are often challenged by the large number of students in their assigned caseload. The Paramedical Student to student ratio varies among communities.

Healthy People 2010 and NASN recommend 1 paramedical student per 750 students in USA. Currently, statistics shows that the ratio in our country (India) is double that, with 1 paramedical Student per 1,500 students. As a result paramedical students often travel to several distant locations. Thus, paramedical students need consistent access to quality health resources throughout their studies.

- Computer skills ranging from novice to advanced user.
- Inability to evaluate Websites with specific criteria.
- Time constraints.
- Difficulty in accessing a computer during the class day.

Learn how to access electronic information to enhance your practice. Have a question, need help with an action plan, and need to know about a syndrome? Find out how to access this information through the specific sites for paramedical students.

The continuing practice is focused on three main sections:

1. Resources from the National Library of Medicine

2. HSLS's Health Information for the Consumer Website
3. A specialized list of resources geared towards paramedical students, accessible from the Heath Information for the Consumer Website

MEDLINE PLUS

The first section is concentrated on how to use MEDLINE *plus*. This section is divided into three categories: 1) Research tools 2) Treatment resources 3) Usability.

The research tools category comprises addressed medical encyclopedias and dictionaries, the health topics index, and PubMed scanned searches. The treatment resources category focuse on clinical trials and prescription and over-the-counter drugs. Finally, the usability of the MEDLINE*plus* Website is discussed. It is explained that this Website includes some full-text resources as well as resources in other languages such as Spanish and that advertisements are not permitted.

The second section focuses on the Health Information for the Consumer Website created by HSLS (The Health Sciences Library System) librarians. The site is structured to promote learning of health and disease topics by starting with dictionaries and texts, then continuing through more advanced topics, such as evidenced-based medicine and decision-making tools. A written description under each topic helps to explain the research tools and print resources. Librarians explain how to use research tools to locate databases and pamphlets under the disease and conditions section. Drug information, medical tests and procedures, and physician directories are also covered. The paramedical students are given time to explore these sites briefly, ask questions and receive one-on-one instruction, if necessary.

Final section, the specialized list of resources created for paramedical students is reviewed. The list is divided into health, government and organization information resources.

On the health information page, Websites such as Band aids and Blackboards** and a peanut-allergy Website†† are examined. The government information page includes the following Websites‡‡: Centers for Disease Control and Prevention, Office of National Drug Control Policy and "Early Warning Timely Response: A Guide to Safe Schools" produced by the Department of Education. Finally, information resources from organizations are covered. The students are introduced to the National Center for Tobacco-Free Kids***, among others.

INDEPENDENT LEARNING EXERCISES

At the end, the participants receive independent learning exercises. The exercises consist of questions that could be answered using MEDLINE*plus* and questions that could be answered using the Health Information for the Consumer Website. The questions range from "Locate some information on the Eye Diseases" to "Locate the recommended childhood-immunization schedule from the Centers for Disease Control (CDC) Website." The goal of the exercises is to reinforce the participants' newly acquired skills from the survey. Contact information for the librarian instructors is provided on the handouts and participants are encouraged to use the contact information if they had questions about survey or the learning exercises.

CONCLUSION

The results of the impact survey show an increase in the ability of paramedical and practitioners to use the Internet to locate reliable and authoritative health information. With the help of Internet they can collect all their information, ready reference and update paramedical datas. At the conclusion of this topic, the college or institute and all the teaching faculties are requested to encourage the students to use internet to locate their subject need and any other related works. They must guide the students and provide meaningful time to use internet within their class rooms or near to them.

REFERENCES

*   *School health services and health science*, January, 2002
*   *American academic of pediatrics*, Vol.108 No.3, November 2002

E-03

Management and Preservation of Information Resources in Information and Communication Technology Era

Sreelath Purushothaman
*Assistant Librarian., Sri Krishna College of
Engineering and Technology., Coimbatore : 641 008*

Dr. M. Tamishchelvan
*Librarian, Sri Krishna College of Engineering and
Technology, Coimbatore : 641008.*

ABSTRACT

*One thing that hasn't changed in the past 100 years
is that libraries need to constantly reevaluate their
services to meet the changing needs of their service
population. Nowadays Information and
Communication Technologies are being increasingly
used in library and information services for the
acquisition, processing and dissemination of
information. Libraires and information centres have*

been using ICT based resources and services like information in electronic form such as texts or indexes on CD ROMs, commercial databases accessed via modem and web terminals to satisfy the diverse information needs of their users. Managing the development, maintenance and delivery of electronic information is one of the major current challenges for library and information services as well as college library and information services. This paper discusses issues concerning the management and preservation of the ICT based resources.

INTRODUCTION

Information resources in this ICT era are increasingly being produced in digital formats. Almost everyone involved in the knowledge production process, prefers the electronic form. The electronic form has revolutionized the way knowledge is produced and disseminated to the end user, usually in a fast, timely and efficient way. For libraries, it is changing the way the librarian acquires, processes and stores information. Most Indian libraries have about 15 per cent of their content in digital format and it is increasing at the rate of about 5 percent per annum. The steady growth of digital information as a component of major research collections has significant implications for college and research libraries. One of the dilemmas facing today's librarians is that they seem to be suffering from management and delivery of information available in digital formats. Librarians should ensure not only the management but also the permanent storage of effective sustainable digital collections and preserve the knowledge available. The reference service definition as stated by Dr. S. R Ranganathan is hereby modified as *"The right information, in the right place, in the right format, at the right time"* to add *"in the right format"*, in the case of information available in the digital formats. Tackling the issues of permanency, accuracy and integrity of stored digital knowledge resources is a real task. Apart from physical deterioration, obsolescence of hardware, software and storage medium and failure to save crucial format information, may cause digital decay and loss of entire content of a digital document. Digital archive experts are trying to save the enormous digital content being generated and stored today for a distant future.

DIGITAL INFORMATION RESOURCE MANAGEMENT

Digital Information Resources Management (DIRM) is the *explicit* and *systematic* management of *vital knowledge* available in digital form - and its associated *processes* of creation, organization, diffusion, use and exploitation. The rules governing the management of Information Resources available in digital format are similar to managing the Information Resources in the print form.

The five key activities for effective DIRM are:

- **Identification** What information is there? How is it identified and coded?
- **Ownership** Who is responsible for different information entities and co-ordination?
- **Cost and Value** A basic model for making judgements on purchase and use
- **Development** Increasing its value or stimulating demand.

Ten Aspects that Add Value to Information

- *TIMELINESS:* Information is perishable. Different information has different half lives ('sell by dates'). Some degrade rapidly
- *ACCESSIBILITY:* Easy to find and retrieve - no long-winded searches, good 'hits'
- *USABILITY:* Ease of use; user can manipulate to suit application

- **UTILITY:** Is suited and usable for multiple applications
- **QUALITY:** Accurate, reliable, credible, validated
- **CUSTOMISATION:** Filtered, targeted, appropriate style and format; needs minimum processing for specified application
- **MEDIUM:** Appropriate for portability and ongoing use
- **REPACKAGING:** Reformatted to match onward use
- **FLEXIBILITY:** Easy to process; can be used in different ways
- **REUSABILITY:** Can be reused; ideally extra use should refine its quality; the more people that can access and use, the better.
- **EXPLOITATION:** Productive maximization of value for money

DIGITAL INFORMATION SERVICE

The services that a typical library should provide for the maximum use of the digital information are:

- Identify sources of important knowledge, both inside and outside the institution
- Catalogue and index material so that retrieval is efficient and effective.
- Maintain and sustain the knowledge repository (the knowledge bank)
- Provide a one stop shop for multiple information needs
- Know who can help - pointers to people as well as information
- Run a client advisory service - offering expertise on sources, their availability, relevance, quality and overall usefulness to the institution.
- Alert users to opportunities for betterment of

knowledge available in the resource centre

- Make valuable connections – helping users who have doubts in particular area to get in touch with those who have solutions i.e. "knowing what we know"
- Create communities - putting users in touch with each other who share similar needs and are tackling similar or related subject area.

Information resource management is to be treated as a strategic asset management where all the activities are related to managing building the asset of information for optimal outcomes.

MANAGING WEB-ENABLED RESOURCES

Digital information available on the internet can be made available to the users by providing the necessary

Infrastructure

Hardware, Software and allied items such as printer, UPS, cable networks, furniture and cooling devices should be made available.

Internet and intranet connectivity: Internet is the first aspect of providing digital information. Intranet helps the organization in providing the information on the desktop. Without the facility to access from remote, it is almost impossible to cater to the information needs of the users.

Contents

The libraries can provide the contents available in the internet to the users by providing the following:

Access to electronic journals, books and other communicable material: The library and information centres can subscribe to electronic information. Users can download the information of their interest. Electronic books have not gained much reference as in the case of electronic journals.

Digital libraries

Digital collection are raw content and digital libraries are systems that make digital collections come alive, make it usefully accessible, useful for accomplishing work and connect them with communities. The collection gain value only when these are surrounded by a matrix of content and interpretation that makes them useful. Therefore it should be ascertained that we develop digital libraries, not just develop digital collections.

Making use of freely available e-books and e-journals

Several free e-books are available on the web which can be accessed freely. Libraries can make use of freely available e-books and e-journals in providing information to the users and also train them in getting information out of these sources.

Consortia arrangement

A library consortium consists of a number of libraries preferably with some homogenous characteristics by subject, institutional affiliation or affiliation to funding authorities that come together with an objective to do certain job collectively. These jobs may include: subscribe to e-resources, include resource sharing, share cataloguing of resources, shared technology solutions, shared core/peripheral collections, shared cataloguing in network environment.

Information Literacy

Poor information and digital literacy is a major problem in developing countries. To keep with the rapid changes in ICT and digital library systems and services, training should be provided on a regular basis in order to help the users keep upto date and thereby make the optimum use of the services and sources made available to them. User education/information and literacy programmes can be very helpful in educating the users on the usage of the information available on the internet.

Training

Establishing and maintaining the best possible customer service is essential for every library. Training is a process of learning, which is structured to impart and develop knowledge, skills and attitude in employees. In-service training can be defined as the process of acquiring and transmitting professional knowledge and practical skills during work. It helps organizations and individuals to develop themselves in consonance with the changing needs of the environment in which they serve, operate and progress.

STRATEGIES FOR PRESERVING DIGITAL OBJECTS

Digital information is produced in a wide variety of standard and proprietary formats, common image formats, and word processing, spreadsheet and database documents. Each of these formats continues to evolve, becoming more complex as revised software versions add new features or functionality. It is not uncommon for software enhancements to "orphan" or leave unreadable, files generated by earlier versions. The threat to digital information has surpassed the danger of unstable media or obsolete hardware. In 1994, the Commission on Preservation and Access and The Research Libraries Group (RLG) formed the Task Force on Digital Archiving. The 1996 Task Force report outlined the challenges for digital preservation and made some recommendations.

The following strategies were proposed as components of a digital preservation program:

- Refreshing data
- Migration
- Emulation

Refereshing data

- addresses the decay, change or obsolescence of physical formats - media on which we store files
- involves periodically moving a file from one physical storage medium to another. Changes to physical storage devices require this to be an ongoing process.

Migration

- involves moving files from one file encoding format to another. For example, upgrading a file type to the newest version of your particular software product

Emulation

- focuses on the application rather than the files produced. Emulation tries to recreate application environments on which the original files can run.

Ideally, a combination of **Refreshing** with either **Emulation** or **Migration** should be adopted as a preservation strategy for digital information objects.

MIGRATION AND DIGITAL PRESERVATION

The migration of digital information refers to the "periodic transfer of digital materials from one hardware/ software configuration to another, or from one generation of computer technology to a subsequent generation." This term is sometimes used to refer to the transfer of information to non-digital media. Migration to new operating environments often means that the copy is not exactly the same as the original piece of information.

Providing information about successive migrations in the form of metadata will assist in determining what changes have occurred to the digital object. The complexity of the migration process will depend on the nature of the digital resource which may vary from simple text to an interactive multimedia object.

Digital electronic resources change formats frequently. This is unlike the paper format which has relatively changed very little since it was discovered as papyrus in Egypt at 3000BC. The electronic document is fairly new and has changed forms since then. If it is not the document changing from MS Word, PDF, html XML etc; it is the software requirement to be able to open and read the document. For example, if the document is in PDF you will need a PDF reader; JPEG would require a JPEG; just as a TIFF formatted document would require a TIFF reader. Another approach to preserving access to digital information entails initially migrating it to standard formats which are expected to be less volatile than the wide array of formats in which digital material may originally be accessible. However, it is important to realize that technical standards are in a state of rapid flux and this strategy cannot be solely relied upon to ensure that digital information remains accessible. The selection of a format for preserving digital information will depend upon what aspect of the resource will be required in the future. For example, decisions need to be made as to whether there will be a need to process or edit a digital resource in the future or if the visual presentation needs to be preserved. Transfer to a more stable digital medium (eg from floppy disk to CD-R) offers a short- to medium-term strategy for preserving access, but still requires the CD-R to be migrated when the technology changes.

Using software which is 'backwards compatible', that is, a later version of the software can decode files created on an earlier version, will simplify migration. Interoperability of systems will also facilitate migration by obviating the need to run a specific program in order to be able to access a digital resource which was created using it. However, these features become harder to achieve with greater software complexity and cannot be relied upon as the software manufacturer may consider that the associated costs are not worthwhile.

Migration can be time-consuming and costly. Data can be migrated every five years. Migration of information raises intellectual property issues and there may be costs associated with this.

EMULATION AND DIGITAL PRESERVATION

The most widely used methods for preserving digital information involve a combination of adopting standards that limit the variety of digital formats that a digital repository accepts, converting digital materials to a standard format when they are accessioned into a digital repository, and migrating the digital information from obsolete to current formats so that the information can be accessed using current hardware and software. Some computer scientists have proposed emulation as an alternative strategy for long-term preservation. According to this approach, emulation of obsolete systems on future unknown computer platforms would make it possible to retrieve, display and use digital documents with their original software. Recent research has begun to demonstrate the feasibility of several different technical approaches that use emulation to preserve digital objects. One purported advantage of emulation is that this approach retains not only the intellectual content of digital information but also the "look and feel" and functionality of the original.

CONCLUSION

The electronic environment is complex. Information is constantly changing all the time. At the moment it should be imperative that institutions especially universities and research institutions should be providing leadership in looking for solutions that will ensure preservation and permanent access to the digital information resources.

User needs should be taken into account when choosing preservation strategies because preservation methods that preserve features, behaviors or attributes of documents in excess of what users need will be costly and wasteful; whereas methods that fail to retain all of the attributes or functionality that users need may preserve digital information that is not useful to researchers.

REFERENCES

* **Kumar, Surendra and Kumar, S.** "Use of ICT in Rural India: A case study of Kishan Call Center", *Library Progress International*, Vol 26, No.2 July-December 2006

* **Kumar, Vinod and Joshi. S.S** (2006) "Role of Universty Libraries and Information Centres in Bridging the Digital Divide", *Library Progress International*, Vol 26, No.2, July-December, 2006

* **Farkas, Merdith.** "The Evolving Library", *American Libraries*, June/ July 2007

* **Sridhar M.R.** "The task of Digital Information Management", *"Deccan Herald"*, July, 19, 2007

* **Haneefa Mohammed K.** "Use Of ICT based resources and services in special libraries in Kerala", *Annals of Library and Information Studies*, Vol 54 No.1, March 2007

* **Lawrence, Gregory W, etal.,** "Risk Management of Digital Information: A File Format Investigation", http://www.clir.org/ PUBS/reports/pub93/pub93.pdf (accessed on September 6, 2007)

* **Kanyengo, Christine W.** "Managing Digital Information Resources in Africa: preserving the integrity of scholarship", http:/ /www.ascleiden.nl/Pdf/elecpublconfkanyengo.pdf (accessed on September 6. 2007)

E-04
Role of ICT: Collection Development-re-defining the Library

Sumuki Padmanabhan
*Librarian, Chevalier T Thomas Elizabeth College
for Women, Perambur, Chennai.*

ABSTRACT

Libraries are now being challenged by the fast moving studies in the new information technologies of multimedia, internet and other virtual computer technologies, that demand changes in the styles, attitudes and skills towards information handling.

Technology especially computer and telecommunication technology have highly revolutionarized the field of library and information services. They facilitate collection, storage, organization, processing, analysis, presentation, communication and dissemination of data.

This paper examines the recent developments in information technology era, its objectives and its impact on library collections. It examines the role of ICT, exposure to ICT and improvements on ICT tools among other things. ICT plays an immense role in information sourcing, generation, processing, storage/retrieval, dissemination and even entertainment. The new challenges of electronic media will change not only the libraries but also professional competencies and personal competencies.

Libraries are in the "Age of Re-" in which technological and social changes increasingly require rethinking, redefining and redesigning our organizations to meet the needs of today better as well as to anticipate the needs of an uncertain future.

INTRODUCTION

Technologically speaking, the twentieth century has been the century of telecommunications, which has provided long-distance travel not for people but for their voices and more recently for text, data, image, graphics, video and sound. At the end of the twentieth century, people are witnessing a new, technology-driven revolution that runs deeper and faster. That is the telecommunications revolution, which paved way for INFORMATION HIGHWAY. Fiber optics and Internet digitization are two important basic concepts.

It is believed that information and knowledge are distinguishing features of the modern society and the main driver of the change is the growing use of information and communication technologies (ICT).

REORGANIZATION IN A CHANGING ENVIRONMENT

In the present IT era, libraries are getting uncertain about their future. How would a library, a noble, classic and knowledge centre shape up in the age of information technology? Emergence of computers and communication technology have great impact on every facet of library activities and information services. In this era, new technologies are replacing the old methods of collection, storage and retrieval. Thus, library automation has reached a stage where the goal of libraries is to ensure integrated online access to the catalogue, acquisition, serials control and circulation.

With the emergence of computers and communication technologies, the strength of information system in the development of modern database has taken new shape. The information originating from a database has become a large segment of electronic publishing that provides a base for procedures, such as retrieving information, drawing conclusions and making decisions.

As we move towards the next millennium, the library and information professionals face the paradigm shifts:

1. Transition from print to electronic media
2. Passive user to active user
3. Demand for accountability on the part of the librarian
4. Concept of networked environment
5. Individual to team work

The goals of information technology – based libraries are to:

1. ´Develop information / knowledge resources focused on patrons' needs
2. Continue to develop a cooperative and user – centered culture
3. Provide human and technologically moderate access to information
4. Continuing education and training.

The ultimate objective of any information system is to provide the users with appropriate information without loss of time. With the advancements in information technology, the users wish to have the right information at their own desk without having to go anywhere, which would save their precious time. Our patron's information needs range from truly simple to extremely complex subjects and it is often hard to differentiate them specifically.

In this situation, the librarian should be proactive in nature. One should not wait for the users to come to the library, rather one should reach out to the patrons and assist them in CD-ROM searching, online searching or Internet use. Thus, maintenance of librarian – user relationship is going to be one of the major challenges of the future. Library professionals have to strive hard to satisfy information needs of the users by

- Disseminating digital information
- Training in use of information technology
- Mastering the contents of world resources
- Creating confidence, comfort zone, smiling, respecting and being proactive and patient in dealing with patrons.

During the last decade the discussion about change in academic libraries focuses most frequently on the ICT developments, the implications of information in digital format, new learning and teaching concepts, new economic models and legal frameworks.

ROLE OF ICT

The need to communicate more quickly and more efficiently has a central focus in our technological society. The economy, industry, education and security of the industrial nations are going to depend heavily on the use of latest means of communication for rapid exchange of information. The main purpose of communication technology is to transmit information in the form of signals between remote locations, using electrical or electromagnetic media.

The major developments in this area are :

- Audiovisual technology
- Teletex and video tex

- E-mail
- Satellite technology
- Fibre optics
- ISDN
- Fax
- Networking
- Teleconference
- Cellular telephones
- Voice mail
- Paginations etc

INDIAN SCENARIO

In India, the networks in the government sector, offering online services on the Internet are:

- Educational and Research Network (ERNET)
- SOFTNET of Software Technology Parks of India (STPI)
- National Informatics Centre Network (NICNET)
- Videsh Sanchar Nigam Limited (VSNL)
- Mahanagar Telecom Nigam Limited (MTNL)

INTERNET SERVICES

There are basically four activities one can do on the Internet. (i.e.) Communication, Document or file transfer, Interactive browsing and Bulletin boards.

Corresponding to these activities there are four basic tools:

1. E.MAIL – Electronic message exchange
2. FTP (File Transfer protocol) - moving electronic documents, images, sounds etc.,
3. TELNET – accessing another computer system's database or archives

4. USENET – global bulletin board service.

In addition to the above, some new tools have emerged that expand upon these four basic activities, such as

1. World Wide Web (WWW) – a hypertext interface to information on the Internet.

2. Gopher – an information browser that lets us retrieve what we find

3. Veronica – an enhancement to gopher that searches many gopher databases.

4. WAIS – a powerful tool for searching some large databases.

5. Archie – a simple but effective mechanism for searching FTP archives.

NEED FOR LIBRARIES TO ACCESS THE INTERNET

There are five reasons, why users access information centres and libraries through the Internet. They are:

- To get help for publishing their information.
- To get help for locating information (online services and catalogues)
- To get help in determining the quality of various information resources.
- For delivery of documents
- To get access to full text documents and information.

The following are some of the possibilities for exploiting the Internet or Intranet for publishing and delivery of information to the users:

1. It can be used for maintaining up-to-date information about library services, collection, staff etc.

2. It is useful for providing access to databases, OPAC, current contents etc.

3. This is useful for preparing union catalogues.

4. It is also used for database indexing and searching.

COLLECTION DEVELOPMENT FOR INFORMATION SERVICES

Collection Development is the first and foremost function of a library and information centre, which can make or mar the effectiveness of an institution. It refers to selection, acquisition, processing, arranging, maintaining and weeding out library material. Due to the advances in science and technology, there is a rapid growth of information in different formats. This has created problems for developing an effective collection in the library. The print on paper is slowly shifting to electronic publishing. The new medium has given a scope for more efficient means of storage, maintenance and quick access from remote places. As a result, libraries need to concentrate on developing electronic documents selectively and get access to electronic information sources using network facilities to serve the users. Some of the different electronic publications to be considered are:

ELECTRONIC JOURNALS AND NEWSLETTERS

Majority of journals are now available in electronic format. These journals are like printed counterparts in that they appear on a regular schedule, have a team of editors and reviewers and focus on a specific topic. Many publish original research.

CD-ROMS

Most of the abstracting sources are now available in CD-ROM. Linking of several CD-ROM workstations through networks enable the users to access the information in a multi – user environment. Now a days, multimedia effects provide better understanding of the content supplements CD-ROMs.

ONLINE DATABASES

Major online vendors like DIALOG, BRS, STN etc, provide access to online databases. These databases include indexing, abstracting and also full text information and can be accessed using a login name and password. Normally, the vendor provides 30 days trial for a client to know the worthiness of a database. Developments in Internet have changed the mode of collection development. A majority of information sources are available on the net. It is possible to identify, select, order and make payment through various web bookshops. The most popular site is <Amazon.com. > which helps us to keep abreast about the latest books of various publishers like Prentice Hall, Oxford University Press, Blackwell and one can procure them by sending e-mail or by using an international credit card.

REFERNCE SOURCES

- Many publishers of various reference sources have hosted their WebPages on the net. The most important reference sources, such as encyclopedias, dictionaries, thesaurus, handbooks, yearbooks, guides etc are accessible on time on the Internet. Examples are

- Encyclopedia.com (*http://encyclopeadia.com*)

- Dictionaries on-line: A web of on-line dictionaries (http ://www.buck well.edu/~r beard/ diction: html)

CONCLUSION

Electronic publishing may not completely replace the existing printed version but both will supplement each other in order to meet the needs of the users. So, library professionals should accept change and adapt to new situation for the benefit and interest of users.

In the years to come, due to the availability of more powerful microcomputers and development of information technologies the process of information dissemination through the library and information centres in the developing world will be speedier and efficient. The users can have easy access to the most current information by interacting with the CD-ROM database of the world literature or having links with the online net works. New in formation technology will enable information services to carry out consolidation and synthesis of scientific information on a very large scale. Internet is changing the notion of the library from a closed place to a virtual library i.e. a library without walls. There is no doubt Internet has brought a tremendous change in the information transfer process very effectively.

REFERENCES

* **Patil, DB and Kooganuramanath, MM.** *Library and Information Science*, New Delhi : Ashish Publishing House, 1994.

* **Feroz Khan.** *Information Society in Global Age.* New Delhi :A P H Publishing Corporation, 2002.

* **Ashok Babu.T, et al.** *Vision of Future Library and Information Systems.* New Delhiu : Viva Books Pvt. Ltd., 2000.

* **Suraj, V.K.** *Multimedia Information Collection in Digital Libraries*, NewDelhi : Isha Books, 2005.

E-05
Role of Internet in Library and Information Services Marketing

M. Ravichandran
Librarian, Mohamed Sathak Engineering College,
Kilakarai - 623 806

R. Jeyshankar
Lecturer, Department of Library and Information Science,
Alagappa University, Karaikudi -630 003

D. Umamaheswari
Librarian, Christian College of Nursing, Ambilikkai – 624 61

ABSTRACT

The foundation for a great marketing plan of library and information services is to examine the library's mission, values and philosophy of service. Then analyze library capabilities and research customer needs to find out what works or what needs improvement. Use the analysis and research to establish goals, select strategies for promotion, develop the marketing plan of action, implement and evaluate how well the libraries meet their goals. Use results of evaluation to make changes or to develop a new marketing plan that responds to changes in the library, in the community, and in the world of information. Marketing is not exclusively for businessmen. It is the "science of strategy," and its main objective is to provide client (user) satisfaction, so it is necessary that the librarians are welcome to act enthusiastically on marketing applications. Telecommunications, Information Technologies and Database Technologies have been key elements in this process.

INTRODUCTION

Marketing of Library and Information Services **(MLIS)** is the process of planning, pricing, promoting and distributing library products to create "exchanges" that satisfy the library and the customer. MLIS is ongoing and dynamic due to the changes in the requirements, patents of the customers and change in library service itself. The MLIS process determines the decisions and activities involved meeting the needs of customers. MLIS requires careful planning and begins with understanding the mission of the library. It can help in developing the mission of the library, establishing a positive image for the library in the community and determining the best way to provide services to users.

INTERNET IN MLIS

As libraries shift more services to the Internet, the library web site becomes increasingly important as a product (service) in its own right and as a major tool in marketing other products of the library. Libraries can use the Web to provide services, to market services or as part of the marketing process. The advent of new technologies such as: dramatic increase of digital storage media, convergence of telecommunication and broadcasting, the availability of wealth of information resources accessible through the Internet and also reduction in cost of computers in the marketplace, make it possible for librarians to introduce IT products and services to fulfill information needs of their customers. Libraries in advanced countries have begun to undertake digitalization projects to convert their national in-prints into digital formats; some make them available through the Internet. Library as "reservoir of knowledge" must market its IT products and services in order to reach out to its potential users. Introducing IT products and services as an integral part of library services, accompanied by good advertisement as well as introducing systematic user education programs will encourage library users to come to library.

IS INFORMATION MARKETING DIFFERENT?

The MLIS-based products and services refer to sources of information and knowledge contents that are available in electronic forms such as books, CDs, videos, journals, journal articles, data bases, films, audio digital products, online publishing, public domain and commercial online databases available through Internet and other propriety databases available through various private network providers. A number of libraries have subscribed to Information sources in CD-ROM. The different types of library services are public libraries, academic libraries, workplace information centres, advisory services, business consultancy services, subject gateways and organisational web sites.

NEED FOR MLIS

- Competition for customers
- Competition for resources
- Maintaining relevance
- Visibility
- Valuable community resource
- Rising expectations
- Survival

- Beneficial to library image

BARRIERS TO MLIS

Most librarians do not market their libraries, since they do not know how to market or do not know how to do it well. The following are the barriers in promoting library and information service products.

Money and attitude: Lack of funds is often used as a reason not to market. However, marketing library services is not simply a matter of spending money on promotion and advertising. Marketing is also a matter of improving the customer's experience of library services. The attitude of the Librarian and the staff as they interact with customers is what shapes customers' experiences and 'markets' the library to those customers. And majority of library staff do not have positive attitude.

Lack of training and education: Often librarians do not promote library services well due to lack of training and knowledge of marketing tools and techniques. Despite the growing literature on library marketing, there remains a lack of familiarity with the total marketing concept among librarians.

Confusion: There is confusion about what the term marketing means. Much of this has to do with the interchangeability of terms such as 'promotion', 'public relations', 'publicity' and 'marketing'. There is also confusion about marketing libraries; the perception is that marketing is a business tool and not applicable to library settings.

Complex and complicated task: Marketing is a complicated problem for libraries because of their wide range of products and services from books to Internet access and an extremely diverse audience that ranges from children to seniors, public officials to business people and students to faculty etc.

Passive vs. active stance: Rather than selling the library on its value and letting people know what the library or information center offers, librarians often wait for customers to come to them. Rather than pushing out responses to anticipated information needs to customers, librarians wait for customers to stop by the facility or stumble across the library web site.

MARKETING MIX IN MLIS

MLIS requires a critical analysis of the marketing mix (the 7 Ps of Marketing mix - product, place, price, promotion, participants, physical evidence and process) to identify the nature, features, benefits and value of the products to the customer. The development of an effective marketing strategy requires the specification of the marketing mix. These concepts are utilized in the for-profit sector, but a good library-marketing plan will also profit by examining products offered and assessing the value of the products to the users. Market research helps to determine what library users are looking for in the way of product features such as variety, quality, design and benefits such as good performance, quality, reliability and durability, users demand in services, systems, programs and resources.

Table 1. 7Ps of Marketing Mix in MLIS

7 Ps	Definition
Product	Products or services of general reference and information service department. This is, of course, the information, reference and ancillary services that add value such as personal assistance, referral services, online database searches, document delivery and interlibrary loan.
Price	Pricing of use of the library is usually that of the time and effort the user spends

traveling to the library, as well as the time and effort spent searching for and examining materials and cost of a foregone alternative activity.

Place
Place of service, based upon knowledge of the market of a library, is essential in order to identify users and their discrete information needs and wants. Also, this location element has effect upon how the library can best access their product offerings. To expand the service area, the library may have branches, bookmobiles or electronic access, FAX and telephone calls etc.

Promotion
Promotion includes utilizing persuasive information about general information services and communicating this information to target market segments that are potential users. Five kinds of promotion include: publicity, public relations, personal representatives, advertising and sales promotion.

Participants
All human actors who play a part in reference and information services delivery, namely the library's personnel.

Physical Evidence
The environment in which the reference and information services are delivered that facilitates the performance and communication of the service.

Process
The procedures, mechanisms and flow of activities by which the reference and information services are acquired.

CONCLUSION

Marketing is the analysis, planning, implementation, and control of carefully formulated programs designed to bring about voluntary exchanges of values with target markets for the purpose of achieving organizational objectives. Libraries will be utilizing the Web to provide services to an increasingly sophisticated and demanding computer user by providing access to the worldwide information that people and organizations need in a timely, convenient and equitable manner.

REFERENCES

* **Shapiro, Stanley J.** "Marketing and the information professional : odd couple or meaningful relationship?" p. 102- 107. In *The marketing in an age of diversity* / Blaise Cronin, ed. London : ASLIB, 1981. y BESSER, H. "The shape of the twenty first - century library. p.

* **Gallimore, Alec.** *Developing an IT strategy for your library.* London: Library Association, 1997.

* **Koelsch, Frank.** *The infomedia revolution: how it is changing our world and your life.* Toronto: McGraw-Hill Ryerson, 1995.

* **Cosette Kies.** Marketing and Public Relations for Libraries, Metuchen, NJ, London: The Scarecrow Press Inc., 1987, pp.181.

* **Wilton Library.** Innovative Internet applications in libraries. Available online: *http://www.wiltonlibrary.org/innovate.html*

* **Curtis, D., Ed.** *Attracting, educating, and serving remote users through the Web: A how-to-do-it manual for librarians.* New York : Neal-Schuman, 2002.

* **Kotler, Philip.** *Marketing for Nonprofit Organizations.* 2nd ed. New Delhi: Prentice-Hall of India,1995

* **Reed, PW.** (1994) " Marketing Planning and Strategy", *Aslib Proceedings*:45.

E-06

The New Challenge :
Trends and Issues in
Acquiring the Digital
Publications

R. Jeyshankar
Lecturer, Department Library and Information Science.
Alagappa University, Karaikudi.

M. Ravichandran
Librarian, Mohamed Sathak Engineering College,
Kilakarai - 623 806

M. Palaniappan
Library Assistant, Central Library and
Information Science. Alagappa University, Karaikudi.

ABSTRACT

This paper deals with the challenges and issues in acquiring the digital resources. Information and Communication Technology (ICT) is moving in the direction of digital. The future promises hand-held reading of these e-resources. The future is speed and flexibility. Every publishing package offered includes a free listing of e-resources in their websites.

E-resources are mushrooming online, on the web and CD-ROM format. This phenomenon is due to the rapid development of information technology including the internet and digitizing techniques. The quantities of e-resources are growing larger and larger although no exact number is available. In addition, considerable amount of resources are now published electronically. This significantly enlarges the size of the electronic resources which have become one of the most important aspects of a digital library.

INTRODUCTION

Rapid advances in electronic information processing, storage and communication technologies have revolutionized the role of world wide libraries in disseminating electronic information services to their users. As a result, libraries are facing new challenges, new competitors, new demands, new expectations and a variety of information services from users tailored to their wants and needs. The new technologies have facilitated the transformation of data into digital format. Over the last few years, information has been produced digitally and libraries have become major providers of information in digital format.

The information environment is greatly changing throughout the world. Present rapid development in electronic system and recent innovation in technology have resulted in changing emphasis in the role of electronic information and its management. The new technologies have facilitated the information of data into digital format. So the library professionals face lot of issues and challenges in acquiring, at the time subscription or purchasing the digital publication.

The developments in the mass storage, computers and communications fields have made electronic resources on libraries varied. Electronic and online resources are making a forceful entry into the libraries. Many libraries, especially the affluent, the special, research and development, engineering institutions and academic institutions are migrating to the electronic resources including CD-ROM, online databases and electronic and online journals and books. This paper deals with problems and issues and challenges at the time of subscriptions.

MEANING OF ELECTRONIC INFORMATION RESOURCES

A general term for electronic information stored online is CD ROMs and on databases or online tools that index, abstracts or provide electronic access to articles, books, dissertations and other types of content. Many of these databases offer limited full text, collections of documents, data and other written material stored in electronic "libraries" or databases and available electronically

Electronic information may be broadly defined as "The information stored in a medium, which requires an electronic device to read its contents". Information is stored in different electronic media such a floppies, CDs, Magnetic Tapes, Video etc. and can be retrieved with the help of other electronic devices such as computer, video player etc. The library resources classified on the basis of CD – ROM and online resources including e-journals have become multimedia libraries, electronic libraries with direct access.

NEED FOR E-RESOURCES

- Selecting, building on and extend research in promising digital library areas.
- Accelerate development, management and accessibility of digital content and collections.
- Create new capabilities and opportunities for digital libraries to serve existing and new user communities, in all levels of education.
- Encourage the study of interactions between humans and digital libraries in various social and organizational contexts.

TYPES OF E-RESOURCES

- 'Full – text' material to cover e-journals, open access, open archive collections, e-books and e-newspapers etc.
- 'Metadata' sources to cover catalogues, indexes and abstracts or sources that provide information about information.
- Multimedia Material
- Websites.

THE NEW CHALLENGES: TRENDSAND ISSUES IN ACQUIRING DIGITAL PUBLICATION

E-Publications : Major Trends

Nowadays varieties of electronic publications are increased in the form of full text, abstracts and index databases. For example, e-journals, e-books etc. A lot of e-publishers have also emerged. The following trends are identified as a challenge to the library professionals at the time of acquiring the e-publications.

- Rapid growth: e-journals in the last 5 yrs; e-books in the next 3 yrs.
- Increasing acceptance of electronic information resources
- Increasing availability of full-text titles
- Links from citations in Abstracts & Index databases to full-text journals and document delivery at the pay-per-article/per-view level
- Expanded access to integrated information
- Market target expanding to include individual subscribers
- Increasing acceptability of access instead of ownership

E- Publications : Major Issues

Nowadays the library professionals meet the following issues at the time of subscribing the electronic resources.

- Pricing models
- Licensing agreements and·copyright
- Authentication and authorization
- Archival access
- Rise of consortia
- Budget issues
- Measurement/statistics of use

COMMERCIAL E-PUBLICATIONS : E-JOURNALS

In the early period databases were published only in CD versions. But nowadays lot of databases, full – text e-journals and e-books are published. It will increase or double in every year.

- E-abstracting and indexing databases (A&I databases) : Going back to the 1980's; e.g. University of California MELVYL System with access to Medline, Psychological Abstracts, and other A&I databases

- E-journals and e-books (full-text) : very small number of scholarly titles available prior to popularization of web – accessible from FTP sites. Today lot of commercial publishers have entered in different subjects.

  - Commercial pilot/experimental projects: e.g. Elsevier's TULIP; Springer's Red Sage as precursor of today's full-text e-journals

COMMERCIAL E-PUBLICATIONS : E-JOURNALS AND E-BOOKS

- e-books/e-texts

— public-domain titles available prior to web (e.g. Project Gutenberg)

— active developments in commercial book publishing in late 1990s with the netlibrary as success story

— appeared to be doing well until late 2001 when declared bankruptcy

— Other publishers who folded their electronic imprints are Time Warnert Trade Publishing, Random House, and Princeton University Press

— Market not quite ready with library as exception.

Dru Mogge (1999) defined growth and development of e-publications as given below -

1. 1st edition (1991) of the (annual) Directory of Electronic Journals, Newsletters and Academic Discussion Lists by the US Association of Research Libraries (ARL) — listed 110 journals and newsletters

2. 4th edition (1994) – included first time serials published on the WWW. Out of 433 journals/ newsletter entries – more than 60 titles listed the web as a method of distribution

3. 5th edition (1995) – listing of 675 journal/newsletter entries with referred scholarly titles increasing from 74 in 1994 to 142 in 1995

4. Nov 1998 – over 6,000 e-journal titles in the ARL e-journal database

E-JOURNALS AVAILABLE IN DIFFERENT SHAPES AND SIZES

At present, many scientific, technical and medical journals are published freely or commercially. So the library professionals should identify the journals which are available freely and commercially to acquire.

- Free with print subscriptions directly from publisher
- Added surcharge over print subscription (e.g. Wiley, 5-15%)
- Free with print subscription through serials vendor, usually for a limited access period, e.g. 3-years (EBSCO Online, Swetsnet Navigator)
- Directly from publisher in aggregated manner for a surcharge, e.g. Academic Press' IDEAL; Elsevier's Science Direct
- Stable aggregated database, e.g. JSTOR, Project Muse, Bio-One
- Unstable aggregated database with full-text journals, e.g. Lexis-Nexis, EBSCO Host, ProQuest
- Electronic-only option with deep discount for print version (e.g. ACM Digital Libraries)

SOME PRICING METHODOLOGIES

The library professionals should be able to identify the various methods of pricing.

- Student FTE
- Site license – regardless of number of users
- Number of concurrent users/logins
- Some may charge additional technology fee or access fee.

LICENSING AGREEMENTS

- An avenue by electronic information providers to protect their investment in addition to relying on copyright laws.
- May be more restrictive than what copyright law may grant, e.g. lending may be controlled/restricted access may limit to one PC archival access
- A new area for librarians 5-6 years ago: various

workshops and model licensing agreements to help in negotiation process of e-resources: ARL (Association of Research Libraries), University of California, ICOLC (International Coalition of Library Consortia)

RISE OF CONSORTIA COLLABORATIONS

This is one of the major issues to procure the e-resources. If more than one library forms a group to procure e-resources, the price will be reduced. So the library professionals should know the Consortium, à consortium of consortia (ICOLC), à consortia efforts -

- Many libraries belong to several consortia
- May have a much wider geographical boundary (INDEST, Infonet).
- Bonding together to leverage negotiation power with service providers and extend mutual support in other areas related to the acquisition/access of electronic information resources.
- ICOLC (International Coalition of Library Consortia) at *http://www.library.yale.edu/consortia/ statement.html* has more than sixty library consortia as members across the globe. It aims to:
- Facilitate discussion among members on issues of common interest
- Keep members informed about new e-information resources, pricing practices of providers/vendors and other relevant issues.

ARCHIVAL ACCESS

This is one of the major issues of acquiring in the printed publications. So the library professionals should know whether the back issues are provided or not at the time of acquiring e-publications.

- Major concern with archival access in earlier days

- Increasing acceptance of access instead of ownership
- Good intentions, but may not be deliverable
- Technology and delivery mechanism problems
- Implications for collection management

AUTHENTICATION AND AUTHORIZATION

It is another important issue the library professionals should be aware of authorized person to keep and maintain secrets.

- Use of passwords for access too cumbersome
- Use of IP address the norm
- Traffic pressure on university's modem pool
- Use of commercial ISPs (Internet Service Providers)
- How to authenticate a user if the user is authorized to access a particular electronic resource
- Vendor-based web access management control programs

E-BOOKS – NETLIBRARY

- November 1999 — 111 publishers providing content for e-books
- June 2001 — 312 publishers participating; equally divided between academic and commercial publishers
- 38,000 titles with highest usage in economics, business, computer science, literature, medicine, health and wellness, technology, history, education, sociology and religion
- Employed librarians with collection development expertise to develop e-book collection
- Platform independent; accessible online or offline via the netLibrary reader

(Lynn Silipigni Connaway, A Web-based electronic book (e-book) library: the netLibrary model, Library Hi-

Tech, vol. 19, number 4, 2001, pp. 340-349)

- Primary access follows a one-to-one approach for digital rights management
- Charges an access fee to cover costs of maintaining a digital library – can be paid as one-time charge or annually
- Enhanced features: embed multimedia data, link to other electronic resources and cross-reference information across multiple resources
- Filed bankruptcy in November 2001
- Now a partner of OCLC

e-reference collections: a more successful model of packing e-books

- Oxford Reference Online — covers 100 key Oxford dictionaries and reference works with coverage across the subject spectrum: from General Reference and Language to Science and Medicine and from Humanities and Social Sciences to Business
- Xreferplus – a "digital reference library" containing 100 reference titles from 21 publishers on a wide array of subjects (http://www.xrefere.com)

E-books - Pricing methodologies (1)

- Print-on-demand
- Monthly subscription fees
- Free browsing of content with fees for downloading and printing
- One-time purchase of content with perpetual access or annual access fees
- Subscription fees with or without ownership
- Some e-book providers work only with libraries and others market to individual end users

E-books - Pricing methodologies (2)

- e-books pricing and access models still going through a trial period
- netlibrary — one-time fee of 155% of print copy cost with single user access for a specified amount of time
- Safari Books Online – offers access to hundreds of leading technology books from Addison Wesley Professional, Cisco Press, O'Reilly, Peachpit Press, Prentice and Hall PTR etc and uses a point system with multiple user access
- Ebrary — offers unlimited access based on an annual fee, but will charge for copying and printing portions of content

California Digital Library's e-book task force identified eight elements for the evaluation of academic e-book usage

1. Content
2. Software and hardware standards and protocols
3. Digital rights management
4. Access
5. Archiving
6. Privacy
7. The market and pricing
8. Enhancement and ideal e-book feaures

True success may have to wait till the availability of e-paper;

Budget issues

- Rapidly growing budgetary commitment to e-resources with heavy pressure already on print serials budget- 95/96 — 3-5% ; 00/01 — 12-15 %; 02/03 — 1-17%+ as is the case with HKBU

- Libraries have been slow to cancel print subscriptions as a result of e-journal access (Study/findings of survey of 299 US libraries by Marian Shemberg and Cheryl Grossman in 1999 — 9 had cancelled 26-50 titles, 44 had cancelled 25 titles or fewer and 163 had not cancelled any
- Interdisciplinary and multidisciplinary nature of aggregated databases require rethinking of collection budget allocation methods

E-Metrics: measuring use of e-resources (1)

- General recognition of need for consistent and comparable statistical data
- A number of international/national professional organizations working to improve situation in the context of measuring library performance in the networked, electronic environment
  - International Coalition of Library Consortia (ICOLC)
  - European Commission EQUINOX Project
  - Association of Research Libraries (ARL)

E-Metrics: measuring use of e-resources (2)

- ICOLC's "Guidelines for Statistical Measures of Usage of Web-Based Information Resources" <http://www.library.yale.edu/consortia/2001webstats.htm>
- Addresses issues such as minimal requirements, privacy and user confidentiality, institutional or consortia confidentiality, access etc.
- Data elements that must be provided for:
  - no. of sessions (i.e logins)
  - no. of queries/searches (a unique intellectual inquiry)

— no. of menu selections (if display of data is through use of menus)

— no. of full-content units (e.g. journal articles, e-books, etc.)

E-Metrics: measuring use of e-resources (3)

- ARL effort: more from performance management and measurement perspective focusing on study of users and uses cost and benefit analysis, study of staff impact and needs; engagement with information providers and their usage data services

- "The problems of definition, reliability, and consistency of data provided by the vendor community alone are daunting. But they are matched equally by librarians' lack of agreement on what is important to collect, how to collect it and how to use what is collected. Most libraries lack experience with the collection and analysis of data related to their investment in electronic resources."[3]

3 Rush Miller and Sherrie Schmidt:

"E-Metrics: Measures for Electronic Resources", Keynote delivered at the 4th Northumbria International Conference on Performance Measurement in Libraries and Information Services.

Model of Effective Selection and Presentation Practices[4]

- Access for attention
  - Selection Policies and Strategic Plans
  - Institutional Finance and Organization
  - Internal Procedures for Initial Evaluation and Purchase
  - Licensing Issues and Practices

- Web Presentation Strategies
- User Support
- Ongoing Evaluation and Usage Information
- Preservation and Archiving
- Toward Integrated Systems for Managing Electronic Resources

CONCLUSION

- E-resources have greatly expanded access to information with powerful search engines and retrieval tools
- Users have desk-top access to information from anywhere through the Web
- The networked digital information environment is here to stay and will continue to grow
- Libraries face technical, financial and organizational challenges, but the enduring values of libraries remain the same: selection, collection, organization, service and preservation of information.

REFERENCES

* **Dru Mogg.** "Seven years of tracking electronic publishing : the ARL Directoryu of Electronic Journals, Newletters, and Academic Discussion Lists", *Library Hi Tech*, Vol.17, No.1, 1999, pp.17-25

* **Lynn Silipigni Connaway.** A Web-based electronic book (e-book) library : the netlibrary model", *Library Hi-Tech*, Vol.19, No.4, 2001, pp..340-349

* **Rush Miller and Sherrie Schmidt,** (2005) "E-Metrics : Measures for Electronic Resources", Keynote delivered at the 4th Northumbria International Conference on Performance Measurement in Libraries and Information Services.

* **Timothy D. Jewell.** Selection and Presentation of Commercially Available Electronic Resources : Issues and Practices, Digital Library

Federation, Council of Library and Information Resources, Washington, D.C. , July 2001.

* **Adrienne Muir**. "Digital Preservation : awareness, Responsibility and Rights Issues", *Journals of Information Science,* Vol.30, No.1.2004, pp.73-92.

E-07
Indest-AICTE@Engineering College

A. Joseph Anburaj
Librarian, KLN College of Engineering,
Pottapalayam, Madurai.11

N. Vasantha Kumar
Assistant Libarian, Thiagarajar School of Management (TSM),
Center for Higher Learning, Thiruppankundram,
Madurai.5.

ABSTRACT

This paper describes availability of E-resources for engineering colleges at

Indian National Digital libraries in Engineering Sciences and Technology (INDEST-AICTE Consortium), members and subscription details.

INTRODUCTION

Library and Information Centers are experiencing huge changes from printed to digital collections. This has led to many changes in traditional library works as well as the role of library professionals to facilitate access to dissemination of information. In this way INDEST-AICTE consortium provides electronic resources to all type of engineering colleges (Government, Government Aided and Self Financing) at nominal cost. At the time of evaluation the INDEST e-resources are considered as alternate sources of printed journals by AICTE and NBA.

THE CONSORTIUM

The "Indian National Digital Library in Engineering Science and Technology (INDEST) consortium" was set-up by the Ministry of Human Resource Development (MHRD) on the recommendation of an expert group appointed by the Ministry under the chairmanship of Prof. N. Balakrishnan, IISc. 38 Centrally-funded Government institutions including IITs, IISc Bangalore, NITs, IIITs, and IIMs are core members of the INDEST consortium. The Ministry provides funds required for providing differential access to electronic resources subscribed by the core members through the consortium headquarters set-up at the IIT Delhi. The consortium was re-named as INDEST-AICTE consortium in December 2005 with the AICTE playing pivotal role in enrolling its affiliated engineering colleges and institutions as members of the consortium for selected e-resources at much lower rates of subscription.

The consortium subscribes to over 6,500 electronic journals from a number of publishers and aggregators. The INDEST-AICTE website (*http://indest.iitd.ac.in* or *http://paniit.iitd.ac.in/indest*) hosts a search interface to locate these journals and their URLs.

MEMBERS

Core Member: All IIT's, IISc, NIT's, ISM, SLIET and NERIST,IIIT, IIITM , IIM's, NITIE

AICTE-Supported Members

AICTE provides funds for access to e-resources to all Government engineering colleges and Technical institutions.

Self-Supported Members

The consortium being an open –ended proposition, invites AICTE-accredited and UGC-affiliated institutions to join hands with the Engineering and Technology Institutions in India and share the benefits it offers in terms of lower subscription rates and better terms of agreement with the publishers.

E- RESOURCES

1. IEL Online (IEEE/IEE Electronic Library)

- It covers current electrical, electronics and computer science engineering literature.
- Documents – More than One Million
- Publications – 12,000
- Journals – 126 (IEEE) + 21 (IEE)
- Magazines, transactions and 600+ conference proceedings
- Web Site : *http://ieeexplore.ieee.org/*

2. American Society of Civil Engineers (ASCE)

- It covers the field of civil engineering, construction and architecture.
- Journals - 30
- Magazines and Transactions
- Web site: http://ojps.aip.org/

3. American Society of Mechanical Engineers (ASME)

- It covers the literature in mechanical engineers, mechatronics, etc.,
- Journals – 21
- Magazines and Transactions
- Web site: http://ojps.aip.org/

4. Springer Verlag's Link

- It covers the literature in basic science and engineering in general.
- Basic science covers Mathematics, Chemistry, Material Science, Physics and Astronomy.
- Journals – 525
- Website: *http://www.springerlink.com/*

5. Digital Engineering Library (DEL)

- It covers 12 Major areas of engineering and more than 200 topics. Includes aerospace engineering, bio engineering, chemical engineering civil engineering, communication engineering, construction and architectural engineering, electrical engineering, engineering math and science, environmental engineering, industrial engineering, material science and mechanical engineering.
- Engineering articles – more than 4000.
- Marks Standard book for mechanical engineers -10th Edition
- Perry's Chemical Engineers Handbook – 7th Edition
- Standard hand book for Electrical engineers – 14th Edition
- Roark's Formula for stress and strain – 7th Edition.
- Website: *http://www.digitalengineeringlibrary.com/*

6. Engineering Science Data Unit (ESDU)

- It provides Engineering Design Data, Methods and Software that form an important part of the design operations of companies through out the world.
- ESDU's vast range of industry – standard design tools are presented in over 1340 design guides with supporting software.

- ESDU consists of 21 titles in 4 major engineering disciplines – aerospace, structural, mechanical and process engineering.
- Website: *http://www.esdu.com/*

SUBSCRIPTION RATE

Sl. No	Resources	List Price in Rupees	Price offered to the consortium in Rs.	Discount in %
1	ASCE Journals	4,43,000.00	1,08,640.00	75.48
2	ASME Journals+ (AMR)	2,85,300.00	97,920.00	65.68
3	IEL Online (Single Simultaneous Access)	52,99,750.00	2,17,060.00	95.90
4	Springer Link	4,11,80,400.00	1,67,590.00	99.59
5	DEL	1,19,904.00	39,170.00	67.33
6	ESDU	64,80,000.00	51,410.00	99.21

SUBSCRIPTION RATE ON PRO-RATA BASIS

Subscription to these e-resources can start from beginning of any month till august 2007 (January to December 2007 in case of Springer Link). Table given in next page.

CONCLUSION

Subscription to on-line journals adds new dimension to the e-resource environment. Libraries and many technical institutions may come forward to subscribe on-line journals to increase the usage among users as well as to reduce the expenditure on subscription to international journals.

REFERENCES

* http://www.aicte.ernet.in
* http://indest.iitd.ac.in
* http://www.aicte.ernet.in/indest.htm

Resource	Rates/Year	Rate in Rs. Pro-Rated for Remaining Months (From Oct. 06 to August. 07) to August 2007									
		From Oct. 2006	From Nov. 2006	From Dec. 2006	From Jan. 2007	From Feb. 2007	From Mar. 2007	From Apr. 2007	From May 2007	From June 2007	From July 2007
IEL	217060	198970	180880	162800	144710	126620	108530	90440	72350	54270	36180
ASCE	108640	99590	90530	81480	72430	63370	54320	45270	36210	27160	18110
ASME	97920	89760	81600	73440	65280	57120	48960	40800	32640	24480	16320
DEL	39170	35910	32640	29380	26110	22850	19590	16320	13060	9790	6530
ESDU	51410	47130	42840	38560	34270	29990	25710	21420	17140	12850	8570

Resource	From Jan. 2007	From Feb. 2007	From Mar. 2007	From Apr. 2007	From May 2007	From June 2007	From July 2007	From Aug. 2007	From Sep. 2007	From Oct. 2007	From Nov. 2007
Springer Link	167590	153620	139660	125690	111730	97760	83800	69830	55860	41900	27930

E-08
Digital Library Access in Enhancing E-Learning

M. Mariraj

Assistant Technical Officer, School of Management, Bharathiar University, Coimbatore – 46.

R. Ramesh

M. Phil Research Scholar, Alagappa University, Karaikudi.

ABSTRACT

This paper addresses and discusses such aspects as what is meant by "e-learning" and how can it be supported by the library environment, the functionality of the digital library and how e-learning resources are included and organized in the digital library.

E-learning has come in to existence for the past couple of years, which uses a network for delivery, interaction or facilitation which are also known as distributed learning or distance learning.

Digital library is also not merely an automated conventional library, where the resources are electronically catalogued and are available only for browsing purposes.

INTRODUCTION

The growth in e learning, in which education is delivered and supported through computer networks such as the internet, has posed new challenges for library services. E-learners and traditional learners now have access to a universe of digital information through the information superhighway. New information and communications technologies, as well as new educational models, require librarians to re-evaluate the way they develop, manage and deliver resources and services.

DIGITAL LIBRARY DEFINITION

Digital Library has been defined in many ways. The real meaning is "Digital library is a managed collection of information with associated services, where the information is stored in digital formats and accessible over a network".

Digital library is a large collection of objects, stored and maintained by multiple sources, such as databases, image banks, file systems, e-mail services and web based repositories.

WHAT IS E-LEARNING

Different terms have been used for e-learning, such as "online learning", "internet learning", "distributed learning", "networked learning", "tele-learning", "virtual learning", "computer-assisted learning", "web-based learning" and "distance learning".

All of these terms imply that the learner is at a distance from the tutor, that the learner uses some form of technology to access the learning materials, that the learner uses technology to interact with the tutor and other learners and that some form of support is provided to learners.

E-learning is meant to be more than just educational websites or computer software. It includes all aspects of electronic delivery – so watching an educational video, using a digital camera, using a computer to edit pictures, text or sounds for a presentation or project, or using an interactive whiteboard in a lesson, can all be considered implementations of e-learning.

ROLE OF DIGITAL LIBRARIES IN E-LEARNING

The introduction of digital libraries into the education process was made easier by distance education, which has developed over the years. With the internet and the worldwide web, distance education programs can mount sets of materials on web servers to support online courses. One of the basic ideas is to join learning materials on various topics, written by many educators, in a digital library of courseware. Digital libraries could have an enormous impact on teaching and learning in the classroom.

INFORMATION UTILIZATION BY E-LEARNERS

e-learners have access to an overwhelming range of information sources available at the click of a mouse: library resources, government information, news sites, advertising and many other forms of resources. Librarians have traditionally selected and organized resources with great care. In building digital libraries, librarians have the opportunity to provide e-learners with direction and to rescue them from information overload.

A digital library can link e-learners to library catalogues, licensed journal databases, electronic book collections, selected internet resources, electronic course reserves and tutorials and to forums for communication and interaction with others. The digital library permits e-learners to access library and networked resources and services anytime and anywhere if an Internet connection and computing equipment are available.

DIGITAL LIBRARIES AND E-LEARNING LINKAGE

The digital library serves mainly as a facilitator in organizing and providing knowledge and resources to its users. Sharing knowledge and information among library staff, researchers, faculty, students and other departments within the institution encourages them to work together, develop their skills and form strong and trusting relationships. A focus on collaboration between the library and the faculty promotes a responsive approach to course design and supports teaching and learning objectives, particularly when this collaboration incorporates student contributions and feedback.

From a research perspective, a number of models can be involved in creating an environment that is responsive to the scholarly information needs of a diverse group of e-learners. Librarians locate, select and describe quality internet resources and provide access to journal databases and electronic book collections, providing e-learners with full-text content from a wide range of online resources and publications, including peer-reviewed journals. Within this framework, the library works with faculty, researchers, scholarly societies and publishers in developing and managing a collection of enriched online scholarly resources. Such a partnership enables researchers to interact with others, exchange experiences and publish their works online. The library role is thus transformed from simply being a provider of library resources, into meeting the ongoing support needs of the parties involved. The library also serves to foster research skills by encouraging students and other learners to search, investigate, discover and take advantage of these valuable online resources.

E-LEARNERS AND DIGITAL LIBRARY RESOURCES

Technology offers opportunities to be innovative, as the following discussion of electronic resources and services demonstrates, but it is important to bear in mind that not all e-learners are equal when it comes to access to computing equipment, the availability, speed and stability of internet connections or the information skills that are needed to make optimum use of digital libraries.

Access to print-based library materials continues to be important, because not all of the information resources that e-learners need are available in electronic format. Many of our most valuable research materials are still print-based. Although there has been a shift away from purchasing print materials to be housed in a physical building and toward providing access to licensed digital resources made available over a computer network, librarians continue to work to resolve issues pertaining to distance delivery of resources that are unavailable in digital format. Online catalogues and indexing and abstracting systems provide e-learners with convenient access to bibliographic information about valuable scholarly documents. When those documents are not available in full-text form online, a demand is generated for delivery from a library's print collection or from the collections of other libraries through interlibrary loans. Typical solutions for delivery of non-digital formats include the use of mail and courier services, the establishment of collections at designated sites and the negotiation of agreements with other libraries through consortia.

Given that a growing number of learners are accessing library collections online, librarians are working to develop an integrated approach for providing access to electronic resources that facilitates retrieval and reduces confusion. A library website can function as an information gateway, an entry point to a range of online resources, with key components being the library catalogue and journal databases. Most online catalogues permit the integration of electronic books and electronic journals, enabling learners to locate items from digital and physical collections with one search. User services – such as the ability to check due dates, renew materials and request materials online – are also provided. Gateways may also organize collections and incorporate directories.

DIGITAL LIBRARY REFERENCE SERVICES

E-learners require more than access to e-resources. Traditionally, a reference librarian acts as an additional type of resource, one who can be counted upon to provide expertise in making sense of library systems and research tools and to offer a helping hand along that often slippery path known as the research process. Digital library users face additional challenges in mining relevant information out of a computer system that "obstinately" returns zero hits in response to a query that does not match the character strings in its database files.

DIGITAL LIBRARY USER INSTRUCTION

Library instruction has always been a significant role that librarians have played. Reference librarians provide tours, introductory and subject-specific classroom instruction, as well as on-the-fly, at-the-point-of-need instruction in the reference department. The new challenge for librarians is to provide library instruction to a growing population of remote and/or distance e-learners. With the increase in digital library collections that are accessible outside the library via the internet, students are visiting libraries less frequently. Telephone and e-mail reference allow reference librarians to provide short and sometimes detailed reference assistance to e-learners but these media are too cumbersome for remote instruction. However, with the advent of real-time virtual reference, librarians now have the ability to provide instruction to remote and distance learners.

CONCLUSION

In this paper, we discussed about necessary interaction between the e-learning and digital library worlds and also some perspective on common services that both of these worlds should draw upon rather than re-developing them. Digital library services are an essential component of a quality e-learning system. As access to internet-based courses grows, an increasing number of e-learners are dispersed around the globe, often in parts of the world where physical access to the collections of large academic and research libraries is impossible. These learners are largely dependent on the quality and academic usefulness of services that the digital library can offer electronically. The strength of digital libraries and digital collections depends on the relationships libraries develop and maintain with the creators, publishers and aggregators of e-resources, as well as with those who use, learn from and evaluate these resources. Providing ongoing technical, reference and instructional support to e-learners requires that libraries redefine their values and services, collaborate with their users and approach their tasks creatively.

REFERENCES

* **Anandan, C and Gangathran, M.** *Digital Libraries from technology to culture*, New Delhi : Kanishka Publishers,2006.
* http://www.aardvark.net
* http://www.flexiblelearning.net
* http://www.jelit.org
* http://www.anziil.org.
* http://www.theatlantic.com
* http://www.diglib.org
* http://www.emeraldinsight.com

E-09
Design and Development of An Institutional Repository at Bannari Amman Institute of Technology : A Case Study

S. Sivaraj
*Head, Learning Resource Centre, Bannari Amman
Institute of Technology, Sathyamangalam, Tamil Nadu*

Dr. S. Mohammed Esmail
*Reader, DLIS, Annamalai University,
Annamalainagar, Tamil Nadu*

Dr. M. Kanakaraj
*Librarian & Head, PSG College of Technology,
Coimbatore, Tamil Nadu*

ABSTRACT

*This paper presents an overview of the design and
development of Institutional Repository at Bannari*

Amman Institute of Technology using *Green Stone Digital Library Software.* It highlights the experiences of the Learning Resource Centre, Bannari Amman Institute of Technology in designing and developing Institutional Repository which were essentially provided as an alternative/supplement to the print and microform collection, in order to satisfy the information needs with greater speed, accuracy and efficiency. The paper will also highlight the use of the Institutional Repository and Internet to enhance the library collection, expand services and improve operations to provide access to a growing array of internal and external electronic resources. Finally, the authors wish to share their experiences particularly with the library professionals of the various parts of India.

INTRODUCTION

The world's universities, museums, governments and other organizations house treasures that have been hidden in archives, basements, attics, print formats and a variety of storage devices. These treasures encompass scientific, technological, cultural, artistic and historical materials generally unavailable to searchers and the public. Institutional repositories[1] are now being created to manage, preserve and maintain the digital assets, intellectual output and histories of institutions. Librarians are taking leadership roles in planning and building these repositories, fulfilling their roles as experts in collecting, describing, preserving and providing stewardship for documents and digital information.

Repositories provide services to faculty, researchers and administrators who want to archive research, historic and creative materials. The open access and open archives movement[2], the need for changes in scholarly communication to remove barriers to access and the increasing awareness that universities and research institutions are losing valuable digital and print materials have begun driving the establishment of institutional repositories. Using open archive models, established metadata standards and digital rights management, important new information sources are seeing the light of day and becoming more generally available.

PURPOSE OF THIS STUDY

The main purpose of this study is to present an overview of the design and development of Intuitional Repository at the Learning Resource Centre, Bannari Amman Institute of Technology. It will also highlight the experiences of the Learning Resource Centre, Bannari Amman Institute of Technology in developing these resources. In addition, the authors wish to share their experiences particularly with the library professionals of various parts of India.

INSTITUTIONAL REPOSITORY SOFTWARE PROVIDERS

The following are some of the better known software developers/vendors[3] offering Institutional Repository software. This is not an exhaustive list but the Librarians might examine these when choosing the system that best suits their needs:

- Archimede
- bepress
- CDSware
- CONTENTdm
- DSpace
- EPrints
- Fedora
- Greenstone
- Open Repository

GREENSTONE DIGITAL LIBRARY SOFTWARE

The URL of the GSDL is: http://www.greenstone.org/

DESCRIPTION

Developed by the New Zealand Digital Library Project at the University of Waikato, Greenstone is a suite of software for building and distributing digital library collections. Greenstone was developed and distributed in cooperation with UNESCO and the Human Info NGO.

AVAILABILITY

- Free multi-lingual, open source software
- Distributed under the GNU General Public License
- Current version: Greenstone v2.72
- Download location: *http://www.greenstone.org/*

FEATURES

- Multilingual: Four core languages are English, French, Spanish and Russian. Over 25 additional language interfaces are available
- Includes a pre-built demonstration collection
- Offers an "Export to CDROM" feature

THE LEARNING RESOURCE CENTER OF BANNARI AMMAN INSTITUTE OF TECHNOLOGY

The Bannari Amman Institute of Technology is an institute of higher learning in Engineering and Research.

The Learning Resource Centre of Bannari Amman Institute of Technology has a two-storeyed air-conditioned building with rich collection of books, journals, back volumes and digital library with 40 computers. It has currently developed a spectacular library web portal and institutional repository using Greenstone Digital Library Software and it is also involved in a research project sponsored by DSIR, Govt. of India. It has organized various short-term courses for the benefit of students and also for unemployed youth to get self-employment. It is an institutional member in British Council Library, DELNET and AICTE-INDEST Consortium, New Delhi.

INSTITUTIONAL REPOSITORY AT LRC, BIT

The LRC has established an Institutional Repository using Green Stone Digital Library Software (GSDL) and the thesis reports of students, syllabus, previous year question papers, function photos, videos etc., are made available in this Institutional Repository.

The web portal of LRC, BIT http://www.lib.bitsathy. ac.in was launched on 18 February 2004. Information on Government, Education, Universities, Scholarships, Competitive Exams, Examination results, Employment, Other Library links etc., are available in this web portal.

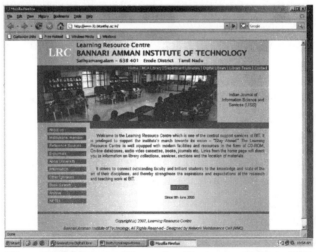

Fig. 1. Web portal of Learning Resource Centre, BIT

The Institutional Repository using GSDL software has been developed and the IR is linked with the LRC web portal to access information through internet.

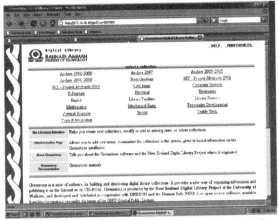

Fig.2. Institutional Repository using GSDL

The number of open access journals, publishing high quality, peer reviewed research is growing. New open access initiatives are regularly being announced, including the recent decision of the Indian Academy of Sciences to make their 11 journals open access and some of the links to open access journals on Engineering and Technology have been made available in the IR. Further, the LRC, BIT subscribes e- journals through AICTE, INDEST Consortium and these e-journals are made available through LRC web portal.

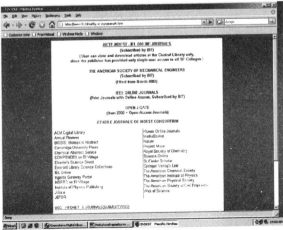

Fig.3. Web portal link to open access e-journals

Bannari Amman Institute of Technology was established during 1996 and there were more than 10000 photos which have been taken during many programmes held from the inception of the institute to till date and these photos, audios and videos are made available in IR using GSDL software. These photos, audios and videos can be accessed, downloaded and printed through intranet.

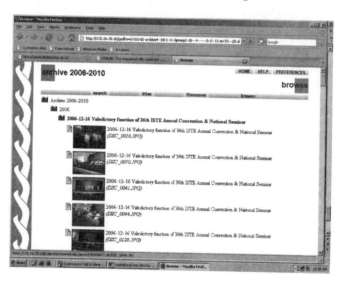

Fig. 4. Photo gallery using GSDL

There are more than 500 abstract of project reports submitted by the students, previous year question papers, syllabus of the programmes offered by the Institute which are made available online using GSDL and these can be viewed, copied and printed through intranet.

Fig. 5. Thesis / Syllabus / articles using GSDL

CHOSSING A SOFTWARE PLATFORM

To choose a software platform for the Institutional Repository, it is a good idea to assemble a team consisting of Institute library administration staff along with information technology staff. Each member contributes expertise on how the system should operate and the features required – whether service features (metadata, submission workflow, content types, etc.) or underlying server issues (operating system, databases, search mechanisms etc.).

This article outlines the issues which the library team might consider as features to look for and the strengths of the top IR platforms currently available:

- Basic technology building blocks
- Product features to look for
- Technology product models
- Other technical aspects of running a service
- Implementation steps
- Cost considerations

- Major IR software providers
- Feature checklists

CONCLUSION

The open access movement and institutional repositories could contribute significantly to economic growth by broadening the market for scholarly publications and research results, especially in Science and Technology. Lower access costs would broaden usage. The knowledge creation and dissemination that lower access costs brought knowledge to people who used that knowledge as the basis of invention and innovation. The ideas and knowledge may be expensive to generate, but inexpensive to use once implemented. The future will bring greater innovation and technologies through open access and institutional repositories.

REFERENCES

* **Clifford A. Lynch.** "Institutional Repositories: Essential Infrastructure for Scholarship the Digital Age" *ARL,* No. 226 (February 2003),pp. 1-7.

* **Mokyr, Joel.** *The Gifts of Athena: Historical Origins of the Knowledge Economy,* New York : Princeton University Press, 2002, pp. 1-27.

* "Institutional Repositories: Enhancing Teaching, Learning, and Research" published by Educause Evolving Technologies Committee (October 2003).

E-10
Agricultural Information Sources in Electronic Environment

R. Jayaraman

Assistant Librarian (S.G), Agricultural College and Research Institute, TNAU, Madurai - 625 104.

Dr. S. Srinivasa Raghavan

Librarian, Bharathidasan University, Tiruchirapalli.24.

ABSTRACT

Tamil Nadu Agricultural University, the pioneer in Agricultural Research, Education and Extension provides valuable information sources and services to the students, scientists and farmers. Full text online journals, secondary database and e-books are the major information sources available through electronic devices. These digital sources not only provide service but also enlighten the users about the recent advances in the Digital Libraries. This paper explores the possibility of using various digital sources to the users of Tamil Nadu Agricultural University Libraries.

INTRODUCTION

Electronic resources are now recognized as being of great importance to even small academic and public libraries and they are consuming an ever increasing share of library budgets, often for monographic acquisitions. CD-ROMs, local area networks, computer equipment, online resources, the internet and other remote databases all provide libraries with vast resources for their user populations. In addition to the benefits of additional access, the information explosion has also produced a considerable amount of confusion on the part of library users and librarians.

As access to electronic information services becomes more widespread, libraries are beginning to lose their monopolies, particularly as far as aggregation and access are concerned. They do however retain strengths in traditional expertise of selecting, organizing and creating access tools for information which are still necessary in the electronic environment especially with fewer barriers to publications and worldwide access. Libraries also continue to play a role both in terms of branding and authority and in the procurement of information.

ELECTRONIC INFORMATION

Electronic journals are periodicals available on-line through Internet or in CD-ROM format. For years, publishers have been providing full-text access to a number of journals on CD-ROM, which requires a significant amount of hardware, time and technical expertise on subscribers end. Electronic journals are blessings and a curse for libraries. To be meaningful in the current information environment and to meet users' ever-increasing demands, libraries must acquire as many appropriate full text resources as quickly as possible and make them easy to use. The integration of electronic journals within the academic and special libraries has brought a revolutionary change in its traditional system.

To facilitate access and to manage e-journals effectively, staff posted in libraries need to be more knowledgeable about the options and they are supposed to play an active role to seek solutions to the issues involved in it and to be more innovative in changing their way of performing various operations. Now days library have embraced electronic journals as a part of serial collection and articles in the e-journals can be down loaded, searched with embedded hotlinks and access by multiple users. As it has become a part of serial development, many libraries have chosen to drop standing print subscription in favor of their electronic counter parts to save time and space but still in India there is a cultural lag, the users feel comfortable and happy in using hard copy of the journals in place of e-journals.

USES OF E-JOURNALS

- Easy to access from all times, from any location – depending on publisher's limitations.
- Save storage costs.
- Mark journals available immediately after its publication rather than awaiting shipment
- Have the ability to access the full text of an article without any hassles e.g. misplaced issue or awaiting return from bindery.
- Cannot be stolen.
- Facilitate users to submit their articles on – line, request instructions for authors or to get rapid access to publishers.
- Request may be made for table of contents (TOC) to be setup directly with the publishers.
- Could be searched, browsed and interlinked with other publications and bibliographic databases may be printed and emailed immediately.

- Availability of TOCs (Table of contents) and abstracts without charges, if free access is not available as part of the library subscription.

- Provide opportunities for enrichment and augmentation of content.

ELECTRONIC RESOURCES FOR AGRICULATURAL SCIENCES-SCIENCE DIRECT

Science direct is a collection of information resources of millions of scientific works around the world. It is a web database of Elsevier Science publishers. The collections are in multi disciplinary content source including research journals. It covers more than 1,700 scientific and technical journals, three million articles and also reports are made available. Access to abstracts of articles and journals' table of content is free for all users.

The Elsevier science publishers publications are in online form in the name of Science Direct Web Editions like *www.sciencedirect.com*.

WEB OF SCIENCE

The web of science provides seamless access to current and retrospective multidisciplinary information from approximately 8,700 of the most prestigious, high impact research journals in world. Web of science also provides a unique search method, cited reference searching. With it, users can navigate forward, backward and through the literature, searching all disciplines and time spans to uncover all the information relevant to their research. Users can also navigate to electronic full-text journal articles.

Launched in January 2005, the web of science initiative makes hundreds of thousands of older, twentieth century scientific journal items available in one place and on one platform for the first time. Approximately 850,000 fully indexed journal articles have been added to web of science, from 262 scientific journals published in the first half of the twentieth century. This comprehensive collection is fully searchable, with complete bibliographic data, cited reference data and navigation and direct links to the full text.

BENEFITS

- Discover who is citing your research and the impact, your work is having on the global research community.
- Uncover the seminal research of an important theory or concept.
- Measure the influence of colleagues or competitor's work
- Follow the path and direction of today's hottest ideas and concepts
- Determine if a theory has been confirmed, changed or improved
- Find our how a basic concept is being applied
- Track a topic through years of research literature
- Verify the accuracy of references
- Locate relevant articles missed through a topic or subject search

Associated products : ISI Web of knowledge current contents connect.

DIGITAL AGRICULTURAL INFORMATION SYSTEM IN ICAR

Digitization means acquiring, converting, storing and providing information in a computer readable format that is standardized, organized and available on demand. Digital technology opens up a totally new perspective. The World Wide Web holds millions of websites and the Internet is a place for research, teaching, expression, publication and communication of information. India has a very large collection of manuscripts in agriculture and allied sciences. They are spread all over the country in different libraries, academic institutions, museums and in private collections and today face a threat of survival. This invaluable heritage has to be documented, preserved and made accessible to succeeding generation, for which digitization is the panacea.

The Indian Council of Agricultural Research, being an apex scientific organization at national level plays an important role to disseminate agricultural information. ICAR fully recognized the importance of information management. As such, in 1961, the Council decided to create a system to record on-going research projects and of late shifted towards digitization of records. An attempt is made here to present below some of the major progress made in this direction along with future vision.

WEB PAGE OF ICAR

ICAR made a beginning by hosting its web page through NIC in February, 1997. It was redesigned in 2003 by ARIS Unit of ICAR. Several new features have been added and existing information has been updated and restructured. Newsletter of ICAR namely ICAR News (Q), ICAR Reporter (Q), ARIS News(Q) now half yearly, Directory of conferences, seminars, symposia, workshops in agriculture and allied sciences and ICAR Telephone Directory are made available online by DIPA. The website is regularly updated. Similarly other ICAR Institutes have also developed their websites and made available their research achievements in digital format to the scientific community.

DIGITAL LIBRARIES IN THE ICAR SYSTEM

Libraries have served as important catalysts in storage, dissemination and retrieval of knowledge. In today's information scenario, vast resources of knowledge available in the form of text and images need digital technology for efficient handling. Libraries today are digital to a large extent around the world, as library in any developed country has a digital catalog, computerized retrievals and are capable of handling online and CD ROM databases and substantial electronic full text information. The major work in the ICAR Library system was done in National Agricultural Library at Indian Agricultural Research Institute with the financial support under NATP Project. The Institute's Library has digitized old and rare books. The library also digitized Ph.D. Thesis database and Bibliography of Indian Agriculture (BIA). Similarly CIBA, Chennai has brought out two CD-ROMs of the Institute's Publications, with the result that all the research findings and achievements of the Institute are now available in CD. Other Institutes' Libraries have also digitized their collection and made available to scientific community.

FUTURE VISION OF ICAR

- Web publishing
- Online Journals/Newsletters of ICAR Institutes
- Availability of Library collection/resources on web site
- Strengthening of Digital Library and information system
- Development of Digital archival system
- Creation and development of crop wise on line databases
- Creation of interactive websites
- Development of online crop based expert systems
- Knowledge management on world wide web
- Conversion of traditional knowledge base to digital knowledge base

CONCLUSION

The new Electronic Information Environment requires

that Librarian's role should be characterized by increased visibility and vitality. Librarians need to be well integrated into the activities of their institutions and the community they serve.

REFERENCES

* Indian Council of Agricultural Research, " Development of Digital Agricultural Information System in ICAR" in *ARIS News*, Vol.8 No.1, Jan-June 2005. pp.1-4

* Knowledge Management in Health Sciences: Newer perspectives MLAI 2004", *National convention*, 9-11 Dec.2004., University of Madras, pp. 354-356.

* **Tariq Ashraf.** *Library Services in Electronic Environment: Changes challenges issues and strategies.* New Delhi : Kaveri Books, 2004. pp.XXI 174-175.

* http://www.sciencedirect.com

* http://http://isiknowledge.com

E-11
MEDLARS [Medical Literature Analysis Retrieval System]

Dr. A. Ganesan
Head and Librarian, Department of Library and Information Science, AVVM Sri Pushpam College, Poondi, Thanjavur Dt.

J. Selvam
Lecturer, Department of Library and Information Science, AVVM Sri Pushpam College, Poondi, Thanjavur Dt.

V. Rajavel
Student, Department of Library and Information Science, AVVM Sri Pushpam College, Poondi, Thanjavur Dt.

ABSTRACT

MEDLARS is an acronym for medical literature analysis and retrieval service in a collection of databases maintained and leased to libraries and research institutions by the National library of medicine (NLM) including MEDLINE, AIDSLINE, TOXLINE, etc. A comprehensive list of NLM data base and resources is available online. The paper highlights the medical literature information availability & growth of MEDLARS.

INTRODUCTION

The National Library of Medicine (NLM) is located just outside Whashington DC in Maryland. It is part of the National Institute of Health, US department of health, Education and Welfare (HEW). One of the three National libraries in the US (with the Library of Congress and the National Agricultural Library), National Library of Medicine is the world's largest research library in a single scientific field.

AIM

The library collects materials exhaustively in some 40 bio medical areas and to a lesser degree in related subjects. The holdings include over 1/2 million books, journals, technical reports documents, theses, pamphlets, micro-film, pictorials and audio visual materials. More than 70 languages are represented in the collections.

MEDLARS become operational in JANURARY, 1964. MEDLARS is a multipurpose system, the prime purpose being the production of index medicus. Since January 1960 index medicines have been published in monthly parts each part being divided into subject and author section arranged alphabetically. Citations are given in full under every entry. In the subject section, under each heading, entries are grouped according to the original languages of the articles, with English language items first, followed by citation for article in other languages arranged alphabetically by languages. Titles in forein languages are translated into English and shown in square brackets together with an indication of the language concerned.

CRITERIA FOR SELECTION OF SUBJECT HEADINGS

- Frequency of term usage in the medical literature.

- Recognition of need for the terms by various users of mash.
- Recommendations by advisory panels on terminology.
- Ability to assign relatively clear and precise definition to the term.

Citation will be found in IM only under the mash headings that appear in larger type. All other entries in the alphabetical list are cross references leading the user directly or indirectly to appropriate IM heading.

OBJECTIVES OF MEDLARS

- To improve the quality of IM.
- Increase the number of articles.
- Increase the depth of indexing.
- Reduce the time of preparation of IM
- Compilation of IM on specialized topics.
- To facilitate quick searching in computer data base.

SELECTION OF ARTICLES

Most journals are indexed cover to cover. Original articles are indexed, as well as editorials and bibliographies. The designation "selective" is applied to those journals which are not exclusively medical, but also general scientific journals such as science and nature, frequently containing bio-medical articles. These journals are selectively indexed for their bio-medical coverage only.

COMMITTEE FOR SELECTION OF JOURNALS

In the selection of journals to be included in MEDLARS, the library is advised by a committee on selection of literature for MEDLARS composed of leading physicians, medical librarians and editors of medical journal.

GROWTH OF MEDLARS DATABASE

As on 1970, the MEDLARS data base comprised of over 1 million citations to bio-medical articles, from January 1964. The database was growing at the rate of about 200,000 citation annually. The articles cited are written in languages other than English.

INDEXING PROCESS

The indexing process involves the careful analysis of articles and description of the context of each by the use of specific subject headings selected from a controlled list. High quality articles are indexed with as many terms subject headings as are needed to describe fully the subject matter discussed. In practice about 10 to 20 terms are assigned for articles on the average. They tend to be long and are rather research oriented.

- Read and understand the title.
- Read the text down to the point at which the author states the purpose of his paper.
- Scan the list, chapter heading, section heading, bold face, italics, charts, plans, x-rays etc.
- Read every word of the summary.
- Closely scan the abstract.
- Scan the bibliographic references.

EXPLANATION OF DATA FORM

The upper part is used to record a full bibliographic description of the article and this forms the basis of the printed citation in IM or in a MEDLARS search. Print out some of the items for eg: translation and transiteration of foreign tittles are always supplied on the data form by the indexer. The language of a foreign article is always indicated. This appears as an abbreviation in IM and can be used as a search parameter in retrieval operations.

PROCESSING THE CITATION

Out put of the completed indexed data is used as input to the procedure that generates the machine readable data base. The subject heading with bibliographic citation for the articles are put into machine readable form by using paper tape typewriters. These machines produce a punched paper tape and proof paper copy. After proof reading, correction tapes go through computers input procedure that transfers input data for each article to magnetic tape. Records arranged in order of account contain author title, journal reference, language, abbreviation and other English subject headings, arranged by the indexer.

MEDLARS SEARCH

Requests are made by medical educators, practioners, researchers and other health professional. Searches are for various purposes.

- To determine the state of research in an field.
- Assist in the preparation of a review article.
- Help solve a clinical problem. About 20,000 medlar searches were compiled in US in 1970. Indexing an article for input to MEDLAR indexes, goes through two stages.
- Deciding what the article is about
- Describing the content of the article by means of MeSH terms.

A search analyst goes through the same two stage process.

- Decide what kind of articles he wants.
- Translate his request into a search statement. In MeSH terms, that can be processed against the citation file.

MEDLARS search is carriedout in two steps

- High speed search.

- Logic search.

The searcher's final responsibility is to review carefully the probability success or failure and then to take appropriate action.

PLANNING OF THE MEDLARS EVALUATION

Began in December 1965, the principal objectives being.

- To study the demand search requirements of MEDLAR'S users.
- To determine how effective and efficient the present MEDLARS
- To recoganize factors users may be satisfied more efficiently and more economically. In particular to suggest means where by new generations of equipment and progress may be used most effectively.

In October, 1971 the library initiated a nationwide on line bibliographic retrieval system as a general service for the bio-medical community. This service was called MEDLINE (MEDLARS on line), which contains about half-million references from the most recent medical journal literature, accessed by terminal located on some 350 medical libraries throughout the ration. By conversing with the computer at NLM using the writer like terminal, a user is able to retrieve almost instantaneously references to the latest journal articles in his area of interest.

The growth of MEDLINE has been dramatic since its introduction in late 1971. There are now several NLM data bases available. It is up dated monthly. It also includes nursing and dental journals not covered in index medicines

SDILINE

Selective dissemination of information on online 18,000 citations are available to participants.

CATLINE

Cataloguing on line. A database contains full bibliographic information for all materials catalogued in the library.

SERLINE

Serials on line, is a database of serial records containing bibliographic and location information for some 6000 current biomedical serial titles. Using **SERLINE** it is possible to identify where specific titles are held by over 100 participating medical libraries.

TOXLINE

Toxiology information online in an extensive file. About 400,000 citations and abstracts in the fields of toxiology and pharmacology are available as they relate to medicine, environmental pollution, health and safety.

MEDLARS was started at the national level and became international. Decentralized input from different countries are sent to NLM for MEDLARS and these countries receive output from MEDLARS in the tape form and do their own searching. The countries which participate in this system are National library of Australia, Canada National science library, France Institute of Medical Research, Japan information center for Science and Technology, Sweden. UK British library world. India can have access to MEDLARS tape through WHO, free of cost in the print out form.

CONCLUSION

The above study reveals that medical literature analysis and retrieval system is a collection of information available in the MEDLARS. Students are very much helped by utilizing MEDLARS.

REFERENCES

* **Kumar, PSG.** *A student manual of library and information science,* Vol.I and II. New Delhi : Kanishka Publications, 2006
* **Kumar, PSG** *Foundation of library and information science / UGC Curriculam.* New Delhi : B.R. Publications, 2003

- Bring out publications periodically highlighting the professionals' research and development activities.
- Enrich library environment by installing appropriate artifacts which reflects cultural and social heritage.
- Explore the possibility of procuring and developing the information available on modern gadgets including software and sharing through networking.

MAJOR ISSUES IN CONSORTIA

- Identification and negotiation with publishers and vendors to provide access under consortium purchase.
- Legal issues involved in contracts and usage of materials within the consortia
- Identifying the necessary infrastructures for access to electronic resources.
- Users of all libraries of the consortia to get equal access to all the information at all time.

Steps in the process of formation of Consortia

1. Prepare and circulate a draft vision document.
2. Scope and area of resource sharing
3. Specific goals
4. Membership aspect
5. Funding sources
6. Services to be facilitated
7. Establish communication amongst members and seek their consensus
8. Develop profiles of each members including availability of infrastructure, IP addresses used, contact persons, contact numbers and email address
9. Identify electronic resources including databases and full text resources for shared acquisition and access
10. Create website and listserv for the consortium

11. Study issues related to terms of contracts for licensing electronic rights of access.

ACTIVITIES OF CONSORTIA

- Reciprocal borrowing privileges
- Expanded inter library loan services
- Referral service
- Mutual notification of acquisitions
- Special communication services
- Assigned subject specialization
- Micro filming
- Central resources dormitory or storage center
- Joint research projects

ADVANTAGES OF CONSORTIA

- Collections of the consortium libraries enable each member library to support scholarly research for its users.
- Cooperative R&D in application of information technology, enhances service & realizes cost efficiencies.
- Staff development and interaction enhance the quality of service
- Increase the cost-benefit per subscription for participating institutions.
- Promote the rational use of funds.
- Ensure continuous and long-term subscription to the subscribed journals.
- Provide opportunities of local storage and hosting of subscribed information resources
- Better terms of agreement for use, archival access and preservation of subscribed electronic resources.

- Widespread support for further digitization of resources, to be shared.

MAJOR INTERNATIONAL CONSORTIUM INITIATIVES

Consortia at the International level have come in different forms and flavors. They range from simple to full-fledged networks. In USA there are more than 100 electronic consortia. Most established ones are : The Washington Research library(http:// www. Wrlc.org), Virginia VIVA (http// exlibris.uls.vcu. edu), Ohio Link (http:// www.ohiolink.edu) Georgia's Galileo(http:// Galileo.gsu.edu/Homepage.) and so on. The consortium institutions are informing their members about electronic information resources, pricing practices of electronic publishers and vendors and other issues of importance to consortium directors and governing boards. The coalition also meets with the information provider community to discuss product offerings and issues of mutual concern.

In Europe two models are important, one is library purchasing consortia and the other access schemes. In Germany there are three major consortia models in operation.

- Regional consortia for higher education libraries
- Regional consortia for multi type libraries instituted for higher education libraries
- Multi institutional research library consortia.

In China, China Academic Library & Information System is highly centralized integrated consortium. (http:// www.calis.edu.cn) The consortium serves about 700000 students over 27 provinces in China.

In Japan, Association of National University Libraries, Japan (ANUL) is playing an active role in academic communities.

CONSORTIA INITIATIVES AT NATIONAL LEVEL

Consortia in India are catching at a faster pace among the academic institutions. It is high time that the academic libraries can take the advantages of electronic information easily accessible to its user community.

Selected list of consortium are detailed below:

INDEST - AICTE CONSORTIUM

The Ministry of human resources Development (MHRD) has set up the Indian National Digital library in Engineering Science and Technology (INDEST) consortium. It has commenced its operation in 2002 at IIT Delhi. The consortium subscribes to full text electronic resources and bibliographic databases 38 institutions including IISc, NIT, REC, IIM, and few other institutions funded by MHRD are members.

The consortium also welcomes other institutions under self supported category. 462 engineering colleges, and other educational institutions have joined the consortium. The total membership has now gone up to 560. The consortium supports setting-up institutional repositories in member libraries , promoting submission of Electronic Theses and Dissertation in member libraries , providing technology support to member, fostering joint archives and storage facility, facilitating shared Digital Library projects development providing for common union catalogue for books and so on.

UGC- INFONET CONSORTIUM

The UGC has initiated E journal consortium in the year 2004 in order to access a large number of scholarly journals from reputed publishers, aggregators and society to universities in India. Under this scheme 4000 full-text scholarly electronic journals from 25 international publishers are made accessible to 100 universities in the first phase of its implementation. The programme is also extended to all affiliated colleges. The programme is executed by INFLIBNET, Ahmedabad.

Currently the UGC-INFONET E journals consortium subscribes to good number of journals few of them are listed below

a. American Chemical Society

b. American Institute of Physics

c. Annual Reviews

d. Biological Abstracts

e. Chemical Abstracts Service

f. Emerald library science collections

g. Institute of Physics publishing

h. JSTOR

i. Nature

j. Royal Society of Chemistry

k. Springer Link Journals. Etc.

FORSA

FORSA is a group of different libraries from institutions where astronomy is one of the main areas of research. The FORSA was launched in the 1980 with an objective to compile Union catalogue of scientific serials, annual and other irregular publications, reference tools, compiled theses holding, holding of duplicate issues of journals, directory of libraries and facilities available in member libraries.

CSIR E – JOURNAL CONSORTIUM

The CSIR E journal consortium was the first major and formal consortium at the national level. The consortium started with an access to Science Direct for all of its 40 laboratories in 2001. This consortium is wholly funded by CSIR and is monitored by NISCAIR.

DAE CONSORTIUM

The Department of Atomic Energy (DAE) Consortium caters to the information requirement of 36 institutions including BARC, TIFR and SAMEER. Funded by the Department of Atomic Energy (DAE), Govt. of India, the Consortium subscribes to e-resources from 4 publishers (including Science Direct, Springer, Math, and SciNet) for providing access to around 2,000 e-journals. Established in 2003, the Consortium is administered by BARC, Mumbai.

IIM CONSORTIUM

The IIM Consortium is an initiative from libraries of all the six IIMs in India. The consortium commenced its activities in 2002 with subscription to electronic resources on cross-sharing and cost-sharing basis. A resource subscribed by the IIMs on cross-sharing basis includes journals from Wiley Inter Science and Springer journals. All IIMs are core members of the INDEST – AICTE consortium.

CONCLUSION

Consortia became a major force in information delivery and they need to focus on their obligation to further the common aspirations of libraries and librarians to provide equitable and affordable information to all. They need to become real players in the creation and dissemination of scholarly communication. But wide disparity in the availability and use of academic and research information still prevails among different universities and research institutions in India. The government should make an attempt to provide necessary infrastructure like network connections to access the electronic resources and also support the training programmes for librarians for information retrieval and consortia building activities. This will definitely bring economy, efficiency, equality in information availability and use.

REFERENCES

* **Achyutha Rao H.R. and RT.D. Gandhi R.** "Mysore city library consortium", *National Seminar on Modernisation of library services in university libraries.* (1989).

* **Bostick, Sharon L.** "Academic library consortia in the United States: An introduction". *Library Quaterly,* V 11, 2001, pp. 6-13.

* Forum for Resource Sharing in Astronomy and Astrophysics (FORSA), [http://www.iiap.res.in/library/forsa.html].

* Indian National Digital Library in Engineering Sciences and Technology (INDEST) Consortium, New Delhi. [http://paniit.iitd.ac.in/indest/].

* Indian National Digital Library in Engineering Sciences and Technology (INDEST) Consortium, New Delhi. [http://paniit.iitd.ac.in/indest/].

* **Krishnan, S.** Consortium -CSIR Experience [http://www.iiap.res.in/library/proc.html]

* **Kumbar, T S.** E-Resources subscription for the University System: UGC/INFLIBNET initiative [http://www.iiap.res.in/library/proc.html]

* **Narayana, Poornima; Goudar, I.R.N.** A model for scientific and technical Information consortium: Case study of CSIR.

* **Nfila, Reason Baathuli; Ampen, Kwasi Darko .**" Developments in academic Library consortia from the1960s through to 2000: a review of the literature", *Library Management,* Vol.23 (4/5), 2002, pp. 203-212.

* **Patil, Y M.** Sharing E-journals in a Consortia Environment: A Case Study of FORSA libraries. [http://www.iiap.res.in/library/proc.html]

* **Prem Chand,** (2005), UGC INFONET E-journal Consortium: Role of INFLIBNET. Caliber 2005, Cochin University of Science and Technology (Kochi) on February 2- 4, 2005.

* UGC-Infonet E-journal Consortium [http://www.inflibnet.ac.in/econ/index.htm].